McDonnell Douglas F-15 Eagle

Other titles in the Crowood Aviation Series

McDonnell Douglas
F-15 EAGLE

PETER E. DAVIES AND
TONY THORNBOROUGH

The Crowood Press

First published in 2001 by
The Crowood Press Ltd
Ramsbury, Marlborough
Wiltshire SN8 2HR

British Library Cataloguing-in-Publication Data
A catalogue record for this book is available from the British Library.

ISBN 1 86126 343 0

Acknowledgements
In compiling this book the authors are very grateful for the assistance of Arnold Engineering Develop-
ment Center, Ben Backes, Capt Ken Baldry, USN (Ret), Capt Haridev Basudev, USAF, Todd H.
Blecher (Boeing), Col Mike Casey, USAF, Brad Elward, Phil Evans, MSgt Jesse Hall, USAF, Lt Col
John J. Harty, USAF (Ret), Kevin Jackson, Capt Peter Kerr, USAF, Col Jack Leslie, Jack McEnroe, Col
George M. Monroe, USAF, Maj Claude S. Morse, USAF (Ret), SrA Jason Passmore, USAF, Capt Mike
'Starbaby' Pietrucha, USAF, John Poole, Capt Lawrence Pravacek, USAF, Lt Col Jeffrey G. Randolph,
USAF (Ret), Raytheon, Lt Col John Roberts, USAF (Ret), Mick Roth, James E. Rotramel, Gp Capt
M.J.F. Shaw, CBE, RAF (Ret), Capt Herman Shirg, USAF, MSgt Louis P. Sirois, USAF, Gregory S.
Spahr, Bettie E. Sprigg, Capt Kelly Sullivan, USAF, Norm Taylor, Douglas R. Thar, Ronald van der
Krogt, Maj Mark 'Tex' Wilkins, USAF, Capt White, USAF, the 'Phase' maintainers of the 48th FW.

Special thanks to Tony Cassanova, TSgt Mike Kaplan, USAF, and Col Ron Thurlow, USAF (Ret.).

Typefaces used: Goudy (*text*),
Cheltenham (*headings*).

Typeset and designed by
D & N Publishing
Baydon, Marlborough, Wiltshire.

Printed and bound in Great Britain by Bookcraft, Midsomer Norton.

Contents

Introduction

Rarely has any aircraft lived up to its name as convincingly as the F-15 Eagle. As a substantial bird of prey, with keen vision and powerful flight giving it mastery of the air, or as a symbol of American pride and patriotism, McDonnell Douglas's masterpiece has certainly ruled all the skies it has entered during the last quarter-century. In aerial combat, since June 1979, around one hundred of its enemies have fallen without loss to the graceful, grey fighter. Only in comparison with that other American 'eagle', the modest ten-dollar coin, might the parallels run short. In paying for their F-15s the US taxpayers had to adjust to unit costs that, at around $22m per copy in 1979 dollars, were about four times more expensive than their predecessors. In turn, the Eagle's replacement will quadruple that sum again, with each F-22A Raptor costing at least $100m.

As prices have risen numbers of aircraft have declined, so that each F-15 had to be vastly more capable than the far more numerous F-4s and F-106s that preceded it. The F-22A, of which only 339 are currently expected, will probably have to fulfil the tasks that around 600 'light grey' F-15s were performing in 1999. Raptor will certainly have to earn the 'air dominance' label that its designers claim for it.

If the USAF manages to win funds for more Raptors they would eventually replace those Eagles of a darker feather, the F-15E 'Strike Eagles'. When the USAF elected to retire its superb, though ageing F-111F strike force it chose to take advantage of the F-15's considerable growth potential, allied with new developments in digital night/all weather attack systems. F-15E with its LANTIRN system quickly became the USAF's premier strike/interdictor and it

will continue in production thirty years after the Eagle first flew.

Like all classic designs the Eagle was right first time and its predatory appearance has altered hardly at all since it entered squadron service, although its engines, avionics and weapons have steadily improved. It has also been the safest fighter in USAF service, with a 'strike' rate of 6.9 in its first 145,000 hours of flight compared to 13.8 for the USAF F-4 Phantom and 14.5 for the F-14 Tomcat over the same period. Eagles have returned to base after airborne incidents that have removed large portions of airframe; in one case an entire wing.

All but one of the air forces that have purchased F-15s have used it actively in combat and it rapidly attained air superiority, its chief purpose, in battles over Syria, Iraq and the Balkans during some of the most intense air-to-air fighting since the Second World War. Although it never met the hordes of Soviet Bloc MiGs and Sukhois that it was originally designed to repel over Central Europe's potential battlefields, the Eagle has engaged and conclusively defeated Foxbats, Fulcrums and Floggers in those post-Cold War conflicts. In so doing, it proved the real efficacy of the previously disappointing AIM-7 Sparrow missile and demonstrated true 'beyond visual range' (BVR) air superiority tactics. At the same time F-15Es showed that a couple of guided bombs, accurately targeted, could consistently wipe out pinpoint targets that would previously have required a formation of heavily laden bombers rather than a pair of fighters that could also defeat any aerial opposition to their attack. The same F-15Es, flying patrols over the 'no fly' areas of Iraq since 1991 have worked as SEAD partners with

F-16CJ Wild Weasels, steadily eroding Saddam Hussein's air defences every time he challenges overflights by Allied aircraft.

In the continental USA Eagles re-equipped many Air National Guard units and they joined regular USAF F-15 squadrons in defending US airspace out to its extremities from Alaska, Iceland and Hawaii. For the Japanese, the Eagle's long endurance and powerful radar 'sight' have also made it an ideal air defence fighter for their needs. Israeli pilots were so eager to enjoy the Eagle's combat edge that they willingly accepted a batch of used Research and Development aircraft to give them early membership of the elite F-15 club. Israel was still receiving a specially modified 'Strike Eagle', the F-15I in 1999. The country's fighter pilots claimed the first fifty-five air-to-air 'kills' for the Eagle, without loss, and added their range of domestically produced missiles to its powerful talons.

As well as introducing many new technologies in its structure, avionics and engines the F-15 has also been used to test even more advanced concepts such as tail-mounted, thrust-vectoring engine nozzles, new digital electronic control systems and even self-repairing flight control systems. Some of these revolutionary developments will become operational in F-22A and its possible successors.

For some years America seemed to have the wrong fighters and tactics for the wars it was compelled to fight. Many lessons were learned and remembered in the design of the F-15. Since it first flew the St Louis nest in 1972 it has consistently shown itself to be ideally suited to the situations it has had to face.

P.E. Davies and A.M. Thornborough,
Bristol, 2001

CHAPTER ONE

F-X

The F-15 Eagle's immediate predecessor and America's principal fighter in the Vietnam War, the F-4 Phantom has sometimes been portrayed as a rather unmanageable heavyweight, outclassed in a dogfight by the nimbler MiGs of the North Vietnamese. In fact, when flown with the right tactics, an aggressive approach and adequate warning of attack it could deal with those opponents more than capably, as US Navy pilots proved in 1972. After *Top Gun* initiatives instilled effective ACM procedures they were able to destroy more MiGs in one month than they had scored during the entire war up to that point. In 1972 Navy and Marine crews shot down twenty-six MiGs, losing only three of their own number to the opposing fighters. More reliable weapons would have increased that total considerably: the disappointing AIM-7 Sparrow was used for only one of those kills. Despite these successes the F-4's overall air-to-air performance was seen as inadequate, and rather unfairly so since it was not designed for the close-in fighting that the rules of engagement of Vietnam forced upon F-4 pilots. The usual need to identify enemy aircraft visually before engaging with missiles, thereby avoiding the risk of 'blue on blue' hits, largely ruled out the use of the aircraft's primary AIM-7 Sparrow missile armament as the launch range to its target would have been too short for it to home and detonate successfully.

Other critics pointed to the Phantom's lack of a gun in all but its USAF F-4E version as a major handicap for the resultant close-in air fighting. Five of the F-4E's twenty-one aerial victories involved its inbuilt cannon, though twice as many gun kills were by F-4C/D aircraft using a strap-on external cannon. Forty of the USAF's total of 138 kills (29 per cent) involved a gun. For the Israeli Air Force in 1973 the figure approached 65 per cent. The Navy's dedicated gunfighter, the F-8 Crusader used its 20mm weapons for one complete kill and a combination of 20mm and missiles for two others. Phantoms destroyed

150 North Vietnamese aircraft against a probable loss of forty-nine to MiGs, though the majority of its victories came rather late in the war, largely due to changes in training routines and a belated realization that the F-4 could be a competent 'dog-fighter' as well as an attack aircraft, a role in which the Air Force and Navy had used it most extensively.

From the evidence of these rather mixed messages USAF planners began to envisage the Phantom's successor, a process that began in 1965, soon after the F-4's combat debut. As the war progressed they saw that the type could perform attack, air superiority and reconnaissance-type missions for all three US armed services, thereby vindicating in Government eyes the concept of 'commonality' that reigned in the Pentagon at this time. This policy was also meant to produce a 'common' fighter/attack/fleet defence aircraft, the TFX (F-111) for the USAF and USN and the project's failure to produce more than a strike bomber from this original proposal did nothing to curtail the quest for commonality in later projects, including the Phantom replacement initiative.

Also in its fighter inventory at this time were the F-105, soon to be phased out after heavy losses in battle and the specialist, missile armed F-102 and F-106 air defence interceptors, linked to a complex ground-control network. Missing from the line-up was a dedicated air superiority fighter, uncompromised by the 'common' requirement to perform other missions. In its previous major engagement, the Korean War, the USAF had relied heavily upon its F-86 Sabre as a true air superiority antidote to the MiG-15. As defence analysts observed the battles in South-East Asia it was clear that this type of fighter was not, after all, outmoded. The main difference between simple day-fighters like the F-86E and the complex, multipurpose jets of the 1960s was cost. Aircraft like the F-105 and F-4 took enormous sums to build and operate, and they were being lost in large numbers to the most primitive forms of air defence, often

while attacking targets of limited strategic importance. Inevitably the US Defense Secretary, Robert McNamara, chief proponent of commonality, sought cheaper solutions for the taxpayer. Ideal replacements were seen to be light, cheaper tactical aircraft such as the A-7 Corsair (another 'common' USAF/USN project) and F-5 Freedom Fighter. The USAF was encouraged to accept 454 A-7D Corsairs and in so doing it won McNamara's permission to initiate the F-X study for an F-4 Phantom replacement, optimized for the Air Force's fighter mission.

From April 1965 the USAF began design studies for its ideal air-to-air fighter, concentrating on higher thrust-to-weight ratio than the F-4 and much better air-to-air capability. Armament proposals centred on an improved version of the F-4's radar/infrared guided missile mix. A buy of around 1,000 copies was anticipated to counter the expected improvements in Soviet bloc fighter technology as well as the hordes of earlier-technology MiGs that would be faced in the event of a European conflict. Once the concept entered the political arena its pure air-to-air basis did not survive long before Congress overruled senior USAF personnel and demanded a secondary air-to-ground capability for their money to give the aircraft maximum utilization. This decision influenced the eventual specification of the aircraft's avionics and airframe structure and fortuitously made possible the long-term development of an attack variant, the F-15E. However, at the time this compromise was seen as a minor price for the Air Force to pay for the right to their own fighter, rather than having to share another common design with the USN as McNamara would have preferred.

Once the basic F-X requirement was formulated, a Request for Proposals (RFP) was issued to thirteen companies on 8 December 1965 resulting in contracts to Boeing, Lockheed and North American on 18 March out of the eight who responded. The McDonnell Douglas proposal was not favoured with a contract from the initial

Concept Formulation Study (CFS) but the company began its own F-X study under former F-4 Project Manager, Don Malvern.

All of the initial CFS proposals were turned down, partly because they were compromised too heavily by the air-to-ground requirement. Most were reminiscent of the TFX, with swing-wings, four under-fuselage AIM-7s, advanced nav-attack avionics and twin podded turbofans powering an aircraft weighing in excess of 65,000 lb (29,484kg). At this point another influence was brought to bear on USAF thinking as the CFS team continued its deliberations through 1966. Maj John R. Boyd, author of the Fighter Weapons School's tactics manual *Aerial Attack Study* had developed a concept known as energy manoeuvrability based on his studies at Georgia Technical College and later at Eglin AFB. Using early USAF mainframe computers he analysed the performance of a selection of fighters by studying their potential and kinetic energy in manoeuvring situations, at various altitudes, weights and airspeeds. His findings, when published in May 1964, provided engineers with an accurate tool to assess and compare the combat performance of any design proposals. Application of these ideas to the F-X conundrum produced revised targets. The 65,000lb (29,480kg) weight (close to that of the stately A-5A Vigilante bomber) was reduced to below 40,000lb (18,144kg); maximum speed came down from Mach 2.7 to a more practical Mach 2.4 to economize on structural materials and thrust-to-weight ratio was set at 1:1. Variable-sweep wings were still preferred.

By July 1967 the F-X Concept Formulation Package had become pretty firm and in the same month it was energized by the appearance of the prototype MiG-25 Foxbat at the Domodadovo air display in Russia. Analysts judged the Soviet fighter to be a generation ahead of the US fighter inventory. Designed to counter the still-born XB-70 Valkyrie bomber (and possibly the SR-71 Blackbird too) the MiG-25 was built for sustained Mach 3 performance, smashed a number of world performance records between 1965 and 1977, and in 1991 was to be the probable cause of the Coalition Forces' only air-to-air loss in Operation *Desert Storm*. Although it didn't mature as a multipurpose type until 1978 the MiG-25's extraordinary performance was an unpleasant surprise to the West, as the MiG-15 had been in 1950.

The effect of the MiG-25 revelation was to increase the emphasis on air superiority in the F-X specification and a reduction in the air-to-ground factor. A new request for bids went out to seven companies on 11 August 1967 followed by contracts for McDonnell Douglas and General Dynamics and the inclusion of company-funded submissions from North American, Lockheed, Fairchild-Republic and Grumman. While these companies refined their bids through 1968 another change of emphasis occurred when the USN dropped their troublesome, overweight F-111B programme and pushed for a different solution to their fleet air defence fighter requirement via the VF-X project. Fearing that the Department of Defense, under an incoming President would see this as another opportunity for a cost-saving common programme that might blunt the F-X initiative, the USAF accelerated its programme by deciding to bypass the usual prototype stage in favour of going straight to a production 'fly before buy' aircraft. In order to make its needs as different

Every inch a classic from the day it was rolled out, F-15A 71-280, the first Eagle, at St Louis on 26 June 1972.

Jack Morris via Norm Taylor

as possible from VF-X it also pushed the air superiority priority and insisted on a single-place cockpit, knowing that the Navy wanted a two-seat pilot and RIO arrangement, as in the F-4. Lt Gen John Burns (former CO of the 8th TFW Wolfpack), argued that the two-man concept was essentially a Navy idea, suited to their F-4 'interceptor' but inappropriate for the USAF where both F-4 crewmen were officially pilots. Single-seat fighter pilots had not taken kindly to the F-4 in many cases and there was a resurgence of the 'wild blue yonder' fighter pilot philosophy for the F-X.

In its final stages the F-X Development Concept Paper also called for twin engines, a cockpit that gave first-class, all-round visibility (not the F-4's strong point), a 260mi (418km) radius on internal fuel and an inbuilt gun. The issue of the Concept Paper took place against a background of another internal USAF debate about the basic purpose of F-X. Fighter analyst Maj John C. Boyd and Pierre Sprey (working directly for the Secretary of Defense) strongly advocated a much lighter, simpler fighter, citing the vulnerability of more sophisticated designs to cost overruns, technological shortfalls and poor reliability. Boyd, architect of energy manoeuvrability, was unconvinced that a heavy, complex F-X would meet the performance targets. Their arguments were persuasive to those seeking to maintain front-line fighters in sufficient numbers in the face of ever-increasing unit costs. Their point of view led eventually to the USAF's separate Lightweight Fighter programme and the F-16 at half the price of the F-X. However, that evolution was still some way ahead and this last-minute attempt to derail F-X served to harden opinion defensively behind the well-established F-X proposals for fear of losing funding to a cheaper aircraft. The word in the Pentagon was, 'the only way a second lieutenant can make it to first lieutenant is to swear allegiance to the F-X' (or F-15 as it became from 12 September 1968).

Eight companies received RFPs on 30 September 1968 (the August 1967 line-up of companies plus Northrop) though GD, one of the first contenders to become involved in the F-X endeavour, was ruled out soon afterwards. Three months later, Contract Definition Phase contracts went to North American, Fairchild-Hiller and McDonnell Douglas. It was a demanding specification, requiring the fighter to be able to fly to Europe without air-to-air

refuelling; a first for any fighter aircraft that arose from the need to provide rapid reinforcement to USAFE units in an emergency. Low wing-loading was to give buffet-free flight at Mach 0.9 and the twin, self-starting engines were to push the fighter to a Mach 2.5 top speed. Maximum take-off weight was 40,000lb (18,144kg) and the airframe was to have a 4,000hr fatigue life (with a 'scatter factor' of 4, so that 16,000hr would be possible) and maintenance man-hours per flight hour (mmh/fh) were not to exceed 11.3 to 1. The latter was to be achieved mainly through the use of line-replaceable units (LRUs) for the avionics. Low mean-time between failures (mtbf) for radar units had been the main reason for poor aircraft availability in Vietnam. Armament was still the eight missile-plus-gun arrangement, built around a far-reaching pulse Doppler radar with look-down, shoot-down capability. One-man operation of this complex system would be facilitated by advances in cockpit design allowing the pilot to work heads up rather than reducing his awareness of the combat situation outside by peering at inaccessible instruments or searching for switches to set up complex armament or radar procedures. To satisfy the followers of Pierre Sprey and John Boyd (by now known as the Fighter Mafia) it was decreed that the F-15 should rely heavily on proven, low-risk technology to minimize the possibility of cost overruns or failed systems. Major components were therefore to be supplied from ongoing Government-funded development programmes. On the list also (another legacy of Vietnam) was high survivability in combat, including low-vulnerability flight controls, fuel and electrical systems as well as structural integrity. The achievement of an Israeli pilot, several years later, in bringing home an F-15D with an entire wing missing showed how well the winning contractor satisfied that requirement.

While evaluating the three manufacturers' proposals the USAF Source Selection Evaluation Board, headed by Col Benjamin N. Bellis had to bear in mind the F-15's likely opponents. Agile MiG-21s (improved versions of the fighters that had led some Vietnam-hardened pilots to advocate a purchase of the type for USAF air defence purposes) still comprised the bulk of the fighter force in the Warsaw Pact countries and their allies. The F-15 would have to manoeuvre with them, relying on superior performance, armament

and tactics to compensate for the numerical superiority of the MiGs. At the same time it would need excellent long-range radar and missiles to deal with the new breed of Soviet BVR fighters with their advanced weapons systems. Balancing the speed required to see off a MiG-25 and the agility to fight through a pack of MiG-21s attacking from both high altitude and from the 'deck' required some extremely difficult design decisions. Pressure from the 'Fighter Mafia' for a single-engined aircraft was countered by the F-15's need to haul an eight-missile load (over 3,000 lb (1,360kg)), its heavy fire-control system and a fuel load sufficient for Transatlantic deployment. No existing engine could have provided the necessary power and there was no time to develop one.

Col Bellis, fresh from the SR-71 programme, gave the three contestants from January to June 1969 to work on their proposals. His team at USAF Aeronautical Systems took from July to December of that year to assess them. On 23 December 1969 there were celebrations in St Louis when the McDonnell Douglas submission was declared the winner.

Airframe

Their F-15 came out at roughly the same size as its F-4 predecessor, though its shoulder-mounted wing of 608sq ft (57sq m) (the F-4's was 530sq ft (49sq m)) and 300sq ft (28sq m) greater overall top surface area made it seem more massive. Weight saving through the use of simpler structural components and titanium or composite materials for around a quarter of the airframe meant that it was 6,000lb (2,722kg) lighter than the F-4E Phantom. The internal structure and equipment was also not as densely packed as it was in many other contemporary designs. Don Malvern's team tunnel-tested 107 wing designs out of 800 paper proposals. Using three wind tunnels the wing designs were put through over 22,000 hours of tests, five times as long as the process that produced the F-4's distinctive 'cranked' wing. Although some of the test items included swing-wing variants, favoured by Grumman for their VF-X/F-14 Tomcat, but strongly opposed by Col Boyd on grounds of weight and complexity, McDonnell Douglas tended towards a fixed wing. The chosen design used a 45-degree leading edge sweep that had proved to be an excellent compromise for high and low-speed handling on many aircraft from the F-100 (originally called Sabre 45) to the F-4. Optimized for flight at Mach 0.9 the wing used no high lift devices on its leading edge, employing instead a high degree of conical camber over its 42.8ft (13m) span. Its low wing loading (56–60lb/sq ft) gave a turn rate of 11.8 degrees per second, only 1 degree less than the F-16, and reduced landing speed to 120kt for a much softer touch-down than the F-4's. Its zero angle of incidence gave maximum acceleration by reducing the drag caused by rapid lift production. The wing was designed to take quite substantial g loading with any one of its three main spars in each wing fractured. Overall, the fatigue life requirement for the F-15 was 300 per cent higher than that of the F-4, which required structural reinforcement from quite early in its service life.

F-15A 71-0286 with the F-15 Joint Task Force at Edwards AFB on 16 June 1975. This aircraft tested carriage of the AN/ALQ-119 ECM pod on its outboard wing pylon, revealing adverse effects on aircraft handling. Jack Morris via Jim Rotramel

(Below) **The Number One F-15A assigned to the AFFTC at Edwards AFB. The original wingtip and horizontal stabilized outlines were retained until March 1974.** Norm Taylor Collection

Additional lift came from the fuselage, built in three sections. In the forward section consisting of a nose barrel and two vertically joined side panel assemblies were virtually all the avionics and over 80 per cent of the wiring. From the outset the cockpit area was designed with space for a second seat or additional equipment growth without the need for extensive re-design. The centre fuselage, extending from just behind the pilot's clamshell canopy to the front faces of the engines, housed the gun system, Sparrow missile equipment and fuel. The wings were

attached to a truss construction that carried the structural loads around the twin, side-by-side air ducts to save the weight of a separate wing-support framework. The intakes had variable geometry to enable the aircraft to reach Mach 2.5 with 'nodding' ramps pivoting at the lower lip of the intake. Their overall shape was reminiscent of the intakes on the North American A-5 Vigilante, but also of the MiG-25's. They enabled air to be captured and directed efficiently into the duct at high angles of attack of up to 24 degrees by pointing downwards to match the aircraft's attitude.

As a bonus, their flat upper surface acted as a canard area, increasing the effectiveness of the horizontal stabilizers. Intake angle was regulated automatically by a computerized air inlet control (each inlet was controlled by an independent air inlet controller). The incoming air was then shaped by three automatically variable ramps in the 'roof' of each inlet duct with a bypass door (Door 33) and bleed-air vent. The first and second ramps were perforated to allow air to filter through while the long rear section smoothed the airflow for its passage to the turbine face.

In the rear fuselage section was a continuous titanium structure containing both engines that could be drawn out rearwards for maintenance. A titanium keel area acted as a firewall between the engines and also supported the tailhook. Mounting lugs for the twin vertical stabilizers and the all-moving horizontal stabilizer were included. Twin tails were chosen (unlike the second choice North American's that had one) for better yaw stability at high speeds and high angles of attack. Initially, shorter vertical stabilizers were combined with ventral stabilizers but the latter affected cruise drag badly and were deleted from the drawings in April 1971 in favour of taller tails.

Hydraulic fluid leakage from AAA damage had been a major cause of combat losses to fighters in South East Asia. For the new fighter twin hydraulic systems incorporated a sensor system that could immediately identify leaks and isolate the damaged circuit. The tail (stabilator) control system, the main flying control for roll and pitch control in supersonic flight, could also draw power from a utility hydraulic system. Self-sealing fuel lines were used and the fuel tanks were kept away from the engines to reduce fire damage risks, rather than being situated above the engines as in the F-4. Using a range of advanced materials and construction techniques McDonnell Douglas engineered a light, strong airframe, parts of which (including the boron composite tail surfaces) were fatigue tested to 16,000 hours. Lacking these technical advantages in the USSR, Mikoyan-Gurevich had to use tempered steel for 80 per cent of the MiG-25's main structure to resist Mach 3 air friction temperatures of 300°C (572°F).

While the F-15 design team, headed by George Graff with Don Malvern as Programme Manager, refined their plans, preparations were made to integrate the USAF-selected engines, radar and armament.

Eagle Power: F100-PW-100

Producing an engine that would allow a comparatively large fighter like the F-15 to enter a loop at 150kt, accelerate in a Mach 0.9, 5g turn without afterburner, fly at Mach 2.5 and cross the Atlantic without a tanker was an unprecedented challenge. The requirement for massive power to give a thrust-to-weight ratio the right side of 1:1 suggested an engine of around 23,000lb

(10,430kg) thrust; roughly the same as the massive Tumanskii R-15B-300 used in the MiG-25. Fuel economy for long range implied a low-bypass turbofan using lightweight materials. The USAF's first combat turbofan, the Pratt and Whitney TF30-P-1 eventually became an extremely reliable engine, yielding over 25,000lb (11,340kg) thrust in its final TF30-P-100 version for the F-111F Aardvark. Earlier variants had all suffered a variety of stall problems associated mainly with the F-111's short air intake ducts. The USN had used the TF-30-P-6 in the A-7A, replacing it with the Rolls-Royce/Allison TF41, also used for the USAF A-7D. In the F-14A it was the power source (inherited from the cancelled F-111B) from 1969 until 1988, when re-engined Tomcats began using the new General Electric F110. For much of its time in the F-14 the TF-30 threw up problems with fan-blade loss and fires, causing a number of losses.

With this rather uneven background of turbofan experience, an estimated budget of $2m per engine and the prevailing philosophy of commonality it was inevitable that the DoD should attempt to develop a reliable engine that would power the F-15 and offer a better solution for the F-14A too.

After the April 1968 issue of RFPs, designers Richard J. Coar and R.T. Baseler at Pratt and Whitney drew on their 1965 JTF16 project design, their experience of the TF30 and the extremely powerful J58 of the SR-71 Blackbird. Their goal was an engine that was 1,000 lb (450kg) lighter than the TF30, with about 5,000lb (2,270kg) more thrust but very similar fuel consumption plus more rapid throttle response. In direct competition for the ATEGG (advanced turbine engine gas generator) contract to power F-15 was General Electric's GE1/10 proposal. At that stage the DoD's Joint Engine Program Office wanted a common-core engine, known as the F401, for F-15 and the re-engined Tomcat. All F-14s after the 32nd aircraft would have received the new engine as F-14Bs. From the outset there were fundamental differences between the Navy that wanted another 5,000lb (2,270kg) thrust and the USAF that needed a different afterburner, fan and low-pressure compressor to achieve its specified 22,000lb (9,980kg) thrust. Soon after the F-14 contract was signed in January 1969 it became clear that cost overruns would not permit a substantial F-14B programme and the F401 was confined to a brief test period in 1973–74. On 27 February 1970, P&W won

Proving the in-flight refuelling system, which was to be crucial for the Eagle's many long deployment flights, on 15 January 1973. Norm Taylor Collection

'Ram' engine tests on the F100-PW-229 IPE, simulating conditions at high speed and low altitude, at Arnold Engineering Development Centre (AEDC). Arnold Engineering Development Centre

the contract for the F-15 engine, leaving General Electric to proceed with their design that eventually matured into the F404 for the F/A-18, F101 for the B-1B and F110 as a replacement for P&W's engines in the F-15 and F-16.

P&W's YF100 two-shaft turbofan engine reached mock-up stage in January 1971 and flight-testing in February 1972 within a 'milestone' programme that required it to satisfy requirements at eight stages up to production standard, each milestone triggering the release of new funding. In its prototype versions it developed 23,810lb (10,810kg) of thrust, using a three-stage fan and ten-stage compressor. Two high-pressure stages (running at 13,450rpm) and two low-pressure stages replaced the single 'high' and three 'low' stages of the TF30 and a larger, five-

segment afterburner with 'balanced beam' nozzle was attached. Extensive use of light-weight titanium and advanced cooling techniques permitted a turbine temperature of 2,500°F (1,370°C)with a an overall compression ratio of 23:1. As development progressed the F100 steadily met its deadlines, apart from a 150hr endurance qualification in February 1973 when a blade failure occurred at 132hr during simulated Mach 2.3, 40,000ft (12,190m) running. Despite Congressional disapproval General Bellis agreed to a slight reduction in the parameters for this over-demanding test in order to keep the programme on schedule. In fact, the failure was later attributed to flakes of rust, shaken off the test chamber walls and ingested through the engine so that they coated some of the blades and reduced their self-cooling and

aerodynamic properties. Anyone who has been inside a test chamber with a large jet engine, bucking against its shackles at full throttle, will appreciate how the massive vibration could cause this to happen. On this occasion the afterburner separated from the engine and the entire powerplant behind the fan was destroyed by fire. Another engine had exploded the previous week under similar circumstances.

The YF100 was used in the first five F-15As, subsequent aircraft receiving the production F100-PW-100 with a slightly beefed-up compressor. Contrary to P&W's normal practice the pace of the programme ruled out flight-testing the engine, which the company had planned to do in a B-45 testbed aircraft. Problems that occurred later may have been revealed by this missed stage, despite delays.

Sea Eagles: USN F-15N

When it became clear in 1965 that the US Navy was going to ditch the troubled F-111B Fleet Defence fighter project, McDonnell Douglas sought to repeat their success with the Phantom and build a new fighter for the Air Force, Navy and Marines. Don Malvern headed a team that worked on proposals for the Navy's VF-X requirement, using Pratt & Whitney engines and the advanced Hughes AN/AWG-9 radar/weapons control system that was intended to have at least 50 per cent commonality with the USAF's anticipated fighter/attack needs. In June 1968 when RFPs were issued, McDonnell Douglas prepared their variable-sweep, twin-tailed Model 225 alongside an upgraded, swing-wing Phantom derivative. The victory of Grumman's Design 303 (F-14A Tomcat) had been heavily predicted but Malvern persisted with his design study that already began to resemble the F-15.

(Above) **AEDC performed many hours of tests in their supersonic wind tunnel in 1972 to ensure compatibility of the F100 engine with the F-15's inlet system.** Arnold Engineering Development Centre

An F100-PW-220 'pulled' from an F-15E shows the special handling equipment needed for the task. via Ron Thurlow

By 1971 F-14 costing problems had taken Grumman to the verge of bankruptcy and interest in a naval F-15 alternative was rearoused. McDonnell Douglas assured Deputy Secretary for Defense Nitze that a version of their Model 199-1B (F-15A) could operate from carriers with the addition of wing-folding, a stronger arresting hook, a twin-wheel extending nose gear for nose-tow catapult launch and reinforced main landing gear.

The company's long experience with naval fighters served them well in persuading the Navy that a viable Tomcat alternative could be built with only 2,300lb (1,043kg) of extra weight. However, the Navy's Fighter Study Group 111 that clearly did not favour an 'Air Force Fighter' added a considerable package of extra equipment and the Tomcat's four AIM-54 Phoenix missiles (known as 'the buffalo' because of its bulky shape). The

weight and cost graphs for 'F-15N' immediately soared out of feasible limits.

1973 brought more pressure on the over-budget F-14 and alternatives were again re-examined at the insistence of the Senate Armed Services Committee. F-15N was compared with various cut-priced, reduced capability F-14 alternatives and the swing-wing Phantom, F-4(FVS). A Phoenix-armed F-15(N-PHX) would have weighed nearly 47,000lb (21,320kg), while a navalized Sparrow-firing version was still 4,300lb (1,950kg) over the basic F-15A weight and lacked the F-14's swing-wing to supply safe landing and launch speeds at that weight. 'Blown' BLC flaps, single-slotted ailerons and Krueger leading-edge flaps would have been necessary to provide high lift and reduce approach speed to 136kt. Doubts were also expressed about the narrow-track landing gear's stability for a deck landing and about the pilot's view of the deck on approach because of the aircraft's high aoa.

F-15A 74-110 in June 1976 with the 'attitude deception' paint scheme devised by Keith Ferris. TF-15As 74-0139 and 74-1030 had similar schemes, as did F-15A 73-0111. Colours were FS36440, 36231 and 36118. Jim Rotramel

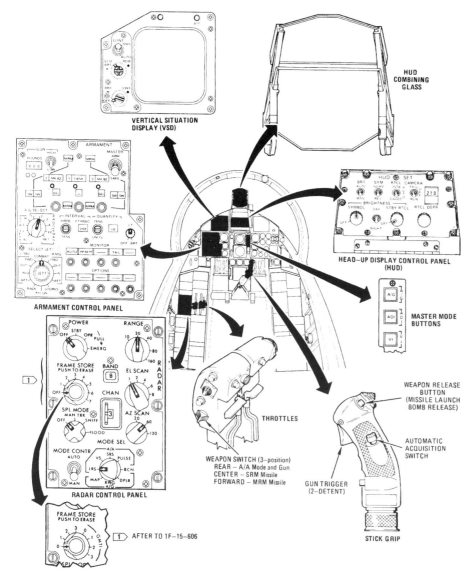

Fire control and display systems.

Another Fighter Study Group was set up and its deliberations eventually produced a formula for the next-generation naval fighter, the F/A-18 rather than an F-15N. Meanwhile, rising concern about the Middle East situation, in which carrier aviation would have been crucial in the event of a conflict involving the USA, reinstated the F-14A as a perceived necessity. Although McDonnell Douglas's Eagle, while still cheaper than a Tomcat, never saw a carrier deck, its linear successor, the F/A-18 Hornet became the true USN Phantom replacement and went on to supplant the A-6, A-7 and some F-14As too.

McDonnell's new fighter needed a name. For the F-4 a company-wide competition produced a range of sobriquets reflecting J.S. McDonnell's interest in the occult, from which he chose 'Phantom II'. A similarly supernatural range of names was put to the test for F-15, together with those suggesting birds of prey (also favoured by the Boss). From these he rapidly selected 'Eagle' before it could be bestowed on the B-1 bomber. Detail design continued through to June 1972 sped on by the company's investment in computer-aided design and following a similar 'milestone' plan to that used for the engine. Within a series of 'cost-plus and fixed-price' incentives, McDonnell Douglas pressed on towards the first milestone in September 1970: the preliminary design review. With the choice of engine settled attention turned to armament and the radar/fire control system to operate it.

Eagle Talons: The Gun

Despite the relatively small proportion of air-to-air kills involving guns in Vietnam it was felt that no future fighter should be built without one. It was considered that the weight and internal space penalty of a 265lb (120kg) M61 cannon plus ammunition might pay off in close combat or when the missiles ran out. At first, the Eagle's primary armament was to be the AIM-82A Dogfight missile, a revised Sparrow designated AIM-7F and a new gun, the GAU-7. Engineered by Philco-Ford this

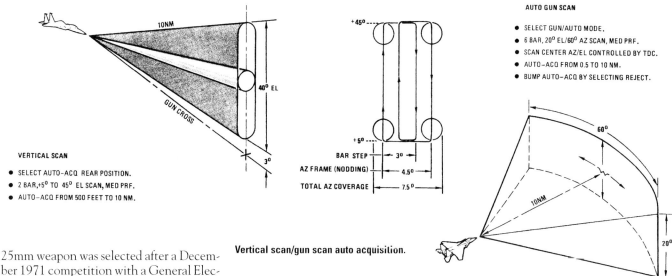

VERTICAL SCAN

- SELECT AUTO-ACQ REAR POSITION.
- 2 BAR, +5° TO 45° EL SCAN, MED PRF.
- AUTO-ACQ FROM 500 FEET TO 10 NM.

BAR STEP — 3°

AZ FRAME (NODDING) — 4.5°

TOTAL AZ COVERAGE — 7.5°

AUTO GUN SCAN

- SELECT GUN/AUTO MODE.
- 6 BAR, 20° EL/60° AZ SCAN, MED PRF.
- SCAN CENTER AZ/EL CONTROLLED BY TDC.
- AUTO-ACQ FROM 0.5 TO 10 NM.
- BUMP AUTO-ACQ BY SELECTING REJECT.

Vertical scan/gun scan auto acquisition.

25mm weapon was selected after a December 1971 competition with a General Electric proposal at Eglin AFB and was to have been fitted to Eagle F5. It used Brunswick caseless ammunition (already rejected by the US Army after separate trials) to save weight and cost, but this was its downfall. There was an unacceptable probability that the ammunition might explode within its feed tunnel to the gun. It also tended to leave high levels of chemical residue. In addition, the gun feed mechanism could not be made to work reliably, partly because detonation of the shells was uneven at the high firing speed of 6,000 rounds per minute. The project had already consumed $100m by September 1973 when the Air Force decided that it could wait no longer. General Electric's design had encountered similar problems. The combat-hardened M61-A-1 Vulcan rotary cannon that the USAF had preferred all along, was installed instead, though mountings for the GAU-7 remained in place in Eagles up to the F-15E. The first four test F-15As had used M61s while awaiting their GAU-7s, firing 21,000 rounds in the first 1,000 test flights.

Locating the gun in the airframe was not easy. Placing it under the nose, as in the F-4E, would have upset the delicate avionics in the nose with vibration. A position further back in the fuselage was considered, though gun-gas ingestion into the intakes ruled this out leaving one of the wing-roots as the best choice. It offered space for the weapon and its ammunition drum while keeping it fairly close to the centre of gravity to avoid recoil-induced aiming errors. It also gave much easier gun alignment in the vertical plane to keep the shells on target. In the F-4E, mounting the gun on the fuselage centreline axis required a slightly

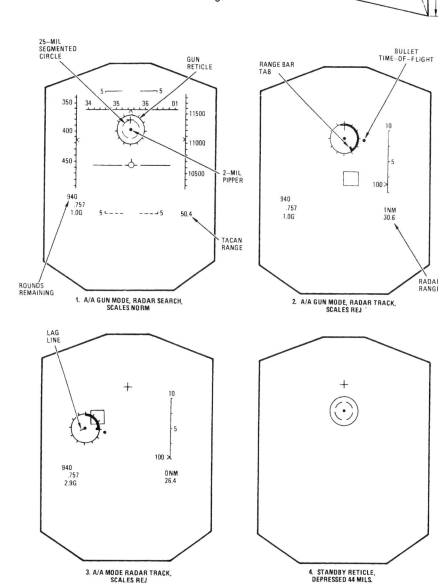

1. A/A GUN MODE, RADAR SEARCH, SCALES NORM

2. A/A GUN MODE, RADAR TRACK, SCALES REJ

3. A/A MODE RADAR TRACK, SCALES REJ

4. STANDBY RETICLE, DEPRESSED 44 MILS.

HUD displays, gun mode steering. USAF

depressed line of fire because of the air-craft's drooping nose profile and therefore a slight nose-up pitch to fire the gun accurately. A wing-root location solved this problem despite being slightly off-axis.

Also included in the first 'milestone' was a radar 'fly off' competition between Hughes and Westinghouse for the F-15's radar. With the award of a contract to the winning Hughes design at the end of August, the main components of the F-15 design began to fall into place.

Eagle Eyes: The An/APG-63 Radar

Westinghouse's AN/APQ-72 and APQ-100 radars, used in the early F-4s were ground-breaking, long-range detection and missile-guidance sets. The APQ-120 was a lighter, solid-state system for the F-4E and the AWG-10 system for the F-4J introduced pulse Doppler, look-down, shoot-down capability as well as pulse search-while-track and continuous wave illumination for

the AIM-7 Sparrow. On good days they were excellent systems but their complexity and unreliability often reduced their availability severely and crews were lucky to be able to lock on to targets at much more than 12mi (19km) for an AIM-7 shot. Hughes had developed the sophisticated AWG-9 (Air Weapons Group 9) system for the F-14A that could track 24 targets at up to 195mi (314km) and attack six of them simultaneously at different distances and altitudes. It could operate in six modes, four of them pulse Doppler, and has remained highly effective for over thirty years.

For the F-15A, the first all-digital fighter, a new long-range pulse Doppler system with look-down, shoot-down capability was required. Whereas Hughes had put together their AWG-9 at their El Segundo, California plant using Navy-funded components their APG-63 for the F-15 used various contractor-funded equipment (CFE) under McDonnell Douglas control. Long-range search was to be combined with more effective control of the chosen AIM-7 missile and also target-finding for the AIM-9 Sidewinder and the gun. Operating in the X-Band frequency range the radar array scanned up to 150mi (240km) ahead, covering an airspace volume to 60 degrees each side of the fighter in azimuth and +/– 10 degrees in elevation above and below the centreline. It could emit and analyse a mixture of high pulse repetition frequency (PRF) and medium PRF signals at the same time. This meant that the pilot received two types of data to help him locate and track his target. The high PRF transmissions (known as Velocity Search), pulsing at up to 10,000 pulses per second, were good for detecting targets at long range, particularly when approaching head-on at high closing speeds. The programmable signal processor (PSP) in later models could filter out 'clutter' and recognize from these pulses a Doppler shift, or slight increase in the number of pulsed wave-forms reaching the target as it closed, causing an increase in the frequency of the signal. From these data, the target's closing rate could be established so that the radar/fire-control system could set up missile launch parameters. However, high PRF was of little use against targets that were being pursued by the F-15 or approaching it from any other angle than head-on. Here, Long Range Search (LRS) mode mixed in medium PRFs that were better for tracking targets that changed speed or direction, and gave better definition against ground 'clutter' returns. The ability

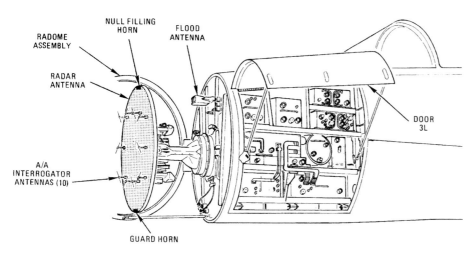

Radar set installation.

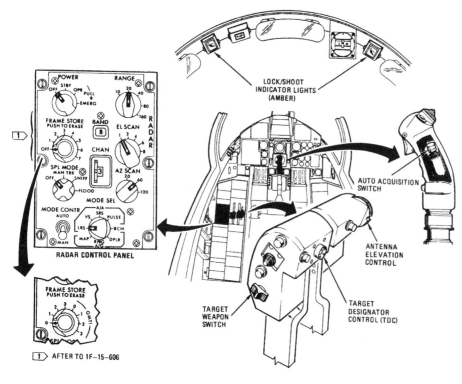

Radar controls. USAF

A/A modes radar search parameters. USAF

A/A MODE	RANGE/VELOCITY SCALES SELECTABLE	ANTENNA SCAN (SEARCH)		VSD DISPLAY
		AZ SCAN	EL BARS	
Long Range Search (LRS) HI/MED PRF ①	10, 20, 40, 80, or 160 NM	120°, 60° or 20°	1, 2, 4, 6 or 8 Bars	④ B-Scan, Space-Stabilized Up to 7 Frame Data Aging
Velocity Search (VS) HI PRF	Search: RNG Scale, 80 to 1800 kts TGT Relative GS ② Track: 10, 20, 40, 80, or 160 NM	Same as LRS		Same as LRS except during search, TGT Relative GS instead of RNG
Short Range Search (SRS) MED PRF	Search: 10, 20, 40, NM Track: 10, 20, 40, 80 or 160 NM	Same as LRS		Same as LRS
Pulse Search LO PRF ③	10, 20, 40, 80 or 160 NM	Same as LRS		B-Scan, Space-Stabilized No Data Aging
Beacon LO PRF	10, 20, 40, 80 or 160 NM	Same as LRS		B-Scan, Space Stabilized
RAM Search MED PRF	35NM Scan Center	(see below)		B-Scan, Space Stabilized Automatic Data Aging

① MED PRF only in 10 NM range: HI PRF only in 160 NM range.

② Velocity coverage in 380 to 2100 KTS in 160 NM range.

③ In PSP aircraft, becomes MED PRF mode.

④ In PSP aircraft, only 3-Frame data aging available.

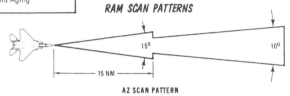

RAM SCAN PATTERNS

15° 10°

15 NM

AZ SCAN PATTERN

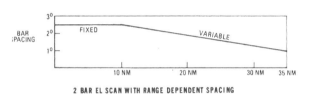

BAR SPACING

3°
2° FIXED   VARIABLE
1°

10 NM   20 NM   30 NM   35 NM

2 BAR EL SCAN WITH RANGE DEPENDENT SPACING

(Below) A Block 7 F-15A destined for the 58th TTW at Luke AFB. Opposing pilots soon called it a 'flying tennis court' since the area of its flying surfaces was significantly larger than the F-4 Phantom's. 73-100 was the first production Eagle in the Compass Ghost Grey colour scheme. It was later painted in RSAF colours for the sales drive in Saudi Arabia. Norm Taylor Collection

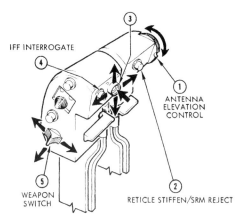

IFF INTERROGATE

ANTENNA ELEVATION CONTROL

WEAPON SWITCH

RETICLE STIFFEN/SRM REJECT

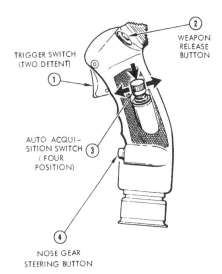

WEAPON RELEASE BUTTON

TRIGGER SWITCH (TWO DETENT)

AUTO ACQUISITION SWITCH (FOUR POSITION)

NOSE GEAR STEERING BUTTON

1. Controls centreline of antenna elevation scan pattern.

2. **Gun mode:** Provides fixed, 1,000ft range signal to primary reticle when held pressed.

   SRM mode: Momentarily pressed to reject selected SRM and select the next missile in the launch sequence.

3. **Not Pressed:** Controls VSD acquisition symbol.

   Pressed: Slaves antenna to VSD acquisition symbol. Initiates acquisition scan. Enables auto-acquire RAM (in Radar search).

   Released: Radar lockon command.

4. **Pressed:** Starts IFF interrogate.
   Selects AIM-9L seeker manual boresight.

   Released: AIM-9L returns to radar antenna LOS.

5. **Rear:** Selects A/A attack mode with gun steering.

   Centre: Selects SRM with SRM steering.

   Forward: Selects MRM with MRM steering.

1. **Trigger 1:** HUD camera operate.

   Trigger 2: Gun fire and HUD camera operate.

2. **Pressed:** SRM or MRM Launch and MRM illumination; HUD camera operate.

3. **Forward:** Alternately selects BST or SS auto-acq. (PSP) Selects RAM search or track.

   Rear: Selects vertical scan auto-acq mode. (PSP) Selects RAM relative alt. display.

   Down: Rejects any acquisition or tracking mode; returns radar to search mode.

   Centre: Spring loaded OFF.

4. **Initial Actuation:** Uncages SRM seeker and enables self-track (UNC on VSD).

   Second Actuation: (AIM-9J/J-1/P/P-1) seeker returns to BST.
   (AIM-9L) seeker returns to antenna LOS (Radar locked on) or to BST (No radar lockon).

to process high and low PRFs is now commonplace and can be incorporated into much smaller radars such as the Blue Vixen in the BAe Sea Harrier F/A.2. Hughes's APG-63 was the first system to offer this facility and this was undoubtedly a major consideration in its selection for the F-15.

APG-63 could interrogate IFF returns from potentially hostile 'plots' using an L-Band antenna and in the 1980s NCTR (non-cooperative target recognition) was added to identify targets without an IFF signature and used for the first time in 1991 during Operation *Desert Storm*. The radar also had a ground-mapping mode for navigation that could also be employed for radar offset bombing. All radar imagery from the 36in (91cm) planar array in the nose, scanning at 70 degrees per second in a selected arc, appeared either on the pilot's Head-up Display (HUD) or on a second display panel, originally called the Multiple Air Navigation Indicator (MANI) on the main instrument panel, that has since been redesignated the Vertical Situation Display (VSD). The processed, filtered signals gave the pilot a much clearer image than previous, cluttered, cathode ray tube

(Left) **Stick grip and throttle controls.**

(Below) **TF-15A (later F-15B) 73-0108 was publicly dedicated by President Gerald Ford on 14 November 1974 as 'TAC 1'.** John Poole

displays that required considerable concentration and interpretation skills.

In the air-to-air mode the pilot received information on target range from a selected scan arc of 20, 60 or 120 degrees in azimuth, with 1, 2, 4, 6 or 8 bars in elevation. A 'bar' represented the width of the scan at the selected arc. The radar would scan that arc at the top of its antenna elevation, move down to repeat the scan at a slightly lower elevation and so on, up to a maximum of six bar scans, each bar covering 1.5 degrees of vertical airspace. A full six-bar scan at the maximum (lateral) arc of 120 degrees in azimuth took around 14 sec. On his small radar control panel, situated between the throttles and the cockpit sidewall, the pilot could use the Mode Select control to switch radar modes. The Eagle employs a number of radar search modes to see what's out there. The primary mode is **Long-Range Search (LRS)** that interleaves both high and medium PRF with each bar scan; at under 10nm range it switches to Medium only and with 160nm range selected it operates exclusively at High PRF. Both offer nose aspect, look-up or look-down but Medium provides tail aspect search as well, at the expense of considerably reduced detection range. It is used whenever GCI or AWACS is unavailable. **Velocity Search (VS)** is a pulse-Doppler, long-range surveillance mode used to provide early detection of reported targets. It furnishes relative target ground speed versus bearing, works exclusively in High PRF and is slightly better than the LRS mode for initial target acquisition, covering targets at speeds of between roughly 80 and 1800kt relative closing speed. However, range data are not presented on the VSD and it is generally effective only against nose-aspect targets. **Short Range Search (SRS)** pulse-Doppler mode is optimized for Sidewinder and gun engagements, employing Medium PRF to pick out targets primarily at shorter ranges against ground clutter, and provides the pilot with both the opening and closing rates for targets. **Pulse Mode** is a Low PRF mode used for back-up search and track in a look-up only manner. It was non-Doppler and was later superseded in Programmable Signal Processor (PSP)-equipped Eagles (those featuring the later APG-63 or follow-on APG-70 radar) by a new Medium PRF Pulse Mode with improved look-up capability, but retaining the same drawbacks of being ineffective in look-down. IFF would be

(Above) F-15A 73-0085 was one of several detached from Luke AFB to the 57th FWW at Nellis AFB in November 1975. Underwing is a Rockwell GBU-8/B HOBOS electro-optically guided bomb, forerunner of the highly effective GBU-15 and AGM-130 that equipped F-15Es from the 1990s. Logan via Rotramel

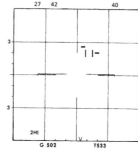

NORMAL SEARCH
PILOT POSITIONS ACQUISITION SYMBOL ON TARGET (OR IN TARGET AREA) AND COMMANDS RAM MODE

Raid assessment mode.

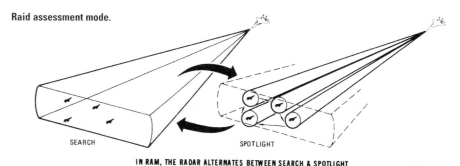

IN RAM, THE RADAR ALTERNATES BETWEEN SEARCH & SPOTLIGHT

ALTITUDE RAM COVERAGE AT DESIGNATED AREA RANGE

AZIMUTH COVERAGE OF SCAN PATTERN AT DESIGNATED AREA RANGE (4.5 NM)

TARGET NOT IN TRACK FILE

SOLID SYMBOL TARGETS IN TRACK FILE

DESIGNATED AREA EL POSITION

DESIGNATED AREA RANGE RELATIVE AZ POSITION (DOES NOT MOVE WITH PERIODIC ANTENNA SCAN)

ALTITUDE OF SCAN CENTER AT DESIGNATED AREA RANGE

RAM MODE CUE

RAM SEARCH DISPLAY

PRIORITY TARGET EL POSITION

RAM MODE CUE

PRIORITY TARGET RANGE

PRIORITY TARGET RELATIVE AZ POSITION (DOES NOT MOVE WITH PERIODIC ANTENNA SCAN)

RELATIVE ALT. SYMBOL

6° CIRCLE REPRESENTS PRIORITY TARGET POSITION

RAM TRACK DISPLAY

(Top) McDonnell Douglas's much-travelled demonstrator TF-15A 71-0291 in Bicentennial colours at Wright Patterson AFB, 23 July 1976. It was the first Eagle to travel outside the USA. Norm Taylor Collection

(Middle) Bearing an MASDC number FH002 on its retirement the third F-15A, 71-0282 tested formation strip lights, flight-tested the APG-63 radar and in 1977 tested the F-15 Advanced Environmental Control System (AECS). Norm Taylor Collection

(Bottom) The faithful 71-0291, in one of its many guises, served as demonstrator for the range of weaponry that had been cleared for the Eagle by February 1979. Norm Taylor Collection

(Above) The 3247th Test Squadron at Eglin AFB, Florida began to use 'AD' codes, signifying 'Armament Division' in 1982, changing to 'ET' in October 1989. F-15A 75-0056 was one of several Eagles used to test new weapons and their associated systems. Norm Taylor

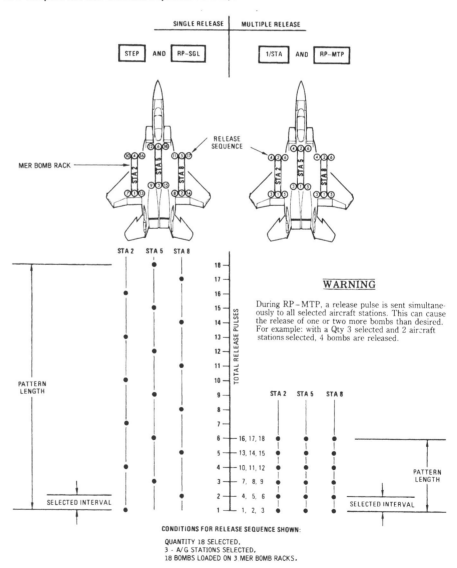

Ordnance release sequences for the F-15C/D in the ground attack mode.

employed between the search and acquisition stages and once acquired the target became a Primary Designated Target (PDT) and was tracked in a Single Target Tracking Mode (STT) by default. Any AIM-7s fired then guided to that target.

Companion radar acquisition modes are used for specific target lock-on preparatory to employment of missiles or guns, and fall under two broad categories; Manual and Automatic. Manual employs the throttle Target Designator Control (TDC) switch to shift the acquisition brackets over the relevant target return on the VSD. Once locked and tracked, this provides steering to target on both the VSD and HUD, as do the automatic modes. These are for separate **Automatic** modes for *heads-up* target acquisition that continue to acquire targets until the pilot rejects that mode or selects another. **Supersearch** uses radar to scan the volume of airspace visible in the HUD in a 6-bar scan at Medium PRF. This would typically be used at BVR at longer ranges or in an IFR

Opposite page:
(Top) An AIM-7M flies straight and true from this 4485 Operational Test Squadron F-15A-18-MC. Coded 'ED' until 1982 the squadron undertook armament trials using a large selection of aircraft types. Raytheon

(Middle) An AIM-120A departs from this Armament Division F-15C-38-MC while aircraft-mounted cameras record its flight. USAF

(Bottom) This Triple Nickel F-15C displays the standard air-to-air armament of AIM-9L Sidewinders and AIM-7F/M Sparrow missiles that Eagles carried until the early 1990s. McDonnell Douglas via Norm Taylor

This Page:
(Above) The McDonnell Douglas ACES II (Advanced Concept Ejection Seat) replaced the IC-7 seat used in F-15As up to Block 17. After this 'through the canopy' ejection from a redundant F-15A airframe two rocket motors power the seat upwards and forwards as the parachute begins to deploy. USAF

(Right) The AIM-120A 'Slammer' introduced fire-and-forget missile technology, vastly increasing the combat capability of fighters like the F-15. Seen here on the LAU-114A/A AIM-9 launch rail it can also be drop-launched from the fuselage missile stations. Hughes

F-15A-3-MC 71-0286 continued to test fuel systems and armament in 1973, still in its International Orange trim. Macair via Norm Taylor

TF-15A-7-MC 73-0110 was delivered to the 58th TTW at Luke AFB and is seen here in January 1975. The raised strake on the airbrake and the borderless national insignia are evident. Norm Taylor

Marked for the 12th Air Force (with headquarters at Bergstrom AFB), this TF-15A (73-0112) carries black-and-white ACM stripes in June 1976. Norm Taylor

environment. **Boresight** slaves the radar antenna along the aircraft's boresight or roll axe and searches in range between 500ft (150m) and 10nm (later 20nm) out at Medium PRF until the enemy is acquired and locked onto, typically where the pilot has sighted the enemy or where such a sighting is imminent, based on a radar search contact. (Before the introduction of the PSP, Boresight mode used a Low PRF if Pulse search had been selected and the pilot flew the Eagle to put the enemy within a 4 degree Boresight steering circle on the HUD.) **Vertical Scan** employs Medium PRF with a 2-bar, 40 degree vertical scan, also at ranges between 500ft (150m) and 10nm (later 20nm), starting at 5 degrees above the fuselage reference line. This would be used primarily in a one-on-one in look-up aspect (and consequently down if the pilot rolls inverted), but also in a situation where an engagement deteriorates into a 'yo-yo', when both the Eagle and its adversary are chasing each other's tails round in circles, allowing the F-15 pilot to get a short-range missile lock in a situation where it is difficult to get enough lead to put the guns on him. **Auto Guns** works in Medium PRF again and features a moveable (via the TDC button) scan pattern about the front of the machine, effective at between 0.5–10nm. This provides a lead-computing aiming reference for accurate shooting.

In addition, PSP Eagles offer a Medium PRF **Raid Assessment Mode (RAM)**, allowing the radar to break-out closely spread multiple targets that might otherwise appear as just one target return, at ranges of up to 35nm, and to create separate track files on up to four of them (later expanded). One may also be singled out for Single Target Track for a missile launch. The spotlighted area is selected using the normal TDC lock-on procedure on any target in the VSD, and selecting RAM mode. In this mode the system scans the small 'spotlighted' volume around the designated area while simultaneously scanning a broader swathe of sky around it. Further 'special' modes designed to reduce detection of the Eagle and/or to work in a countermeasures-saturated environment are also available, comprising **Sniff** and **Flood** modes. Engaging Sniff causes the radar to cease transmitting at the end of its current Bar scan, but to continue receiving. Targets that are radiating noise-jamming can then be acquired and will be shown on the VSD, using Angle-of-Jam reception methods, and Home-on-Jam to derive firing solutions

TF-15A 73-0109 of the 55th TFTS in January 1975, the only Air Superiority Blue F-15 to have its white 'LA' codes overpainted in black. Jim Rotramel

for missiles. Flood engages a Medium PRF antenna pattern (or Low PRF if the radar is working in a Pulse mode) effective out to 2nm for accurate air-to-air gunnery, as well as providing automatic acquisition for missile attack in a dogfight situation.

All missile-ready, optimum steering and launch cues are furnished on the HUD for timely launch of weapons within their prescribed firing parameters. There are separate displays for the key types of AAMs (Sidewinder, Sparrow and AMRAAM) that are periodically updated using new Operational Flight Program software to cater for the exact performance characteristics of new sub-marks as they enter operational service.

In the later APG-70 radar the pilot could switch to Track-While-Scan (TWS) or High Data TWS (HDTWS) so that he could still track the Primary Designated Target (PDT) and keep an eye out for more targets. With the advent of AMRAAM it became possible to designate Secondary Designated Targets (SDTs) as AIM-120s can be unleashed in sequence against multiple, separate targets. The search modes also underwent evolutionary changes for APG-70. Velocity Search remained, plus Range While Search (RWS) in High, Medium or Interleaved modes, essentially similar to LRS/SRS. Range Gated High (RGH) mode provides data purely on high- and low-closure rate targets. A High PRF

Acceleration in the vertical plane, the F-15's speciality. Author's Collection

ACS Aircraft

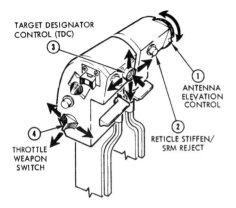

TARGET DESIGNATOR
CONTROL (TDC)
(3)

ANTENNA
ELEVATION
CONTROL
(1)

THROTTLE
WEAPON
SWITCH
(4)

RETICLE STIFFEN/
SRM REJECT
(2)

1. Controls antenna elevation in radar ground map mode.

2. **ACS Aircraft**: Cages HUD Velocity vector and pitch scale to zero drift if AUTO or CDIP is not selected.

   PACS Aircraft: Not used.

3. **Not Pressed**: Control of antenna azimuth scan centre (radar ground map mode).
   Controls azimuth scan centre when radar is in narrow scan RBG map or BCN modes.
   Controls position of acquisition symbol in DBS full and sector scan.

   Pressed: Rate control of HUD target designator (radar in A/G ranging mode) or rate control of VSD cursor (radar in ground map mode); control of VSD target designator in DBS modes.

   Release: Designates air-to-ground target.

4. **Rear**: De-energizes A/G, VI, or ADI mode status.

   Centre/Forward: Allows selection of A/G, VI, or ADI master mode.

5. **PACS Aircraft**: Cages HUD Velocity vector and pitch scale to zero drift if AUTO or CDIP is not selected.

PACS Aircraft

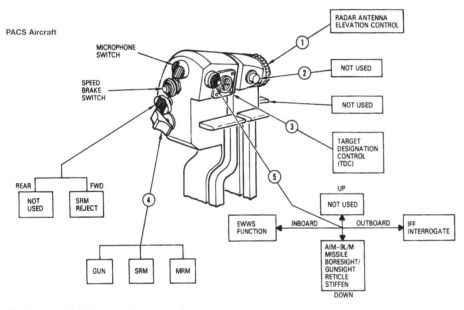

MICROPHONE
SWITCH

SPEED
BRAKE
SWITCH

RADAR ANTENNA
ELEVATION CONTROL
(1)

NOT USED
(2)

NOT USED

TARGET
DESIGNATION
CONTROL
(TDC)
(3)

(5)

UP
NOT USED

EWWS
FUNCTION — INBOARD — OUTBOARD — IFF
INTERROGATE

AIM-9L/M
MISSILE
BORESIGHT/
GUNSIGHT
RETICLE
STIFFEN
DOWN

REAR — FWD
NOT USED — SRM REJECT

(4)

GUN — SRM — MRM

Throttle controls in the ground attack mode.

Vector mode can be used and this doubles the time it takes to complete the scan, the extra data and processing time being used to pick up tiny, and possibly first-generation-stealthy, targets at very long range. Acquisition modes were given increased range to reflect the newer missiles' capability.

Other, non-weapons modes included **Beacon**, to interrogate and home onto other aircraft (such as a tanker) or a ground-based beacon transponder, using B-scan format (air-to-air), or Plan Position Indicator (showing ground returns for air-to-ground) for IFF identification. Pilots would often use this as a quick way of homing onto the 'base' beacon after a mission. Sniff mode could be used actively or

passively to detect sources of radar noise jamming that were interfering with the APG-63's other modes. The radar could also be employed in three air-to-ground modes, a legacy of the earlier requirement for the F-15 to have a secondary attack capability, by switching to A/G on the radar panel. DRLR, a Doppler function, pointed the antenna 15 degrees down and scanning 45 degrees left and right to read ground speed from its returns, thereby providing the central computer with updates for navigation. In Ranging mode (RNG) it could also read slant ranges off points on the ground for the plan position indicator (PPI), or, using low PRFs 'read' the ground for mapping purposes.

These modes actually gave the F-15A a considerable bombing capability, using six delivery modes to release a wide range of weapons from three MER-200 bomb racks. Early flight test experience indicated bombing accuracy superior to the A-7D and F-111A and considerably better than the F-4E. All air-to-ground data appeared on the HUD without preventing a quick switch to air-to-air if needed. In Automatic mode the system would compute ballistics and automatically release in level, dive or dive/toss delivery, giving steering coordinates to the target and radar offsets on the HUD. Alternatively, the pilot could initiate manually, focusing on a continuously displayed impact point in his HUD, generated by computer ballistics. Back-up modes provided similar delivery profiles in the event of a failure in the HUD, central computer or armament control set. Another mode handled delivery of guided weapons and Mk 84 bombs with either laser or electro-optical guidance were cleared for the F-15A. Proposals for other weapons included GBU-15, SRAM and Harpoon.

A complete F-15 avionics system was extensively flight-tested in a WB-66 bomber prior to installation in an Eagle so that it operated very close to its design targets from the start. The entire avionics evaluation programme was conducted using only one radar set that held up well throughout.

Throughout the first part of 1971 political opposition still sought to prevent the Eagle from hatching. As the enormous costs of the F-14 Tomcat and F-15 programmes became more visible the House Appropriations Committee continued to try to foist the F-14 onto the Air Force on the pretext that it could perform the USAF mission and carry the Navy's Phoenix missile. Other Congressional pressure groups continued to agitate for lighter, cheaper fighters, paving the way for F-16. Meanwhile, the F-15 programme stayed on target, easing past more 'milestones' in April and May and achieving its sixth target; engine and inlet compatibility, in February 1972. Remarkably for an aircraft of that era it was also 390lb (177kg) under its 40,000lb (18,144kg) target weight. On 26 June the first aircraft, 71-280 rolled out under its own power at St Louis, on time and below budget. Chief Test Pilot Irving L. Burrows took the fighter for its first flight on 27 July, fourteen years after the first F-4 flew, having prepared thoroughly in the very advanced McDonnell Douglas flight simulator.

The APG-63 radar scanner. USAF

(Above) The slender nose-gear, seen here on an F-15A, has had small modifications to cope with the extra weight of later, heavier Eagles. Author's Collection

(Above right) Early F-15A-style wheel with the 'Macair' logo on its hub. Author

F-15Cs had a different design, although it was interchangeable with the earlier pattern. A new design was introduced for the F-15E and this is not useable on previous Eagles. Author's Collection

Testing Time

Twenty pre-production (not prototype) aircraft were budgeted; twelve for the contractor's initial tests (Category I) and eight for the USAF's Joint Test Force of TAC and Air Force Systems Command (AFSC) pilots (Category II). After making its maiden flight at Edwards AFB 71-280 (aircraft F1) initiated the first of the three manufacturer's test stages using aircraft F1 to F10 and the first two-seat versions, TF1 and TF2. F1 explored the basic flight envelope and handling with external stores and it was joined in September 1972 by F2 (71-281) that became the main engine test airframe. Basic handling tests were assisted by a ⅛th scale remotely piloted replica of the F-15. Dropped from an NB-52 the model performed stall and spin tests under NASA (Dryden) supervision so that these characteristics were well understood before test pilots flew the real thing. By August 1973 Irv Burrows, Pete Garrison and their team had made 1,000 flights, exceeding Mach 2.3 and 60,000ft (18,300m). Both aircraft survived the test programme, F-1 going to Lackland AFB Museum and F-2 to Langley AFB.

The AN/APG-63 was first installed in Eagle F3 (71-282) for radar and calibrated airspeed tests from November 1973, while F4 (71-283) performed structural tests and F5 was first with the M61 gun and external fuel tanks. Further development of radar and weapons control systems fell to F6 that joined the Air Superiority Blue painted test force in June and F10, in which integration of the radar, avionics and Tactical Electronic Warfare System (TEWS) was accomplished. F7 joined the external stores handling tests before serving as a ground systems trainer while F8 was used to refine the fuel system and for spin tests with an anti-spin parachute container attached to the rear fuselage. Up to 29 October 1973 each of the eleven test aircraft in use had averaged fourteen flights per month. Irv Burrows reported that minor adjustments had been made in the Control Augmentation System to damp down the effects of sudden, small control stick movements to avoid the danger of pilot-induced oscillation. He commented on the tendency to 'weather vane' on landing in a crosswind, requiring the nose to be lowered as quickly as possible thereby partially negating the usual nose-high landing run using the aircraft's considerable surface area as an aerodynamic brake to slow it down instead of

F-15A 73-0113 of the 461st TFTS in June 1976 with no national insignia and a false canopy marking beneath the nose. This aircraft was sold to Israel in 1992.
Jim Rotramel

fitting a brake 'chute. Holding a high angle of attack on touchdown bore the risk of a tail-scrape and a shower of sparks to get the attention of those watching from the control tower. After a few such scrapes the HUD was modified to give a flashing warning when the angle reached 13 degrees nose-up, allowing another 2 degrees before contact was made. Changes were made in the compression of the main gear legs, allowing them to absorb most of the landing load on touchdown and to the rudder-aileron interconnect that had tended to raise the wing on the windward side when the rudder was used to correct a 'weathervane' motion, making the situation even worse. Crosswind landing tolerance was increased to 30kt. Additionally, the nose gear steering was made more sensitive.

Family Model

The other two Category I test aircraft were the first two 'twin tub' TF-15As, 71-290 and 71-291. From then on every seventh aircraft off the line was a two-seater, later designated F-15B. Addition of the second cockpit position in the 'growth' space behind the pilot added 800lb (363kg) and required removal of the Northrop AN/ALQ-135 ECM boxes from that area. In other respects it resembled the single-seat F-15A. A second seat proved invaluable for a wide variety of development tasks, and in the case of 71-291 for McDonnell Douglas's F-15 sales effort. This aircraft became the best-known Eagle after its world sales tour and its work as a company

demonstrator before it became the Strike Eagle/F-15E concept demonstrator. T1 (71-290) was to go through many changes of configuration in its long career, appearing as the Advanced Concepts demonstrator, F-15 STOL/Manoeuvring Technology demonstrator, F-15E cockpit testbed and NF-15B with ACTIVE technology vectoring nozzles and canard foreplanes.

Following completion of Cat I the USAF performed Cat II from 14 March 1974, though Air Force pilots had already flown some of the Category I sorties. Col Wendell Shawler, Director of the Joint Test Force, was first to do so for a 75min flight starting at 9am on Saturday 18 August 1972. The programme showed that Don Malvern's engineers and designers had just about got it right, with only twenty-three small engineering change proposals (ECPs) recommended. Some involved details such as rerouting wire bundles or redesigning bolts. Three involved external changes based on the exhaustive flight-testing routines. Minor flutter in the horizontal stabilizer was cured by cutting back the inboard 4ft (1.2m) of each stabilizer to a distance of 16in (40cm). The resulting 'snag' reduced the coefficient of pressure and slightly altered the moment of inertia, eliminating the flutter. Aircraft F4 flight-tested the ECP and it was applied to F1-3 also.

The Eagle's distinctive 'cutaway' wingtips were literally sawn away to cure a severe buffet problem at high g in the high subsonic speed range at around 30,000ft (9,000m). It was established that the rear area of each squared-off tip was creating too much lift in that condition, causing

John Poole was one of the initial cadre of personnel assigned to the F-15 Program at Luke AFB from July 1974. He spent two years there supporting the OT&E program and pilot training.

'The OT&E program began immediately the aircraft arrived at Luke and within some short period, we had the assigned aircraft and the program was well underway. The OT&E program continually evaluated not only the aircraft performance from the pilot's perspective but also the maintenance and supportability. Much time was spent in evaluating the Built In Test (BIT) system designed into the various avionics systems in the aircraft. Of concern was the ability of the aircraft systems to alert the maintenance personnel when something was wrong. In the nose-wheel well was the Avionics Status Panel (ASP) which through a series of mechanical indicators (red or white coloured balls) referred to as 'Bit Balls', indicated if a system had a fault. Red if bad, white if good. The system was supposed to work very simply. If one looked at the panel after flight and a 'red' ball was shown against a particular system, one was supposed to be able to open the panel where the system LRUs were located, and see a further indicator (on the LRU itself), in this case 'white if bad', remove the offending LRU and with a quick operational check of the system, return the aircraft to service. Without going into a very lengthy explanation, the system had its problems. As an example, one very large controversy was never fully resolved. What if the pilot reported no faults and the system said an LRU was faulted? The perfect situation would be to change the offending LRU and fly. We quickly found that the best way was to power up the 'faulted' system and complete a thorough check ourselves.

I remember one very spectacular 'Scramble' test to demonstrate the minimum time for the crews to enter the aircraft, start up and launch. It was the first time we had seen the aircraft in a 'Scramble' type launch and it was impressive. Later, we were to see many such actual scrambles and they never failed to impress everyone. One of the OT&E pilots was a member of Air Defense Command and at that time, the aircraft was still being considered for introduction into the Air Defense fleet and so his interest in evaluating the intercept capabilities was very important to the program. The OT&E folks were tasked to test every capability of the aircraft and our maintenance folks supported them on all deployments. They operated from Edwards AFB to test the capability of the aircraft against the SR-71A and of course the Hughes folks were very interested in making sure that the radar worked and that plenty of spare parts were available in case of failure (the Hughes people came to Edwards with a large number of 'extra' radar LRUs to insure that the system was always at full capability). They were quietly told to take the extra parts back to the factory and properly deliver them as spares. There was to be no 'extra' parts support during the test program to skew the support posture of the program.

Wing maintenance personnel supported the OT&E program during several visits to Nellis AFB and other sites. On the first Nellis visit, the tasking involved air to ground testing and not many days after arrival, a message from HQ TAC came that said to stop the air-to-ground phase of the OT&E testing with the aircraft. Immediately the pilots got the message; the 'Caterpillar' hats (from the company who makes earth-moving equipment) very quickly disappeared, never to reappear! Needless to say, we were

John Poole (right) with TAC-1. John Poole

very happy to see the mission return to the single 'air-to-air' tasking. The air-to-ground capability was never removed from the software and the Israeli Air Force quickly made good use of that capability.

One of the most important phases of the OT&E program occurred at Eglin AFB in 1975 and involved among other things, compatibility testing of the AIM-7F with the F-15. The AIM-7F was a new missile and all of our test assets were flown in on an F-4C support aircraft from the factory in California. Our pilots tested the aircraft against various targets including helicopters and B-52s. Some of the testing involved launching against various drone targets, probably the most impressive was the BOMARC [Boeing IM-99A ramjet-powered unmanned interceptor]. The BOMARC was originally designed as a long range, high altitude air defense weapon and when phased out, became a target drone capable of speeds in excess of Mach 3 above 60,000ft [18,000m]. From our vantage point on the flight line at Eglin, we could see the BOMARCs as they were launched from their site on the beach, west of Eglin. What a sight to see them climbing vertically from the launch pad toward their target track, far out into the Gulf of Mexico. To support the BOMARC shots, the F-15 'shooter' aircraft would have already launched, refuelled from the KC-97 tanker and would be in position for the GCI site to vector him toward the target as it flew its preprogrammed profile. The timing for these missions was critical because once the BOMARC launched, the F-15 either had to go or the mission was lost along with the drone. These missions were critical to demonstrate and evaluate the capability of the individual parts (AIM-7, APG-63 Radar and aircraft) to perform as an integrated weapons system against a wide variety of threats. The results of the shots were classified but, from the debrief of the pilots after each mission, we knew things went very well. As maintenance personnel supporting the program, our tasking was to insure that each time the aircraft launched, it launched with a trouble free radar system. Our radar technicians, crew chiefs and other maintenance personnel did an absolutely fantastic job and never once did we lose a mission for maintenance.

Another experience (non-OT&E) early in the program involved the first visit of the Eagle to another country supported only by Air Force maintenance personnel. The Air Force was invited to participate in the 1975

Canadian International Air Exposition and the Cleveland Air show the same week. So, two aircraft were deployed to Trenton, Ontario and with tanker support, an F-15 supported both shows each day. The two aircraft sent to Canada were an Air Superiority Blue aircraft and the first production 'Grey' Eagle, 73-100. The 'Grey' aircraft had less than 25 total hours since delivery and our Canadian friends could not believe that we would bring a 'new' aircraft to support the air show. What an experience for everyone: the local population really enjoyed the daily flights at Trenton, everyone was treated very well and the aircraft performance was excellent. The Canadians loved the performance of the aircraft with its very tight turns and vertical climb capability. The aircraft were configured with three external tanks and when we arrived at Trenton, we took off the two wing tanks and flew with the centerline only. The effects of the Grey painted aircraft versus the Blue aircraft were unbelievable. Remember at Luke, it was clear blue sky almost every day. The Blue aircraft really stood out against the dark clouds while the Grey aircraft just disappeared! The aircraft flew non-stop from Luke to Trenton and returned the same way.

The OT&E Program was mixed in with our normal flying program at Luke and all maintenance activity on the OT&E aircraft was carefully tracked to gain a baseline for reliability and maintainability. I am sure that some software changes in the radar system were driven by the data gained from the OT&E program. Also, we were constantly trying to find ways to improve the troubleshooting procedures and to find ways to supplement the BIT programs of the various systems.

The airplane was much easier to maintain than the Phantom or F-111. The systems were much more reliable and in general more maintainable. The access panels, for example could be opened with a coin. (We had a special tool to unsnap the locking screws). I enjoyed giving tours and briefings on the aircraft and during those sessions, I would offer to open the avionics access panel to show the various LRUs. However, I would say that I had forgotten my special tool to open the panels. I would then ask someone in the group for a coin which of course, I would use to open the bay door!! I must say it was always quite impressive that one could gain access to the avionics bays of the aircraft without requiring any special tools!'

One of the first batch of USAFE Eagles, F-15A 76-0011 for the 36th TFW at Bitburg. Author's Collection

vibration severe enough to alarm the test pilots. A standard wing fence solution was tried without effect. Finally, an area of 4sq ft (0.37sq m) was cut off each tip diagonally and the gap was sealed with wood and filler. The revised, raked tips appeared on the factory line for all production F-15s and they were retrofitted to the test Eagles. Finally, the airbrake had caused buffet too when extended so its area was increased from 20 to 31.5sq ft (2.9sq m) that allowed its previous almost vertical extension angle to be reduced without reducing the amount of drag it created. The longer brake needed an external stiffener rib on the first thirty production aircraft, deleted when the structure was made more rigid. By mid-1974 the programme had encountered few aircraft problems and F-15As were rolling off the line more cheaply and with 32 per cent fewer assembly man-hours than originally assumed. The use of large, integrally machined parts, including bulkheads each weighing 145lb (66kg) and machined from a 1,250lb (567kg) titanium block. As a further weight-saving, McDonnell Douglas was contracted in May 1971 to design a boron wing for the aircraft, saving another 400lb (181kg), but this was cancelled in 1975.

There was, however, one increasingly worrying series of discoveries concerning the behaviour of the F100 engine in combat-type flight situations. Col Bellis's team had been charged with commissioning an aircraft with minimum-risk technology, but the F-15 nevertheless had a highly innovative radar and cockpit and an engine that pushed the limits of compression, internal temperatures and responsiveness in combat very hard indeed. Although the F100's 'milestone' points had been passed, albeit with slight relaxation of the final one 1973 brought a series of engine fires and compressor failures. Mostly, these were connected with rapid throttle movements at high altitude leading to engine stalls and afterburner blow-outs. In the hands of experienced test pilots none had led to an accident: the F-15 was the first US fighter to reach its first 5,000hr without a serious mishap and it flew 7,300hr before the first loss and 30,000hr before the second. Problems with the F100 caused delays

while P&W fine-tuned the engine to make it more tolerant of rapid throttle movements in manoeuvring flight. Sadly, the stall-stagnation difficulty persisted into service life and it has required an ongoing series of improvements throughout the Eagle's career to date.

As the first batch of F-15 pilots became used to their new aircraft they quickly appreciated that they were riding a genuine fighter with superior energy, turning and acceleration. It had a cockpit that was easy to use and gave visibility through 360 degrees, even including downward vision through its bulged Lexan canopy. It had the ethos of a weapon that could restore the morale of pilots, still somewhat jaded by the experience of Vietnam. However, even the most optimistic of them could hardly have forecast that USAF Eagles' kill-to-loss ratio in their next major engagement would be 34:0, or that Israeli pilots would use early F-15As to destroy fifty-seven enemy aircraft (including three MiG-25s) without loss, or even that the Eagles' overall kill to loss ratio by the end of the century would approach 100:0.

CHAPTER TWO

Ready Team

Red-and-white ACM markings were an attempt to make the Air Superiority Blue F-15As (including this one, 73-0103) more visible against a sky background. 73-100 had yellow and black stripes and TF-15A 73-0112 had a black-and-white pattern. This paradoxical burst of colour on the monochrome Eagles was sadly short-lived. Norm Taylor Collection

Fledglings

It was appropriate that the 555th *Triple Nickel* Squadron should become the first USAF recipient of the F-15A. The top-scoring squadron in Vietnam, with 40 MiGs downed between 23 April 1966 and 28 December 1972, it had included Col Robin Olds, Capt Steve Ritchie and Capt Chuck DeBellevue among its multiple MiG-killers and accumulated a wealth of fighter experience. In practice, its famous identity was transferred in number only to the 58th TFTW at Luke AFB from July 1974 though many former Vietnam F-4 pilots were among its first 'Eagle Drivers'. Selection for the squadron was considered a privilege. Cat.II R&D testing was finished by 14 November 1974 when the 555th TFS CO, Lt Col Ted Laudise received the first Eagle from Edwards AFB, TF-15A 73-108, labelled TAC-1 and flown in by Lt Col Ted Laudise with Lt Col Art Bergman in the

back seat. The presence of President Gerald Ford and the USAF Chief of Staff, Gen David Jones, and the TAC Commander, Gen Robert J. Dixon, underlined the significance of the occasion. From March 1975 the test program passed to the Air Force Test and Evaluation Center (AFTEC) and then, from 1977 to the 422nd Fighter Weapons Squadron at Nellis AFB, where Category III Follow-On Test and Evaluation (FOT&E) continued. AFTEC's team at Luke, under Lt Col Art Bergman, included seven TAC, ADC and AFSC pilots flying six F-15s on loan from the 57th FWW at Nellis, including TAC-1. They developed ACM tactics at Edwards AFB and against USN *Top Gun* instructors at MCAS Yuma as well as flying weapons and ECM trials at Nellis and Eglin AFB.

At Luke the 4461st TFTS activated on 23 June 1976 as the second F-15A training unit, becoming the 461st TFTS *Jesters* in July 1977. With *Triple Nickel* they began to

prepare the pilots for the first operational Wing. In due course two other training units formed within it at Luke; the 550th TFTS *Silver Eagles* in August 1977 and the 426th TFTS in January 1981. The 58th TFTW was renamed 58th TTW on 1 April 1977 and on 29 August 1979 the training role passed to the 405th TTW, also at Luke. The last F-15A training mission was flown at the Arizona base on 15 November 1991 by former 555th TFTS CO Lt Col Dennis Granquist, whereupon all Eagle instruction passed to Tyndall AFB, leaving the 58th TTW to concentrate on the F-16, with an appropriate code change from LA to LF (Luke Falcon) in the process.

By 1978 Luke had received forty-six F 15A/B models for its three training squadrons, under *Ready Team*. Pilots had found the Eagle an easy aircraft to learn, with few vices and spectacular performance in ACM. It was, for example, the first fighter capable of supersonic performance in a climb. OT&E trials at Edwards in April–May 1974 pitted the F-15A against F-4Es and F-5E Aggressors (simulating MiG-23s and MiG-21s respectively) and the F-15 pilots began to earn their nickname, 'Ego Drivers' by winning forty-five out of forty-six engagements. At low altitudes the match was closer as the F-15's large, draggy wing gave it a very small

slightly lower rate of roll than was intended it could make cold meat of most fighters with its enormous excess power and acceleration even if it lost the advantage of using its BVR missiles first.

Spares shortages had caused some delays in the training schedule early in 1976 and there had been disappointingly low maintenance life-span on some components

example, we had our entire spares complement for a full wing of aircraft (72) delivered prior to the January 1977 arrival of the first three aircraft. The same thing occurred at Soesterberg as well.

There were still minor airframe discrepancies to resolve. An RWR fairing at the tip of the left vertical stabilizer was subject to so much vibration that the cables leading to the ALQ-128 antenna tended to fracture. A simple solution was found by installing a styrofoam tube to contain the cable and its connections. At first, ground crews were told to avoid using their usual cadmium-plated tools because they could react with the large areas of titanium metal used in the F-15's structure. Large quantities of tools were replaced, but soon afterwards it was decided that the risk was inconsiderable and the remaining original tools were reapproved.

Engine maintenance man hours, in particular, had been much higher than expected and stall-stagnation problems, leading to fires, continued to occur. Acceleration times for the engine were slower than predicted and pilots sometimes had difficulty in restarting their engines after a stall because the fuel/air mix was too lean, or after an afterburner blow-out because it was too rich. Blow-outs occurred mainly at high altitude in rarefied air. With fuel still pumping out of the afterburner supply rings to feed a non-existent flame a stream of raw fuel would eventually work its way back to the hot end of the core engine and ignite with an explosion, sending a high-pressure wave back through the engine. This would stall the fan blades, that in turn stalled the compressor. High pressure air then flooded out of the intakes, 'unstalling' the engine, but the process would repeat itself in a very rapid cycle. The result was a rough and alarming ride for the pilot and probable overheating in the stalled high-pressure turbine if raw fuel ignited there. Engine temperatures would then rise beyond the self-cooling ability of the compressor blades causing severe damage. If heat damage had not occurred a relight was possible if achieved fairly quickly as the engine spooled down more slowly than expected. At the least, expensive parts had their lives shortened, turbine blades often needed replacing (fifty-four such failures had occurred by 1979) and inspection had to be done more frequently than planned. Reducing the engine's maximum attainable gas temperature by 80° F brought some benefit. Stall problems were exacerbated in

Luke AFB's F-15 squadrons worked hard to train the first generation of Eagle drivers in the mid-1970s. One of their 555th TFTS F-15As, 74-0117, leaves for another training sortie. In 1974 it was passed to Israel as part of a post-Gulf war 'compensation' package. McDonnell Douglas via Norm Taylor Collection

speed advantage over the slender F-5E. Although a full missile load brought top speed down from Mach 2.3 to around Mach 1.85 this was still well above the speed at which medium and close-range air-to-air fighting took place. The Eagle's designers had concentrated on manoeuvrability, so lacking in most Vietnam-period fighters and although the F-15 had a

causing a reduction in the 'sortie production rate' per aircraft of about 50 per cent at times. John Poole:

Part of the impact of spares on the training program at Luke was simply one of priority. Once the 1st Fighter Wing at Langley and the 36 TFW at Bitburg began their build-up, the priority for spares went to the combat units. At Bitburg, for example, we had our entire spares complement

ACM when pilots would accelerate to a target and then rapidly throttle back to avoid over-running it. It might have been of some small comfort to Engine Shop workers to know that the early MiG-25 engines had a lifespan of 150 hours.

Although similar engine problems were not new they drew unwelcome attention to the F-15 programme at a time when the cost-cutters were still out to cancel it. Critics became more vociferous when the F100 was adapted for use in the General Dynamics F-16A. Although this reduced engine unit, already inflated by the cancellation of F-14B, the F-16's development flying in 1975–76 showed that it had none

fuel at sea level and less at altitude. There was also a reduction in fuel flow at the maximum afterburner setting and this eliminated many of the blow-outs. An unwelcome consequence of these changes was the partial loss of the engine's smokeless exhaust. Highly visible smoke had been a big disadvantage in earlier jets and the F100 was meant to be a clean engine. Sadly, engine problems continued to occur until the digital F100-220 became available in 1985. John Poole recalled:

> One thing that continually caused the engine community problems were the 'Turkey Feathers' at the rear of the engine. These outer, moveable

Heads Up

For trainee pilots at Luke learning to master the new fighter, the HOTAS (hands on throttle and stick) control technique introduced with the F-15 was one of the biggest challenges, but it also conferred enormous advantages. Pilots of Vietnam-era fighters had been far too vulnerable and missed too many opportunities or warnings because they had to spend so much time setting up switches or checking dials in the cockpit instead of keeping an eye on the situation outside. In a single-seat fighter 'situational awareness' is particularly vital. Setting up a change of missile in the F-4B, for example,

Kelly AFB, Texas hosted a visit by this 57th FWW F-15A-14-MC on 10 September 1977, still with its white tailcodes. C. Eddy via Norm Taylor

of the problems with the F100 that dogged the Eagle. P&W and McDonnell Douglas continued to modify the fuel control system, adjust throttle travel and modify the airflow splitter for the fan duct. They also introduced borescope inspection for turbine blades, a great time-saver. One simple modification that brought considerable improvement in afterburner reliability, was a barometric device that controlled the fuel flow to the afterburner spray rings at rates dependent upon altitude: more

panels modulated (moved), along with the inner panels, as the power changed and the afterburner was used. They seemed to constantly deform and jam, tearing and bending. Some thought that the problem was magnified by high speed but I never saw that officially stated anywhere. The only corrective action was to remove and replace them. This problem continued for several years and finally a decision was made to remove the outer panels, thus ending the problem. The impacts appeared to be minimal, other than looks as now the inner hardware was exposed.

required an impractical series of contortions as USMC aviator Manfred 'Fokker' Rietsch explained:

> Switching from SW (Sidewinder) to SP (Sparrow), you had to find the second switch from the left on the lower front panel among many other similar switches. We ended up putting a rubber hose, known as a 'donkey dick' on this weapons switch to let us find it without looking down. All weapons information and control was inside the cockpit. The TACAN and IFF

F-15A 73-0088 of the 555th TFTS, the first Eagle to be lost in an accident. Jim Rotramel

Evening sun catches a Nellis-based 57th FWW Eagle. Ron Thurlow

controls were on the right console, great for vertigo 'in the soup'. There were tiny oil and hydraulic gauges way down between your feet that you couldn't read at night.

This kind of environment might have been tolerable in an interceptor, focused on a straight-ahead attack on a distant target but life in a dogfighter had to be easier and faster. (This situation improved with the later F-4 models, but was not limited to the F-4. The F-105 had much the same problem if the pilot was caught in 'Air to Ground' cockpit configuration and found a MIG out front.) Eagle drivers were, after all, flying the fighter that TAC Commander Gen Momyer had described as having, 'more potential than a pilot can physiologically take'.

John Poole worked on the pilot training programme:

One of the first things we saw was the difference between the 'old heads" acceptance of the HUD and HOTAS systems, and the young kids. One must remember that the complexity of the systems was hard for everyone to master. Most had come from a two-crew system (F-4) and now had to learn to use radar/HUD and the HOTAS as well as remembering the other complexities of the aircraft. Some of the old heads did not initially like the HUD but quickly adapted to it and the vast amount of information it offered in a 'heads up' situation. The young pilots really took to the HOTAS system. Since they were the first-generation 'computer gamers' the system was easy to learn. The 'old heads' (ex-Phantom pilots with South-East Asia experience) were very good with the system once they had gained experience of it. I saw some gun-camera film that was very impressive.

HOTAS, dreamed up by McDonnell Douglas designer Gene Adam, was one of the company's most important innovations with the F-15 and it has found many other fighter applications. Essentially, it allowed a pilot to control the aircraft using the throttle quadrant and the control stick, locating all the other crucial switches and buttons without moving his hands from those two controls. Developing skills akin to those required to finger a wind instrument, a pilot

Although the gun has not been used very much in combat, pilots regularly practise with it. The wing-root location of the gun muzzle places it behind the engine inlet, avoiding gun-gas ingestion problems. Author's Collection

F-15A 76-0063, the 461st TFTS 'Boss bird'. USAF

learned to distinguish them by touch and by position relative to their hand. With his left hand he could locate on the throttle's left lever a radar antenna elevation control thumb wheel, gun/missile reject switch and countermeasures dispenser control for the ECM system. The bulkier right throttle also included the weapons mode selector (gun/AIM-9/AIM-7), speed brake switch, IFF transponder interrogator control, UHF radio, intercom mike switch and a radar target designator control to initiate radar lock-on to a target once it had been 'bracketed' by the acquisition 'gates' on the radar scope. Within an inch of his finger tips were a rudder trim switch and two finger-lift engine cut-offs that would get the engines turning for a start when the throttles were 'off'.

Held snugly in his right fist was a bunch of switches on the control column stick grip. They included the gun trigger (with two detents; one for gun camera or video and the second for gun and camera. It was important to get this right!), a Nose-Wheel Steering button doubling as AIM-9 uncaging and slaving control, the Radar mode auto-acquisition/air refuelling receptacle release switch (used to 'go boresight', or to 'undesignate' a target, or to go quickly to 'Supersearch' mode) and the CAS/Autopilot disengage paddle switch. At the tip of the stick grip were the main trim switch and weapons release button. Thus the pilot had literally at his fingertips the controls for most flight situations and was free to concentrate his attention on the HUD and the world outside.

F-15A HUD

Although the F-15A's cockpit instrumentation was fairly conventional, in keeping with its contractual 'low-risk' technology, it did include a head-up display unit as the pilot's main source of vital information. In use since 1967, the HUD was rapidly becoming indispensable to the fighter pilot. Navigation, radar, weapons and comprehensive flight information could be presented to him in the form of verbal or symbolic data, projected at infinity within his normal line of sight. In the F-15A the philosophy of keeping the pilot's attention out of the cockpit was taken a stage further by positioning the radio and

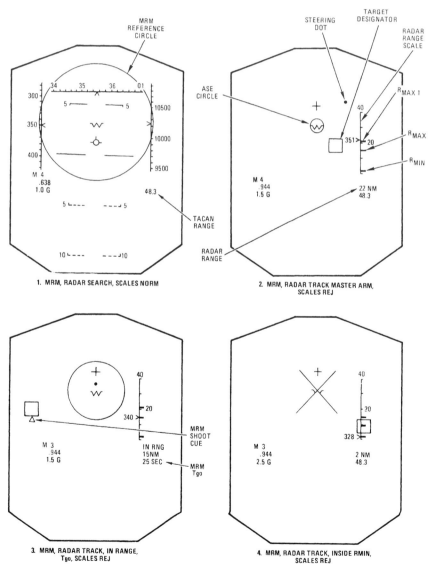

HUD displays, MRM steering. USAF

An F-15C four-ship prepares to roll out for another mission from Bitburg. USAF

transponder communication controls just below the HUD so that he could switch frequencies without taking his eyes off the HUD for more than a second or two.

McDonnell Douglas Electronics Company designed the F-15A HUD. Its 20 degree field of vision (12–17 degrees when looking straight ahead) was quite narrow compared with the Kaiser holographic raster scan video HUDs of later Eagles but the compactness left the pilot with a clear 'optical' view ahead to each side of it. Its standard symbology gave him magnetic heading, indicated airspeed and Mach number, barometric altitude and g load, all generated by the Air Data Computer and Attitude Direction Indicator (ADI). The F-15A's 'natural' HUD mode was air-to-air, and the HUD repeated information that was mostly displayed on his radar screen too. He was presented with airspeed and altitude on two 'ladders' at each side of the screen, with rate of closure to target indication on another vertical line, Mach number and g load. A steering circle and dot (the dot had to be in the circle prior to missile release) appeared in the centre. There was also a velocity vector line showing the Eagle's flight path and a pitch scale line showing its attitude relative to the horizon. 'In range' and 'time to impact' logos appeared if missiles were selected.

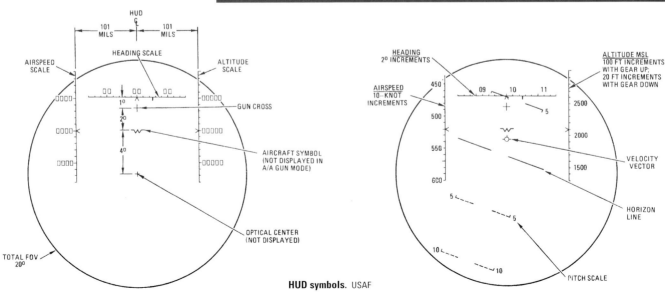

HUD symbols. USAF

IFF information could also be selected. An array of dipole aerials on the planar radar scanner would transmit at L-band frequency when the pilot pushed the IFF button on his throttle. 'Friendly' returns would show the potential target to be harmless, via a diamond symbol on his HUD and radar screen, or a rectangle for a 'hostile' or 'uninterrogated' plot. In this case he could then transfer his attention to the HUD where he would be shown aim points and maximum/minimum range for either AIM-7 or AIM-9, the latter being shown as SRM (short range missile). Alternatively, selecting GUN, with a 20-mile (32km) radar range conjured up a boresight cross sight, a target designator box lead-computed to 2,250ft (686m), a 'rounds remaining' ammunition counter and a horizon reference line. Choosing 'air-to-ground modified the sight reticule to show a displayed impact line, radar offset aim points and the air-to-ground target indicator box.

Weighing only 60lb (27kg) the HUD included a reloadable 16mm cine camera, or video in later aircraft. It projected its data via a cathode ray tube onto a combining glass through collimating lenses. An automatic brightness control maintained a constant contrast between the HUD symbology and the ambient light level of the sky. There was a standby lead computing gyro to generate a basic gunsight reticule if the central computer failed.

McDonnell Douglas designers placed the pilot high in his cockpit – some described it as having the canopy rail at waist height. The nose ahead of the pilot fell away sharply into a predatory 'beak' and the fuselage behind him was cut away allowing him full rearward visibility to each side of his headrest. He looked forward through a one-piece polycarbonate (later stretched acrylic) windshield that could withstand a 4lb (2kg) birdstrike at 335kt. The huge canopy had to be made in two pieces with a narrow joining frame as it was not possible to make a large enough single sheet of the material for manufacturing it. For the F-15B a more bulged rear section was all that was required. In both cases the outward bulge of the transparency allowed a considerable degree of downward view. This was a considerable improvement on the F-4, where frequent banking and rolling was needed to obtain a reasonable view below and to the sides.

Having acquired his target initially on his radar display or visually the pilot then had a choice of weapons to deal with the threat. If the original proposals for F-X had

Poised in clear, blue Alaskan skies F-15A 74-0105 was an early delivery to the 21st CW at Elmendorf AFB. USAF

Maintenance was often carried out in crowded shelters on USAFE bases. A fixer checks this Eagle's flying controls by torchlight. USAF

An F-15A/B section from the 58th TFS overflies Germany during a *Coronet* deployment to Europe in 1979/80. Norm Taylor Collection

Eagle Talons: Missiles

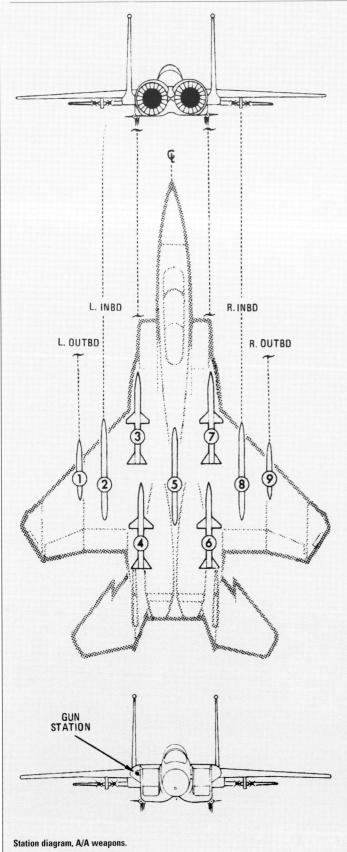

L. INBD   R. INBD

L. OUTBD   R. OUTBD

GUN STATION

Station diagram, A/A weapons.

The infrared AIM-9 Sidewinder and AIM-7 Sparrow were the first effective missiles of their kind, with origins dating back to 1951 and 1946 respectively. Both were originally US Navy projects and they were developed through the 1960s to become the standard armament for both Navy and Air Force tactical fighters, apart from a brief period when the early F-4D models used the AIM-4 Falcon. These was plenty of opportunity to test and develop them in South-East Asia, though the statistics were not encouraging and did not bear out the high experimental and training 'scores' achieved in far less stressful environments. In Vietnam, 612 Sparrows were fired, scoring or contributing to 56 kills (below a 10 per cent success rate) and 454 Sidewinders racked up 81 victims, mainly in the final year of war, for an 18 per cent overall success rate. The malfunction rate for AIM-7 was so high at 66 per cent that USN F-4 crews virtually abandoned it in the final stages of the conflict, relying on their secondary AIM-9 armament instead. In many cases the failures could be attributed to the difficulty of setting up and firing the missile correctly, to poor tactics or to inadequate maintenance procedures. The figures were alarming, nevertheless, and the USAF and USN combined to force ahead the development of truly effective missiles. Lacking the funds for rapid development of completely new types, it was decided to focus on perfecting the existing weapons. The first real breakthrough came with the AIM-9L Sidewinder that took forward the dogfighting capability of the earlier AIM-9E/G models.

Nine Lima
Available in 1976, the AIM-9L remedied many of the missile's previous shortcomings. It had a much improved proximity fusing system (DSU-15A/B) using a ring of eight gallium arsenide laser diodes to ensure detonation at the highest possible speed against a manoeuvring target. The small lasers emitted a pattern of radiation resembling the spokes of a wheel and known as whiskers. A target that interrupted any of these laser beams would trigger the warhead. The WDU-17 annular blast-fragmentation (ABF) warhead was increased to 25lb (11kg), using pre-formed rods that were designed to tumble in flight, increasing their chance of penetrating the target. The rocket motor's TX-683 solid propellant was housed in a star-shaped chamber to increase its burning area. Its DSQ-29 guidance control section used an argon-cooled, indium-antimonide seeker head giving genuine all-aspect capability. Previous Sidewinders were fired in a tail-chase combat but AIM-9L could be launched head-on. Using an AM/FM conical scan device developed in Germany by Bodensee Geratetechnik, the highly sensitive seeker was far less susceptible to standard IR-missile avoidance tactics such as decoy flares. It could also resist 'sun capture': previously a target aircraft could often shake off an AIM-9 by flying towards or across the sun, giving the missile a hotter target to track.

A set of pointed double-delta BSU-32/B foreplanes gave greater manoeuvrability. After its USN combat debut in 1981 the Lima performed extremely well from Royal Navy Sea Harriers in the Falklands conflict, with 23 kills from 26 launches, although most were actually from 'dead six' tail-chase positions. Over 16,000 AIM-9Ls were built for the USAF, USN and other users and they eventually gave way in production to the AIM-9M with a reduced-smoke Mk36 Mod 9 Bermite-Hercules rocket motor and better infrared countermeasures resistance. The seeker head, with a closed-cycle cooling system, was even more sensitive. AIM-9M formed the basis for the AIM-9R (formerly AIM-9M Improved) missile that has an imaging infrared (IIR) system giving clearer target definition.

Although AIM-9 development may have 'peaked out', the USAF could still modify some existing AIM-9L/M variants. From 1978 the AIM-9M and AIM-9P were produced in several sub-variants as updates of the earlier AIM-9H/J, the first Sidewinders with solid-state electronics and squared, double-delta manoeuvring fins. AIM-9P applied to earlier missiles upgraded to AIM-9L standard but using the AIM-9J fins and shorter-burning motor. AIM-9M/P missiles gave the F-15 force in Operation *Desert Storm* twelve of their forty-four air/air kills. Three sub-variants of the AIM-9P were developed; the AIM-9P1 with an active optical proximity fuse, the P2 with reduced-smoke motor and the P3 with a longer-life warhead. The basic simplicity of the Sidewinder means that further mix-and-match updates to existing stocks can keep the missiles current for many years. This, in turn, has meant that a completely new replacement weapon has been slow to attract funding. F-15s have carried AIM-9J/Ps on LAU-114 launchers but the AIM-9L/M is the more usual load.

The ultimate Sidewinder may well be the GM-Hughes/Raytheon AIM-9X Evolved Sidewinder SRAAM (short-range air-to-air missile), originally known as the 'Boa' or 'high off-boresight' variant. This adds to the existing AIM-9M missile improved fins, a thrust-vectoring system designed originally for the Sea Sparrow and JDAM (joint direct attack munition) technology that could give the missile a turn radius as tight as as 200m. Its development was spurred by the Soviet AA-11 Archer (R-76) missile that has been an effective weapon since 1986, offering off-boresight targeting at 60 degrees from the aircraft's boresight line each side. AIM-9X is designed to operate with the Boeing Joint Helmet-Mounted Cueing System (JHMCS), a much-improved version of VTAS. This system was under test at Edwards AFB in 1999 (making its first guided flight from an F-15 on 1 September) with the F-15 Combined Test Force, whose Advanced Projects Flt Cdr Capt Mark Spillman estimated that JHMCS would, 'change the nature of fighter aircraft combat for U.S. pilots'. The helmet projects information such as altitude, airspeed, heading and target information on a visor within the pilot's field of view, overlaying the HUD imagery. Targets tracked by radar or an aircraft's IRST (infrared search and track) system also appear and there are cueing symbols that draw the pilot's eyes to his target. He doesn't have to look at his HUD, inside the cockpit, or even straight ahead through the windshield. The system then confirms seeker lock-on and fires the missile. AIM-9X has a new imaging seeker that operates far beyond visual range and it can be launched at targets that are at a high angle off the F-15's heading. Using JHMCS a pilot can track the target visually, cue the radar to it and slave the AIM-9X's swivelling seeker head to the target without having to change the aircraft's heading. The missile and helmet system are due for service entry with F-15 and F-16 units around 2002. September 1999 saw the first firing from an F-15C in a head-on, slightly offset shot.

Sparrow

Disappointing results with the AIM-9E Sparrow, standard armament for the F-4 from 1963–69, led to the so-called 'dogfight' version since the missile could rarely be fired in its design BVR mode. Echoing US experience in Vietnam, the Israeli Air Force found that in the 1973 Yom Kippur War less than seven of their 335 claimed kills involved the AIM-7, although F-4s were their principal fighter. In virtually all fighter-on-fighter combats the engagement never involved a BVR phase before the fight began, at which stage short-range missiles or guns were the only choices. AIM-7E-2 'Dogfight Sparrow' was intended to make the weapon viable against manoeuvring targets at shorter range, rather than the large, distant bomber targets for which it had originally been intended. The improvement was insufficient and a complete redesign was needed, although this had to be effected within a missile of the same configuration and size so that it would still fit into the F-4's recessed launchers. With the F-15, designers opted instead for external mountings on the lower edges of the fuselage so that the aircraft would not be limited to missiles of only one size. The revised Sparrow also needed longer range, since it had been intended for head-on launches against closing targets. If it was launched in a high-speed tail chase of a target at the outer limit of its range parameters the rocket motor could burn out before the missile caught up with its quarry.

AIM-7F, the primary weapon for the Eagle was developed between 1966–69 and produced from 1974 and was in most respects a new weapon although it used the same 12ft (4m) long airframe. It offered so many improvements, particularly at lower altitudes that it was also specified for the new F/A-18 until the AIM-7M was ready in 1982. In the AIM-7F model the 88lb (40kg) warhead was moved forward, using space created by miniaturizing the avionics for the Autopilot and homing device. Its Mk 58 rocket motor could then be increased in size, stretching the missile's range from 30mi (48km) to over 60mi (96km). At the same time its minimum firing parameters were reduced so that it could be used after its carrier aircraft had entered visual range. AIM-7F also had improved resistance to radar countermeasures. In the AIM-7M, responsible for thirty-four air-to-air kills during *Desert Storm*, a new monopulse seeker (similar to the one used in the British Skyflash adaptation of the missile), a radar-operated active fuse, shorter 'warm-up' time and more concentrated fragmentation warhead were among

many features to help improve reliability. AIM-7M was a further significant improvement and it belatedly earned the missile a reputation for high kill probability and far greater reliability, particularly among pilots who had initially seen their aircraft as 'gun and Sidewinder' fighters by default.

From the F-15A pilot's position, setting up an AIM-7F launch required the radar/HUD display to be set at MRM (medium-range missile) giving him data on the number and status of missiles aboard his aircraft and a calculation of the missiles' firing range limits (R max an R min) in the circumstances. An IN RNG (in range) message appeared at the bottom left of the HUD combining glass when the target was between these two limits and a seeker circle and target box symbol were displayed. AIM-7Fs tuned themselves when the radar was engaged, MRM selected and the 'master arm' switch engaged. They took two minutes to warm up, initiating a 'standby' command on the display. The computer automatically bypassed any Sparrows that did not respond at this stage and 'good' missiles would get a 'ready' indicator on the armament panel. The pilot then used his radar display to lock up the radar target blip, transferring his attention to the HUD thereafter for the rest of the launch sequence. A press of the red weapon release button on top of the stick would initiate launch of an AIM-7 and he then had to maintain radar lock on the target for a set countdown time, indicated in his HUD, for the missile to acquire and home on its target.

AMRAAM

Despite its success in the Gulf, Sparrow required replacement by a new medium-range missile and development of AIM-120 'Slammer' began in 1975. In 1981 Hughes received a full-scale development contract and controlled the project through some difficult development work (particularly on the software) until the firm was absorbed into Raytheon Defense Systems in 1996/97. At the height of its test programme, when overruns in cost had threatened cancellation, four AIM-120s were ripple-fired from an F-15C and shot down four manoeuvring, flare-and-chaff emitting QF-100 drone fighters within seconds. The missile entered service with the 58th TFS during its *Desert Storm* deployment when a batch of fifty-two missiles arrived for the Squadron's F-15Cs. Many 'captive carries' were made to test the missiles' software and compatibility but none was fired.

Of similar length to the AIM-7, AMRAAM (advanced medium-range air-to-air missile) is lighter, more slender and has smaller guidance fins. It can be hung on AIM-9 launch rail positions, although it still takes its initial targeting and course information from the launch aircraft's sensors. AIM-120 has its own active radar with a seeker resembling a miniature APG-63 and can therefore seek targets independently. After receipt of initial targeting and mid-course correction data from the F-15, it is 'free' to use its own radar and Northrop Inertial Reference Unit and IFF interrogator in the terminal phase of the attack (approximately the last 10mi (16km) of a 31mi (50km) range), allowing the launch aircraft to move to other business. Its 154lb (70kg) rocket motor emits comparatively low smoke levels and the 50.6lb (23kg) Chamberlain Manufacturing ABF warhead fragments into 198 rectangular projectiles ejected in a circular pattern that intensifies in the sector of the circle containing the target. It has either proximity or contact fuse options. Its guidance radar uses High PRF for long range or Medium PRF in look-down mode.

Its first kill was on 27 December 1992 from an F-16D during OSW and it went on to score three kills with its first three launches in anger. F-15s initially used AIM-120A although the field-reprogrammable AIM-120B (via the aircraft's data bus) became available from 1994 and the AIM-120C (with reduced-size control surfaces to fit into the F-22A weapons bay) appeared in 1997. Improved Phase II and Phase III missiles will have reprogrammable ECCM, aimable warhead projectiles, ring-laser gyros, GPS and bigger motors. On F-15C/Es the missile is usually carried on the outboard wing pylon rails (Stations 2B/8A) and on the rear fuselage or rear upper CFT mountings.

gone ahead he would have reached for the AIM-82A missile switch-setting as first option in a medium or close-range fight. Although the AIM-9 Sidewinder had been the more effective of the two missiles used on the F-4, it was decided that a new, more manoeuvrable dogfight missile should be developed for the F-15 and other fighters.

Contracts for the missile were issued – and cancelled within a year. General Dynamics, Philco-Ford and Hughes all received contracts to design and build a prototype short-range missile that would be more agile than the Sidewinder and improve on its actual and predicted kill rate of between 18 per cent and 28 per cent in USAF

service. After five months of extravagant claims for the missile's likely performance and some heated unarmed combat between manufacturers, politicians and cost analysts the contracts were cancelled in favour of the Hughes AIM-95 Agile that was in turn cancelled. An improved version of AIM-9 was specified instead.

AIMVAL/ACEVAL

The enormous advances in fighter technology initiated by the F-15 programme caused a rethink of the USAF's air combat strategy. Early in the OT&E programme it was apparent that, one-on-one, no US or Soviet fighter stood much of a chance once an Eagle had got on its tail. Pilots of AV-8As or Sea Harriers were among the few to claim consistent success in that situation in later years. The Eagle could out-run or out-turn all the others. In the reverse situation either a near-vertical climb and reversal, or a sustained high g turn would usually give the Eagle pilot the advantage. Comments about the fighter being able to make 'aces out of hamburgers' began to circulate among its disgruntled victims. Against the T-38/F-5E Aggressors an F-15A would pull more than 14 degrees per second in a turn compared to the opponent's 11 degrees. From January to October 1977 the USAF and USN conducted a lengthy and complex study of air combat under the direction of F-4 pioneer RADM Julian S. Lake at Nellis. AIMVAL (air intercept missile evaluation) sought to assess current and future air-to-air missiles in realistic conditions, while ACEVAL (air combat evaluation) pitted the F-14 and F-15 in some 2,300 sorties against aggressor forces in varying numbers, so that pilots faced single or multiple adversaries in gruelling furball dogfights. Unsurprisingly the F-15's clear advantage in a one-to-one combat was significantly narrowed when it met two or more opponents. Some pointed to the F-14's advantage in having two pairs of eyes to monitor the fight: a good RIO could spot threats that his pilot might miss as he was too busy 'rowing the boat'. Certainly, the workload in the single-seat F-15A was still considerable despite the many cockpit improvements, particularly with a number of concurrent threats. When Eagles were 'shot' during AIMVAL/ACEVAL it was usually by an unseen 'enemy' while they were setting up an attack on another aircraft. The Eagle's considerable size in plan view was a disadvantage compared with smaller fighters. Also, F-5E drivers developed a radar lock-breaking manoeuvre by flying across the Eagle's line of flight, a tactic that continues to baffle most radars to this day. Clearly, the 1970 USAF TAC-Avenger computer study that worked out the kill probability of an F-15 vs a MiG-21 with the same armament at 955:1 in the

A trio of fully armed USAFE Eagles take their turn on the KC-135 tanker. Bill Thompson

Eagle's favour was a little optimistic, or a reflection of the primitive computer technology of the day!

The exercise also brought an end to the USAF's 'welded wing' tactical formation for fighters, in which a close formation of four aircraft supported a dedicated 'shooter' in the quartet and stuck to his wing, come what may. For the F-15 era a version of the more flexible USN technique of using two fighters, widely separated in line abreast and giving mutual support and equal kill opportunities, was worked out.

For the budgeters, AIMVAL/ACEVAL proved the worth of a mix of complex, costly fighters (F-15) and simpler but effective ones (F-16) as a means of preventing the Eagles from being 'mobbed' by numerous opponents, as it surely would have been in a frontal conflict with Warsaw Pact forces. While this may have impacted upon the total buy of F-15s it allowed the aircraft to remain viable in its designated air superiority role, firing its BVR missiles from a distance and only engaging more closely if it had to do so.

Seeing the Target

One improvement recommended by the analysts of AIMVAL/ACEVAL was the visual target acquisition system (VITAS), essentially a development of the Navy's Honeywell VTAS of the early 1970s. In both systems the pilot had an eyepiece (known as a 'granny glass') attached to his helmet. The aircraft's radar and weapons system could be slaved to this sighting device so that a pilot could lock on to a target by looking at it. Lights on the canopy rail gave confirmation of a lock and of appropriate missile range parameters. As part of AIMVAL its six F-15A participants each had the VITAS equipment installed, together with some software changes in the radar/computer. Its air-to-ground programme ('Box 081') was taken out and replaced with an interface to the VITAS and to a pair of 'concept missiles' that the aircraft carried on LAU-7 launchers. These were essentially missile simulators that were linked to the ACMI range computers to project the characteristics of hypothetical air-to-air missiles. The radar was also given a search-while-track function, enabling it to track a target while searching for another, and 'Expand mode', allowing it to 'look around' the target and see whether radar blips were single or multiple targets. A familiar Soviet tactic was to fly two pairs of fighters closely together so that they appeared to be only two single aircraft on radar. On good days this software change lets the radar 'see' two such targets 500ft (150m) apart at 20mi (32km) and it was later incorporated into the upgraded APG-63 for the F-15C.

AIMVAL/ACEVAL also demonstrated the benefit of an Electro-optical or optical back-up system for visual identification of targets in the air. From 1972 late-build F-4Es had received the Northrop AN/ASX-1 TISEO (target identification system, Electro-optical) installed in their left wing-root. Developed from the *Rivet Haste* and *Combat Tree* programmes in Vietnam this device peered ahead of the aircraft with a video camera and could zoom in on distant targets for a visual ID, slaved to the radar if necessary. The pilot could make a quick, long-range radar lock, switch to TISEO to lock up the target optically and then break radar lock, so that the target had only momentary warning of a radar detection. This valuable system had been included in the original F-15 proposal but fell victim to the cost-cutters at an early stage. AIMVAL/ACEVAL

showed the benefits of such a system. F-14As, equipped with the Northrop TVSU (TV sight unit), a version of TISEO beefed up for aircraft carrier life, were able to identify visually targets at almost 9.5mi (15km) rather than the 2 to 2.5mi (3–4km) possible with the naked eye. This factor was crucial to many of the F-14 lock-ons and led to the Navy's adoption of a modified version (TSU) with an added infrared detection facility for later Tomcats.

However, when forced to close to AIM-7F range both F-14 and F-15 crews were often detected visually by Aggressor aircraft (at about 5mi/8km, usually) before they could acquire the elusive F-5s visually at 3mi (5km). Denied TISEO, F-15 pilots had already experimented with telescopic rifle sights bought from hunting rifle shops and fixed beside their HUDs, (some of the AIMVAL/ACEVAL pilots who were among the first deployed to Soesterberg in the Netherlands took this scope with them) but in 1978 the USAF tested the Perkins-Elmer Eagle Eye III, a solid-state zoom TV camera capable of transferring its imagery onto the pilot's radar display via a 2ft (60cm) long, 10in (25cm) diameter lens. Trials took place at Nellis by the Air Force Avionics Laboratory and the Tactical Weapons Center. This system also fell victim to the accountants, leaving some pilots to resort once again to their Leupold rifle scopes.

FAST and Far

A further outcome of early service experience with the F-15 was the development of conformal fuel tanks (CFTs) to extend the aircraft's range. Practice high-speed interceptions with a full weapons load and afterburner take-off followed by a max speed climb showed that the aircraft had a tactical radius of less than 100mi (160km) on internal fuel. Reconciling this with the design objective of an unrefuelled Atlantic crossing required a novel solution. F-15 was already plumbed for three 600gall (2,728l) external tanks for what McDonnell Douglas called its 'long-range intercept or combat air patrol' configuration. These added to the 1,759gal internal fuel load to give a total of 2,979gal (13,542l) (around 19,300lb (8,754kg)). It was still necessary to increase that load significantly without adding to the considerable subsonic drag of three external tanks.

From the earliest days of the F-15 project the idea of conformal tanks or pallets,

attached beneath the wing roots, had been investigated. They could contain fuel and/or a variety of sensors and mission equipment. J.S. McDonnell had always sought to build versatility into his basic designs and all his fighters after the FH-1 Phantom had been produced in a specialized reconnaissance version. For F-15 the company proposed 32.5ft (10m) long conformal containers equipped with cameras and other recce sensors, or ECM plus fuel, or cargo carriers, gunpods, chemical spray tanks, a 'buddy' tanker arrangement, even an augmented thrust JATO-type take-off booster. Crucially, the designers allowed for conformal carriage of ordnance or missiles on the outer 'edge' of each pod, anticipating the F-15E *Strike Eagle* configuration of later years. The main ingredient in all these exciting proposals was JP-4 fuel, in varying proportions to the other potential contents within the 227cu ft (64cu m) of additional space they offered. Two of the units, christened FAST PACKs (fuel and sensor tactical package) could hold 1,538gal (6,992l), only 17 per cent less than the three standard external 'bags', and without any significant increase in subsonic cruise drag at all. Also, they left the wing pylons free for other ordnance. In 1974 prototype units were built including a rapid installation system enabling a standard bomb loading truck with an adaptor to offer up the tank while maintainers fitted two bolts. An electrical input and two fuel connections were joined automatically as the unit slipped into place. Stressed to 7g (filled) and 9g (empty) the units could not be jettisoned but their fuel could be passed through the aircraft's fuel dumps in an emergency.

To prove that the F-15 had thus achieved its Transatlantic range, TF-15A 71-291 hauled its total load of 32,319lb (14,660kg) of fuel – internal, three tanks and FAST PACKs – from the runway at Loring AFB, Maine on 26 August 1974, climbed to 33,000ft (10,000m) and flew the 2,650nm to RAF Bentwaters, England in 5hr 15 min, arriving overhead at 41,000ft (12,500m) with 3,800lb (1,724kg) fuel remaining. The pilots were Irv Burrows, Chief test pilot for McDonnell Douglas and Col Shawler, F-15 Test Director. Two years later the faithful '291 made a world sales tour in Bicentennial colours. In 2.5 months it flew 34,000mi (55,000km) to England, Germany, Japan, Korea, the Philippines, Hawaii and back to Luke AFB. En route it became the first fighter to cross Australia without refuelling.

Streak Eagle

Like its predecessor the F-4 Phantom, McDonnell Douglas's F-15 was an obvious contender for some Official World Records. Phantoms had achieved a remarkable twenty-five performance records from 1959 onwards. The Eagle's best chance was seen to be the time-to-climb records for jet aircraft, inspired by computer predictions that it could easily beat the Phantom and MiG-25 Foxbat records. In January 1975 the 17th aircraft, F-15A-5-MC 72-119 was prepared for the task while McDonnell Chief Experimental Test Pilot, Pete Garrison developed the flight profiles requiring the aircraft, for example, to make a supersonic 80 degree climb and reach 30,000ft (9,000m) in 50sec. In several of the profiles the F-15 had to be accelerating through Mach 1 only 23sec after its wheels started to roll. Some minor modifications were needed to the aircraft, an attrition replacement Cat II test machine that had not been required for OT&E as there were no losses.

While '119 was still on the production line some 2,800lb (1,300kg) of net weight were saved by omitting its radar, radio, gun, tailhook, compass, one generator and the utility hydraulics plus flap and speed-brake actuators. In keeping with its name, Streak Eagle was denuded of paintwork, saving another 40lb (18kg).

Added, with a 1,000lb (454kg). penalty, were full-pressure suit support equipment for the pilot for flights above 50,000ft (15,240m), a battery radio, a pitot boom with alpha and beta vanes, rearward-looking video, standby attitude gyro and radar compartment ballast. The arresting hook was replaced by a cable hold-back device to release the Eagle for take-off once it had gone to full power. Maj 'Mac' MacFarlane, Maj Roger Smith and Maj David Peterson were the Streak pilots. In early test-runs the aircraft's acceleration was so rapid that the undercarriage could not be retracted fast enough after lift-off to avoid exceeding stress limits on the doors and the sorties had to be scrubbed.

Over a five-week period at Grand Forks AFB, North Dakota, the three pilots systematically worked their way to eight new records, exceeding the previous figures by between 15 and 33 per cent. Take-off runs, depending on fuel load – just enough for each flight – were often around 4,000ft (1,200m) and on one of Maj Peterson's launches he accelerated faster than a Saturn V rocket up to 49,000ft (15,000m). Peak altitudes over 100,000ft (30,500m) were reached as the aircraft went ballistic and fell back, restarting its 'blown out' engines at 55,000 ft (16,800m).

THE 1975 RECORD FLIGHTS (times are measured in seconds from release of brakes)

Altitude	Time	Pilot	Date	Previous record holder
3,000m	27.57	Maj R. Smith	16 Jan	F-4
6,000m	39.33	Maj W. MacFarlane	16 Jan	F-4
9,000m	48.86	Maj W. MacFarlane	16 Jan	F-4
12,000m	59.38	Maj W. MacFarlane	16 Jan	F-4
15,000m	77.02	Maj D. W. Peterson	16 Jan	F-4
20,000m	122.94	Maj R. Smith	19 Jan	MiG-25
25,000m	161.02	Maj D.W. Peterson	26 Jan	MiG-25
30,000m	207.80	Maj R. Smith	1 Feb	MiG-25

F-15A-6-MC 72-0119, modified as 'Aquila Maxima' for the *Streak Eagle* record flights. Behind the pilot's seat is a white UHF antenna. The gun port is sealed and an instrumentation boom is attached to the radar-less nose. Removing the paint saved only 40lb, but every ounce counted. Boeing/McDonnell Douglas

Eyes and Ears

McDonnell's team proposed a dedicated reconnaissance Eagle from the outset. Initially, this would have followed the usual Company policy of developing a camera nose to replace the existing structure. It would also have housed sideways-looking radar, a multi-spectrum scanner and TV camera. The Air Force rejected this as being too expensive, preferring to stick with its dwindling RF-4C fleet until the early 1990s, by which time dedicated tactical reconnaissance aircraft had been largely replaced by satellite or RPV imagery. Various FAST PACK alternatives hardened into the F-15R *Peep Eagle* Reconnaissance Technology Demonstrator Pod, housing a range of cameras and other imaging equipment including synthetic aperture radar mapping and capable of downloading data direct to a ground station. The pod was flown in '291 in 1987 and the same aircraft test-flew several Wild Weasel SEAD configurations as McDonnell Douglas tried to sell a successor to

(Above) The 49th TFW at Holloman AFB traded in F-4Ds Phantoms for F-15As from 1977. One of their F-15As is seen visiting Lambert Field, St Louis. Norm Taylor

their F-4G Wild Weasel IV to the USAF. 71-291 flew with an F-4G-type chin pod under its nose for the APR-38 SEAD system used by the F-4G Phantom. Various other Weasel configurations were funded by the USAF, which was very interested in a purchase on several occasions. In the end it was obliged to take the cheaper F-16C as the basis of its SEAD tactical aircraft.

57th FWW F-15A 74-0136 at Nellis AFB in January 1979. Ron Thurlow

First Fighter

Throughout 1975 Luke AFB echoed to the roar of F-100s as its 58th TFTW trained the pilots for TAC's first operational F-15 Wing, the 1st TFW at Langley AFB. Its Commander, Col Larry D Welch, accepted his first F-15A, 74-083, temporarily named *Peninsula Patriot* (with a paper label on its nose), on 9 January 1976. It was flown in by Col Richard Craft, Commander of 27th TFS, the first operational squadron. In fact, the very first aircraft on charge had been an F-15B on 18 December 1975 for ground-crew familiarization after the Wing moved from McDill AFB in June. It was perhaps the maintainers who were to face most of the problems with the new aircraft at that stage, though 'pilot production' at Luke had also been slowed down by low aircraft availability. Engine stall-stagnation and the resultant maintenance overload on the Engine Shops that had still not received the diagnostic equipment for the job, was still the main handicap. A number of teething difficulties with the radar and fire control unit also took time and effort while fixes were devised.

Although the reliance on line replaceable units (LRUs) with BIT testing meant that aircraft were not grounded because of one failed avionics unit, the removed unit had to be tested and repaired once it had been slid out of the F-15. Lack of suitable equipment on site meant that less than half could be fixed without being returned to their manufacturer. This caused an increasing shortage of workable 'black boxes', cannibalization of parts from other

A line-up of 8th TFS F-15As (possibly inviting a visit from Santa Claus?) for *Red Flag* in July 1982. Ron Thurlow

Taxiing out with only a centreline tank and ACMI pod, F-15C 84-0003 of the 53rd TFS is set for an ACM or DACT session over the North Sea. Jim Rotramel

aircraft and therefore groundings by default. Avionics Intermediate Shop (AIS) test stations were available for automatic diagnosis of a fault in an LRU. However, many of the avionics units were still in an evolutionary state and many minor variations occurred between components so that standard AIS diagnosis did not always work. The problem was compounded by a shortage of suitably qualified specialists at Langley and a massive training programme was undertaken at the base. Spares shortages hit the production line too when labour disputes among two P&W suppliers interrupted engine production. Some new, engineless F-15As had to be stored at Robins AFB in 1979 and deliveries of new engines to Langley were protracted. The cumulative effect over a number of years was that Langley failed an ORI (operational readiness inspection) in 1980 and a planned *Coronet Sight* deployment to Gilze Rijen, Holland had to be cancelled.

Col Welch's hard-working pilots went through a slightly accelerated course at Luke since the air-to-ground phase was cut out from November 1975 because of delays in ordnance clearance. Even so, the 1st TFW began its operational life about twelve pilots under strength. Once at Langley, aircrew began a 75-day training programme, concentrating on about thirty air-to-air sorties each. Among them were six local air defence sorties, a reminder that the 1st TFW was also tasked with this secondary mission because of its proximity to the Headquarters of TAC and CONUS

A rare and subdued example of F-15 nose-art: the 36th TFW Commander's aircraft (76-0036) was named 'Eiffel Eagle' in 1979. Author's collection

NORAD. The pressure was on to demonstrate the new fighter's mettle and the 27th TFS *Fightin' Eagles*, arguably the oldest USAF fighter squadron and former home to First World War ace, Frank Luke, showed its face at many other bases and took part in a *Red Flag* exercise in July 1976.

The 1st TFW had long since earned its distinctive, non-standard FF (*First Fighter*) tail code. It had been the first US aerial unit to destroy an enemy aircraft in the First World War, the first group-level unit to conduct aerial combat and the first to fly jet fighters; the Lockheed P-80 in July 1946. Its second squadron to convert to the F-15A by the end of 1976, the 94th TFS *Hat in Ring*, numbered Eddie Rickenbacker and eleven other aces among its World War I roster. In 1977 the third unit, the 71st TFS *The Mailed Fist* received its 24 F-15A/B Eagles and the Wing achieved Initial Operational Capability (IOC). An eight-aircraft Detachment was kept at Nellis for *Red Flag* use, when pilots tested their skills against F-4s, F-106s, A-4 and F-5E Aggressors in 528 DACT sorties by the end of January 1977. Everyone was eager to take on the mighty Eagle and see if it lived up to its name. In the following year the *First Fighter* squadrons began to establish the Wing's role as a forward deployable unit, sending a detachment to Japan, Korea and the Philippines in the first half of 1978 for *Coronet Condor*. At the end of the year a twelve-aircraft detachment flew to Riyadh, Saudi Arabia via Torrejon, Portugal and the Sudan as *Coronet Eagle/ Prized Eagle*.

To add to its already onerous challenges Langley was tasked with Operation *Ready Eagle I*, the preparation of another three squadrons for the first USAFE F-15 Wing, the 36th TFW at Bitburg, W. Germany. They had to be combat-ready on arrival in Europe after nothing more than a local 'theatre checkout'. Training of maintenance personnel ('Eagle Keepers') began in September 1976 and by 15 April 1977 Langley had succeeded in putting the requisite 522 trained 'fixers' in place at Bitburg in time for the arrival of the first familiarization F-15As (75-049/50/53) on 26 January 1977. It was fortunate that there were highly experienced specialists available to see the project through. One of them was John Poole, who described how his background enabled him to enjoy this high-spot in his 30-year career:

Involvement in one of the greatest fighter programmes in history. My specialty was Automatic Flight Controls and Heading Systems. My experience was varied over many aircraft, including the F-4, F-101B and older aircraft. I was also fortunate to receive factory rep tech training on the A-7D and F-111A. To be selected for the F-15 program one was required to have had training and practical experience on the F-111 Integrated Avionics Systems. This requirement was levied to ensure that personnel understood the concept of Integrated Avionics and would therefore be more suited and easier to train for maintaining the first new, specifically designed air superiority fighter in many years. I was selected as one of the initial cadre to be assigned to the F-15 at Luke AFB and moved my

family there in July 1974. Getting settled at Luke and attending the required Field Training Detachment for training and orientation on the F-15 systems was very exciting. We organized our Shops and facilities with some rather 'high visibility' to various USAF Generals and civilian dignitaries and prepared ourselves for the arrival of the first aircraft in November. Then the excitement really began. I spent two years at Luke supporting the development of the pilot training program and OT&E. I was then selected as one of a small cadre to go to Bitburg and convert the 36th TFW from F-4Es to the F-15, another very 'high visibility' program. When the first three aircraft arrived at Bitburg we had an initial cadre of approximately 140 personnel in place and already working to prepare the Wing for transition. The Field Training Detachment (FTD) had to be up and ready to support the training requirement since the follow-on personnel, beyond the cadre, were not all F-15 qualified. The Flight Simulator was delivered by C-5A Galaxy and our Intermediate Level avionics automatic and manual rest equipment was also flown in. The Type 4 Precision Measurement Equipment Laboratory (PMEL), providing calibration standards and support for most of the test equipment used on the aircraft, required set-up and calibration as well. Two of the initial three aircraft were assigned to various training and checkout procedures and the other one was used to keep the few F-15 pilots qualified. The aircraft rotated between flying and training. The real secret to getting the first squadron operational was the quality of the personnel and the 'can do' attitude of everyone there. It was a big team effort and we believed in the aircraft and its capabilities and were determined to make sure nothing went wrong. A very important part of the team was the delegation of McDonnell Douglas Technical Representatives assigned to support the maintenance team. They were just as much a part of the team as anyone else and devoted many long hours assisting the various maintenance disciplines.

Within approximately 14 months after arrival at Bitburg, I was asked to go to Soesterberg in Holland as Senior NCO of Avionics Flightline Maintenance for the conversion of the famous 32nd TFS from the F-4E to the F-15. I was allowed to pick six personnel from those at Bitburg and the remainder came from the *Ready Eagle* program. Unlike the transition at Bitburg, we lost the Phantoms very quickly and our Alert line was supported by personnel and aircraft from the 1st TFW. Our Dutch friends were very noise-conscious (but tolerant) and the aircraft produced quite a noise 'footprint' on a full afterburner takeoff, which occurred on every scramble.

F-15B 76-0139, marked for the 832nd Air Division Commander and based at Luke AFB.
Author's Collection

(Above) With impressively synchronized undercarriage retraction, a pair of 8th TFS F-15As blasts off from Nellis AFB in June 1980.
Boeing/McDonnell Douglas via Norm Taylor

(Below) The Bonn Convention established that the 32nd TFS should intercept any unidentified aircraft that penetrated West Germany's northern border. In wartime it would have sought to maintain air superiority in the 2 ATAF region. Two of its F-15Cs show off their agility in 1982. Norm Taylor Collection

Bulldogs and Wolfhounds

Although some would argue that the F-15A was a little quieter than the F-4E, residents of Camp New Amsterdam (Soesterberg) learned to live with it from November 1978 until 13 January 1994 when the last three F-15As left the base. At Bitburg, preparations continued while pilots coming off F-4Es joined the first 32 to qualify on the F-15, after receiving 20 to 25 upgrade sorties with the 94th TFS at Langley. Among this group, half came from existing F-15 squadrons at Luke and Langley, the rest from F-4Es or other types. The first pilots attained mission-ready status on 14 January 1977 and by 25 April all, including Brig Gen Fred Kyler, the 36th TFW CO were ready to deploy to the German base. This was delayed slightly by the late arrival of parts of the F-15 Tactical Electronic Warfare System (TEWS) and the need to replace some unreliable fuel pumps. Early F-15s had operated without the TEWS but it was more urgently needed for European operations.

Eventually the first cell of three F-15As left Langley on 27 April, followed by three other cells and their air-spares at half-hour

intervals. They touched down at Bitburg 7.5hr later after several air refuellings. Brig Gen Fred Kyler flew in the first F-15A (75-051) and the 525th TFS *Bulldogs* had 23 aircraft. The 22nd TFS bade farewell to their last F-4E on 26 February 1977, six weeks after the arrival of their first F-15A and they were operational on the new fighter by 30 June. Bitburg's *Tiger* squadron, the 53rd TFS converted by 9 November completing the establishment of the first overseas Eagle Wing.

A posting to Bitburg meant a move to the sharpest edge of NATO's Central Front and a commitment to be first in battle if the Cold War turned hot. Situated in the Eifel region, the rather cramped base had housed the 36th TFW since 1952 after it moved from Furstenfeldbruck with F-86F Sabres. Like the Sabre, the F-15A had a purely air-to-air role in USAFE. It would have been the first defence against shoals of Soviet bloc low and medium-altitude attackers and its base would have been the target of many a ballistic missile. At peak strength the wing owned 73 F-15A/B Eagles, the two-seat 'twin tubs' being used for orientation and VIP flights, but NATO's fighter force needed more Eagles to redress the imbalance in forces brought about by large numbers of more advanced Russian fighters.

The re-equipment of the 32nd TFS at Soesterberg involved yet another task for the Langley Wing. *Coronet Sandpiper* took eighteen F-15As from the 71st TFS to the Dutch base to cover for the 32nd TFS while its pilots converted at Luke AFB under *Ready Eagle II*. Among the arriving Eagles were the first two 'permanent' F-15As destined for the 32nd TFS; 77-074, flown in on 13 September 1978 from Langley by the 32nd TFS CO, Col Albert L. Pruden Jr., and 77-075. The first quartet of 71st TFS aircraft to land included 75-059, piloted by Col Neil L. Eddins, who had taken command of the 1st TFW. Another F-15A, 76-059, developed fuel system problems over the Atlantic and was effectively towed across by a tanker that pumped in fuel slightly faster than the F-15 was venting it out.

Soesterberg passed its F-4Es to other units (many going to Ramstein) and rehearsed its mission to defend the Netherlands and areas of Northern Germany within the 2nd ATAF, Sector 1. Having served as part of the 36th Day Fighter Wing, the 32nd had moved to the 86th FIW from April 1960 until 1968, using the F-100C Super Sabre until it was replaced by the Convair F-102A in 1961. F-4E

F-15A-18-MC 77-0064 of the 4485th TS joins a line-up of 1st TFW and 3247th TS Eagles in October 1984. Author's Collection

MiG kills from the Vietnam War appear on 76-0078, the mount of the 550th TFS CO, Lt Col John Madden. With the 555th TFS he shot down a MiG-21 on 12 October 1972 and two MiG-19s on 9 September 1972 with 'top scorer' Capt Chuck DeBellvue as his WSO. Jim Rotramel

In overall Gloss ADC Grey, Lt Col Madden's F-15A 76-0078 still has the original borderless national insignia and Silver Eagles tail flashes. Jim Rotramel

Phantoms were phased in from August 1969. Its 'CR' tail code should officially have read 'SR'; the 'S' for Soesterberg and 'R' as the first squadron letter in the 'R, S, T' sequence used for USAFE units. Since 'SR' was already in use by the 62nd TAS's C-130Es in Tennessee, 'CR' was used, referring to Camp New Amsterdam, the base's correct name until 1987. Others thought the code signified 'CRown', an allusion to the unit's close links to the Royal Netherlands Air Force. The 32nd TFS 'crown' badge and orange ribbons linked it also with William of Orange, first Prince of the Netherlands. Its 'Wolfhounds' nickname was also illustrated in the badge, with a drooling wolf cartoon designed by Walt Disney Studios in 1942 when the Squadron was a submarine-hunting unit in the Dutch East Indies. Bitburg's *Bulldogs* also had their canine mascot, a real bulldog called Pexer who was flown to Bitburg in a helmet bag, going supersonic en route.

The *Wolfhounds'* speedy and effective transition won them the Air Force Outstanding Unit Award in 1978 and 1980, and the Hughes Trophy in both 1979 and 1980. The Hughes Trophy is awarded annually for the most outstanding air defence squadron in the USAF and this was the first time it had been awarded to a unit in two consecutive years. For the squadrons at Bitburg and Soesterberg the availability of DACT training with Aggressor aircraft was a major ingredient in their success. Experience with AIMVAL/ACEVAL and the 57th FWW at Nellis led to the formation of the 527th TFTAS at RAF Alconbury in 1976 that reached full strength with twenty F-5Es and some battle-hardened pilots by June 1976. Spangdahlem's Phantoms had already established a DACT arrangement with the 527th when Bitburg's first twelve-Eagle detachment arrived at Alconbury on 12 September 1977 to make a similar arrangement. They kept aircraft there for six weeks, rotating crews and returning in December and in February/March 1978 with five F-15As. Before the 36th TFW's deployment to Aalborg, Denmark for Exercise *Oksboel* another dozen Eagles flew from Alconbury to challenge the F-5E pilots in gut-wrenching manoeuvres (John Poole recalled seeing wrinkles in the skins on the top of some aircraft) over the North Sea. Eagles from Soesterberg also visited Alconbury frequently

The landscape below these 32nd TFS *Wolfhounds* F-15As leaves little doubt about their immediate area of responsibility. Boeing/McDonnell Douglas via Norm Taylor

with two or four-aircraft detachments. Dog-fights with MiG-simulating F-5Es were often conducted en route to Alconbury or on return to Bitburg or Soesterberg. Further, more regular practice in air combat was available via ACM with other F-15As, but the Aggressors gave the most realistic opposition because their pilots were trained in the most current Soviet fighter tactics for 'inside BVR' combat.

The competitive demands of these ACM sessions put pressure on the 'Eagle Keepers' too. John Poole:

The deployments in support of the various ACM detachments were a challenge for two reasons: availability of spare parts and the fact that we didn't want to lose a fight to anyone! Our maintenance folks worked very hard to make sure each aircraft was 100 per cent prior to each mission. While on detachment, the maintainers worked much harder and more as a close team, therefore learning more about their systems. Without the luxury of extra parts, they wanted to make sure that the correct part was removed the first time. All 'removed' parts had to go back to home base for in depth checkout/repair and we didn't like to send 'good' parts back.

It was during these demanding sorties that problems with the F100 engine began to reassert themselves. The initial training of the first seven F-15 squadrons had taken place with remarkably few accidents, despite the pressure on time and aircraft availability at Luke and Langley. In the first of the stateside incidents the pilot of F-15A 73-088 had noticed smoke in his cockpit over the Gila Bend Gunnery Range near Luke AFB on 14 October 1975. He turned off both generators, inadvertently knocking out the main fuel tank boost pump. The emergency pump failed to take over, the aircraft flamed out and was flying too low for a restart, leaving the pilot no recourse but his IC-7 ejection seat. AIMVAL/ACE-VAL also led to a crash on 28 February 1977 when F-15A 74-129 of the 57th FWW hit a 'Red Force' F-5E over the Nellis Range. Again, the pilot was able to eject, but in December another 67 FWW Eagle crash cost the life of the 433rd FWS CO. This was still an unprecedentedly good record for a complex, new fighter and none of the mishaps implied serious problems with the aircraft, but 1978 brought a spate of mishaps, six of them to Bitburg aircraft and most attributable to engine problems. Extracts from the USAF accident

Going vertical: an Elmendorf Eagle demonstrates the principle of excess thrust and escapes the inhospitable environment of Alaska. Boeing/McDonnell Douglas

F-15A 77-0141 of the 57th Wing displays the *Satan's Angels* insignia of the 433rd FWS, formerly an 8th TFW *Wolfpack* unit with many MiGs to its credit in the Vietnam War. Ron Thurlow

43rd TFS F-15A 74-0108 visits Shaw AFB in December 1986. The 'Big Dipper' tail band and low visibility insignia are distinctive. Norm Taylor

F-15A-18-MC 77-0083 cruises serenely back to Soesterberg after an ACM session. The centreline tank rapidly became a fixture on operational Eagles. Norm Taylor Collection

summaries show that there were common causes in several of them:

17 April 1978

The mishap aircraft [75-059] was No. 3 in a three-ship DACT mission against four F-5Es in the Aggressor Training Area, 125 NM north-east of RAF Alconbury. During the engagement, No. 3 called, 'Bingo minus 1' indicating that his remaining fuel was 100lb (45kg) below the pre-briefed fuel state. The F-15s disengaged and began recovery. Two minutes later No. 3 called 4,000lb (1,814kg) fuel remaining but none in his feed tanks. The starboard engine then flamed out, followed two minutes later by the port engine. Anticipating complete loss of control the pilot ejected at 14,000ft (4,267m), sustaining minor injuries.

15 June 1978

Adler 53 [76-047] was one of two F-15s on a DACT mission against two F-5Es en route to Bitburg and had just begun conversion to a gun attack on the lead F-5 when he called to terminate the engagement. Flames were observed coming from both engines. *Adler* 53 established a glide and reported one engine had stagnated and the other refused to start. After descending through haze the pilot ejected safely, 3.5 minutes after the problem arose [and was recovered by a trawler].

6 July 1978

The accident F-15 [76-053] was in a flight of four en route to an ACT/air refuelling mission. After take-off from Bitburg the aircraft formatted for a standard instrument departure. Shortly afterwards, the departure radar failed. Radar contact was then re-established, by which time the flight was flying level in cloud at 7,000ft (2,130m). Shortly afterwards, *Adler* 24 called 'Four is lost wingman', indicating he had lost contact with the flight. [*Adler* 23 also lost contact, re-establishing it at 9,500ft (2,900m), above the clouds.] A radar, radio and visual search failed to locate *Adler* 24. The aircraft crashed 13 nm NNW of Bitburg with the canopy still on.

19 Dec 1978

Growl 17 [75-063] was in a three-ship ACT mission. Combat started when *Growl* 17 made a radar lock on *Growl* 18 and began a rear attack. The aircraft closed on its target, attempting a high-angle gun shot. *Growl* 18 saw *Growl* 17 overshoot and burst into flames and called, 'Punch out. Punch out!' *Growl* 16 saw a parachute shortly before the aircraft hit the ground.

28 Dec 1978

The mishap aircraft [75-064] was on an ACT mission. After the third engagement the pilot entered a chandelle manoeuvre. The wingman reported fire coming from the engine nozzle area, probably from the starboard engine. The pilot cut the afterburner on the port engine, shut off fuel to the other engine and entered a shallow dive to maintain airspeed. During the recovery the left engine wound down and attempts to air-start both engines were unsuccessful. The pilot ejected safely.

A sixth F-15A, 76-073, was reportedly damaged by fire on 7 June when the port engine failed after selecting afterburner. In four of these accidents stall-stagnation was clearly at the root, brought about by pilots making rapid throttle movements during ACT. Engine or fuel system failures were also implicated in the other cases and P&W

redoubled the efforts to modify the F100 further and increase its reliability. The Bitburg Wing, working hard and successfully to get the Eagle into USAFE service, rode out these disappointments. In part, the problem originated in the Wing's requirement to be prepared for combat conditions in Europe. On transfer from the USA the F-15's engines were trimmed to a higher fan turbine inlet temperature (FTIT); the 'combat' setting. This tended to cause overtemperature in the F100s and turbine failure. The sight of Eagles thundering down the runway, spitting sheets of fire and bits of turbine from their rear ends became less common after the engines' FTIT was 'turned down' to Stateside settings again.

In other respects, the Eagle proved to be a much easier aircraft to keep on the line than its predecessors. Large jobs such as engine changes could be done far more rapidly and one of the longest – changing a radar antenna – took only one and a half hours. However, it was an unpleasant job and was sometimes necessitated by fractured hydraulic lines behind the antenna. The fluid then sprayed all over the inside of the radome in a minor disaster known as a 'nosebleed' and the mess had to be carefully cleaned up.

As part of NATO's' first line of defence Bitburg mounted Zulu Alert flights, aiming to get airborne inside five minutes from the warning hooter, as did the 32nd TFS. At Bitburg this required modifications to the shelters previously occupied by F-4s. Inward-opening doors that could not be used with the larger Eagle inside the shelter, had to be replaced with one-piece sliding versions. This still left only 6in

(15cm) clearance each side of the aircraft. In order to ensure scrape-free entry to the shelter, metal wheel tracks were fitted to the floor and a cable system allowed the aircraft to be winched back into its lair at the end of a sortie. The primary Zulu Alert consisted of four aircraft that had to be 'perfect' aircraft from the maintenance viewpoint. Two back-up Eagles were kept ready in shelters to the rear. Soesterberg's Alert facility was a little easier to operate because after the primary Alert aircraft had left via the huge 'garage door' at the front of the barn a second pair could be brought in from the rear of the structure. Gen Collar, the tough but humane Wg Cdr at Bitburg in its early Eagle days, was fond of 'firing off' the Alert aircraft as a public relations exercise whenever the base had important visitors. They were treated to the spectacle of two Eagles hurtling down the runway well within the 4min limit and then performing high-velocity climbing turns to avoid the civil air route that passed over the base. On occasion, the frequency of these 'publicity' launches gave the 'Eagle Keepers' headaches, particularly when the first launch occurred so soon after the aircraft's arrival that there were only three airworthy examples on the base. At Bitburg, Alert turnaround time had to include an allowance for INS realignment since the aircraft had to be shut down before being towed back into its shelter. Even the small difference in the location of the aircraft outside rather than inside the shelter would upset the INS navigational calculations unless it were realigned with the correct co-ordinates before flight.

Active F-15 units had a few F-15B/D 'twin tub' models on strength for training, familiarization and check rides or hack duties. 79-0004 belonged to the 32nd TFS and was later transferred to the Royal Saudi AF. USAF

By 1980 another strategy had been evolved to make the best of the F-15's capability as part of a Mixed Fighter Force (MFF) with other NATO participants to maximize their effect against a Warsaw PAC onslaught. Discussions 'over a few beers' between RAF Phantom FGR.2 crews from Wildenrath and the pilots of the 32nd TFS resulted in the Eagles and Phantoms, with their superior BVR weapons, acting as the frontal 'battering ram' against an incoming strike force of less radar-capable F-4F, F-104 and F-5s that would have followed behind to mop up any intruders that had slipped through.

Crested Eagles

In the USA other new F-15A/B units continued to form. At Holloman AFB, on 20 December 1977 a flypast by six F-15As led by four Phantoms marked the end of the New Mexico-based 7th TFS *Bunyabs*' conversion to the Eagle. The other two based squadrons, the 8th TFS *Blacksheep* and 9th TFS *Iron Knights* followed in 1978 and the Wing achieved IOC by 4 June. Eight aircraft went to the November *Red Flag* and ten attended *Maple Flag* at Cold Lake in Canada the following May. The 49th had a long-standing commitment as a forward-deployable reinforcement for NATO and made many a *Crested Cap* deployment to Germany with its 'HO'-coded F-4Ds in the 1970s. A pair of 49th TFW Eagles had made a record-breaking 6,200mi (10,000km) flight in 14hr, with six in-flight refuellings, in February 1980. Several pilots reported that their ejection seats were even harder

than those in the F-4. Nevertheless, long flights became routine for the Wing when it began Rapid Deployment Force duties for a year from July 1980. After a cancelled *Coronet Turbine* opening deployment to Lahr, Germany in August of that year the Wing sent in twelve 7th TFS aircraft to Lahr as *Coronet Sloop* and a similar number of 9th TFS aircraft to Aalborg, Denmark as *Coronet Compass* in August 1981, and another to Jever. *Crested Caps* took their Eagles back to Lahr in August 1983 and similar deployments continued throughout the 1980s, including *Coronet Scout* to Gilze Rijen and *Coronet Fang* to Wittmund, each with a dozen aircraft. On that visit F-15A 77-091 sustained wing damage when a pylon was accidentally jettisoned in flight, while 77-138 was more seriously wounded by an engine fire and had to return to the USA by C-5A Galaxy.

At Eglin AFB, Florida the 33rd TFW received its first Eagles (77-068 and 77-156) on 21 September 1979 for training purposes and 'squadron' aircraft from 15 December. By 21 June 1979 it had a full complement of aircraft. Its 58th TFS *Gorillas* reached IOC on 23 May 1979, followed by former F-4E unit the 59th TFS *Golden Pride* (formerly an ADC unit) and the 60th TFS *Fighting Crows* by the end of 1980. Cold War European deployments were very much a part of the 33rd's agenda too, with the *Gorillas* making their first deployment in October 1979 by sending eighteen aircraft to Bremgarten as *Coronet Eagle*. Another six visited Misawa, Japan in April of that year and *Crested Cap* deployments were made to Bremgarten and Sollingen in August/September 1982. Large deployments to Lahr in

phase with the 49th TFW continued in the 1980s: 24 *Golden Pride* Eagles arrived in August 1985 and a similar package from the 58th TFS made the journey in September 1987 in *Coronet Phaser*. The message to the Eastern bloc countries was very distinct: at the slightest hint of aggression USAFE fighter forces could be rapidly doubled by units that were used to the European environment and able to deploy there at very short notice.

Training on the F-15A to supply the thirteen front-line units continued at Luke, while the 57th FWW pushed on with development work at Nellis using some of the original OT&E aircraft until new-build F-15As were available. Weapons delivery profiles, air combat tactics and EW strategies were all the responsibility of the 422nd TES (Test and Evaluation Squadron), while the 433rd FWS had a vital role in training F-15 pilots in advanced flying techniques. Like the Navy's *Top Gun* programme the plan was to put at least one graduate from this course into each operational squadron so that he could pass on his expertise in air combat tactics. The 433rd received its first F-15A (75-042), flown in by the CO, Lt Col Dave Jacobsen on November 1976 and five other F-15A/B by the end of the year. It ran four-month classes, each with up to six students. One other TAC unit, the 31st TFW at Homestead AFB was scheduled to join the F-15A flyers in 1983, but a change of plans kept it on F-4s until its transition to the F-16 'Viper' in 1985-6. For the other F-15 wings their next big evolution was the introduction of a more potent Eagle, the F-15C.

Tyndall AFB began F-15 training in 1986 and its 325th TTW included the 2nd FS with yellow tail stripes. 74-0102 previously flew with the 58th TTW and 57th TTW in 1978. Norm Taylor

CHAPTER THREE

Better Birds of Prey

F-15C

So much of the Eagle design was right first time that the second single-seat version, the F-15C was largely a refined F-15A that improved the aircraft's endurance and took advantage of the rapid advances in avionics technology. Its airframe had some local strengthening to cope with weight increases and a stronger undercarriage with new main

wheels for the same purpose. Most of the extra bulk came from 311gal (1,414l) (2,021lb) (917kg) of additional fuel in an enlarged Goodyear fuselage tank and two internal wing tanks that were extended rearwards to hold an extra 73gal (332l) (475lb) (215kg) each. The major range boost came from conformal fuel tanks (CFTs)that had been tested on F-15B 71-291 and were made standard for the F-15C. The Israeli

AF, an eager purchaser of the potent fighter, had expressed a considerable interest in CFTs from the outset and this helped to guarantee the development and production of the units. Whereas the Type 1 CFT on '291 was fuel-only, production models were equipped for tangential carriage of weapons along their outer, lower edges. Installation (and automatic fuel line/electrical connection) was performed by sliding the tanks up

Eagle 78-0468, the first F-15C model, on an early flight over St Louis. Later, at Edwards AFB with 'ED' codes it test-flew CFTs with bomb-loads. Norm Taylor Collection

stabilizing 'rails' built into the F-15C's flanks and securing two bolts. CFTs added another 9,750lb (4,423kg) of fuel.

Also included in what was originally called the Production Eagle Package (PEP-2000) to change the aircraft to F-15C standard were an extra UHF radio (*Have Quick* secure radios in later models), improved ECM and a new seat. The F-15A's IC-7 ejection seat was replaced by the more advanced McDonnell Douglas ACES II (advanced concept ejection seat), also used in the F-16, A-10 and B-1B. By 1995 the seat was ensuring 80 per cent survival rates among those who had cause to use it and the manufacturers claimed a perfect safety record for the seat on the occasions on which it had been used within its design parameters. Tested in an early OT&E F-15A, the zero-zero unit was installed in all Eagles after Production Block 17. ACES II can select one of three ejection modes automatically, depending on the circumstances of the emergency. At low speed (therefore, probably, low altitude or ground-level, zero-zero ejection), it produces a parachute within 1.8sec after the 700lb (317kg) of vectored thrust from the gyro-controlled rocket catapult have blasted the seat from the cockpit. A second, stabilizing rocket ignites to keep the seat's attitude correct relative to the ground. In Mode 2 (high speed) a drogue chute slows the seat before the main canopy is deployed, avoiding damage to both parachute and pilot. Mode 3 delays the parachute deployment process if the aircraft is at high altitude so that the

Better Engines

Evolutionary improvements in the reliability of the F100 engine brought about the F100-P-220, the powerplant for the F-15C, although it was not ready for the first batch of aircraft. Dry thrust was slightly reduced by 300lb (136kg) from the 14,670lb (6,655kg) of the F100-P-100, with a 400lb (180kg) cut in afterburning thrust to 23,450lb (10,640kg). Although this might have seemed a curiously retrogressive move pilots found acceleration and performance actually improved because of the engine's more efficient power and fuel distribution. Several problem areas with the first F100 version were largely resolved with the introduction of digital electronic engine control (DEEC) using a 16-bit, 8.5kb computer. The system was test-run in 1983 and it gave far better management of the fuel supply. Digital engines are much more responsive to rapid changes in power setting, easier to trim and less inclined to stall. Their performance is constantly monitored and an engine diagnostic unit (EDU) immediately identifies any abnormalities and records them for maintenance purposes. A new, less complex main fuel pump was less susceptible to breakdowns and lasted twice as long. New technology enabled turbine blades to be manufactured using a 'single crystal' method in which cooling of the steel could be controlled so that their crystalline structure was aligned in one direction, giving improved heat resistance. Together with the slight reduction in overall engine temperature this meant that engine fixers would less often have to face the sight of compressor blades reduced to ragged stumps by engine overheating. Afterburner cooling was improved and a new light-off detector automatically 'supervised' the previously troublesome afterburner lighting and relighting process, preventing fuel from flooding into an unlit afterburner. The new -220 engine didn't become available until 1986 but many of its improvements were applied to the majority of earlier -100 units. The only externally visible difference was the removal of the seventeen covers ('turkey feathers') that protected the complex activating rods for the engine nozzles. A Technical Order had already specified that these could be removed from -100 engines to simplify maintenance. The F100-P-220 was built without them. With the new-variant powerplant pilots could enjoy unrestricted use of the throttle and better transonic acceleration with a very-much reduced chance of stall-stagnation, power loss or fires.

pilot isn't suspended in an airless environment with only his 10-minute emergency oxygen supply.

Other cockpit equipment comprised a video recorder for radar and 'gun camera' imagery in place of the cine camera and an overload warning system that gave audible warning of excessive g, but allowed the pilot to pull up to 9g rather than the previous 7.3g limit.

The first of these definitive single-seat Eagles, F-15C-21-MC 78-468, flew on 26 February 1979 followed by its two-seat equivalent, F-15D 78-561 on 19 June. Later that year important modifications were made to the AN/APG-63 radar. The addition of a first-generation programmable signal processor gave better filtering of 'clutter' from ground returns, improved track-while scan and the ability to distinguish closely-formatting targets at distance, i.e. the software improvements tested in AIMVAL/ACEVAL. Perched on an avionics rack behind the big access Door

CFTs can be attached using a normal bomb truck with an adaptor frame. The 'Fast packs' add very little drag though their weight penalty inevitably causes some degradation in manoeuvrability. Boeing/McDonnell Douglas

3L the digital PSP's primary function was to enable the radar to be instantly updated with new modes or weapons parameters merely by changing the software package. It also enabled the pilot to switch 'lock' from target to target more rapidly. Tested in F-15A 77-084 the improved radar was retrofitted to earlier F-15Cs that left the line before it was ready.

Shogun Eagles

The first batch of F-15Cs was destined for the 18th TFW at Kadena AFB, Okinawa although the aircraft went initially to Eglin AFB and the 33rd TFW. F-15A/B models had been in use at Eglin from December 1979 and the first F-15C (78-470) arrived on 3 July of that year to commence *Ready Eagle III*, the supply of F-15Cs to Kadena. The 67th TFS *Fighting Cocks*, formerly a pioneering F-4C *Wild Weasel* unit in Vietnam, were first to convert at Eglin, returning their new aircraft to Kadena from 26 September 1979. Next were the 44th TFS *Vampires*, who had fought through the Vietnam War in F-105s from 1964 to 1970 before moving to F-4Ds. Their conversion was complete by the end of 1979, making way for Kadena's third squadron the 12th TFS *Dirty Dozen* that made the transition from January 1980.

Pacific Command (PACOM) covers the largest geographical area in the USAF's remit, extending from the US west coast to Africa and from the North to the South Pole. In the 1980s it contained the 7th AF in Korea, the 5th AF in Japan and the 13th AF in the Philippines. The allocation of the longer-ranging F-15C to the Pacific as a first priority reflected this scope, as did the decision to allow the 18th TFW a total of eighty-two Eagles when Bitburg, NATO's premier Cold War defenders had only seventy-eight at their peak. Based since 1954 at the largest PACAF facility, the 18th TFW is the only USAF Wing never to have been based in the continental USA. In the 1980s it had its own tanker squadron, an Aerospace Rescue and Recovery Squadron, an RF-4C recce unit (which donated its 'ZZ' tailcode to the 18th TFW) and from the mid-1990s a based AWACS unit. In 1989 the 26th AS Aggressor Squadron relocated from Clark AFB to Kadena and continued to provide DACT training, although it was disestablished soon after converting to the F-16C later that year. *Shogun Warrior* F-15Cs have mounted Alert Detachments at Osan AFB, South Korea and frequently

Unlike its F-4 ancestor the F-15 offers spectacular visibility from its rear seat. This Kadena-based F-15D takes a fill from a Stratotanker. USAF

took advantage of their maximum ferry endurance of 15 hours (with tanker support) to fly to the extremities of their area of responsibility. Eight aircraft visited Whenuapui, New Zealand in September 1984 for Exercise *Triad '84*, acting as the 'Blue Force' with RNZAF BAe Strikemasters and facing an 'Orange Force' of 8th TFW F-16s, RAAF Mirages and RNZAF A-4K Skyhawks. The Wing sent eight aircraft on the long transit to *Red Flag* in November 1986 and appearances at Nellis and the *William Tell* air-to-air gunnery meets became a regular occurrence, as did participation in *Pitch Black* exercises in the Southern Hemisphere. One such took place in August 1991 when fourteen aircraft visited Darwin to fly with RAAF and a number of units from South-East Asian nations. Participation in large scale *Cope Thunder* exercises, which were moved from Clark AFB in the Philippines to Elmendorf in Alaska in 1991, occupied up to fifteen Eagles at a time from July 1992 onwards. The 1996 *Cope Thunders* involved twelve Eagles in March and another dozen in May. More locally, the 18th TFW sometimes shares exercises with Japanese Air Force units, visiting Chitose with twelve Eagles for *Keen Edge 95* with several other PACAF squadrons and repeating the exercise in 1999 to work with Chitose's 2nd Kokudan F-15Js.

With the end of USAF operations at Clark AFB in 1991, Kadena's importance in the area was enhanced and the political instability in Korea and Indonesia together with uncertainties about Taiwan have ensured that its twin, 12,000ft (3,660m) runways have been kept busy. However, the *Shogun Warriors* did not escape the drastic cuts that reduced USAF strength in the 1990s. In 1992 the Wing heard that it would lose eighteen aircraft. The axe didn't fall until 5 November 1999 when the 12th TFS was inactivated, distributing its aircraft to the other two units and returning some to the USA. This reduced the 18th TFW to around fifty aircraft, all of which were sent to the Korean Airlines facility at Pusan South Korea for programmed depot maintenance (PDM).

Eagles on Ice

At Elmendorf, two squadrons of the 21st TFW (formerly 21st Composite Wing) received Eagles to defend the State of Alaska and an area of Northern Canada. Its NORAD duties began in October 1982 giving the squadron responsibility for about half a million square miles (1,295,000 sq km) of frozen wastes from the North Pole to the Aleutians as 'Top Cover

A Bitburg F-15C takes its place in a gathering of NATO 'big hitters' including an RAF Phantom FGR.2, a 48th
TFW F-111F and a Belgian Mirage 5. USAF

Among the competitors at the 1988 *William Tell* was an immaculate ex-36th TFW F-15C, 79-0041,
representing the host 43rd TFS at Tyndall AFB. Norm Taylor Collection

A quartet of Kadena F-15Cs in Mod Eagle scheme formats with the other members of the air superiority team, the E-3 AWACS and KC-135 tanker. USAF

for America'. The squadron also mounted Alert facilities at King Salmon Airport on the Aleutian chain and Galena Airport. Most of the 'trade' was with Soviet reconnaissance aircraft. There were about fifty interceptions of Bear-G and Bear-H snoopers annually in the late 1980s, falling to nineteen in 1991. A pair of 962nd AWACS E-3A Sentries on detachment from Tinker AFB co-ordinated the intercepts.

AK-coded F-15Cs proved well able to cope with the harsh climate of Alaska despite having to operate mainly from open flight-lines, with hangarage for maintenance. There have been no serious accidents in the decade since 1990. Training facilities included an instrumented ACMI range for Alaska-based units and for the use of *Cope Thunder* exercises. Until 1988 there were two Elmendorf-based T-33As flying electronic warfare simulation sorties but defence cuts forced their replacement by contract-hire civilian jets. Two bare-base facilities could also act as forward-operating locations (FOLs), including one known as The Rock, at Deadhorse. Their unpopularity with pilots just might have been reasoned away by

quoting BGen Billy Mitchell's 1935 observation, 'Alaska is the most strategic point in the world. He who holds Alaska holds the world'. Americans have not forgotten that it is the only area of the continental USA to have been attacked. Japan occupied some of the outlying islands in 1942. The 3rd FW's air defence posture, shared with the 18th FS at Eielson AFB – the coldest base in the USA – is still relevant.

The Wing's 43rd TFS *Hornets* exchanged their FC-coded F-4E Phantoms for ex-1st TFW FY 74 F-15As from 1 March 1982 working up to a maximum of twenty-two aircraft by April 1983 and anticipating the formation of a second squadron at Elmendorf. This did not happen until May 1987 when the 54th TFS *Leopards*, an old ADC squadron, was revived and received ex-71st TFS F-15C/Ds. At the same time the 43rd TFS accepted eighteen ex-36th TFW F-15Cs plus others from Langley AFB and returned its last F-15A on 12 August 1988. Most of its earlier returnees went to the 199 FIS, Hawaii ANG. An August 1990 reorganization saw the end of Alaskan Air Command as it became the 11th Air Force

within PACAF. Shortly afterwards the combination of political pressure and volcanic activity forced the 3rd TFW to vacate Clark AFB. Its F-4E-flying 90th TFS *Pair o'Dice* had been scheduled to receive the new F-15E and it was logical to add these aircraft to the Elmendorf Wing, transferring the 3rd TFW title with them. On 19 December 1991 the 21st CW became the 3rd FW. The Wing's two F-15C squadrons remained untouched until another relabelling changed the 54rd TFS to the 19th TFS *Gamecocks*, a title formerly applied to an F-16 unit at Shaw whose Wing had in turn adopted the identity of a former USAFE F-111 Wing, the 20th FW. Although this set of squadron identities survived through the rest of the 1990s, the aircraft continued to change. In June 1998 it was decided to standardize the variant of F100 engine in use at Elmendorf to simplify maintenance and spares holding, so its forty-three F-100-P-100 powered F-15Cs were progressively exchanged with those of the 33rd FW *Nomads* at Eglin that used the -220 version like Elmendorf's F-15Es.

PACAF membership took the Elmendorf Eagles on numerous long-distance

The combination of airbrake, big wing, high angle of attack and careful judgement that makes a braking parachute unnecessary for an F-15 on landing. This Kadena aircraft was arriving at Clark AFB for a May 1980 exercise *Cope Thunder*. Ron Thurlow

F-15C 84-0004 was the fourth aircraft to receive the MSIP updates on the St Louis production line. In service with the 33rd TFW, MSIP Eagles won first place in the 1986 *William Tell*. Boeing/McDonnell Douglas

deployments throughout the 1990s as well as hosting incoming deployments for *Cope Thunder*. The *Leopards* flew to Korat RTAFB, Thailand in June 1995 for the ten-day *Cope Tiger* exercise involving Thai, Singapore AF and other PACAF units. Luke AFB hosted *Tandem Thrust* for PACAF squadrons in July 1992 attended by twelve Eagles from all three squadrons, while four Eagles flew to Murom AFB in Russia in August 1996 for an exchange with an Su-27 unit.

Back in the USA

Although the 33rd TFW's first batch of F-15Cs were only on temporary tenure before moving to Kadena, the Wing received its own F-15Cs from 23 February 1983 after a three-year period flying the F-15A/B batch previously operated at Soesterberg by the 32nd TFS. Eglin's Eagles continued their tradition of frequent deployments with the new birds, having pioneered the concept of full-squadron deployments to Bremgarten and Lahr in Germany with their F-15As. Lahr received all twenty-four of the 58th TFS F-15Cs for *Coronet Phaser* in September and October of 1987, four of their Eagles staying behind to join the 36th TFW's 'Eagle update'. The large-scale approach was also used for the Wing's *Red Flag* training at that time with twenty aircraft at Nellis in November 1986. The size of these operations perhaps reflected the 33rd TFW's occupation on one of the largest bases in the USA. Covering 720sq mi (1,865sq km) of Florida terrain, plus another 100,000sq mi (259,000sq km) of range area, mostly off-shore it also housed the 3246th Test Wing (later 46th Test Wing) and the munitions test organization that became the Air Armament Center.

Red Flag continued to provide crucial, realistic combat training throughout the 1980s and 1990s and pilots learned to make full use of their fighter's dominant 1.3:1 thrust-to-weight ratio to allow them to take the initiative in combat, or get out fast if things fell apart. The 33rd TFW sent detachments of between ten and twenty Eagles to at least one of the *Red Flag* events each year.

In parallel with *Red Flag* there were exercises such as *Long Shot '94* at Nellis. At very short notice the contending teams were given 'bombing targets' at some distance from their home bases. Routes, attack

(Above) Bitburg Eagles lived in hardened shelters that made NATO bases less vulnerable, though when Eagles hit similar shelters in Iraq during *Desert Storm* the structures offered little protection against direct hits from directly above by Paveway LGBS. USAF

An 18th TFW *Shogun Warriors* F-15C under tow at Clark AFB in December 1979 with safety covers and tags in place. Ron Thurlow

(Below) A Holloman AFB F-15A at Nellis AFB for a *Red Flag*, February 1983. The 9th TFS flew 'A' model Eagles from November 1978 until it reverted to F-4Es in 1992 as training unit for Luftwaffe Phantom pilots. Ron Thurlow

profiles and weaponry would have to be decided in a matter of a few hours and the teams would recover to Nellis afterwards for debriefing. *Maple Flag XXI* at Cold Lake, Alberta took Eagles to Canada to train over vast, sparsely populated areas of terrain, often at low altitudes. Eight 33rd TFW aircraft flew with CAF Hornets, RAF Harriers and USAF FB-111As, A-7Ds and F-16s with a Detachment of 57th FWW Aggressors to catch the unwary. European deployments continued to take much of the 33rd Wing's time through the early 1990s. Two twelve-aircraft packages went to Soesterberg on *Coronet* exercises in 1990 and 1992. Both *Coronet* and *Crested Cap* reinforcement exercises involved some intensive flying for the visiting squadrons

(Top) Unnaturally close for Eagles, this pair would be about a mile apart on a typical CAP mission. Eagle airframes stay remarkably clean in service, lacking the frequent fluid leaks of previous fighters. A little staining from the two dump vents under the fuselage booms is the only blemish. Boeing/McDonnell Douglas

(Bottom) The final Block 23 F-15C, 78-0550 against a bleak Alaskan backdrop, surrounded by its support equipment. Kevin Jackson

with a normal pattern of two four-ship launches in the morning and another two in the afternoon, each on 90-minute DACT, CAP or ACT missions. Other 'foreign tours' were associated with duties in the Gulf area and related detachments to Keflavik. Despite its key role as a forward-deployable Wing, the 33rd also took cuts in the 1990s drawdown process when the 59th FS was forced out of business by the 1997 Quadrennial Defense Review. Six F-15Cs were spread between the other two squadrons and the rest were transferred out.

The switch to F-15Cs for the Langley Wing began in November 1981 and the Wing resumed its normal pattern of deployments. October 1983's Cuban-inspired coup in Grenada took the 33rd TFW's Eagles to Puerto Rico, leaving the 1st TFW to provide air defence for the south-eastern USA. European commitments took 'FF' Eagles on seven of the nineteen F-15 deployments to NATO bases up to 1979, developing better working (and drinking) relationships with their hosts. *Coronet Mohawk* to Bremgarten in August 1986 included a visit to the Tactical Air Meet at RAF Waddington by half of the eight deployed F-15Cs, while *Accord Express* at Aalborg, Denmark in September 1987 (a test of NATO's ACE Mobile Force) also allowed 71st TFS Eagles to indulge in a little DACT with the 527th AS F-5Es over the North Sea. A longer trip in November 1989 for *Coronet Trooper* was a part of that year's *Bright Star* exercise in Egypt. More locally, the Wing's aircraft escaped to Wright-Patterson AFB in September 1989 to avoid *Hurricane Hugo*!

Training procedures at F-15 bases continued to evolve during the 1990s, but the basic skills required for interception and gunnery still dominated the routines at Langley. In the mid-1990s the base was launching up to ninety sorties a day; 4,000 per year, an average of twelve a month for each pilot. After orientation flights a pilot could expect two BFM (basic flight manoeuvres) sorties, two for interception, four for practice ACM and air combat tactics and five sessions in the simulator before he reached full combat readiness. Larger mock combats might involve up to twelve aircraft fighting it out over the sea off the Virginia coast. Big ACC exercises such as *Long Shot '95* included representation from Langley's 27th TFS at Nellis where they joined other F-15 delegations from the 4th TFW, 366th TFW and two ANG units. High-flying F-15Cs acted as fighter cover

AIM-7 was chosen as the F-15's primary BVR weapon despite its disappointing performance in Vietnam. More sophisticated variants, coupled with the F-15's radar/fire-control system, proved to be extremely successful in combat. Armourers here are assembling a missile for a *Shogun Warriors* F-15C. USAF

A pair of Dash 229 engines can generate almost 60,000lb (27,216kg) of thrust for takeoff and allow an F-15 to cruise supersonically without afterburner. This Eagle appears to have an afterburner problem on take-off. USAF

for strike packages of A-10As, F-16s, an F-117A and four F-111Es (making their final appearance) together with B-1Bs and B-52s from former SAC units that had swelled the ACC roster at these events. In all, 117 aircraft took part in this massive exercise, with

the attackers attempting to score direct hits on specially constructed brick buildings while F-15s saw off the opposing fighters. The winners on that occasion were an 8th AF team including an Eagle contingent from the 2nd FS at Tyndall AFB.

USAFE Update

Re-equipment of USAFE F-15 squadrons with the F-15C began with the 32nd TFS between May and November 1980. Their first six aircraft, touching down from 13 June onwards, were FY 78 models, later passed on to Bitburg in 1980, but they had acquired twenty-six FY 79 Eagles by the end of 1985, rising to thirty in mid-1989. Tail number 79-032 naturally became the squadron 'Boss Bird' with a large 'droolin' wolf' design adorning its nose. Transition to the new model was complete by February 1981, the last three F-15As having departed to Eglin under *Ready Switch* on 14 November 1980. A further eight FY 81 aircraft were delivered in 1983 enabling the squadron to be split into two flights, one with green fin bands outlined in orange and the other with the reverse design. At that time larger paint jobs were often done by European contractors, including BAe Warton for a time in 1988 while PDM work for European Eagles was done in Spain at CASA, Getafe as a trade-off for the use of the Torrejon base by USAF squadrons. When that arrangement ended some PDM work went to Israeli Aircraft Industries.

Operations from the Dutch base still focused on the same air defence priorities with interception practice using squadron F-15s as, for example, MiG-23 Floggers, flying low to attack Holland's port facilities from the north while other F-15Cs rose to intercept them. On one occasion the Flogger was genuine, but pilotless. A MiG-23 that had taken off from Kolobrzek in Poland lost engine power on climb-out, prompting the pilot to eject. His MiG recovered its energy, climbed to 37,000ft (11,280m) and overflew West Germany. The Soesterberg Zulu Alert launched and was prepared to shoot it down if it threatened populous areas. After an hour aloft the MiG ran out of fuel and crashed into a house, killing the occupant. The 1980s were a time of big NATO exercises, such as *Salty Hammer* in 1988 that had nine Soesterberg F-15Cs as part of an air defence line-up to face forty F-16Cs from the Hahn Wing, making saturation attacks on UK airfields. Other NATO engagements for the *Wolfhounds* included *Sure Fire* at Sembach, Germany that was an annual weapons loading and combat turn-around competition. *Excaliburs* ran through several years; the April 1988 event at Lakenheath put 32nd TFS Eagles on CAP for a force of 3rd and 17th AF strikers attacking the Spadeadam range in northern England,

while navigation and weapons delivery skills were assessed by the adjudicators. Regular two-week *Red Star* courses were held at Alconbury by the Aggressors and these always attracted F-15s from Bitburg and Holland. Further variety came from exchanges with other NATO squadrons including 12 Squadron at RAF Lossiemouth in July 1992, Spanish EF-18As from ALA 12 in November 1992 and the Mirage F1Cs of EC-12 in August 1984. The Mirage experience proved valuable and was repeated in 1990 when members of the 32nd FS prepared to face similar aircraft from Saddam Hussein's Air Force.

A further exchange of equipment became necessary in September 1990 shortly after the squadron had returned from a Weapons

F-15C 79-0036, the 36th TFW 'Wing' aircraft, received this special colour scheme in 1986. It hinted at the far more spectacular scheme used by the wing's *Skyblazers* F-100 Aerobatic Team in 1961. Author's Collection

Training Detachment to Tyndall AFB. The deteriorating situation in the Gulf resulted in twelve Soesterberg F-15C/Ds being sent to join the Saudi Air Force, while the remainder of the Dutch-based F-15Cs went back to Tyndall, but to stay. A lack of replacement F-15Cs led to a decision to re-equip with the equally capable MSIP F-15A, the first of which was passed on from the 49th FW at Holloman AFB on 22 October 1991. The aircraft was 77-132 and its serial made it a suitable replacement 'Boss Bird', complete with nose art.

MSIP and TEWS

The last batch of F-15C/D Eagles came from FY86 funding but the Eagle was obviously due for at least another decade of service

while the long, costly debate over its likely successor continued. Production of the F-15C/D had been limited to 575 units, including 129 for Israel and Saudi Arabia, some of which were based on F-15E airframes. Attrition had been unexpectedly low and a substantial number of F-15A/B airframes from the 412 produced were still in good shape. With new-build aircraft costing around $35m each it clearly made sense to maximize the useful life of all the existing Eagles, given that all the single-seat models were very similar and could be updated to much the same standard with 'production line' update kits. These could be tailored to individual aircraft depending on their age. This approach made it possible to keep 116 F-15A/Bs in USAF service at the end of 1997, alongside 406 F-15C/D models and the project was known as the Multi-Stage Improvement Program (MSIP), run jointly by McDonnell Douglas and Warner Robins ALC.

MSIP projects were designed for both F-15A/B (MSIP I) and F-15CD (MSIP II) from 1982. Although MSIP I was cancelled to reduce costs many earlier Eagles received substantial parts of the MSIP II improvements. A major focus of the programme was the F-15's avionics package including its tactical electronic warfare system (TEWS) and improvements to this had already begun in 1978 with the addition of agile trackers to the F-15A's Northrop AN/ALQ-135 internal countermeasures set. In many respects this actually represented the final stage in the installation of the original EW system that was delayed for several years after the F-15A entered service.

(Above) The 1990s brought another round of markings revisions and the darker Mod Eagle scheme began to appear on Eagles after MSIP or PDM treatment. F-15C-31-MC 81-0033 of the 94th FS made a 'fuel/food' stop at Shaw AFB on 12 March 1996 en route to Langley AFB. Norm Taylor

(Below) In June 1983 the 1st TFW marked an F-15C for each of its three squadrons and the Wing Commander. Two squadrons, the oldest in the USAF, originated during the First World War and the 71st TFS traces its history back to the Second World War. Boeing/McDonnell Douglas

(Above) A less colourful, but equally striking scheme adorned F-15C 84-0021 for the 1991 *Tiger Meet* and the 53rd TFS 50th Anniversary.
Author's Collection

Nose to nose with the 53rd's Tiger Meet F-15C.
Tony Thornborough

FOX FIRE
MiG-25 FOXBAT
                                                    AI
SLOT BACK II
Su-27 FLANKER
            HIGH LARK I/II
            MiG-23 FLOGGER B/K
SLOT BACK I
MiG-29 FULCRUM
            JAY BIRD
            MiG-21 FISHBED
            & MiG-23 FLOGGER E

LAND ROLL SA-8 GECKO
            STRAIGHT FLUSH
                Illumination
STRAIGHT FLUSH SA-6 GAINFUL
        LOW BLOW SA-3 GOA   SAM TTR

FAN SONG B/F   FAN SONG D/E
SA-2 GUIDELINE SA-2 GUIDELINE
                PAT HAND SA-4 GANEF

    FIRE CAN   AAA
    WHIFF   FLAP WHEEL
                    GUN DISH ZSU-23/4

    BAR LOCK GCI   THIN SKIN   EW, GCI
LONG TRACK   Height Finder

F-15 ICS radar bands. USAF

				1.5 - not yet implemented				3				F-15E ICS
				1			2			C only		F-15A/C ICS
A	B	C	D	E	F	G	H	I	J			NATO Bands

0MC   0.5GC   1GC   2GC   3GC   4GC   6GC 8GC 10GC   20GC

'Full Dimensional Protection'

From the outset the F-15 was designed to be self-sufficient in dealing electronically with enemy SAM, AAA and AI radars and missiles, equipped with a combined Radar Warning Receiver (RWR) and Internal Countermeasures Set (ICS), designed to give it relative immunity from attack during high-altitude CAPs. Over the past two decades this suite has evolved into today's integrated Tactical Electronic Warfare System (TEWS), tailored to the Eagle's expanding mission requirements, particularly interdiction.

Pods

The Northrop-Grumman AN/ALQ-135 ICS portion did not begin appearing on the aircraft until 1977, three years after the machine had entered operational service and during the IOT&E phase of Eagle development other solutions were also explored. As an interim measure, the F-15A was designed with two outboard wing pylons that existed mainly for the carriage of the USAF's standard TWT-based Westinghouse AN/ALQ-119(V) noise/deception radar-jamming pods. Their effect on handling characteristics was so severe in the air-to-air role that the installation was cancelled and the pylons were deleted. The AN/ALQ-119(V)-16 or -17 could be carried on the F-15A centreline (Station 5) after 1977 and was used by export customers who, for security reasons did not receive the full ICS provisions. Similarly, export F-15B/Ds were wired to carry the AN/ALQ-119(V)-15 'long pod' that has added modules to cover a wider frequency spectrum. These aircraft lacked the ICS altogether as it was ousted by the fitting of the second seat and controls. Another standard TWT-based USAF noise/deception-jamming pod, the Project 669 Westinghouse AN/ALQ-131(V), was cleared for export and used by Israeli and Japanese F-15s, although increasingly these were replaced by locally produced items and internal systems. The USAF never used them on its Eagles operationally, although the aircraft has been qualified to carry them including the Raytheon-modified ALQ-119, the AN/ALQ-184(V) that became operational during 1987 and that offers greater reliability and increased Effective Radiated Power over its predecessor. Early in the F-15's career the pods were deemed to cause excessive drag and

F-15Cs on the St Louis line in June 1981. Forty-eight aircraft were included in the FY81 order and sixty in the previous year, plus eighty-five for Israel and Saudi Arabia. Twenty years later USAF production continued at about four per annum. Boeing/McDonnell Douglas

An AIM-9J/P series Sidewinder is made ready for *William Tell* '84. Sunshield covers on the F-15's wheels are part of the attention to detail that scored points for the competing teams. USAF

(Above) F-15 and F-16 have been a winning partnership for the USAF and both aircraft have achieved success in combat, though the F-16 has generally taken the ground-attack mission. USAF

(Below) A Wolfhound F-15 awaits its pilot. Author's Collection

(Left) Eglin Eagle 85-0103 departs Patrick AFB with burners ablaze in April 1997. John Gourley

to occupy valuable hardpoint space. The centreline pylon, in particular, is needed for the external fuel tank that is virtually a fixture on F-15s and causes very little drag penalty. McDonnell Douglas therefore pressed ahead at an early stage with rendering the F-15's electronic combat systems completely internal, based on the company's original concept.

TEWS

In its modern guise, the TEWS consists of the following units, assembled into an integrated, largely automated system providing what the USAF describes as 'full dimensional protection':

The Loral AN/ALR-56 RWR, installed from the beginning, was progressively upgraded to ALR-56A format in 1981 and to ALR-56C with the advent of the F-15E, that had it fitted from initial manufacture, F-15A/Cs being updated on a retrofit basis. This is the central listening unit in the system, operating primarily via four High Band antennae installed in the wingtips and vertical stabilizers, with a Low Band antenna under the nose. Its function is to receive and analyse threat emissions from other radars in aircraft, SAM installations or AAA in the C through J Radar frequency Bands, store the data and compare it with its internal library of threat signal information in order to identify the emissions and thus choose a suitable response. Increases in the installed computer speed and capacity have made the ALR-56 ever more able to deal simultaneously with an increasing range and number of threat signals and to prioritize those threats faced by the aircraft for hand-off to the ICS for selective jamming – a feature known as 'Power Management'. A pilot only has to switch the system 'on' or 'off' and observe the data it feeds him. Threat warnings are displayed on a CRT via warning lights and through the headset audio. They are jokingly referred to as 'squeaks' but are actually the primary cue in a heads-up environment. The dashboard display shows the type and bearing of threats relative to the aircraft in alphanumeric icon form and tells him whether the threat has been scanned or locked onto by the system, if the pilot chooses to look down at it. The full system was installed from 1977 onwards but it took several years for it to appear in all aircraft.

The *Northrop AN/ALQ-135 ICS* works with the ALR-56 as already noted, although also autonomously using its own Set-On facilities in emergencies, selecting the most appropriate frequencies and signal modulations in direct response to enemy SAM and fighter radars in order to deny them accurate targeting information or down-link command guidance. It is flight-line programmable using Pre-Flight Message (PFM) software adjustments and can cope with multiple waveforms simultaneously.

The 18th FW sends its F-15s to Korean Air Lines at Pusan, Korea for PDM and includes an Alert duty in Korea among its wide responsibilities. USAF

Originally the F-15A/C's ICS operated in two overlapping radio-frequency Bands. Band 1 (covering the E to G radar Bands) was installed primarily to fox *FAN SONG* SA-2 SAM and *FIRE CAN* AAA radars. Band 2 (embracing the G to I Bands) thwarts *STRAIGHT FLUSH* SA-6 among others. Blade antennae under the nose, fore and aft of the nose landing gear, catered for both. The ALQ-135's 'black boxes' (in fact, light blue-green) comprised six LRUs installed behind the pilot including three amplifiers and three control oscillators/exciters to generate the jamming radiation that kept the F-15 out of trouble at CAP altitudes. As the F-15E expanded the Eagle's operational repertoire to lower altitudes, well beyond the FEBA (forward edge of the battle area), so the demand for higher frequency threat Band coverage emerged. The later ALQ-135B fitted in part of the F-15E 'Strike Eagle's' ammunition bay provided the aircraft with Band 3, catering for the H-J Radar Bands in which the modern panoply of low-level, short-range AAA and SAMs operate. Portions of the system were retrofitted to F-15Cs also. ALQ-135B began its Early Operational Assessment just prior to Operation *Desert Storm* and was aimed at thwarting newer radars such as the SA-8 *GECKO's* 'LAND ROLL' acquisition and tracking radars and

SA-6 *GAINFUL's* 'STRAIGHT FLUSH' target illumination radar. It also disrupts enemy fighters' AI radar sets, offering what the USAF has described as 'robust jamming against pulse-Doppler radars' to permit F-15E crews to focus on their strike missions. The main distinguishing feature of this modification was a radome on each fuselage boom of the F-15E (on the tip of only the right fuselage tail boom in the case of the F-15C that needed only part of the package), with forward jamming antennae located in the strike Eagle's wing roots. A squarer-shaped radome was substituted in the mid-1990s. The F-15C also adopted antennae ahead of the windshield and ventrally, behind the main radar radome in each case. Plans have been afoot for nearly a decade to add Band 1.5 jamming capability to the F-15E under TEWS Phase 3, thus providing the strike variant with complete coverage in the E through J Bands. This is now in production after completing trials in October 2000 and is being fitted to selected F-15Es.

As a last-ditch measure, the F-15 features *Tracor AN/ALE-40 chaff and flare Countermeasures Dispensers (CMD),* since upgraded to the ALE-45 standard. Also under the control of the ALR-56 (although the automatic function is never used because it depletes the chaff too rapidly – manual dispensing is the primary method), this set operates the four CMDs containing up to 240 cartridges of chaff and 120 flare 'square shooter' cartridges. Only forty-eight of the larger MJU-10 flares can be loaded and only if no chaff is carried. A normal F-15E load-out might be 120 chaff and twenty-four MJU-10 flares. CMDs are located in the F-15's belly, ahead of the main landing gear wells and are nicknamed 'icecube trays', which they closely resemble. Flares are popped out to decoy heat-seeking missiles such as the A-11 ARCHER, and man-portable or amphibious vehicle-based SAMs such as SA-7 STRELA or SA-9 GASKIN. Chaff's function is to provide a last-second alternate radar-painted target for semi-active or active radar-homing missiles (AIMs and SAMs such as SA-6 GAIN-FUL). The CMD was built into F-15C/Es and retrofitted to MSIP F-15A/Bs, based on successful Israeli experience in equipping its F-15Bs with 'square shooters' for long-range strike and escort duties with these defensive pyrotechnics. To boost capacity, the entire USAF F-15 fleet is shortly to receive the Swedish BOL dispenser, current funding plans calling for four pylon-mounted dispensers per aircraft offering a total of 640 expendable countermeasures rounds.

The final piece of magic is the *Magnavox AN/ALQ-128 electronic warfare warning system (EWWS)* installed early in the Eagle's career. This highly sensitive system essentially extends the coverage provided by the ALR-56 to provide precise warning of enemy fighter activity, to help discriminate between friendly and enemy fighters and thus assist with air-to-air engagements by helping to prioritize 'bandits' for BVR missile engagements. It was prototyped in Vietnam as Project *Combat Tree* on USAF F-4D/Es and the equipment is housed in a pod on the top of the left fin (replaced by a weight on export Eagles where the system was deleted) and an antenna on the left nose, flush with the surface.

Weasel Eagles

With its integrated electronic combat suite it comes as no surprise that McDonnell Douglas have long since advocated the use of the twin-seat Eagle as a *Wild Weasel* SEAD (Suppression of Enemy Air Defenses) platform, toting additional radar-sniffing apparatus to ferret out radar sites and then hand off target data to AGM-88 HARM (High-speed Anti-Radiation Missile) to destroy them. Based on its experience in equipping the Eagle's forebear, the F-4G Phantom, with the McDonnell Douglas /IBM AN/APR-47 Weasel Attack Signal Processor and Homing & Warning Computer under Project *Advanced Wild Weasel*, the St. Louis Corporation's Advanced Projects Office installed the equipment in its Lambert Field-based demonstrator F-15B 71-0291 and test-flew the package amid great secrecy. At this juncture the F-15E Strike Eagle was entering production with the F100-PW-229 IPE (Improved Performance Engine) beginning with F-15E number 134. This offered superb low-altitude performance, ideal for 'Weaseling'. However, in the end the USAF elected to continue with its F-4G Phantom AN/APR-47 Performance Update Program/Operational Flight Program enhancements to enable it to fully utilize HARM and the *Weasel* Eagle project was not funded. The demonstrator aircraft was quickly demodified for other tasks.

In 1997 St. Louis' resident F-15 test platform emerged once again from the hangar, this time with the new LR-500 system on board as part of an effort to endow the machine with *Wild Weasel* Precision Direction-Finding (PDF) capabilities. Like

The *Dirty Dozen*'s Squadron aircraft in Mod Eagle paint prior to the unit's deactivation on 5 November 1999. USAF

the APR-47, the all-up PDF system offered full 'Range Known' HARM targeting, where the missile is at its most lethal, using new conformal antennae arrays fitted flush either side of the aircraft's nose and in front of the pilot's windshield, but also able to determine range in a fraction of the time it took the F-4G to undertake the task. More-over, the LR-500 was demonstrated to be sufficiently accurate to offer the potential to hand-off target position to the APG-70 SAR, which could then programme AGM-154 JSOWS to demolish the radar site, rather than just trash the radar dish with a HARM. The aircraft was also to feature modified LANTIRN pods offering laser output tuned to damage enemy electro-optic systems and AAA gunners' eyes, a programme still being examined behind closed hangar doors for technical and eth-ical feasibility. However, an overall lack-lustre response from the Pentagon – which since *Desert Storm* has been increasingly enamoured with 'Stealth' at the expense of electronic combat support aircraft – result-ed in its termination at St Louis. The USAF did not want to tie up F-15Es in the new role and the proposed F-15C PDF vari-ant that followed was deemed by Boeing's top engineers to be too task-saturated for a solo crewmember as it could only offer lim-ited HARM capability. The SEAD equip-ment has since been revisited in LR-700 form, but chiefly for use aboard the pro-posed Boeing twin-seat US Navy and Marines F/A-18G Growler electronic com-bat jet.

Despite being combat-proven and already boasting TEWS, SAR, E-O and PGM capability it is now highly unlikely that the Eagle will ever fulfil a dedicated SEAD function. However, the aircraft has performed ably in the DEAD (Destruction of Enemy Air Defences) role, using LAN-TIRN FLIR and laser for PGM delivery, either rolling in on the smoke trail of a SAM launch or relying on handoff from other sensors. In this capacity the aircraft has actually achieved a higher SAM-kill rate than the F-4G Phantom's replace-ment, the HARM Targeting System-equipped Lockheed-Martin F-16CJ.

Future additions to TEWS, still under development, are likely to include a Mis-sile Approach Warning System working in infrared or ultraviolet, which can see the plumes of enemy missiles' rocket motors, along with the use of AESA radars as active jammers, transmitting pencil-beam disruption at selected radar threats ahead

McDonnell Douglas' *Wild Weasel* SEAD project, using elements of the F-4G Phantom's countermeasures set. Boeing/McDonnell Douglas

The LR-500 antenna array on the F-15D *Wild Weasel* Demonstrator. A similar array appeared on each side of the fuselage and in front of the windshield. Author's Collection

radar bandwidth, better MTBF figures and the ability to track faster-moving targets at greater range. It used the same antenna as the APG-63. The heart of the system, the central computer was given a fourfold memory increase and three times the processor speed. This steady upward spiral in 'brain power' meant that later F-15Cs had ten times the capacity of the original F-15As.

Provision was also made for joint tactical information distribution system (JTIDS) Group A terminals, providing a secure data link to an AWACs or J-STARS aircraft or to a ground station for automatic, voiceless transfer of battlefield data and imagery to the cockpit. The 391st FS, 366th FW had the first JTIDS-equipped F-15Cs.

In the cockpit MSIP II put the Eagle pilot in a more modern environment with a Sperry multipurpose colour display (MPCD) in place of the old armament panel, revised throttle controls and a video recorder control panel. Weaponry enhancement allowed for the carriage of the AIM-120A AMRAAM 'Slammer' to replace the AIM-7 Sparrow (*see* Chapter 7). MSIP kits were assembled by McDonnell Douglas and distributed to Warner Robins ALC and to Korean Airlines who performed MSIP updates for seventy-five Kadena-based F-15C/Ds.

Up to 1990 the Soesterberg Eagles had enjoyed an excellent safety record since converting from F-4Es in 1978, which was only marred in the squadron's last years by the loss of 81-049 in April 1990 during DACT over the North Sea. One aircraft (81-048) had been sufficiently damaged by an engine fire in 1986 to warrant return to Warner Robins for repair, while a second (79-033) was less badly damaged at 'Deci' during an ACT deployment in July 1989. The MSIP F-15As, fourteen of which were taken aboard by June 1992, proved even more reliable than the C models, despite their basic age. Although Soesterberg had anticipated a second squadron to be established there in 1991 the spectre of defence cuts had already begun to reduce the 759 US military bases worldwide. Glasnost and down-sizing made Soesterberg a candidate for the trimmers in 1993. The unit's aircraft departed in fours between October and 13 January 1994 to Otis ANGB, Massachusetts for the use of the 101st FS. After thirty-nine years in Holland the 32nd FS shut up shop, leaving a souvenir in the form of F-15A 74-083 for the Royal Netherlands AF Museum.

A night-flyer's view of the F-15C cockpit. Instrumentation was still mainly analogue with a couple of VDUs. Boeing/McDonnell Douglas

of the aircraft without any other give-away transmissions. Fibre-optic towed decoys (FOTD) are also under consideration. These offer a more realistic false target than chaff that is virtually stationary once ejected and easily differentiated using Moving Target Indicator methods and modern micro-processing. The FOTD will be fed jamming signals to its TWT-Amplifier based on instructions from the TEWS via the fibre-optic tether, so that if the enemy uses ECCM (electronic counter-countermeasures) such as track-on-jam its missiles will chase the towed expendable decoy and not the aircraft. These can be installed on wing pylons with only a minor drag penalty and reeled out in high-threat areas. These updates will maintain the Eagle's edge well into the future.

Some of MSIP II involved bringing the F-15 fleet up to the same standard of EW equipment, modifying individual aircraft ad hoc. Another major update that affected only the F-15C/D was the installation of the Hughes AN/APG-70 radar with a PSP operating at three times the speed of the first-generation model and with much increased memory. This improved version of the APG-63 allowed a big increase in

Zulu

Bitburg's conversion to the F-15C began slightly later than its Dutch-based neighbour. The first three machines that were ex-32nd TFS FY78 airframes, swept into Bitburg during August 1980 and the 22nd and 525th Squadrons had completed transition by May 1981 with the 53rd TFS close behind. These jets were progressively exchanged for newer FY84 'tails', with the 53rd TFS passing on their earlier models to Elmendorf and Langley. F-15Cs took over the Zulu Alert stalls at the German base, with four aircraft on standby for the five-minutes-to-takeoff, quick-reaction alert (QRA). A primary pair would launch first to meet an unidentified intruder, with a second pair immediately brought up to readiness to replace an aircraft that developed a fault, or to meet a new and different threat. In the mid-1980s the QRA averaged five launches a week. Real (Alpha) alerts were uncommon and usually involved shepherding a lost commercial aircraft out of the area. The remainder were practice (Beta) launches, but treated equally seriously and pilots were

not told they were on a practice sortie until they had wheels in the wells. To help identify their targets pilots at that time resorted to the 'Eagle Eye' rifle sight, bracketed to their HUD. Pilots on QRA had to do 24-hr shifts a couple of times a month. G-suits had to be worn, but they could be removed to decrease discomfort after 1700 hours as the chance of a QRA reduced at that point. When the hooter sounded they descended the fireman's pole to the hangar, clambered into pre-flighted Eagles, started up and rolled out of the 'shed' for quick final checks before accelerating the 500ft (152m) to the end of the runway. Without stopping, they would then do a maximum power take-off.

In wartime the majority of the Squadron's aircraft would have flown CAP ahead of large strike formations of F-16s and other tactical aircraft attempting to hold back the fast-moving Warpac armoured divisions. With so many other allied aircraft over the FEBA the issue of accurate IFF became crucial and, in retrospect, most engagements with hostile aircraft might well have ended up as 'gun and Sidewinder' battles, as launching BVR missiles in any

direction other than straight ahead of the strike force could have run the risk of a 'blue on blue' casualty.

In the opening phases of an operation Eagles would have formed a 'wall' ahead of the strike force, aiming to pick off at long distance any approaching strike aircraft or their fighter cover. Launching 'in the face' AIM-7s would have been the opening gambit and then engaging in Sidewinder/gun mode with those that managed to get in closer. Another primary mission would have been HVA (high value asset) escort; the vital protection of AWACS, central controller of the air action. ABCC (airborne command and control) HC-130H Hercules would also count as HVAs, providing threat warnings, directing aircraft to targets and coordinating SEAD operations, but they would only get F-15 or F-16 escort if their situation was particularly hazardous.

Perched on CAP at around 30,000ft (9,144m) two elements of F-15Cs, separated by a mile (1.6km), would await AWACS warning of an incoming threat. A quick radar 'sniff' of the target would locate it and, closer in, a second brief use of the radar would allow the pilot to close for a visual identification using his 'Eagle Eye' and make an AIM-9 launch at about six miles (9.6km). Low-flying intruders, hugging the terrain and ready to make a pull up and launch missiles up at the F-15s, would hopefully be picked up by the APG-63's moving target indication (MTI) function. Designed to pick up any low-flyers including slower-moving helicopters the MTI was in the habit of locking the radar onto motorway traffic until it was reset to ignore movers at less than 130 mph (209km/h).

The three Bitburg squadrons had a busy regime of deployments, exercises and weapons training detachments (WTDs). Batches of aircraft flew back to Tyndall AFB for WTDs on which they would periodically fire a live missile at a drone target. Whole-squadron deployments to Decimomannu in Sardinia continued for ACT over the Mediterranean ranges. Smaller numbers attended the regular NATO interair force sessions: tactical leadership programme (TLP) meetings at Jever, tactical air meets (TAM) at Gilze-Rijen, as well as the annual Transatlantic migrations for *Red Flag* and *Green Flag* training. When the 527th AS F-5Es at Alconbury began to fall apart from fatigue the Squadron converted to F-16Cs in June 1988, moved to Bentwaters and was inactivated like the other overseas Aggressor units at the end of

F-15C 79-0035 of Eglin's *Fighting Crows* shows its paces at McDill AFB in May 1999.
John Gourley

1989. This gave USAFE squadrons a little over a year to train with this much more capable simulator of new-generation Soviet fighter tactics. The Aggressor pilots went through a new course called *Have Grip* to learn MiG-29 and Su-27 strategies and build them into their DACT routines.

Bitburg had been one of many units to benefit from the 527th AS's *Red Star* DACT courses with F-5Es. The 1986 exercise used six Eagles and much of the Aggressor Fleet in complex engagements that sometimes put four Eagles against fourteen F-5Es in battles that provided realistic experience of a mass Soviet-type assault. This philosophy pervaded *Hammer/Priory* exercises too. Twelve Eagles CAPped for a series of 3rd, 16th and 17th Air Force 'guerrilla strike packages' making saturation 'raids' on British targets, while others provided air defence against them. In the 1987 version, over 280 'attackers' made for their target range areas in a two-hour period at the height of the exercise.

Such expensive wargames were inevitably first to go when the Cold War began to fade in 1990–91, but USAFE units were soon to follow. Bitburg's end was foreshadowed by the inactivation of the 525th FS on 1 May 1992, just over a year after its participation in Operation *Desert Storm*. The other two squadrons survived until February 1994 when the 22nd ceased flying and began the process of reforming at RAF Lakenheath alongside the 48th FW F-15E squadrons, as the 493rd FS. Reassignment to the 52nd FW at Spangdahlem was the outcome for the 53rd FS *Tigers*. Ten of its aircraft moved to the new base on 25 February 1994. Both squadrons had retained their state of operational readiness throughout the transfer stages. At Bitburg, thirty-five Eagles were put through a 10-day inspection to restore them to 'as new' condition, including a respray. Apart from the Eagles destined for 53rd FS use with new 'SP' codes they were then returned to the USA, mainly to Eglin and Tyndall. The base closed on 15 April 1994 after its last operational aircraft returned from Incirlik, Turkey where they had been flying *Provide Comfort* sorties over Northern Iraq in the aftermath of *Desert Storm*.

From the original roster of F-15A Wings the only one that didn't convert to the F-15C was the 49th TFW at Holloman AFB. Its decade of active deployments on *Coronets* to Europe in the 1980s had taken twelve-aircraft detachments to Gilze-Rijen (*Coronet Bullet*, *Shooter*, *Scout* and *Mescalero*)

and Wittmund (*Coronet Fang*). After the Gulf War its 9th FS made several deployments to Dhahran and Tabuk to relieve the 36th FW and 33rd FW detachments that had manned *Southern Watch* patrols (*see* Chapter 7). Prior to that, the Wing's 7th FS had been inactivated on 13 September 1990 while the other two squadrons began to

receive MSIP II F-15A/Bs. Shortly afterwards the Wing was redesignated as the successor to the 37th FW as sole operator of the F-117A Nighthawk from January 1992. Both 8th and 9th Squadrons were accordingly inactivated on 30 September 1992 and the last F-15 left Holloman on 5 June. Most were passed on to Tyndall AFB.

Generally similar to the F-15C, the front cockpit of 'ET' coded F-15D 84-0045 at Daytona in October 1996. John Gourley

(Below) **The F-15D front cockpit, right console in 84-0045.** John Gourley

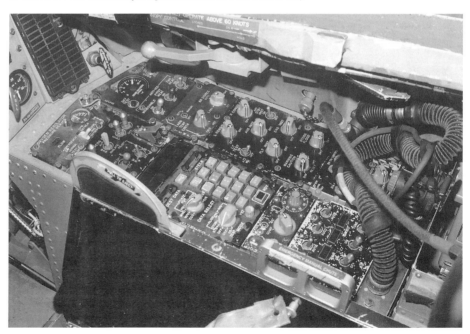

CHAPTER FOUR

Export Eagles

Baz, Akev and Ra'am

Although Iran was the first potential customer for the F-15, Israel was only a year behind it in evaluating the aircraft. A team of pilots test-flew TF-15A 71-290 to the limits in September 1974 as potential successor to the F-4E and the stopgap, Mirage-derived, short-ranged Kfir. They tested its interception capability by taking off and climbing to 30,000ft (9,150m), then accelerating to 0.9 Mach, all within 1min 40sec. At the other end of the speed range they showed that the Eagle could be looped at 150kt. The aircraft's performance in a mock combat with an Edwards-based F-4E impressed the Israeli delegation sufficiently for them to order twenty-five aircraft, though the Israel Defence Force/Air Force (IDF/AF) wanted twice that number. The F-15's high cost was a political obstacle and there was a strong lobby in favour of the equally expensive F-14A (combined with a purchase of Harriers) to match Iran's acquisition of Tomcats. Benny Peled, the Chief of Staff of the IDF/AF, wanted a mix of F-15s and the forthcoming, but cheaper F-16 to build up numbers.

At Edwards AFB the F-15A had demonstrated a convincing superiority in both high and low speed ACM and intercepts, fitting it perfectly for the type of operations that the IDF/AF had mastered in the Six Day War of 1967, the War of Attrition with Syria and Egypt up to 1970 and in the bitter lessons of the Yom Kippur War of 1973. During the last of these, Israeli F-4s and Mirages often engaged in extensive dogfights with opposing MiGs that involved up to sixty aircraft. Yom Kippur had been won, but at a probable cost of 115 Israeli aircraft including thirty-five Phantoms. A year on from that the IDF/AF's 'Hadish' selection team wanted the best fighter they could get, almost irrespective of price.

In order to keep costs to $24m per aircraft ($30m including stores and equipment) and in the interests of rapid delivery, the US Government agreed to sell four F-15As from the Cat II OT&E force (72-116, -117, -118 and -120), suitably refurbished and repainted in the Compass Gray scheme but retaining 'early-build' features such as the small airbrake. A fifth OT&E F-15A (72-120) arrived in 1982 as an attrition replacement. Ongoing support came from the existing McDonnell Douglas infrastructure in Israel that had helped to keep the country's F-4s and A-4 Skyhawks flying.

The only real area for concern was the F-15's range. Although air defence missions over Israel's borders were no problem the air force was used to flying fighter cover for longer strike/interdiction missions. The possibilities of FAST PACKS for long-range escort and penetration missions were extremely attractive and Peled's team pushed hard for the Type 1 (fuel-only) conformal tanks to be developed, even offering to buy the development models used on TF-15A 72-291.

Delivery of the first quartet of F-15As under the *Peace Fox* programme took place on Friday, 10 December 1976 at Tel-Nof airbase and they arrived in the afternoon for an acceptance ceremony that unfortunately continued into the Sabbath, causing such strong objections from political factions that Itzhak Rabin's government was forced to resign. Commentators noted that the F-15 was the first fighter in history to shoot down a government. Certainly, the Eagle's qualities as a gun platform were a high priority with the first five IDF/AF pilots as training began in the USA (lacking their own F-15 simulator, Israeli aircrew continued to visit

F-15A 644 Barak of 133 Sqn at Tel Nov. Israel's Rafael Armament development Authority in Haifa developed a range of Shafrir and Python air-to-air missiles for its fighters, based on the AIM-9, but in some cases rivalling the AIM-9X and Russian AA-11 in performance. Simon Watson

the United States for that phase of their training). When the first six Israeli pilots visited St Louis they spent hours with the Macair test pilots trying to glean every possible detail of their new aircraft. Experience had taught them that guns had a higher kill probability than missiles in a close-in fight. As they adapted to their new fighter it quickly became clear that it totally outclassed the Mirage derivatives in dogfighting and in every other area.

Phase II of *Peace Fox* involved the delivery of nineteen new-build F-15As (76-1505 to -1523) in 1976, followed by a pair

of F-15Bs (76-1524/1525) the following year. They were known as 'Baz' (Eagle) in IDF/AF service and were immediately allocated to a high-pressure training programme. It was not long before they were in action under their squadron leader, Col Eitan Ben-Eliyahu. After Syria's invasion of Lebanon and support for the PLO in 1974 the ensuing civil war spilled into Israel in March 1978 provoking a counter-invasion of PLO camps. F-15 pilots flew their first combat sorties but the Syrian Air Force did not engage them. The September 1978 Camp David agreement

between Israel and Egypt increased PLO incursions into Israel, provoking air strikes near Sidon from 27 June 1979 by IDF/AF F-4s and A-4s with an F-15A escort at 20,000ft (6,100m) under E-2C Hawkeye guidance. When twelve Syrian MiG-21s rose to intercept the morning strike on the 27th four fell to the Eagles and another to a single Kfir C-2. The Syrian pilots had split their formation, with six MiGs at 15,000ft (4,570m) and another six flying cover and hoping to ambush opposing fighters.

The Baz leader, who was Commander-elect of the IDF/AF Fighter School, allowed the Syrian MiG formation to pursue the Israeli Skyhawks while the Eagles deliberately feinted a turn away from the battle and out to sea. While the MiG-21s concentrated on their A-4 targets the Baz escort quickly turned back and engaged. From ten miles away F-15As from the Flight School at Hatzerim base took advantage of the effective Israeli jamming of the MiGs' communication and GCI, lit their afterburners and locked up several of the lower-flying MiGs for AIM-7 launches. According to Syrian reports the AIM-7s failed to make contact. In the close-in scuffle that followed, the F-15 squadron leader's wingman, Col M., fired an AIM-9L in a beam attack on a MiG-21, breaking it in half and scoring the Eagle's first-ever air-to-air victory and his seventh. A second MiG (also flown by a Syrian wing commander) fell to Col Ben-Eliyahu, who became CO of 133 Sqn, the first Baz unit. It was his fourth air-to-air kill; he shot down two MiGs in 1973. The other two Eagle victors were

(Top) F-15C deliveries were made in *Peace Fox III* with eighteen aircraft destined for 106 squadron. 840 'Commando' displays six Syrian kill markings as a reminder of the destruction wrought by Israeli fighters over the Bekaa Valley. Simon Watson

(Above) F-15A 636, one of the batch of *Peace Fox I* Block 5-10 aircraft sold to Israel in 1978 and 1992. Boeing/McDonnell Douglas via Norm Taylor

Menachem Einan and a pilot with the call-sign 'Tzuri'. Celebrations at Hatzerim that night were helped along by five bottles of whiskey from the Minister of Defence.

Another four MiG-21s fell to the Eagles on 24 September when a single RF-4E reconnaissance aircraft came under attack by a Syrian formation. F-15A 692 (76-1520 nicknamed *Galaxy*) was one of the victors. A MiG was claimed on 24 August 1980 and two more on 31 December. Hostilities continued into 1981 while the Baz unit revised its training syllabus to include overwater ACM after losing the largely empty Sinai training area under the Camp David pact. On 13 February the F-15 met for the first time the fighter it was designed to match – the MiG-25 Foxbat. Once again, an RF-4E probing flight near Beirut triggered the action. The two Phantoms were supersonic at 40,000ft (12,190m) when they were alerted to the Syrian MiG-25Ps climbing to intercept them from 60mi (96km) away. They turned away, leaving a chaff cloud and following a prearranged flight pattern that allowed an F-15A to approach at lower altitude and climb unseen through the jamming caused by the chaff and by their own internal and dispensed ECM. At 20,000ft (6,100m) the F-15A pilot, the CO of the 133 'Twin Tails' Squadron, released an AIM-7F in a classic front-quarter attack at 25mi (40km), destroying one of the Foxbat-Es. Russian sources claim that another engagement took place later that day when two F-15As were ambushed by MiG-25Ps after they had set up a couple of MiG-21s as bait for the Eagles. The leading Foxbat-E was allegedly shot down but his wingman claimed one of the F-15s by firing a pair of R-40 missiles at 25mi (40km) range. Israel has denied this loss that would otherwise have been the only F-15 air-to-air shoot-down to date. Another MiG-25P was shot down on 25 July 1981 over Akura while attacking an RF-4E.

Israel's acquisition of the F-15, and from November 1980 the F-16A, made possible Operation *Babylon*, the long-intended pre-emptive strike on the French-built Osirak nuclear reactor at 'Tammuz 1' near Baghdad. Between 1960 and 1981 the Israeli government steadily amassed information showing that the plant was intended to produce nuclear weapons and decided to take unilateral, self-protective action. Despite international objections, France continued to supply enriched uranium that Israel considered to be irrelevant to the plant's claimed purpose as a 'civilian research centre'.

F-15As including 844 and 822 in immaculate formation over ancient Masada.
Boeing/McDonnell Douglas

The range of the F-15 and F-16 was vital for the 1,000mi (1,609km) flight without having to involve the IDF/AF's two vulnerable KC-130H refuellers over hostile territory. An attack, renamed Operation *Opera*, by eight F-16As from the 101st squadron was planned for 7 June 1981. A Sunday was selected to minimize casualties at the plant. Six CFT-equipped F-15s from 133 Sqn, forward-based at Etszion and led by their CO, were to escort the F-16s. The strike force crossed Saudi Arabia at an altitude of 100 to 300ft (30–90m) and climbed to 5,000ft (1,520m) from where each F-16A dived to release a pair of Mk84 2,000lb (907kg) bombs in a CCIP attack on the reactor complex. Fourteen of the sixteen weapons exploded, destroying Saddam Hussein's plan to make Iraq a nuclear power. On arrival at the target the Eagles divided into three pairs to fly BARCAP at 20,000ft (6,100m) near Iraqi fighter bases around Baghdad, just as their USAF counterparts were to do a decade later. Saddam's fighters were taken by surprise. All Israeli aircraft returned intact with the Eagle pilots perhaps a little disappointed that they had met absolutely no opposition. This was also a matter of rather more sombre significance to the officers above the rank of Captain in the local area-defence Iraqi fighter units. On the orders of Saddam Hussein they were all shot dead.

F-15I-57-MC 94-0299, a *Peace Fox V* Eagle, wears USAF markings and the insignia of the *Hammers* during pre-delivery training in the USA. Kevin Jackson

Later in 1981 the IDF/AF received the first of eighteen F-15Cs (named Akev, or buzzard) and eight F-15Ds for 106 Squadron under *Peace Fox III*, with deliveries to Tel Nov AB from 26 August 1981 through to the autumn of 1982. Modifications to these and all previous Israeli F-15s included deletion of nuclear delivery capability and substitution of Elta AN/ARC-109 radios for the USAF AN/ARC-164. The AN/ALQ-128 EW system and its fin-tip pod were also removed but ALQ-119, ALQ-131 or the Israeli-produced AL/ L8202 pods could be carried externally. An IC-7 seat replaced the ACES-II model but Israeli Eagles were the first to have chaff/flare countermeasures dispensers installed. Five more F-15Ds (90-275 to -279) were acquired under *Peace Fox IV* in 1989 for attrition replacement and these were based on the F-15 airframe that was the only production model at the time. F-15Ds were used operationally with a navigator in the rear seat.

On 6 June 1982, the day on which 106 Squadron declared IOC on the F-15C, the Lebanon War began, triggered by the attempted assassination of the Israeli ambassador in London. The build-up to a major conflict had been steady. Syria moved SA-6 SAM batteries into the Bekaa Valley to deter Israeli attacks on PLO and Syrian bases, while rocket attacks on northern Israel continued. Air battles over the Bekaa in defence of IDF/AF photo-Phantoms continued and the Syrians lost two MiG-23BMs on 21 April 1982 and a pair of MiG-21s on 26 May over Beirut. Sensing another impending Syrian invasion of

Lebanon, Israel mounted a massive armed occupation of Lebanese ports preceded by heavy air attacks on terrorist headquarters and arms dumps. The invasion was slowed by the extensive SAM batteries in the Bekaa, including SA-2, SA-3 and SA-6 sites backed by Soviet-manned ZSU-23 AAA. Bad weather had delayed the Israeli plan to eliminate these threats but recce flights continued, as did air combat engagements that cost the Syrians another MiG-23 on 7 June and six MiG-21s on 8 June, mostly hit by missiles from Baz escorts. The 7 June shoot-down was by Maj Offer Lapidot in Baz 658 (76-1506 *Typhoon*). He fired an AIM-7F that failed to reach the target although it was correctly launched and he followed up with a Python 3 launched at around 2,000ft (610m) AGL.

On the following day the IDF/AF began a major air onslaught against the Bekaa SAM and radar complex that by then included an estimated 400 AAA guns and 200 missiles, all protecting pro-Syrian forces. Israeli Air Force leaders saw it as the greatest test they had ever faced. They had the benefit of a specialized SEAD weapon, an updated, longer-range version of the AGM-45 Shrike called *Purple Fist*, plus limited quantities of Maverick (Rafael *Pyramid* version,) Standard ARM missiles and (allegedly) some GBU-15 glide-bombs. However, the force relied primarily on conventional bombs to demolish the sites. First, F-4Es took out the GCI radars with stand-off weapons and then other attackers hit the radars controlling the SAM sites. Large formations of up to forty A-4s, F-16s, F-4Es and

Kfir-C2s pulverized the area while specially equipped Boeing 707s supplied very effective stand-off jamming of the Syrians' GCI radars, preventing a co-ordinated fighter response. They came anyway and anyhow. The IDF/AF Air Wing Commander, Avihu Ben-Nun estimated that one hundred Syrian MiG-21s and MiG-23s were panic-scrambled and (ironically) sent to protect their own anti-aircraft defences. Meanwhile, those defences had used their radars in a vain attempt to track Israeli attackers, thereby attracting Shrike anti-radar missiles. They also released smokescreens that paradoxically helped the Israeli strikers to find their locations. The F-15 CAPs were ready to meet the Syrian fighters. Under E-2C Hawkeye control they awaited the approaching waves of MiGs and had the rare opportunity to use AIM-7F missiles to down several before engaging at closer quarters with AIM-9Ls, Python 3 missiles and, for 7 per cent of the kills, 20mm gunfire. At least twenty MiGs fell in the mêlée, adding to seven that had been destroyed earlier in the day.

There were no Israeli losses though one Baz was severely damaged. A pilot listed as 'Major R' was in a four-ship CAP that met two MiG-21s. He and the number four aircraft fired AIM-9Ls at them but were then bracketed by very intense AAA and short-range SAMs. One MiG disintegrated and Major R pursued the other, but then saw a third MiG at closer range that he downed with his third missile. He then made the classic error of watching his blazing victim plummet into a field, giving the defences the opportunity to launch an SA-7 missile that hit his right tailpipe. On one engine, he managed to gain enough altitude to cross the mountain ridge and safety in Israel, landing at Ramat David airfield. He had flown for twenty minutes in an F-15 with 400 shrapnel holes, a major fuel leak and a wrecked engine.

By the end of 9 June, seventeen of the nineteen Syrian missile batteries had been incapacitated. The following day air battles flared up again as Israeli armour pushed on towards Beirut and came under air attack. Another twenty-six Syrian MiGs were eliminated by the IDF/AF fighter force. June 11 brought a UN truce but not before another eighteen Syrian aircraft were shot down. After seven days of vicious air combat Israeli pilots claimed eighty MiG-21s, MiG-23s and Su-20s plus five helicopters. One of the MiG-21s was added to the total for Maj Lapidot, flying 658 *Typhoon* once again. Although thirteen Israeli losses were admitted, they included no Eagles and forty of the enemy had fallen to the mighty Baz.

An uneasy peace settled on Lebanon but, although the PLO had been driven out, they continued to attack Israelis abroad. From a new base in Tunisia they launched an assault on a yacht in Cyprus, killing three Israelis. The response was characteristically swift and unexpected, a long-range strike against the Tunisian PLO camp by eight F-15Ds (and two F-15B 'air spares') on 1 October 1985. Two-seat Eagles were used so that each aircraft could carry a navigator for the long over-water flight. Type 1 (fuel-only) CFTs were carried for the 2,400mi (3,862km) round trip to Khamam al-Shatt. On the F-15's first-ever mission as a bomber the two four-ships carried guided weapons and AIM-9Ls on their six-hour flight, requiring three refuellings from the IDF/AF's Boeing 707 with its Sargent Fletcher drogue refuelling system and an Israeli-produced, TV-guided version of the 'Flying Boom'. Weather conditions remained clear en route and over the target. The Eagles, led by Brig Gen Giora Rom, attacked a number of buildings including Yasser Arafat's command centre, killing seventy-three people and demonstrating the long reach of Israeli retribution.

F-15C/Ds entered the fray after the main action of the Lebanon war, destroying two more MiG-25s on 25 June 1982 and a MiG-25P on 31 August. Two more MiG-23s were brought down by AIM-7Fs

from an F-15D flown by Nir Ronen on 19 November 1985 when they attempted to interrupt an RF-4E mission. Sporadic activity continued for the rest of the 1980s though the IDF/AF's F-15 air-to-air score remained at 56.5:0 with several of the aircraft credited with four kills and one, F-15C tail number 840 (80-129 *Commando*), with six. In the 40-year period from 1948 the IDF/AF claimed an extraordinary total of 796 air-to-air victories, mainly against Syrian and Egyptian pilots.

Wingless Eagle

Among the high-scorers in the battles around the time of the Bekaa conflicts was an F-15D, 957 *Skyblazer* that destroyed four MiGs but survived a different kind of aerial encounter on 1 May 1983. It was one of a pair of Eagles involved in a DACT session with four A-4N Ahit (Skyhawks) over Nahal Tzin in the Negev Desert training area. *Skyblazer* was in collision with an A-4 that pulled up inverted into the Eagle's underside during a four-ship ACM engagement and exploded in a blaze of fuel as its young pilot baled out. The student pilot flying the F-15D realized that his aircraft was losing fuel and descending in a spiral at 300kt. He re-engaged the stability augmentation system, which had tripped out, and regained level flight with the stick pulled far back, full right rudder and right

aileron. Deciding to stay with the aircraft he noted that the hydraulics, avionics and instruments were all functioning but later pointed out that he should have had a special warning light that read 'Wing Missing'! In fact, the entire right wing had been sheared off at the root but the plume of fuel from its ruptured tanks had hidden this alarming situation from him. Overruling 'Eject' calls from his instructor, whom he outranked, the pilot realized that the one-way valves in the fuel system would retain some fuel in the other tanks even though his digital fuel gauge registered 'empty' and he slowed down to attempt to gain better control and assess the chances of recovery. At that point the airfield came into view so the pilot took a chance and lowered the tail-hook and undercarriage. His wingman confirmed that they had extended, but at 250kt the one-winged bird wanted to spin to the right and ejection seemed the only solution again. As a last resort he lit the afterburners, taking a chance that there might still be leaking fuel that might ignite. The speed rose to 270kt and the aircraft responded again. He kept the Eagle on a steady approach, called for the emergency recovery barrier and touched down at 260kt only 5min after the collision. Landing at twice the normal speed was enough to shear the F-15's arresting hook's overstress link after the arresting chain ran out fully but heavy braking stopped the one-winged bird 33ft (10m) before the barrier.

F-15I 217 with a full complement of Paveway II LGBs. Colours are FS 30219, 33531, 34424 with Light Compass Ghost Grey 36375 undersides. Simon Watson

F-15A 667, relegated to the IDF/AF Museum but still bearing its *Squadron of the Double Tail* badge and its former FMS serial 76-1509, looks ready for another fight. Simon Watson

The pilot rose in his cockpit, turned to shake hands with his instructor and took aboard for the first time the missing expanse of wing.

McDonnell Douglas allegedly responded to enquiries about the incident with the information that a one-winged landing was impossible – until they saw the photos. F-15D 957 was repaired, returned to action a few months later and went on to score a further MiG. Its missing wing was later found in one piece. Another F-15 was involved in multiple bird-strikes with a flock of storks soon after take-off on 19 March 1981. One was ingested into the left engine causing a fire. Once again, the pilot stayed with his aircraft and recovered it safely.

Although Israel has so far acquired no further F-15C/D Akevs the Baz inventory was increased by the addition of seventeen more ex-ANG after the Gulf War. They were offered to Israel at a nominal cost in recognition of that country's restraint when bombarded by Saddam Hussein's Scud missiles. These FY73/74 F-15As were retired examples from the Hawaii, Missouri and Louisiana ANG squadrons. They lacked the updates that have taken most other Baz aircraft to something approaching MSIP standard and they were intended primarily for training, storage for attrition replacement and spare parts, although

at least five have seen operational use. The rest of the Eagle force was subjected to a 1998 contract with Elbit systems (via its EFW subsidiary at Fort Worth) to update their cockpits with digital flat-panel display units and new software as 'Baz 2000'.

Thunder

Israeli confidence in the F-15, boosted further by its outstanding success in Operation *Desert Storm*, led to further orders, but this time for the F-15E (*see* Chapter 6). The determination to procure this attack version dated back to 1987 when Gen Amos Lapidot, Commander of the IDF/AF, wanted an MSIP programme for the existing Baz and Akev force and a new purchase of Strike Eagles, as the F-15E was then known. In fact, the next purchase was another attrition replacement batch of five F-15D-50-MC two-seaters. The McDonnell Douglas response to an F-15E request was the F-15F, a single-seat development using some of the F-15E avionics, LAN-TIRN pods and F100-PW-229 engines. This was similar to the downgraded F-15E offered to Saudi Arabia, but both proposals were blocked by Congress. Further suggestions included the F-15H and F-15XP, also simplified F-15Es but with two seats.

Finally, in January 1994 Congress approved the sale of a slightly modified F-15E, the F-15I (for Israel) including some Israeli-produced equipment. The new aircraft was a 'tie-breaker' in a long-running contest between the F-16ES 'Enhanced Strategic') with long-range CFTs, and the F/A-18. Although the IDF/AF had come to regard the F-16 as its principal and most numerous strike aircraft, the attraction of a sophisticated, long-range interdictor with the targeting capability of the F-15E was strong, even at twice the price of an F-16. Israel was particularly aware that Iran had developed its Shihab ballistic missile that was capable of reaching Israeli cities. The F-15I's 2,800mi (4,500km) range put Tehran within its reach.

A contract signed in May 1994 secured twenty-one F-15I Ra'am (Thunder) aircraft, serials 94-0286 to 94-0306, to be delivered at one per month under *Peace Fox V*. Roll-out of the first machine was on 6 November 1997 and its first flight was booked for 12 September. Boeing's Joe Felock, with WSO Maj Rick Junkin, USAF, took the aircraft to 40,000ft (12,200m) and Mach 2, pulling a few 9g turns en route. Testing and stores clearance trials took place with the AFFTC at Edwards AFB, using the first F-15I, 94-0286. The first two Ra'ams were flown into Hatzerim AB via Sigonella on 19 January 1998 escorted in by a pair of F-15Ds and two RF-4Es. A new squadron, No. 69 Tayeset Ha'patisham (*The Hammers*) converted from the F-4E Kurnass to operate the new aircraft and it had received ten by the end of 1998. Subsequent deliveries were via Lakenheath, UK using USAF tankers, though one pair that arrived during the 1999 Kosovo Crisis was 'tanked' by the IDF/AF's own Boeing 707 as USAF refuellers were in short supply. *The Hammers* embarked upon an intensive training programme with an emphasis on night attack. Three F-15Is in full 69 Sqn markings and three-tone camouflage were flown by Israeli crews straight from the factory to Nellis AFB for Red Flag 99-1 before flying on to Hatzerim.

Equipment for the Ra'am included the Lockheed Martin AAQ-14 LANTIRN targeting pod (*see* Chapter 6). AAQ-13 navigation pods had already been bought

for IDF/AF F-16s but 23 new AAQ-14s were purchased for $74.2m. ECM was provided by the Israeli-designed Elisra SPS-2100 integrated set in place of security-restricted US items. It provided passive radar and missile warning functions together with active jamming. Elta built the secure-voice radios and Elbit the 'DASH' helmet-mounted weapons-aiming sight. This is used with the off-bore-sight Python 4 missile that, like the Python 3, is a domestically produced variant of the Sidewinder. With the F-15E's Kaiser holographic HUD and an upgraded APG-70I radar, plus 'Dash 229' engines (with 'turkey feathers' retained) the F-15I is one of the most capable Eagle variants. Israel took the Ra'am into action for the first time for attacks on suspected terrorist camps in Lebanon in February 1999.

Tied to the deal was a long-term arrangement for the supply of CFTs, cockpit side-panels, access doors and vertical

stabilizers that makes IAI the largest supplier of airframe components to Boeing. It could also be a reason to extend F-15 production for Israel and other Middle Eastern customers just as the orders seemed to be running out. Israel has already taken up its option for four additional F-15Is under *Peace Fox VI* (94-307 to -310) having received the last of original batch on 14 September 1999.

Saudi Eagles

One of those customers could be Saudi Arabia's air force (Al Quwwat al Jawwiya as Saudiya) that has operated Eagles since 1981. The Royal Saudi Air Force, founded in 1950 had relied on its force of BAe Lightnings for air defence from 1966 onwards but age and attrition necessitated their replacement. The Saudis wanted F-14 Tomcats to replace what they saw as a

(Above) **840 'Commando' shows the twin red chevrons of 106 Sqn inside its fins.** Simon Watson

(Below) **F-15D 1319 (80-0112) of 13 Sqn RSAF at Dhahran, one of sixteen 'two-seaters' supplied under Project *Peace Sun*.** McDonnell Douglas via Norm Taylor

(Above) F-15A 73-100 as the fictitious '0107' in Saudi markings during sales negotiations with Saudi Arabia in June 1980. Eagles replaced Bae Lightnings as Saudi Arabia's air defence fighters alongside twenty-four Tornado ADVs.
Boeing/McDonnell Douglas

F-15C 1311 (80-0091) and 1306 (80-0096) with AIM-7s and AIM-9Js on a border patrol. Saudi Eagles lacked the ALQ-128 RWR but ALQ-135 sets were supplied in 1990 before the Gulf War. Boeing/McDonnell Douglas

a thorough demonstration of the type and deliveries of Saudi Eagles begun in August 1981 for 13 Sqn at Dhahran. Congress placed some political restrictions on the sale, limiting the numbers of Eagles in Saudi Arabia to sixty at any one time and rationing CFTs in order to keep Israel nominally out of range. Two attrition replacements from the total order for sixty-two aircraft were kept in the USA as part of this agreement. 'Sensitive' electronics were also deleted, particularly the AN/ALQ-128 and AN/AL-135 EW suite. Deliveries of the F-15Cs were made via Bitburg and were completed in May 1992, including an extra twelve *Peace Sun VI* F-15C/Ds that Congress approved in April 1991. This request had been refused in 1989 and was then approved as long as the aircraft were retained at St Louis as attrition replacements. The Gulf War changed all that.

Saudi Eagles first saw action on 5 June 1984 when two McDonnell Douglas F-15Cs destroyed two McDonnell Douglas F-4Es of the Iranian Air Force over the Persian Gulf after they had intruded into Saudi airspace. When Saddam Hussein threatened Saudi Arabia in 1990 the 'sixty aircraft limit' was lifted on the eve of hostilities and

defensive shield against Russia, previously provided by the Shah of Iran's F-14 fleet. When he was overthrown the Saudis wanted their own Tomcat 'barrier'. Despite strong Congressional opposition from those who wanted to preserve Israeli air supremacy, the US Government approved

the sale of forty-six F-15Cs (80-062/106 and 81-002) and sixteen F-15Ds (80-107/121 and 81-003) under the FMS *Peace Sun* programme, with AWACS support from five Boeing E-3As from 1982. In January 1979 the 94th TFS, 1st TFW deployed a dozen Eagles to Saudi Arabia to provide

twenty-four additional F-15Cs were urgently transferred from USAFE units (*see* Chapter 7), forming No. 42 Squadron at Dhahran. Saudi Eagles also had ALQ-135 protection installed at this stage. MSIP updates have been carried out on a number of the F-15Cs. Of the seventy-nine F-15Cs and twenty-three F-15Ds delivered, six are known to have been struck off. Some of the Saudi aircraft were used (with LA codes) for

training RSAF crews at Luke AFB predelivery. Three squadrons were formed: No 5 at King Fahd air base (Taif), No 6 at King Khaled (the former Lightning base at Khamis Mushayt) and No 13 at King Abdul Aziz (Dhahran).

A Saudi request for a strike version of the F-15 was met with the F-15F (single-seat, downgraded F-15E) proposal. Objections from the pro-Israeli lobby in Congress

undermined this prospect and 114 Tornado IDS and ADV aircraft were bought from the European Panavia consortium instead. However, the chance of keeping the F-15 production line open coupled with the news that Israel was to be allowed an F-15E variant caused a change of policy. In May 1993 permission was given for seventy-two F-15XP (later F-15S) Eagles costing $9 billion including support – the largest ever FMS deal. The aircraft is very similar to the F-15E with *Have Quick II* secure radios, full ECM fit, LGB and Maverick capability. Enough LANTIRN pods and CFTs with ordnance pylons have been supplied to equip forty-eight aircraft for the attack role while the rest have 'Dash 4' CFTs equipped with AIM-7 launchers to give priority to air defence. The first F-15S flew on 19 June 1995 and deliveries via Lakenheath have usually run at four per month with the last pair (93-0867 and 93-0919) arriving there on 28 July 2000. This delivery cycle had to be reduced to a monthly pair when oil prices sank in 1996–97 to keep within budget. On one memorable occasion on 20 April 1998 the delivery batch included two Saudi F-15S and a pair of Israeli F-15Is in the same formation across the Atlantic to Lakenheath. Once they had completed tanking over the eastern Mediterranean they parted company for their respective air bases.

In March 2000 Saudi Arabia expressed an interest in the purchase of another twenty-four F-15S aircraft to replace the country's remaining F-5Es, bringing the RSAF total up to 165 Eagles.

Saudi Eagles flew many CAP missions during *Desert Storm*, one of which resulted in the shooting down of a pair of Iraqi Mirage F.1EQs. USAF

RSAF F-15C 601 (80-0062) lifts off for a CAP during Operation *Desert Storm*. The titling on the nose is in the same green shade as the tail insignia though later ex-**USAFE** aircraft were hastily stencilled with the required logo. USAF

Eastern Eagles

The Eagle's second FMS customer, Japan, is the largest Eagle operator outside the USA with 213 purchased. In 1975–76 the Nihon Koku Jietai (Japanese Air Self Defence Force: JASDF) checked out the Western world's eligible fighters in the search for a potential replacement for its F-104J Starfighters. Evaluation of the F-15A/B took place at Edwards AFB in the summer of 1975 and again in 1976. It was clear that the aircraft could operate successfully with Japan's F-4EJ Phantom fleet, coping with the fast high-flyers, low-level intruders or more sophisticated Soviet aircraft that might be beyond the Phantom's powers. Of the other 'finalists' the F-14 was rejected as being underpowered and heavy on maintenance and the F-16 lacked the required BVR interception capability. The decision-

(Top) The first F-15J for the JASDF, 02-8801, poses outside the St Louis plant. 801 is the individual aircraft number and the other three digits indicate the year of procurement (0 for 1980); the F-15's two engines (2) and its all-weather role (8). Boeing/McDonnell Douglas

(Middle) F-15J 02-8801 in service with the Air Development and Test Wing at Gifu. Author's Collection

(Bottom) F-15J 62-8873 rolls out for another training session with 202 Hikotai, formed in 1981 as the F-15 OCU, a function it had previously served for F-104J training. Author's Collection

making process was so elaborate and protracted that an extra batch of Phantoms had to be procured to tide the JASDF over, but in April 1978, nearly three years after the basic decision in favour of the F-15, a licence-production agreement was set up for Mitsubishi to build F-15s. The company was already engaged in licence-building 127 F-4EJs up to May 1981 and the new F-15J contract worked in the same way: an initial small batch was supplied from St Louis (as kits in the case of the F-4EJ) with Japanese-based production of the rest. McDonnell Douglas produced two FMS-funded single-seat F-15Js and twelve F-15DJ two-seaters under *Peace Eagle*. They supplied eight other F-15Js on 11 September

(replacing the AN/ALQ-135), and APR-4 RWR in place of the ALR-56. Production continued up to the target of 213 rather than the original figure of 123. The last, an F-15DJ was delivered on 10 December 1999 for 201 Hikotai (Squadron) at Chitose AB.

Japan has followed the example of other Eagle-flying nations in devising an extensive modernization programme for its F-15 fleet. The projected F-15J/DJ 'Plus' will have IHI-produced F100-IHI-220E engines (available since 1996 instead of the standard –220 that was installed from 1991 onwards) and GCI data-link. Other additions will include an improved ejection seat, radar updates approximating to APG-70 standard and the locally produced

and 1983 respectively and they defend the northern sea approaches including the 200mi (320km) stretch to Russia's eastern coast. At Iruma the Central Air Defence Force includes 6 Koku-dan at Komatsu and 7 Koku-dan at Hyakuri, one each side of Japan's main Honshu Island. Hyakuri's squadrons on the eastern side of Honshu include 204 Hiko-tai with its distinctive eagle tail-insignia and 305 Hiko-tai. Komatsu is home to 303 Hiko-tai the first unit to convert from the F-4EJ, five years after Eagles began to replace the country's F-104Js. The second squadron in 6 Koku-dan is 306 Hiko-tai.

At Kasuga is the Headquarters of the Western Defence Force controlling the 5th

Another F-15J of 202 Hikotai based at Nyutabaru. Author's Collection

1982 as knock-down kits for Mitsubishi Heavy Industries. After the maiden flight of the first US-built F-15J (USAF serial 79-280) the aircraft was passed to Edwards AFB where it was extensively tested by JASDF pilots alongside the second aircraft, 79-281. The pair then flew to Japan in March 1981 for further induction work.

Eagles then followed the F-4EJ onto the Mitsubishi production line with the first one (12-8803) airborne on 26 August 1981. Manufacture involved a range of Japanese companies including Fuji, Shin-Meiwa, Kawasaki, Nippi and Sumitomo. The F100 engine was licence-built by Ishikawajima-Harima Heavy Industries (IHI), with other engine parts from Kawasaki. Build standard was essentially similar to the F-15C/D but with domestically produced electronics in the form of the J/ALQ-8 ECM system

AMRAAM-equivalent 'fire and forget' AAM-4 missile. Longer-term, Japan's F-15s may be modified with limited amounts of replacement structure using 'stealth' materials. A new external pod is under development that would enable F-15s to defeat radar jamming when conducting anti-shipping missions or escorting other aircraft in that role. Also, the J/ALQ-8 system is due for improvement and expendable countermeasure capacity will be increased. Longer-term, a new FLIR/IRST target detection system may be installed.

The F-15 serves in three sections of the JASDF's Koku So-tai (Air Defence Command). The Northern Air Defence Force, based at Misawa AB controls No 2 Koku-dan (Wing) at Chitose on Hokkaido Island, with 201 and 203 Hiko-tai (Squadrons). They converted from the F-104J in 1986

Koku-dan, whose Rinji F-15 Hiko-tai was the first to receive Eagles at Nyutabaru AB in December 1981 and acted as the OCU, evolving into 202 Hiko-tai the following year. This squadron changed identity again on 6 October 2000 when it was replaced by a new fighter training group, Dai 23 Hiko-tai, also at Nyutabaru and flying twenty F-15DJs. Also defending Japan's western approaches is the 8th Koku-dan with 304 Hiko-tai at Tsuiki that switched from Phantoms in April 1990.

The best-known of all JASDF Eagle squadrons is the Hiko Kyodotai, Nyutabaru's aggressor squadron that works with the OCU. It began life with the Mitsubishi T-2 (that proved inadequate for the task) and adopted seven F-15DJs, each with a distinctive paint scheme rather like US aggressor units. Its cobra-marked Eagles

F-15J '889 of 201 Hikotai is prepared for a training sortie. Author's Collection

provide expert ACM over the southern ocean training areas. Current F-15 squadron strength is around 12 to 15 F-15Js with two or three two-seaters per unit, although 202 Hiko-tai OCU understandably has eight F-15DJs. Most units also operate a few Kawasaki T-4 trainers.

When Japan opted for the F-15EJ Phantom it had to do without the aircraft's inflight refuelling system, in keeping with the 'local air defence' principle behind its purchase. When its successor the F-15 was chosen the requirement was for longer-ranging CAPs to counter faster, low-flying intruders bearing stand-off weapons.

Although long-term political agreements still rule out a JASDF tanker force, F-15Js have begun to deploy outside their local area. In June 1999 six F-15Js of 305 Hiko-tai flew to Andersen AFB, Guam for *Cope Thunder North* 99, a seven-day exercise involving the F-15Cs of the 12th FS PACAF and Japanese E-2C Hawkeyes. This marked the first occasion on which Japanese fighters had ventured outside Japan's airspace since the Second World War.

A second potential customer in the Far East is the Republic of Korea Air Force (ROKAF) that began evaluation of the F-15E in September 2000 as a contender for

its FX fighter programme. In October, fourteen evaluation flights were scheduled at Elmendorf AFB using three aircraft and the Koreans were offered the F-15K with APG-63 (v)1 radar as a development of the F-15E tailored to their own needs.

Where Eagles Might Have Dared

The high unit cost of the F-15 has always limited its foreign sales potential and McDonnell Douglas never realistically hoped to match the F-4's production figures of well over 5,000 copies. So far the Eagle's run of 1,556 units (to the end of 1999) has been for four customers but a number of other countries expressed serious interest. The McDonnell Douglas sales campaign focused initially on Iran, whose airpower-obsessed Shah was investing extensively in US military hardware at the time. Although he was already committed politically to the Grumman F-14A the Shah attended several demonstrations of both the F-14 and F-15 at Andrews AFB in 1973. However, the F-14A had claimed his attention most obviously. 'Scotty' Lamoreaux, a pioneer on the F-4 who became F-14 Programme Coordinator for the USN, gave a one-hour Tomcat briefing to the Shah that extended to over six hours because of his intense interest in the aircraft. To some extent the penetration of northern Iranian airspace by Soviet MiG-25 Foxbats pushed the contract in

304 Hikotai line up at Tsuiki after conversion from the F-4EJ Phantom. Author's Collection

Eagle head markings identify 204 Hikotai, the first operational F-15J unit, based at Hyakuri. Author's Collection

Grumman's direction and an order for forty F-14As was signed in June 1974.

Several European air forces were seen as likely customers. France did an evaluation in April 1976 and was seen as a strong bet. The demonstrator TF-15A 72-291 was given Armée de l'Air markings for the occasion, but cost and a reluctance to buy outside French industry prevented a deal. West Germany had explored the possibilities of buying up to 200 Eagles in 1975 when it became obvious that the multinational MRCA (Tornado) would not be ready by that date as an interceptor. The cheaper F-4F was chosen, with a continued commitment to the MRCA.

Farther afield, there were hopes in 1975 that Canada would follow up its two demonstrations with an order for fifty aircraft. Australia too was seen as a likely buyer of a similar number. Eventually, both nations opted instead for McDonnell's later F/A-18 Hornet. The most recent hope of a new contract rested on Greek interest in a simplified F-15E variant called the F-15H. The proposal, announced on 8 October 1998, included considerable offset support work for Hellenic Aerospace Industry, following from existing contracts with Boeing. The request for F-15s prompted a similar one from Turkey that usually expects parity with Greece in the supply of US defence technology. Eventually, the Greek order was cancelled on 30 April 1999 with high cost as the main reason.

In September 2000 Boeing began to offer a refurbishment programme for the 116 F-15A/B airframes that were by then in storage at AMARC after service with ANG squadrons. With at least 6,000hr fatigue life remaining and the possibility of F100-PW-220E engines, configuration with air-to-air missiles (including AMRAAM) and air-to-ground ordnance capability the aircraft, redesignated F-15R ('Renewed') would each require rework totalling up to $25m. Upgrades were planned to take the airframes to F-15C MSIP standard. Although the USAF could have used some of these aircraft itself the target customers were Central European countries such as Poland and Hungary where, with US Government consent, the Eagles could compete with new-build Mirage 2000-5, JAS-39 Gripen, and Lockheed Martin F-16 entrants for those countries' fighter requirements. Boeing saw that this option would be more viable than trying to sell the far more costly F/A-18E/F Hornet to these potential customers.

Royal Eagles

Of all the NATO partners the RAF seemed the most likely Eagle customer for several years. Gp Capt M.J.F. Shaw, CBE, recalled the RAF's evaluation of the F-15 in April 1975:

I think I was the first RAF pilot to get my hands on the TF-15A prototype when it toured Europe in conjunction with the E-3A AWACS during its demonstration visit. It came to Bentwaters and I only had one back-seat trip, but its weapons system and handling were streets ahead of those of the Phantom. I was deeply impressed by the pickup ranges of its radar against 'target' F-111s and by the distance at which it could engage such targets. The TF-15's agility, smooth handling and size also made their mark, as did the superb all-round vision from even the rear cockpit. Later that year I was sent, with Sqn Ldr Roger Beasley (from A&AEE Boscombe Down) and Wg Cdr John Tritton (Staff, HQ 11 Group) to the USA to evaluate the F-15 as an air defence fighter. The aircraft had been designed as an air superiority fighter and its virtues were already well known in that role, but it was less certain how it might fit into the UK/RAF Germany air defence environment.

The three of us went to the McDonnell Douglas factory at St Louis where we spent a week doing technical ground school. The Eagle was clearly a great advance on the F-4 with all the latter's handling peculiarities designed out. The airframe was simple, with a minimum of moving parts and the engines were not unlike the Rolls-Royce Spey, with two spools, hydraulic pumps and generators mounted on a separate frame and an aircraft-mounted auxiliary drive (AMAD). The avionics were a development of the AN/AWG-10/12 and the radar had pulse Doppler and pulse modes with a synthetic B-scope display. This was much easier to use than those on which targets were ill-defined smudges. On synthetic displays the target is either there or not there and when it is locked up all the guesswork about its parameters is removed.

We were ferried in the Company's Learjet from St Louis to Edwards AFB where there was a TF-15A. This time, Roger and I were to fly

(Above) F-15DJ 82-8065 in one of the aggressor schemes used by the Hiko Kyodotai at Nyutabaru. On the tail is the unit's cobra head badge.
Author's Collection

The grotesque remains of an RSAF F-15C after an accidental fire in a shelter.
Author's Collection

head-on before having to descend and turn for two Sidewinder stern shots, all before any of the raiders reached my initial CAP position. Most certainly the F-15 would have worked well as an air defence machine, even without the assistance of a worthy navigator in the back seat!

Roger Beasley did five trips on the stick-force-per-g side of the evaluation and concluded that the aircraft's flying qualities were truly excellent. It had a very low wing-loading, a clever wing section, no high-lift manoeuvring devices (it didn't need any) and none of the adverse yaw characteristics that could bite F-4 pilots. John Tritton, our team leader, had one back-seat ride so that he could corroborate what his two compatriots had written about the aircraft. We all agreed that, with a small reservation about the engines (which were prone to compressor surge so that we had to go to 100 per cent military power whenever manoeuvring at high AOA), the F-15 would be an admirable addition to the RAF inventory in the air defence role. However, Pan Am and TWA did not buy Concorde, which meant that the sixty F-15s that we hoped to procure never materialized.

Rumours of an F-15 purchase or lease lingered on as long as protracted delays kept the Tornado F2 on hold. There was even a movement to order F-15s fitted with the Tornado's Foxhunter radar, but by 1978 the Ministry of Defence had ruled out any possibility of an Eagle order.

five sorties each in the front seat, latterly as aircraft commander. My own back-seat pilot, Denny Behm knew all that was necessary to keep novices out of trouble, but hardly touched the stick on any of my sorties. The flights were set up to see if a single pilot (me, in this case) could handle multiple targets. The aircraft, fitted with two prototype FAST PACKS, felt almost neutrally stable in straight and level flight or an unloaded climb. It was over-sensitive in my view, but I was used to the F-4 in which the stick was a wobbly blunt instrument. In a turn, however, it was so smooth that high g-loadings could be applied without buffet or

noise, leaving the pilot free to concentrate on handling the superb weapons system.

From a Combat Air Patrol (CAP) altitude of FL180 I didn't successfully intercept an F-4 target at 5,000ft doing Mach 1.6. The weight of the FAST PACKS hampered the TF-15's acceleration and climb to the extent that, even with a good radar-detection range, I could not get into a head-on Sparrow-launching position and a stern-chase after a 180 degree turn for a Sidewinder shot would have taken forever. However, the TF-15A, carrying four Sparrows and four Sidewinders (plus gun) did cope with a four-ship, low-level raid by four F-5s. I found I could get two Sparrows off

CHAPTER FIVE

Interceptor

Among the last USAF recipients of the F-15A/B were four TAC squadrons that took over the air defence role previously performed by Aerospace Defense Command (ADC). After 1 October 1979 all ADC units were shifted to Tactical Air Command (TAC) and the Fighter Interceptor Squadrons (FIS) became part of ADTAC (Air Defense, TAC) and then, from 6 December 1985, the 1st Air Force, headquartered at Tyndall AFB, Florida. Three of the squadrons were ex-F-106A Delta Dart operators and the fourth had flown the F-4E Phantom from Keflavik, Iceland.

The first squadron to convert to the F-15A (and also the last to relinquish it) was the 48th FIS. As an F-106 unit it had been the first to deploy abroad with the F-106, the last of which headed off for conversion to a target drone on 9 March 1982. The 'Sixes' were replaced by a batch of eighteen ex-1st TFW F-15As, with 76-087 and -088 introducing the Eagle to the 48th FIS at Langley AFB on 14 August 1981.

A month previously, F-15B 75-087 (ex-36th TFW) had arrived for crew training as ADTAC's first Eagle. With progressive Command reorganization the squadron began under the 20th Air Division, passed to the 23rd AD in March 1983 and finally to the 24th AD in 1987. The 48th FIS, known as the *Tasmanian Devils*, stood up as an F-15 unit on 5 April 1982 carrying over the distinctive blue and white tail colours used on its F-106s and briefly replaced these with an 'LY' tailcode in 1988 towards the end of its career under 1st AF control. Normally the squadron maintained three Eagles in the alert 'barns' at Langley AFB and another three on detachment to Tyndall in the same role. ACM skills were kept sharp through participation in Red Flag exercises, with six-aircraft teams in the 1987 and 1990 events. The *Devils'* association with Langley, dating back to 1953, ended when the unit was deactivated on 30 September 1991 and its aircraft were handed over to the 131st FW,

Missouri ANG. It was the last active duty USAF Fighter Interceptor squadron.

On the western coast at McChord AFB, Washington, the 318th FIS had flown Convair F-106s since 1960, converting to the Eagle with the arrival of F-15B 76-141 on a very rainy 10 June 1983. McChord Delta Darts ceased operations on 27 September 1983, by which time nine Eagles had taken up position there. During the squadron's transition its North West USA Alert duty was taken over by two-aircraft Detachments from the 186th FIS, Montana ANG. The squadron's other Alert responsibility at Castle AFB was temporarily delegated to California ANG F-106As. Markings were the distinctive blue star used on its Darts, then blue tail stripes with a smaller star and finally 'TC' codes (for Tacoma, Washington) from February 1988 until the squadron inactivated on 7 December 1989. Most of its F-15A/Bs were passed on to the 123rd FIS at Portland, Oregon.

ASAT Eagles

Vought (LTV) received a 1979 contract to develop missiles that would be effective against low-altitude satellites carrying reconnaissance or weapons systems. Their ASM-135A design used the Lockheed SR75-LP-1 solid-propellant first stage of the Boeing AGM-69 SRAM-A missile, with an Altair III solid-propellant second stage and no explosive warhead. Instead, the third stage of the anti-satellite (ASAT) missile was a 35lb (16kg) Vought 1005 miniature vehicle, 12in (30cm) long, that could destroy a satellite with the kinetic energy derived from impact at 30,680mph (49,360km/h). It homed on its target by using a telescopic, infrared seeker. The missile was 17.8ft (5.4m) long and was carried on the centreline station of a modified F-15A (76-0086) that also carried a datalink to provide course corrections to the missile after launch in a maximum power zoom climb to 80,000ft (24,400m).

For several F-15 units the interceptor role has mainly involved 'seeing off the Bear'. Keflavik-based Eagles are still tasked with that duty though the 57th FS with its IS-coded Eagles no longer flies. USAF via Ron Thurlow

The 57th FS was unusual among F-15C units in regularly installing CFTs. Long-duration flights and the prospect of diversions to UK bases if the Keflavik runways were weather-bound made the extra fuel a necessity. Author's Collection

Captive flights, using 76-0086 were made in 1982–83 and a live launch in January 1984, followed by three launches against infrared 'targets' in space. On 13 September 1985 F-15A 77-084 *Celestial Eagle*, the second ASAT F-15A assigned to the 6512th Test Squadron, launched an ASM-135A and destroyed the Solwind P78-1 gamma ray spectroscopy satellite that had completed its research programme. The result was a major protest from those who felt that the test had violated a US/Soviet treaty precluding the development of anti-satellite weapons. Scientists who were still receiving valuable data from the Solwind vehicle also voiced their discontent.

Despite this, plans to extend the ASAT modifications to twenty F-15As with two ADTAC squadrons (the 48th FIS and 318th FIS) continued. Around eight aircraft had received the new centreline pylons and electronics to carry the missile by the time Congress got cold feet in the face of continued arms control protests and scrapped the programme in 1988. American concern over the threat from Soviet satellites had actually increased by this time and in 1987 a more powerful

missile with a larger booster was studied together with a ground-launched variant based on the Pershing 2 SSM. However, the extension of 'armed conflict' into space had become too sensitive an issue by then. Russia also produced a prototype ASAT using a MiG-31D Foxhound launch vehicle with its other armament removed and endplate finlets for improved high-altitude stability. It employed many of the techniques used in the ASAT F-15A but was confined to trials only.

The shortest-lived ex-ADTAC F-15 unit was the 5th FIS *Spittin' Kittens* at Minot AFB in chilly North Dakota. Its last F-106A, with its eye-catching yellow lighting tail-flashes, flew to AMARC on 5 April 1985. Operating alongside the base's 23rd BS B-52Hs and 91st Strategic Missile Wing, the 5th FIS used its F-15s to defend the central northern region for only three years. After inactivation on 1 July 1988 the unit's Eagles went to the 101st FIS, Massachusetts ANG and the 5th FIS mission was taken over by the F-16 'Vipers' of the 119th FG.

Patrolling the Greenland, Iceland, UK (GIUK) 'gap' from Keflavik NS, Iceland the 57th FIS *Black Knights* was the most

northerly of the air defence Eagle units. As Phantom flyers its pilots had experienced a busy schedule of Tu-95 Bear intercepts from 'Kef' from 1973 onwards. Up to 155 'alpha' intercepts had been recorded annually – followed by 155 formal complaints from the Russians about 'illicit formating with its aircraft'. Keflavik's complement of F-15C/D aircraft began to arrive on 2 July 1985 when 80-033 and (appropriately) 80-057 from the 1st TFW arrived direct from Langley to replace the long-serving F-4Es. The Eagles touched down with 'IS' tailcodes and chequered fin stripes already in place, the first of eighteen FY80 aircraft to be transferred from Langley by January 1986. Their arrival coincided with a surge of Russian transients, 170 being recorded in 1985, to test the new interceptors. The F-15C was chosen over the F-15A partly because of the base's very active role in deterring Soviet intruders but mainly because the variant's conformal fuel tanks were vital for operations from Keflavik. The *Black Knights* invariably flew with them installed since a diversion to another base, if Keflavik was 'socked in' by weather, would involve a long flight, often to the UK. RAF Lossiemouth

At McChord AFB, Washington the 318th FIS traded in its F-106A Delta Darts for F-15As but retained its attractive star emblem until this was replaced by 'TC' codes. Here, 76-0099 makes a live AIM-7 shot and records it on camera. USAF

(Below) Another 318th FIS F-15A, 76-105, in August 1986. Author's Collection

F-106A-era markings were transferred onto 48th FIS F-15As when they re-equipped from August 1981 for a ten-year period of Eagle operations. This F-15B was at Tyndall AFB in April 1982 shortly before the unit's IOC. Capt Doug Barbier via Norm Taylor

was a favourite overnight stay. This situation was exacerbated by Air Forces Iceland's limited access to the CONUS tanker force. In the late 1980s the KC-135 Stratotanker detachment at RAF Fairford was frequently called upon for fuel. However, Keflavik housed its own E-3B/C AWACS Detachment of the 552nd Airborne Warning and Control Wing. Surveillance and interception of Soviet traffic was shared with RAF and Royal Norwegian AF units, with interceptor flights handing on the escort of each visitor as it passed through the 'gap' and down into the North Atlantic.

Iceland Eagles with their 'Slogin' or 'Knight' callsigns, soon took advantage of the USAFE's Aggressor squadron facility. Two F-15Cs arrived at RAF Alconbury on 16 September 1986 to make arrangements for four-ship DACT sessions. WTDs were held at Tyndall AFB from December 1986 onwards and the *Black Knights* commenced

participation in Red Flag from October 1987. Later in the 1980s the squadron also made two-week deployments to Decimomannu, staging through Bitburg. DACT detachments to Bentwaters and Waddington continued into the 1990s. There was also participation in large NATO exercises: *Ocean Safari* in June 1991 included a five-aircraft detachment based at Alconbury and flying sorties of up to three hours over the UK's south-west approaches.

Maintenance of the F-15s also tended towards integration with USAFE arrangements. For several years the unit's F-15Cs were overhauled at the IAI facility at Tel Aviv with other USAFE Eagles, though that contract was terminated in January 1995, two years ahead of schedule, in a change of political attitudes. The work reverted to Warner Robins ALC. Under another contract eight Iceland Eagles were resprayed at British Aerospace's Kemble

(Right) An F-15 pilot, ready to roll. His rifle scope is visible to the left of the canopy bow. Various attempts to install electro-optical sighting devices for long-distance visual ID were abandoned in the 1980s leaving pilots to experiment with their own 'home made' systems such as this. USAF

(Below) Kadena housed the 18th TFW's Eagles and the RF-4C Phantoms of the 15th TRS. Here, a joint operation keeps watch on a Soviet ship. USAF

factory in the summer of 1988. Like other F-15 units the 57th had its share of downtime through spares shortages and engine problems. One former technician with the squadron swore that there were times when the number of serviceable airframes was so small that the alert jets tail-numbers often had to be repainted so that Russian crews would not see the same aircraft continually intercepting them.

The post-Cold War drawdown process didn't affect Keflavik until January 1994 when it was announced that the 57th FS (as it became in 1991) would lose the majority of its aircraft by 1 April of that year. In fact, after forty years holding the line in Iceland the unit survived until 1 March 1995, its last aircraft (80-047) having left to join the Eglin trials fleet on 26 February. Several others went to Tyndall AFB for the 325th FW. From then on the GIUK gap area has been patrolled by detachments of F-15s from other squadrons, more recently alternating with F-16s. The first to take up position came from the 1st FW that sent five F-15Cs on 17 January for a three-month Alert duty. They came equipped with three drop tanks, since the 57th FS had been the only F-15 unit to use CFTs in the air defence role. Relieving this Langley detachment on 22 April 1995 were four F-15As and a single F-15B from the 102nd FW, Massachusetts ANG, the first ANG unit to deploy F-15s to Iceland. Their fairly brief stay ended on 16 May when six Oregon ANG F-15As arrived to split the three-month TDY with the Massachusetts crews. Their chosen external fuel configuration was just two wing-tanks and they had the support of KC-135F/R tankers on TDY. The fourth squadron on this rota was the 59th FS, 33rd FW that supplied six aircraft on 30 June 1995.

(Right) The Eagle's stalky under-carriage makes for a long climb to the cockpit for air and ground crew alike. It also allows steep angles of attack for take-off and landing, and room for the crucial centreline tank. USAF

In 1997–98 the 'Bear Watch' roster again included the 1st FW and 33rd FW but the ANG units were the 101st and 123rd Fighter Squadrons. For the first time F-16s joined the 'circus' when four 523rd FS 'Vipers' did the July-to-September slot that year. At the time of writing the Alert assignment has passed to the 71st FS, replacing a contingent of 94th FS personnel using the same aircraft. Detachments usually comprised four or five Eagles with tanker support and crews usually welcoming the chance to get in plenty of flying. Aircrew can be drawn from the resident 85th Operations Squadron, the *White Knights*, under 85th Group control. Although the Icelandic Government would prefer these detachments to continue there has been pressure within

(Below) Air Force Logistics Command's F-15A 77-0068 was the first of two to be assigned to Warner Robins ALC for test flights, complete with codes to indicate 'Robins, Georgia'. A 'WR' code was also used briefly. Robins performs most F-15 PDM work though some has been done at Sacramento and at a few locations abroad. USAF

Bear Intercept

On 25 June 1999 the American public was reminded that the threat posed by long-range Russian aircraft had not disappeared in the post-Cold war thaw. During *West '99,* the largest Soviet military exercise since the end of the Cold War, two Tu-95MS Bear Hs passed within striking distance of the USA. It was the first time any US pilot had seen a Russian bomber in friendly airspace for eleven years. The incursion coincided with tension between NATO and Russian forces in Kosovo, culminating in the Russian occupation of Pristina airport without NATO consent, and Russian disquiet with what it saw as 'out-of-theatre' operations by NATO in the Balkans. Two Tu-95 Bears and a pair of Tu-140 Blackjacks had taken off from the 22nd Heavy Bomber Division 'Donbass Red Banner' base at Engels, near Moscow. Both Blackjacks turned away and flew along the Norwegian coast, heading back to Russia before they were intercepted by R. Nor. AF fighters. Heading out over the North Pole, the pair of Bears flew to within sixty miles of the Icelandic coast where they were met by two successive pairs of F-15As from Keflavik. The Bears then turned away and completed their exercise that, according to Russian sources, required them to simulate cruise missile launches against 'targets' in southern Russia. The Eagle pilots came from the 159th FW, Louisiana ANG under Col Brod Veillion. One of them was Capt Kelly Sullivan, who takes up the story:

The night before we intercepted the Bears we had just arrived in Iceland. Half of us had been in Norway training with the East Germans and Norwegians and half had been sitting Alert in Iceland. Capt John Bond and I had just gotten off the C-130 from Norway to take our turn at Alert. We were a little tired so we went straight to our dormitories. We weren't in our Alert dorms yet because the people going to Norway weren't leaving until the next day. We didn't have phones in our rooms so they gave us beepers, since we were the 'next up' pilots. Since Iceland was on a twelve-hour Alert status we didn't think anything of wearing a beeper and staying such a distance from the Alert squadron.

About one fifteen that morning something woke me up. I thought it was my beeper. I picked it up, saying 'This isn't right.' So I put it down on my bed, but about that time Col Mike Lopinto burst into the room saying, 'Sully, this is real. There are Bears flying out of Russia and heading this way. Get up. Let's go!' My first thought was, this is a training exercise, but hey, this is my job; I got to go. I asked Lo(pinto) about the twelve hour Alert and he said, 'No, we're on thirty minute alert right now.' So I was really in the go-mode now; still a little groggy, but ready. We went downstairs and Bondo was already there. He had heard his beeper go off but he didn't understand the number and had no access to a phone. We thought we still had plenty of time; no big deal, and I was sure the maintenance people had gotten the word and were getting ready too. Maj Art Hyatt and Lopinto were there to take Bondo and myself to the Alert shack: there was an Alert truck parked right outside the dorms. As we walked out of the building we immediately saw the Alert truck had been blocked in by another truck. We couldn't leave. Lopinto looked in the truck and found a receipt with a name on it so we ended up locating the guy with the help of the front desk. It turned out to be a Navy sergeant who was there for Operation *Northern Viking.* We woke him up and he came down and moved the truck. His excuse was that he couldn't find anywhere else to park. The Operation had been going on for a couple of weeks and this added to our suspicion that the scramble was part of the exercise. Earlier in the week one guy had gone fishing just off the base and got 'captured'. They were playing 'real world'.

When we got to the Alert squadron there were two full-time F-15 qualified people [85th Group] there and the Alert was part of their assignment. They asked us if they could take it. Bondo and I said 'Sure', because they got there five minutes before we did and they were part of the Alert force too. The two pilots were walking out of the door ready to go when I said to myself, 'Wait a minute. This is real … I should be there … I want to be there.' So I was fired up, I was leaning way forward. Without telling anybody I got dressed in my anti-

exposure suit, grabbed my helmet and gear and cruised up to the Ops desk. Bondo was working the desk and asked me, 'What are you doing?'. I replied, 'I'm going to be the spare.' Maj Hyatt drove me out to the Alert barn and I saw SSgt Tracy Morrison who was a very reliable guy, so I waved him over and he helped get my Eagle going along with the other two. I requested permission to go, over the radio but the response was, 'Shut down Three … stand by.' So I shut down and I was just about to climb out when Lopinto came out to the jet and said, 'Hey, you're on thirty minute alert. Stay in the jet'.

In the meantime Bondo had got dressed and made it out to his jet. Evidently there was no tanker available, so they needed both of us. He climbed in and we sat there for about half an hour until we were finally scrambled. We took off in minimum low ceilings. The cloud deck went up to about 12,000ft (3,660m). The intercept went just like we trained. We had GCI to give us vectors and we locked the Bears up on our radars to get situational awareness on where they were in order to make a coordinated interception. Bondo did a real good job working the radar and getting us into position for the intercept. Before you knew it we had pulled right alongside of them. I was Number Four, so I was about a mile in trail of Bondo.

As the full-time F-15 pilots peeled off we assumed position. There were two Tu-95s and we were flying formation with them at about 30,000ft (9,150m). We could see the tailgunner, who had a little leather helmet on that reminded me of a 1940s football helmet. He waved at me and I thought how big, loud and old-looking the Russian aircraft were. Definitely formidable dinosaurs of the Cold War.

After about an hour flying with them the controllers finally told us to skip it. The Bears were headed back to their own airspace and we started back to ours. It was on the way back that I thought about how far north we flew. A helicopter and a P-3 Orion had been sent to support us. The P-3 had a huge raft in case something happened and we had to go down. They had tried to get us within visual range but ended up ten miles behind us. The helicopter was situated on the northern tip of Iceland as backup, so there were backup plans to back-up plans to protect us – that felt really good. It was also pretty amazing flying back over Iceland, but before we knew it we went right into the weather. It was really cloudy and after flying for three hours we had to shoot precision approaches.

After we landed and shut down we were pretty haggard looking , tired and hungry. We went to the dining hall and Maj Gen Bennett Landreneau (our State Adjutant General), Brig Gen Sam Degeneres (the State Air commander) and Col Brod Veillion, our Wing Commander just happened to be in Iceland on a field visit. They had heard all about the interception and were waiting in the dining hall to meet us. It couldn't have happened at a better time. Everything went off without a hitch and it showed how the maintenance guys got everything ready with almost no notice and launched four jets without a problem.

The Admiral commanding Keflavik arrived in the hall, looked at us and asked, 'Who was Number Four?' I said, 'I was, sir' kind of hesitantly because I didn't know what he was getting at. 'Congratulations, son. You are the last person to have a Bear intercept', he told me. At first I didn't understand, but in Iceland it is a big deal to acknowledge the last guy to get an intercept. You get a red star on your locker and a title to carry until someone else gets an intercept. I consider it a blessing to be able to fly Eagles, so the chance to intercept the Bears was just part of what we train to do. In fact the last intercept had been eleven years before and it was a coincidence that the guy who did it had just left Iceland days before after completing a rotation.

That was a Friday morning. Just two days previously I had been flying with MiGs in Norway. It was a pretty interesting week as far as fighter aviation goes.

A further incursion occurred on 16 September 1999 when a pair of Tu-95 MS aircraft approached Alaskan airspace for the first time since 1993. A pair of 54th FS F-15Cs from Elmendorf AFB turned them away 200mi (322km) off the Alaskan coast.

Congress to close Keflavik when the current Iceland Defense Agreement ends in 2001. For the present, defence of the area remains a USAF responsibility under NATO treaties and occupies about fifty personnel for each detachment, including the most experienced pilots in each squadron. As Col Irving Halter, CO of the 1st OG put it, 'It's not considered a mission for the uninitiated since high winds and driving snow often crop up unexpectedly.' One of his pilots observed, 'There's not much daylight. Sunrise is about 11.15am and sunset around 4pm. We fly in perpetual dusk and sometimes the winds and visibility change on a dime'. One side-effect is that pilots are sometimes prevented by poor weather from flying often enough to keep currency on the aircraft. They are usually rotated back to the home base every fifteen days for this reason, while maintainers generally do 30-day tours. In the late 1990s the detachments generated a two-hour Alert commitment around the clock, reduced from a one-hour status in 1995. Appearances outside Icelandic airspace are limited by the number of Eagles on each detachment. The NATO agreement includes the proviso that not less than four aircraft must be available at the base at any time.

Minutemen

The end of the Cold War brought a rapid change in the perception of North America's air defence requirements. The force that began in 1957 as NORAD (North American Air Defense Command) operated with a highly complex network of radars, missiles and over 3,000 aircraft. The latter component was gradually reduced by 1992 to 216 fighters under the control of the Air National Guard and by 1998 it was further reduced to around a hundred aircraft. Among them were three Eagle squadrons dedicated to the ex-ADTAC fighter interception mission and four others operating as tactical fighter units. Eleven other squadrons flew the F-16ADF, specially developed for the ANG interceptor role.

At NAS New Orleans, near the Cajun town of Belle Chasse, the 122nd TFS, 159th

Wearing its 'Satellite Killer' patch, one of several designs used by the two ASAT Eagles, 76-0086 still has its 'turkey feather' exhaust cover-plates. Boeing/McDonnell Douglas via Norm Taylor

76-0086 with a different patch and the bulky ASM-135A anti-satellite missile on its centreline. USAF

TFG, Louisiana ANG became the first Guard unit to convert to the F-15A/B, receiving sixteen early-production aircraft from the 405th TFW. Inheriting its official *Coonass Militia* nickname from its days on the F-100, F-102 and F-4C (together with the Cajun slogan 'Mort Par Chu'd Shahwee – pilote D'Aigle' or 'Death by Coonass Eagle Pilot') the squadron later adopted the more

politically acceptable *Bayou Militia* title after 1993. Some of its pilots had experience dating back to the F-100 and over 5,000hr of Coonass fighter time. By October 1991 the original FY73/74 aircraft had been passed on, some to AMARC as the first F-15s to appear there, and a newer batch of FY77 F-15A/Bs came in from the 49th FW. MSIP F-15As followed in 1993.

The three ANG squadrons that took on the ex-ADC role were the 101st FS, 102nd FW (Massachusetts ANG), the 123rd FS, 142 FW (Oregon ANG), and the 159th FS, 125th FW (Florida ANG). All were known as Air Sovereignty units from 1998. Throughout the 1990s, the nature of their mission changed from intercepting Soviet recce flights to a whole range of activities

The Coonass Militia

The 122nd TFS, 159 TFG, the Louisiana ANG, officially nicknamed – at the time – the Coonass Militia, was chosen to be the first organization world-wide to fly the F-15 Eagle part-time. The unit's pilots had proven themselves in the F-4. Most had a minimum of 1,000hr in a fighter cockpit and many had flown a tour of duty in South-East Asia. The unit's location, NAS New Orleans, allowed most of the huge expanse of the Gulf of Mexico to be used as a training area, unrestricted from the surface to 50,000ft (15,250m). As it was no more than ten minutes from brake release to 'fight's on', no time was wasted airborne and the training available was arguably the best peacetime air-to-air training available on the planet. Other less fortunate units – Air Force, Navy, Marines, Air Force Reserve and even the Royal Air Force – would cycle through on TDY for one or two weeks at a time to get a taste of this 'full up' training and a taste of the 'Cajun cooking' on the ground.

When the unit was selected to park the Phantom and transition to the Eagle, there were a number of active-duty managers who said that the concept was folly, that the F-15 could not be employed effectively by a part-time force, and that adequate proficiency could not be maintained. It was soon proven, however, that when the pilot force was hand-picked, motivated and already fighter-experienced, not only could proficiency be maintained but it could be maintained to a degree unmatched by any active-duty USAF unit. The Coonass Militia refined old tactics, developed new ones and quickly became the recognized authority on F-15 employment. The squadron installed self-funded VTRs in each aircraft (an installation to be copied later by the USAF), allowing for two-hour colour 8mm video tapes of both the HUD and VSD (radar scope) with audio to be used at flight debriefs. Equipment in each briefing room would display all four VSD tapes, or all four HUD tapes, simultaneously on a split screen allowing for very effective debriefs. In addition, the squadron eventually got a repeater display of the ACMI information from the ANG training site at Gulfport, Mississippi allowing for very effective mass debriefs similar to those at Red Flag. Since this force of part-time pilots experienced very little turnover the pilots stayed in the F-15 cockpit year after year and got better and better – and all for part-time wages. It was a very efficient use of US defence expenditure and the military got a lot of 'bang for the buck'.

To maintain this proficiency the average part-timer Coonass pilot (prior to 1994) would participate for 5–8 days a month, at his discretion. This would allow for six to twelve training sorties and participation in the required ground training. In addition, participation in the unit's two-week 'summer camp' was expected. This was frequently held down the highway in Gulfport. TDY deployments would be available throughout the year also, and participation was always voluntary. These would include deployments to *Red Flag* or *Green Flag*, Cold Lake, Alert in Keflavik, drug interdiction Alert in Panama and various smaller Stateside deployments in support of air-to-air training scenarios developed by other agencies. Regular destinations were Cherry Point MCAS, NAS Key West (Florida), NAS Dallas (Texas) and NAS Miramar, California.

Beginning in 1994, as the ANG and Reserve forces picked up more and more of the active duty US military commitment around the globe, the line between the active and ANG/Reserve forces blurred considerably, making the ANG pilot's schedule much more crowded than in the past. This, coupled with the normal retirement attrition, changed the make-up of the squadron rapidly as it now became the 122nd GS, 159th FG known as the Bayou Militia.

The JP-5 Dilemma

When the 159th TFG first received the F-15A/B from the USAF in 1985 there was a labour-intensive maintenance transition period, as the men and women of the 159th maintenance teams worked to bring the airplanes up to ANG standards. For example, our pilots didn't taxi an airplane from the parking spot to fly a training sortie unless *all* combat-essential systems were OR (operationally ready). If a system did not BIT (built-in test) check after engine start, maintenance was frequently able to replace a malfunctioning unit prior to taxi. But if a quick fix was not available, and a spare part was not preflighted and ready to go, then the sortie was lost to an MND (maintenance non-delivery), a rare occurrence.

An unexpected problem developed, however. The only fuel available at NAS New Orleans was JP-5 and these F-15s had been fed a steady diet of JP-4 since new. When fuelled with JP-5 our F-15s developed chronic fuel leaks which eventually resulted in the necessary resealing of the fuel tanks in all our aircraft, adding to the already intensive maintenance workload. Within a year, however, all twenty-six of our F-15s were up and running to ANG standards and the MND was almost a thing of the past. Imagine our chagrin, therefore when in 1991 our '73 series airplanes were transferred to Israel and we received '77 series F-15s as replacements from the USAF. Our maintenance folks were back to square one again and had to bring this 'new' fleet of aircraft up to our standards, including resealing all of *these* fuel tanks! The local opinion was, 'Why didn't we just give the Israelis the '77s?' but of course, no-one ever asked us!

Lt Col J.G. Randolph, USAFR (Ret).

including drug traffic interdiction and anti-terrorist measures. In 1998 Massachusetts pilots began to use night-vision goggles (NVG) to assist with the surveillance of illegal drug trafficking aircraft that usually fly without navigation lights. Practice with the ITT Electro-Optical Products NVGs over the Cape Cod training area known as 'Whiskey 105' required the Eagle pilots to turn off their own cockpit and navigation lights. Massachusetts F-15s defend the north-eastern USA, having taken over the role and aircraft of the 5th FIS in July 1988 plus the alert duties of the 49th FW when that unit stood down. Conversion was completed by 1 April 1988 after the delivery of F-15A 76-058 began that process in September 1987. Their initial complement was eighteen aircraft, reduced to fifteen after March 1994. Operating from Otis ANGB the squadron occasionally encountered Tu-95s when flying from the Cape Cod area and also on detachment to Keflavik in May 1996 where they used the old 57th FIS 'Knights' call-sign for their alert duties.

At Portland International Airport, Oregon the 123rd FS *Redhawks* traded the last ANG F-4C Phantoms for FY76 F-15As (most coming from the 318th FIS) from 24 May 1989 onwards. Their first F-15B (76-139) flew in on 1 October 1989 and transition was completed by 30 June of the following year after $17m was spent on new facilities for the fighters. The *Redhawks'* area of responsibility stretched from Northern California to the Canadian border with an Alert facility at McChord AFB, Washington. ACM skills were honed in exercises such as *William Tell*, where the unit won the top Lodeo award in October 1996 with full marks for weapons loading and combat turnaround. It also took its turn on Northern Watch duties at Incirlik, Turkey in April 1998 (*see* Chapter 7) and at Keflavik in 1995–96. *Redhawks* also joined with the 122nd FS for the Panama emergency.

The third Air Sovereignty squadron, the 159th FS, proudly flies its jaguar's head insignia and lightning flash, symbols of the local football team, from Jacksonville, Florida. Unusually, the squadron had previously flown the F-16ADF from January 1987 onwards but the superior radar and BVR capability of the F-15A was needed for its defence of the south-eastern USA. Eagles began to arrive late in October 1995 (F-15B 76-125 was the first) and the unit established Eagle alert detachments at Tyndall AFB and NAS Key West, though the latter moved to Homestead AFB once F-15 transition was complete. Although the Florida ANG is one of the busiest squadrons in the effort to intercept drug-running aircraft it also joined the

Keflavik rota in April 1998, making visits to several other USAFE bases at the time. The following year it stepped in to reinforce NATO's northern flank at Rygge, Norway for an exercise in June 1999.

Oregon's other ANG fighter unit, the 114th FS, 173rd FW also converted from the F-16 ADF, receiving F-15As from June 1998 to become the ANG's F-15 training unit. To assist in this task it received seven additional F-15A/Bs in mid-2000. Its syllabus includes both interception and battlefield air superiority (BAS) training. When Tyndall AFB's 325th FW becomes the F-22 Raptor Training Wing, all F-15 instruction will be done at Klamath Falls by the 173rd FW. A specialist in the BAS mission is the 110th FS, 131st FW based at Lambert St Louis Airport, Missouri. Firmly associated with St Louis by its 'SL' tailcodes and St Louis arch tail logo the squadron has flown home-grown McDonnell Douglas products since 1979. *Lindbergh's Own*, flying from the McDonnell home field, exchanged their F-4E Phantoms for a batch of F-15A/Bs in May 1991 commencing with F-15A 76-030 from Eglin AFB. IOC was attained on 15 September when the last F-4E departed for FMS service. Like other ANG units they

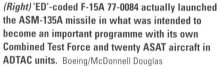

(Right) 'ED'-coded F-15A 77-0084 actually launched the ASM-135A missile in what was intended to become an important programme with its own Combined Test Force and twenty ASAT aircraft in ADTAC units. Boeing/McDonnell Douglas

(Left) In a shrinking USAF, long deployments have become more common as units move around to meet the needs, making the tanker force even more vital. USAF

have participated in exercises such as *Gunsmoke '95* and taken a turn on *Northern Watch* in January 1996, also relieving the 494th FS at Incirlik in February 1997. A deployment to Karup, Denmark in September 1999 took seven F-15As and an F-15B (callsign 'Trend') on an exercise that also required the squadron to operate from Laage AB against German F-4Fs and MiG-29s. By the summer of 1995 the original complement of F-15As had mostly been retired to AMARC and more recent machines were acquired from the Georgia, Louisiana and Hawaii Guard squadrons.

(*Above*) A 'dark grey' F-15C leaps aloft for a practice interception/DACT sortie with an ACMI pod underwing. USAF

A 48th FIS Eagle at Langley AFB in June 1983. Ron Thurlow

(*Below*) Georgia ANG's 128th TFS took over a batch of early Eagles to replace F-4D Phantoms for its battlefield air defence role, including F-15B 73-0112. The unit patch and motto; *Vincet Amor Patriae* appear on the right intake. Norm Taylor

(Above) An unusual Edwards AFB line-up of seven pre-production, Category I F-15As with 'Macair 1', the first Eagle in the foreground. The date was 28 July 1973. via Norm Taylor

The 555th TFS *Triple Nickel* was the first operational F-15 squadron and 76-0079 was one of their Block 16 F-15As. Boeing/McDunnell Douglas via Norm Taylor

(Below) A predatory trio of 58th TTW F-15As slows down for the cameraman during a training flight from Luke AFB. via Norm Taylor

(Above) F-15A 77-0149 was appropriately the 49th TFW 'Boss Bird'. Ron Thurlow

Red and white ACM stripes on F-15A 73-0103 in December 1975. Jim Rotramel

(Below) FY79 F-15Cs from the 36th TFW. All were transferred to the Royal Saudi Air Force in August 1990. USAF

(Above) Not the paintless Streak Eagle but a Kadena-based F-15C-22-MC (78-0516), caught by the rising sun. USAF

TF-15A (F-15B) 71-0291 in its Bicentennial scheme at Lambert Field, St Louis on 12 August 1979. Jim Rotramel

The sleek, purposeful lines of this Elmendorf F-15C are relatively unhindered by bulky CFTs and external tanks. USAF

The insignia of the *Hammers* (69 Sqn) decorates the desert-camouflaged tail of F-15I 217, loaded with LGBs and missiles. Simon Watson

(Below) The Mud Hen flies by night. Luke F-15Es on the flightline. USAF

(Bottom) Redhawks F-15A MSIP 76-0106 in lo-vis finish. USAF

(Above) Nimble performances from a pair of Luke F-15Es despite their full warloads of live Mk 82s and AIM-9 missiles. USAF

(Left) An F-15C over some inhospitable terrain during Operation *Desert Storm*. USAF

(Right) F-15C 83-0039 of the Tactical Air Warfare Centre at Eglin AFB, Florida. USAF

(Below) Showing only a pale shadow of their previously colourful Hawaii ANG markings, a pair of 199th FS F-15As; 74-0099 is in the lead. USAF

A 48th FW F-15E, carrying AGM-130A stand-off weapons and AIM-120 AMRAAMs, leaves Aviano for an *Allied Force* mission. USAF

(Below) 57th FWW F-15Es from Nellis AFB hold steady over the Nevada mountains. The second aircraft is marked for the Nellis Weapons School. USAF

An Elmendorf F-15C in Mod Eagle scheme enhanced by the setting sun. USAF

(Below) F-15E 91-0314 from the 494th FS, with a heavy burden of LGBs and missiles, en route to a target in the former Yugoslavia. USAF

The Crew Chief of F-15C 84-0015 unplugs his intercom from the connect/control section in the BIT panel box under the aircraft's air intake. The Eagle will then be free to fly. Peter Davies

As darkness approaches another night mission during *Allied Force* gets under way. USAF

(Above) Bitburg Eagles 79-0058 and 79-0019 command the air over Germany. USAF

(Below) The first flight for the S/MTD F-15 on 10 May 1989. Lee Whitney/ McDonnell Douglas

(Above) Eagles have stood Alert duty at USAF bases throughout the world since the late 1970s and will continue to hold the line until they are completely replaced by F-22A Raptors in 2010 to 2015. USAF

Pilots have a rare opportunity to launch live missiles when they attend Weapons Training Detachments at Tyndall AFB. F-15A 76-0119 of the 48th FIS looses an AIM-7 in October 1982. Norm Taylor Collection

Further east in Georgia the 128th FS, 116th FW became the first ANG unit to move on from the F-15A that it had operated in the BAS role. After flying fighters for twenty-two years the squadron made its last F-15 flight on 30 August 1995 when F-15A 75-024 lifted off from Dobbins AFB. This heralded in a change of identity to the 128th BS with the B-1B Lancer and a move to Robins AFB. The squadron had flown, in fairly quick succession, the F-100D, F-105G, F-4D and from 28 March 1986 the F-15A. The 405th TTW supplied the first aircraft, 74-128. Many of its stable mates came from the 36th TFW at Bitburg as it transitioned to the F-15C. Like other ANG squadrons it received, but seldom used, tail-codes on the formation of ACC. Georgia's aircraft were allocated 'GA', Florida's 'JZ' and Oregon's 123rd FS 'OR'.

A Used Phantom Driver Moves on to the Eagle

Lt Col Jeffrey G. Randolph, USAFR (Ret) describes his initial reactions to the F-15:

After 2,000 hours flying the F-4C/D/E the transition to the F-15 was an easy one for me. Aircraft systems logic was very similar and the aircraft was remarkably easy to fly; not easy to employ effectively at first, but easy to fly. A number of operational differences were immediately apparent, however.

The first thing that got my attention in the F-15 was the character of the GE F100 fanjet engines versus the J79 turbojet engines in the F-4. In the F-15 there was seldom a need to touch the throttles prior to takeoff. There was so much residual thrust at idle that speed control while taxiing was merely a matter of brake modulation – just release the brakes to come out of the parking spot and ride them all the way to starting the take-off roll. And if using the afterburners for takeoff (seldom needed) you could feel each of the five stages of afterburner as they lit in quick succession.

Once in flight the fanjet challenge was in flying precise, fingertip formation. Flying close formation in the Phantom was a snap, as the aircraft was rock-solid and the turbojet engine response was instantaneous. Those of us used to that immediate reaction to the slightest throttle movement in the F-4 had to learn to factor in the momentary time-lag from throttle movement to thrust response with the fanjet in the F-15. In addition, coming from the rock-solid Phantom, the new Eagle pilot felt like the airplane was 'skittering' around more, as if it were on a sheet of ice, due to the wing loading and enhanced flight controls. Both these problems were easily overcome with some experience in the airplane and the Eagle driver never got tired of the seemingly endless reserve of power always available from those F100 fanjets.

The Jet Fuel Starter (JFS) was a welcome addition to the Eagle as we Phantom drivers were dependent on some sort of 'outside intervention' to get started. We needed either an external air-start cart (the most common) or the seldom-used but quite exciting black powder 'cartridge starts'. Also, the JFS in the F-15 was quite conventional and didn't present any of the potential ground hazards inherent with the hydrazine arrangement in the F-16. Other welcome differences noticed immediately on the first flight in the F-15 included the increased seating height, into a bubble canopy, greatly increasing pilot visibility; the ergonomic improvements in the cockpit whereby all important switches and controls were literally at your fingertips and the Heads-Up Display providing infinitely more information

than the Lead Computing Optical Sight System (LCOSS) in the F-4. The air conditioner was actually effective on the ground (unlike the F-4's), there was a complete absence of immediate action or 'bold face' emergency procedures to be memorised by the pilot and, best of all, was the radar.

The APG-63 was the heart of the F-15A/B. Unlike the radar in the F-4 that remained essentially unchanged after rolling out of the factory, the F-15 radar could be upgraded – and frequently was – with entirely new capabilities in a matter of minutes with a software change. Usually these challenged the pilot to learn some new switch functions to take advantage of the new capabilities. The best difference, however, was that the APG-63 only showed you the targets, and it showed you all the targets. If you didn't see a suspected target you were looking in the wrong place. It was that simple. When you locked onto a target in the F-15 the information immediately with reference to that target was akin to sitting in the target aircraft cockpit. In fact, at any given moment in an air-to-air engagement there was more accurate information available to the Eagle pilot than he could possibly assimilate and the individual pilot quickly learned where to get the information most useful to him personally, at a glance, in the heat of battle.

The last major difference obvious to the experienced F-4 pilot was the remarkable Integrated Flight Control System in the F-15. The pilot never trimmed the aircraft as it was constantly trimming itself. Although the F-15 had the advantage of not being fly-by-wire the F-15 flight control computers used the airspeed, altitude and angle of attack (AOA) information to enhance pilot inputs to the flight controls. For example, in the low airspeed/high angle of attack flight regime, as might be experienced in a 'dogfight', the experienced F-4 pilot learned, usually the hard way to neutralize the ailerons and 'rudder' the airplane through any manoeuvring. Any aileron input would result in an opposite direction 'nose rise/nose slice' dramatic departure from controlled flight. In the F-15, however, if an inexperienced pilot in the same flight regime introduced lateral stick movement (aileron), unbeknown to him he would get no aileron whatsoever, but instead would automatically get both rudders deflected in the direction of the commanded turn, augmented by differential (split) horizontal stabilizer movement. The aircraft would smartly manoeuvre where 'Lt Hamfist' wanted it to go and he would think himself a master aviator. Thanks to superb flight control computer augmentation the F-15 made even an inexperienced fighter pilot look good!

The 122nd TFS, Louisiana ANG *Bayou Militia* adopted 'JZ' codes and 'Jazz' callsigns to associate them with their home-base, New Orleans. '093 was an ex-32nd TFS Eagle. Norm Taylor

Two other ANG squadrons were scheduled to receive Eagles. One, the 188th FS *Tacos* of the New Mexico ANG began to convert in 1991 but a shift of policy substituted the F-16C/D. The other, the 199th FS Hawaii ANG became one of the longest-serving F-15A users. Hickam AFB, where the squadron shares space with commercial air traffic, resounded for many years to the squadron's F-4C Phantoms with their individual Hawaiian names. It was the first F-4C air defence unit and, after deployment of a Georgia ANG F-15A detachment, it began to convert to the Eagle in March 1987 using aircraft from the 43rd TFS at Elmendorf. These were replaced by twenty-six ex-49th TFW F-15A/Bs in 1992. Hawaii ANG ('HANG') Eagles have the attractive 'lei-style' tail-stripes of their predecessors and the squadron maintains many local traditions, such as the crew-chief's pre-takeoff salute; a fist with the outer digits extended to mean 'no ka oi, bra' - 'looking good, brother'. The squadron still operated mainly MSIP FY77 aircraft into the new century and spares were becoming harder to find as delays in the re-equipment of front-line F-15 units with the F-22A meant that F-15Cs were slow to filter down to ANG units. However, the squadron has pioneered the use of night-vision goggles for night training in air combat. It has also helped to bring the Link 16 Fighter Data Link (FDL) into ANG use. This is a jam-resistant, digital information system that enables the F-15 to take aboard an enormous amount of surveillance and command information from a variety of airborne and ground sources and share it with other aircraft, sometimes as common radar imagery. The system will be in place with front-line F-15C and F-15E squadrons by the end of 2002 and with ANG units in roughly the same period.

Training involves DACM with MCAS Kaneohe Bay-based F/A-18Cs and other visiting Guard units. Typically, the based Eagles would commence proceedings with a 'HANG ten' departure; four aircraft taking off at ten-second intervals, hauling up the gear and pulling up into a vertical climb out of sight. Although their primary task is air defence of this mid-Pacific island chain where memories of the December 1941 Japanese attack still linger, since 1994 the 199th FS has also deployed as far as Keflavik, when it took on the April 1999 duty. Six aircraft flew to Singapore in December 1997 for Exercise *Commando Sling* and three to Incirlik in 1994 and 1996. The first of these was a 90-day TDY shared with the 122nd FS, Louisiana ANG and it gave the USAFE crews who had been manning the *Northern Watch* a Christmas break. In 1991 the HANGmen thought they might become the first Guard unit to receive the F-15C but, like other ANG squadrons, they have stayed with MSIP F-15As that will have several more years of useful life. For Period One of the April 2000 *Red Flag* (at that all six participating F-15 squadrons came from the ANG) they wore 'HH' tailcodes. However, trips away from the island are a comparative rarity and the

The 199th TFS's famously colourful tail markings (indicating the sea channels, warriors and mountains of the Hawaiian islands) were almost lost in the tone-down of markings in the 1990s. Ex-49th TFW F-15A 76-0118 stands ready at Hickam AFB, Hawaii in April 1997. Norm Taylor

squadron's main off-base function in recent years has been to fill in for 18th FW at Kadena if one of its two remaining F-15C units is required elsewhere in the world.

William Tell and Tyndall

When the F-15 RTU work at Luke AFB ended in 1994 the training role passed to the 325th TTW at Tyndall AFB, Florida that had already been managing ANG F-15A instruction since August 1984 as an extension of its work at the US Air Defense Weapons Center. In 1991 it became the 325th FW, controlling three squadrons; the 1st FS *Griffins*, 2nd FS *Second to None/Unicorns* and the long-established 95th FS *Mr Bones*. All but the 1st FS were former ADC F-106A/B squadrons and the 2nd FS maintained its secondary CONUS air defence role.

Tyndall's speciality was air interception training, providing an essential component between basic Eagle conversion at Luke and the 'front line' units. It was (and is) uniquely qualified to provide realistic practice in live missile firing over its huge offshore sea ranges using drone aircraft targets. Originally these were QF-100 or PQM-102 pilotless drones, succeeded by QF-106As that began to arrive at the same time as the F-15As. The first Eagle, 73-103 was flown in by Gulf War leader Brig Gen Chuck Horner who was then CO of the Air Defense Weapons Center. More recently pilots have had the dubious privilege of shooting down the Phantoms of the preceding generation, converted to QF-4s and provided by the 82nd ATS, 475th WEG at Tyndall's 'droneway'.

From 1993 the base took on all F-15C/D indoctrination as part of the Air Education and Training Command. The last F-15B was withdrawn on 22 September 1996. Tyndall regularly detaches up to fourteen aircraft to *Red Flag*, *Green Flag* and *Gunsmoke* exercises as part of its programmes. From October

(*Above*) Guarding its 'birthplace' at Lambert Field, St Louis this F-15A belongs to the 110th FS, Missouri ANG with its St Louis (SL) codes and *Lindbergh's Own* patch. D. Olson via Norm Taylor

Florida's 159th FS has flown from Jacksonville since 1946, beginning with P-51Ds and currently flying the Mustang's supersonic equivalent, the F-15 after eight years on the F-16A/B. F-15A 75-0039 formerly served with the 325th FW and the Georgia ANG. Norm Taylor

(Top) The 122nd TFS CO's F-15A-12-MC (an ex-1st TFW aircraft) at Shaw AFB in November 1985. Norm Taylor

(Above) A neat pair of 48th FIS F-15A-17-MCs flying near Langley AFB, Virginia. Norm Taylor Collection

(Left) Reflecting their increasing adoption of 'front-line' roles in the 1990s ANG squadrons began to wear their assigned tail-codes more often. Georgia's 75-0024 poses for the camera of David F. Brown. via MAP

1999 the Florida ANG was integrated into the 325th FW to help with the training of F-15 crews by putting a total of thirty-three pilots into the Tyndall squadrons under the command of Col Charles Campbell, but within the 325th FW so that students would not know the difference between active or Guard instructors. The motive was to alleviate the pilot shortage in active duty F-15 squadrons and about twenty pilots from the 325th were released from training duties and returned to active units as their ANG replacements became available. The best-known of Tyndall's functions was its hosting of the *William Tell* Competition. This dated back to the USAF's Annual Gunnery and Weapons Meet that included a rocketry section from 1954 to accommodate the new F-86D Sabre and F-94C Starfire with their semi-automatic, collision course radars and FFAR rockets. In 1958 the event moved from Yuma, Arizona to Tyndall as Project *William Tell* and took aboard the supersonic Convair F-102A together with teams from USAFE and ANG squadrons. The variety of aircraft types required different competition categories to be established. From 1959 to 1965 the event was bi-annual, introducing the F-100, F-104A, F-101, F-106 and the Q-2C Firebee air-launched drone. The latter became part of more sophisticated combat simulations based around the semi-automatic ground environment (SAGE) data-link control system used by ADC interceptors. Suspended from 1965 and 1970 because of the Vietnam War the competition resumed up to 1976 when the introduction of the F-4 as an ANG interceptor

meant another category reorganization and appropriate target simulation for the Phantom's AIM-7 and AIM-9 missiles. From then on *William Tell* became largely an F-4 meet, using PQM-102 drones from 1978 and EB-57s to provide an EW element with chaff and ECM. The construction of Tyndall's ACMI range allowed complex ACM scenarios to be added to the original interception menus.

The F-15 entered the competition in 1982 with five squadron teams, whereupon the event partially reverted to its original concept with the reintroduction of a gunnery category. Teams usually included four Eagles plus a spare.

William Tell F-15 Participants

October 1982 Event: 18th TFW (Winners. Carried Shogun logo and artwork); 48th FIS; 33rd TFW; 49th TFW. This was the last event to include the CF-101 Voodoo.

October 1984 Event: 33rd TFW (Overall winners, top F-15 team, top in weapons loading and maintenance); 32nd TFS (with 'drooling wolf firing a missile from a bow' art on right intake); 49th TFW; 18th TFW; 1st TFW, 318th FIS.

October 1986 Event: 1st TFW (each aircraft named after a city in the Langley area); 18th TFW, 33rd TFW; 36th TFW; 48th FIS. F-15 teams competed against ANG F-4 teams and a CAF CF-18 entry that took the overall Top Gun award.

October 1988 Event: the last *William Tell* to include the F-4. Top Gun award went to the 49th TFW F-15A team. The competition was then suspended until 1992 because of the Gulf War, the first cancellation since Vietnam. The 1990 event would have been an all-F-15 affair apart from the Canadian Hornet team.

October 1992 Event included the following four mission profiles:

PROFILE 1 (Missiles), involving two elements of two aircraft firing a live AIM-7 each at a target drone in a set sequence of actions (2,500 points per pilot. Total: 10,000 points).

PROFILE 2 (Gun). In this, two elements of two aircraft fired 20 mm at an AGTS-36 target towed by another F-15 (1,250 points per pilot, 5,000 total).

PROFILE 3 (Mass Raid). This involved four aircraft with external tanks against incoming B-1Bs, B-52s, F-111s and ECM-simulating Learjets. Pilots also had to de-conflict with 'friendly' fighters within the strike group. The defending F-15s, under the direction of a ground-control Weapons Director Team, had sixteen simulated missile shots between them to destroy sixteen intruders inside the 45-minute timescale (2,500 points per pilot, total 10,000 points).

PROFILE 4 (Lane Defence) Two F-15 elements scrambled within five minutes to a CAP position for lane defence against four QF-106s entering the area at different

A Tyndall-based F-15A of the 1st TFTS, 325th TTW. By 1984 this aircraft had spent most of its career training 'Ego Drivers' with the 58th TTW and 405th TTW at Luke AFB. Norm Taylor

The Oregon ANG managed to make the most of its art-work in the toned-down 1990s. Its two squadrons include the 114th FS that has taken over an increasing share of F-15 training. API

altitudes, times and intervals. The defending Eagles had to destroy all four targets inside five minutes (Total 50,000 points including an allocation for ground crew and bonus points for 'kills' within 3.5 minutes).

Overall points were also awarded for maintenance, munitions loading and the Weapons Director Teams.

The F-15 teams were: 18th FW (callsign 'Shogun', winners of Profiles 3 and 4, maintenance and weapons loading. In first position overall); 1st FW (callsign 'Freedom', came second); 33rd FW (callsign 'Nomad', came third); 36th FW (callsign 'Baron', won Profile 1 and came fifth); 101st FS (callsign 'Flash', came eighth). Top Gun pilot: Capt Jeff Pritchard of the 18th FW.

October 1994 Event (40th Anniversary of the Competition). Mission profiles were the same as for 1992 except that in Profile 1 an AIM-120 replaced the AIM-7 live firing. Eight teams competed and the 18th FW won again, with Capt James Browne of the 52nd FW as Top Gun. The 52nd FW was the only USAFE team that year.

October 1996 Event: Defence cuts compressed the competition into six days with three 'flying' days, rather than the two-week period of previous *William Tells*. The four Profiles were cut to two:

PROFILE 1 a two-v-four + one engagement and PROFILE 2 live missile firing.

In the first of these a two-ship element had to identify the four 'hostile' aircraft and avoid the '+ one' that was a friendly fighter in among them, emphasizing the vital importance of accurate IFF in contemporary air combat. The engagement was 'guns only'. For the 'live fire' component a two-ship launched a missile each at a QF-4 or QF-106 drone. Weapons loading was based on a 'static load' rather than the previous 'integrated combat turnaround' (ICT). Teams came from the 33rd FW, 325th FW, 18th Wg, 48th FW, 142nd FW and Oregon ANG. A further sign of the times was the reduction team sizes to three Eagles as ACC exercises became increasingly consolidated into *Red Flag* and *Air Warrior* events at Nellis AFB.

Decorated with a Cape Cod designator on its centreline tank and a DUC Award ribbon, this Massachusetts ANG F-15A awaits its pilot. Author's Collection

CHAPTER SIX

Mud Hen

J.S. McDonnell's policy in producing fighters was always to make his company's designs as adaptable as possible with minimal change to the basic airframe. His F-101 Voodoo, F2H Banshee and F-4 Phantom had appeared in both reconnaissance variants and others that were optimized to deliver a wide selection of air-to-air and air-to-ground weapons. The F-15A had already demonstrated a considerable air-to-ground capability that McDonnell Douglas and Hughes Aircraft decided to develop as a company-funded project called Strike Eagle. This initiative received encouragement from the USAF, and in particular from Gen Wilber Creech, from the outset. During his period as Commander of TAC from 1978 Creech had done much to raise standards of maintenance, availability, morale (and thereby retention of skilled personnel) throughout the USAF. Among other initiatives he reintroduced the idea of a Dedicated Crew Chief (DCC) for each aircraft, personalizing the relationship between maintainer, aircrew and aircraft in ways that had been lost in the USAF's 'corporate' post-war approach. He recognized that having a highly effective, sophisticated but easy-to-maintain strike aircraft like the Strike Eagle would restore TAC's cutting edge. As the concept evolved in 1978 the Air Force wrote its Tactical All-weather Requirements Study around Strike Eagle that it envisaged as a long-range, night, strike/interdictor. The slogan, 'Not a Pound for Air to Ground', devised to preserve the Eagle's dedicated air superiority role in its earlier years, was conveniently shelved as TAC refined its specification for a replacement for the General Dynamics F-111 Aardvark.

Holding the line in Europe since 1970, the F-111E and more sophisticated F-111F were a major component in the West's deterrent force but the ever-increasing numerical strength of the Warpac forces meant that USAFE's two F-111 Wings, each with about seventy-five aircraft, needed reinforcement and eventual replacement.

Company TF-15A 71-0291 emerged in yet another guise as the Strike Eagle demonstrator, with CFTs, an enormous load of 250lb (113kg) bombs on MERs and prototype F-15E avionics. Its 'slime and sludge' Euro 1 colour scheme befitted its role as 'Mud Hen' or 'Beagle' (bomber Eagle). Boeing just call it an Eagle. Boeing/McDonnell Douglas via Norm Taylor

Ford Aerospace/Loral's AN/AVQ-26 Pave Tack laser/infrared targeting pod conferred a unique night/all-weather attack capability on the F-111F that was to demonstrate its crucial operational value in Operation *Desert Storm* towards the end of its USAF service. Strike Eagle required at least the same degree of accuracy with PGMS at night and comparable speed and range in order to interdict key choke points and supply bases behind enemy lines, slowing a major Warpac advance into Western Europe while reinforcements were brought in from the USA to push it back. Although there was some pressure to reopen the F-111 production or 'update' lines to provide the

extra aircraft the Aardvark had many detractors in positions of power. There was also a considerable lobby for Strike Eagle with its more advanced avionics and engines, easier maintenance and 'commonality' with other F-15 variants. Crucially, the Strike Eagle was essentially still an F-15 fighter and could defend itself against air-to-air opposition, obviating the need for fighter escort. Although speed, guile, low altitude TFR and a couple of AIM-9s had given the F-111 a good chance against hostile interceptors the new generation of Soviet fighters with look-down/shoot-down missiles had decreased its survivability unescorted.

One of the F-111's strongest cards was its long range. It could haul 6,000lb (2,722kg) of ordnance over a 1,000nm combat radius, putting over 30 per cent of potential Central European targets within its striking distance. McDonnell Douglas Conformal Fuel Tanks (CFTs) were clearly essential for the shorter-legged F-15 derivative, but its projected combat radius was still to be significantly less at 680nm. There were also concerns about the F-15's wing that was designed for fighter combat at medium and high altitude whereas the F-111's 'swing wing' could be swept back to angles between 54 and 72.5 degrees to provide the smooth 'Cadillac' ride that its crews had enjoyed since its combat debut in 1968. F-111 pilot Maj Dick Brown enthused: 'You can go from 300kt to 800kt and, with your eyes closed, you wouldn't know. There's no

through better instrumentation and control systems the ever-increasing workload for navigation, weapons delivery and air-to-air fighting by night and day had become far too much for a single crew member.

McDonnell Douglas and Hughes Aircraft decided to field a 'Strike Eagle' concept demonstration aircraft, based on the faithful second prototype TF-15A (72-0291). This versatile airframe had already shown the Eagle's bombing ability during tests in the mid-1970s, before the F-15's strike capability was temporarily deleted from the USAF's agenda. As the Advanced Fighter Capability Demonstrator, '291 adopted a 'slime and sludge' European 1 green/grey camouflage scheme and flight-tested iron bombs, GPU-5 gun-pods and AIM-9 missiles among other combined warloads. Weapons pylons had been included in the range of optional CFT

identify vehicle-sized targets at a 30-mile range. Coupled with a ground moving target detection facility this equipped the aircraft to take on hostile armour on the move using PGMs. An APG-70 version without the SAR or moving target facilities was produced for MSIP F-15C/Ds and in July 1997 an F-15C flew with the APG-63(V)1, a further APG-70 upgrade with improved ECCM, larger processing capability and expanded BIT to reduce operational costs. By that stage the APG-63 and APG-70 had become virtually standardized units using parts from the same supply network.

Among the items tested on '291 was the AN/AVQ-26 Pave Tack pod, mounted on the left forward CFT pylon. Its data were displayed in the rear cockpit on one of the four cathode ray tube display panels (CRTs) that became the core of the new cockpit concept devised for the aircraft. However, the USAF was already funding a new navigation/targeting pod system that was lighter and more advanced than the 13.5ft (4m) long, 1,227lb (560kg) Pave Tack that had, in any case, been limited to a production run of only 160 units. Martin Marietta (Lockheed Martin) developed the Low-altitude Navigation and Targeting Infrared for Night (LANTIRN) system using two pods to provide the F-16 and A-10A with night-attack capability, giving them a better chance of completing their missions over heavily defended battle zones. The system eventually equipped a number of F-16C-40 'Vipers' but its primary candidate in the 1980s was seen as the 'Strike Eagle', by then known as the F-15E.

Although the production F-15E bore a close external resemblance to the F-15D, almost two-thirds of the internal structure was redesigned for the new role. Primarily, the airframe was strengthened to last out the required 16,000hr fatigue life and cope with the 9g loads in turbulent conditions with a heavy burden of weapons and fuel. The large increase in maximum take-off weight from 68,470lb (31,058kg) for the F-15C to 84,000lb (38,102kg) for the F-15E necessitated larger Bendix main landing gear wheels (36 × 11-18 against 34.5 × 9.75-18 on the F-15C) and some gentle bulges in the main undercarriage doors to house them. A new, doorless arresting hook could handle the increased weight in an emergency landing and more powerful generators supplied the uprated electrical power requirements. Much of this energy flowed to the new avionics in redesigned forward bays, including space provided by

71-0291 in standard Compass Ghost Grey carrying the very effective AN/AVQ-26 Pave Tack target acquisition/designation pod. Norm Taylor Collection

change, even in feel on the control stick.' F-15's wing inevitably gave a bumpier ride at low level, though it improved with a bomb load aboard. Airsickness has always been an occupational inconvenience for 'Strike Eagle' (F-15E) back-seaters, as it was for their F-4 predecessors. However, as Col Mike Casey observed, 'It is never so rough that you can't carry out normal cockpit duties – very much like the F-4.'

Like its F-111 and F-4 predecessors the 'Strike Eagle' had to be a two-seater. Despite the increase in digital automation and the simplification of many cockpit routines

configurations from the start. Initially, only one per CFT was tested but the full complement of six per 'tank' was flight-tested on F-15C 78-0468 in 1983. Weapons separation trials continued at Eglin AFB with two CFT-equipped F-15Ds and at Edwards AFB.

Hughes's contribution to the project centred on an enhanced APG-63 radar using the same antenna as the original radar but offering improved stability, dynamic range and detection ranges. Crucially, the new APG-70 radar provided synthetic aperture (SAR) mode enabling it to

LANTIRN and APG-70

Although the F-15E's APG-70 radar gives it a prodigious all-weather attack capability it is the partnership with the Martin Marietta (Lockheed Martin) LANTIRN (Low Altitude Navigation and Targeting infrared for Night) and Kaiser wide-angle holographic HUD that created the aircraft's unique interdiction capabilities. For a total external weight of 950lb (430kg) the twin-podded system enables 600mph (965km/h) attacks at altitudes of 500ft (150m) or less in darkness. Evolved from an early-1980s requirement to turn the F-16C and A-10A into night-capable attackers (reducing daytime losses over the hypothetical European battlefield) the system was actually prioritized for the F-15E, with Block 40 F-16Cs as the second 'customer'. The need to replace F-111F as the USAF's prime striker pushed F-15E to the front of the queue, while the A-10A remained 'day only'.

(Below) **Development work for LANTIRN included trials with the General Electric Firefly III system, based on the Martin Marietta ATLIS II laser acquisition/tracking system, seen here on F-15B 77-0166 of the AFFTC at Edwards AFB.** Norm Taylor Collection

(Bottom) **A pair of AN/AAQ-14 targeting pods in their transport cradles.** via A. Thornborough

F-15E crews can use the APG-70's synthetic aperture mode to make accurate radar maps. The radar's mapping performance (particularly its processor speed) was greatly enhanced, compared with the APG-63, and the detailed 'patch' maps of the target area that it can produce in a few seconds are of very high resolution in synthetic aperture mode. Mapping also requires very frequent inputs of navigational data from the INS to give exact positions for the terrain features included in the map. Altitudes above 1,000ft (305m) are needed to provide the correct 'grazing angle' for the radar beam to return signals of sufficient strength to provide the required resolution. While mapping of targets as far away as 160mi (260km) can be achieved, the highest resolution is obtainable at shorter ranges. For synthetic aperture to yield results the radar has to be 'looking at' a mapping area at least 10 degrees off the aircraft's direction of travel.

LANTIRN is packed in two independent pods mounted on pylons beneath the F-15E's intakes. The AAQ-13 Navigation Pod (6.5ft (2m) long × 1ft (30cm) in diameter) is mated to the starboard pylon and has two main sections. The larger area is occupied by a Ku-band terrain avoidance/following radar manufactured by Texas Instruments. Its narrow-beamwidth antenna is housed in a small radome and integrated with a receiver/exciter unit, power supply and an interface with the APG-70. The test versions of the pod supplied terrain-avoidance cues onto the Kaiser HUD and the WSO's MFDs, but production models offer fully automatic TFR commands to the F-15E's flying controls and throttles. Minimum

altitudes down to 200ft (60m) for 'hands off' flight can be set (as in the F-111). AAQ-13 also contains a FLIR for night/poor weather that projects an IR image of the terrain ahead onto the HUD. Essentially, it enhances the view ahead sufficiently to allow the pilot to fly 'heads up' at low altitude without recourse to radar and its consequent tell-tale emissions. AAQ-13 completed its OT&E phase in December 1984 and entered full production in November 1986 with USAF deliveries beginning on 31 March 1987.

Under the port intake hangs the AAQ-14 Targeting Pod. Slightly larger (98.5in (250cm) × 15in (38cm)) and heavier at 542lb (246kg) than the AAQ-13. This attack sensor pod is in some ways a smaller version of the AN/AVQ-26 Pave Tack pod. Its nose-mounted sensor turret houses an 8.1in (20.6cm) aperture, high-resolution FLIR that has variable magnification for long-range target acquisition, shorter-range target detection and tracking (at a 6 × 6 degrees view) or closer-range target selection at 1.7 × 1.7 degrees vision. Alongside it, is a laser to designate for LGBs (in coded pulses) or to give accurate rangefinding for conventional munitions. It can also provide automatic lock-on for AGM-65D Maverick IIR missiles. AAQ-14 entered production in 1990. Both pods can also be used on the F-16C/D with minor interface alterations.

The AEDC wind-tunnel tested over 500 aircraft/ stores configurations for the F-15E under the SEEK EAGLE weapons certification programme from 1985 onwards. Arnold Engineering Development Centre

taking a chunk out of the Number 1 (forward) fuel tank. The consequent 330lb/ 51gal decrease in view of the total fuel load of 5,295gal with CFTs and three tanks is insignificant.

More radical restructuring took place in the rear fuselage that was completely redesigned to accommodate either the P&W F100-PW-220 or the GE F110-GE-100 in case a re-engining programme could be initiated. Advances in moulding titanium alloy, a notoriously difficult and costly material in its previous applications, allowed more complex structures to be moulded so that the required numbers of components and fasteners were much reduced, saving weight and money. As MSgt Bettig, at Lakenheath's F-15 Phase Maintenance area pointed out:

> The engine bay is built for ease of maintenance, unlike the F-4 where it could take three days to do a motor change. This one is set up with a clean bay that has no built-in fire-retarding foam and is easy to inspect and access. A good team can change a motor in four to six hours. The thin titanium engine bay doors weigh a half to two-thirds those on an F-4 that used to take two people to lower them.

In 1984 it seemed that the F110 might be specified for 'Strike Eagle', in view of the F100's continued stall/stagnation problems, as it had been for the Grumman F-14B/D Tomcat. In fact all F-15s apart from an F110 testbed (87-0180) have used the Pratt and Whitney engine.

A further engine variant was introduced with the F100-PW-229 that was used in production F-15Es from August 1991 onwards, aircraft 90-0233 being the first recipient. Known as the Improved Performance Engine the -229 took maximum afterburning thrust up to 29,100lb (13,200kg) compared with 23,450lb (10,637kg) for the 'tuned down' -220. Its improved digital engine control unit

The *Silver Eagles* CO's aircraft releases a deadly dozen Mk 82s in June 1989 using its AN/APG-70 radar in place of the scarce LANTIRN pods. Boeing/McDonnell Douglas

A CFT awaits hanging on a 4th TFW F-15E-43-M Con 16 October 1998 at Seymour Johnson AFB. Norm Taylor

(DECU) permits much faster throttle response; around 4sec from idle speed to maximum thrust. There is better reliability and some improvement in fuel economy. Engine shop technicians have lost work, but not sleep, over the fact that the -229 is a self-trimming powerplant and doesn't require the lengthy 'trim runs' of its predecessors to adjust it to its optimum performance.

Prior to the decision to put the F-15E into production there was a final, competitive stage in the process as the USAF launched its 1982 Dual Role Fighter (DRF) competition. The main opposition came from General Dynamics' F-16XL supersonic cruise and manoeuvring prototype (SCAMP), although the Panavia Tornado was also considered. Lack of air-to-air capability and the political disadvantages of its European origins ruled out the Tornado, but the GD proposal was more attractive. Two F-16XL prototypes were built, a single-seater (that would have become the F-16E in production) and a two-seater (F-16F), using a radically cranked arrow-shaped wing and an extended F-16 fuselage to give the aircraft increased speed, weapons load (15,000lb (6,804kg) total) and improved manoeuvring. The USAF ran its DRF evaluation until May 1983 and the F-15E was declared

the winner on 24 February 1984, relegating the F-16XLs to NASA research work.

Among the deciding factors were the cheaper development costs of the F-15E, using a proven, low-risk design, and its greater growth potential. With the prospect of an order for 400 aircraft McDonnell Douglas started work on three aircraft in July 1985, flying the first (86-0183) on 11 December 1986 with McAir test pilot Gary L. Jennings at the helm. 'E001' wore the Gunship Grey (FS36114) colour scheme of all subsequent F-15Es but it retained the rear fuselage structure of earlier F-15s. The second aircraft (86-0184) introduced these engineering changes. 86-0185 was the first definitive production 'Mud Hen' airframe; 86-0186 with full production configuration and F100-PW-220 engines was the first to be delivered to the USAF when it reached the 33rd TFW at Eglin AFB in August 1986 for trials.

Luke AFB received the first squadron aircraft; 86-0186 and 86-0187 that joined Lt Col Trotter's 461st TFS *Deadly Jesters* with the 405th TTW from 18 July 1988. Formed from the 4461st CCTS in 1997 the squadron had flown the F-15A/B and then the F-15D from January 1983. It was joined as an F-15E training unit by the

550th TFTS, whose F-15Es began to show up on 12 May 1989 and the 426th TFTS that trained Eagle crews from 1 January 1981 until 29 November 1990. The 555th TFTS *Triple Nickel* also converted to the F-15E towards the end of 1992, but by that time the 405th TTW, established with Col Chuck Horner as its CO, had been redesignated the 58th FW within the 19th AF Air Education and Training Command. A further reorganization on 1 April 1994 renamed the Wing as the 56th FW with two fighter squadrons, the 461st FS and 550th FS, the 555th TFTS having disbanded on that date. However, the 461st FS only survived until 4 August 1994 leaving the 550th to close out F-15E training at Luke in March 1995. From then on all F-15E instruction passed to the 333rd FS within the big F-15E Wing, the 4th FW at Seymour Johnson AFB.

F-15Es were at first in quite short supply, partly because of budgetary cuts. The first large batch of forty-eight, ordered in FY87, was reduced by six and then matched by another forty-two in FY88. There was growing pressure to limit or even cancel further production in order to preserve funds for other, more costly Air Force projects and thirty-six F-15Es, ordered for FY89, were

The front 'office' of F-15E 87-0184 /LF on display at Daytona in November 1993 – a very different configuration from earlier 'steam gauge' Eagles.
John Gourley

(Below right) **An F-15E crew's cockpit imagery at night. The width of the Kaiser holographic HUD and the clarity of the FLIR imagery on the rear MFDs are particularly impressive. On the right central unit is a synthetic aperture radar (SAR) 'patch' map, used for targeting.** Boeing/ McDonnell Douglas

cancelled only to be reinstated when funds were forced back into the programme. By March 1989 TAC had received only sixteen aircraft for training purposes.

Equipment of the first operational Wing, the 4th TFW, began on 29 December 1988 when Seymour Johnson's long-serving F-4E Phantoms started to move out. Like the 1st TFW the Wing had an illustrious past with its Second World War RAF *Eagle* Squadron, a score of 502 enemy aircraft in the Korean War and long experience with the F-105 and F-4. Its first F-15E, *Spirit of Goldsboro* began the transition process for the 336th TFS *Rocketeers*, leading to IOC at the beginning of October 1989 with twenty-four F-15Es. Former F-4 crews were delighted with their new aircrafts' performance, revelling in the ability to accelerate in a climb, unlike the F-4 that began to lose speed as soon as the stick was pulled back. The F-15 was virtually 'unspinnable' unless it had a serious cg problem through fuel imbalance and it had suffered very few accidents (4.7 per 100,000hr up to 1980) or equipment failures, because of its multiple redundant systems.

Like all F-15s the Strike Eagle/F-15E had two independent flight control systems. Primary control is a triple-redundant fly-by-wire system, used for the first time in an American fighter. It can automatically adjust to compensate partially for a lost or damaged control surface and it automatically varies control stick pressures to allow for the speed of the aircraft. The second, independent back-up control system is conventional, mechanical and uses hydraulic actuators on each control surface. In the F-15E the cg is a little further forward than in previous Eagles requiring an adjustment to pitch authority. Either system will fly the Eagle, though the two normally work together. Hydraulic systems are tripled for extra safety. With the loss of either PC (power control) hydraulic system plus all electrical power and utility hydraulics, control could be maintained using the tailerons for pitch (together) and roll (differentially), assuming that one rudder and one aileron could still operate. Loss of PC-1 and PC-2 hydraulics left the utility hydraulic system to power all primary flight controls. Loss of the mechanical control system meant that the control augmentation system directed the aircraft in flight, using rudders and tailerons only. Secondary flying controls, the electric flaps and hydraulic airbrake, would also be available if their respective systems were intact. A hydraulic system also controlled the aircraft's three-ramp air intakes.

The *Rocketeers'* entry to the TAC Gunnery Competition, *Long Rifle VI* at Davis Monthan in June 1990 earned them first place, with second position going to the F-15Es of the 405th TTW. Next to reach IOC at Seymour Johnson were the 335th TFS *Chiefs* on 1 October 1990 with the 334th FS *Eagles* joining them on 18 June 1991. The 333rd FS Lancers moved in from Davis Monthan AFB, where it had flown A-10As, to take over as the F-15E training squadron, an evolution that was completed by November 1994 With eighteen aircraft it provided a basic seven-month course for new pilots and WSOs with a variety of short courses to bring experienced crews up to speed.

Seymour Johnson's Eagle flyers practised ordnance delivery, when trainee WSOs could learn their trade on the limited number of LANTIRN pods that were initially available. At $3.2m each in 1996 values, roughly the price of a complete jet fighter twenty years previously, each AAQ-14 targeting pod became a major funding item. A syllabus was established in time to prepare the 4th TFW for Operation *Desert Shield*, for which the *Rocketeers* (or *Rockets* as they are more commonly known) and *Chiefs* were required to deploy within a very short time of completing transition to their new aircraft. By late 1994 an established training regime was in place at the North Carolina base. Although the new Eagle had earned the nicknames 'Beagle' and 'Mud Hen' in recognition of its terrain altering habits, almost half of the twenty-five daily sorties from the base concentrated on refining air-to-air skills. Night sorties accounted for a substantial proportion also, with at least two multi-aircraft launches per night, while WSOs tended to average more flight time than pilots on the bombing range schedules. Crews trained hard, usually averaging far more than their statutory minimum of night flights per month.

Air-to-air training usually involved either two-ship or four-ship formations running intercepts on each other (2 vs 2 in the case of a four-ship) and then practising basic fighter manoeuvres (BFM). Much of this was by day but some night engagements were specified. One variation involved a pair of Eagles flying a night attack profile with the other two flying solo intercept tactics on them during a mission of about ninety minutes including half an hour on the

An AN/AAQ-13 navigation pod on a 57th FW F-15E's pylon. The flat FLIR window is above the TFR radome. via A. Thornborough

LANTIRN pods, three external tanks and CFTs already make a formidable load for this 492nd FS F-15E before any offensive ordnance is hung. Norm Taylor

range. Air-to-ground training took place over the Dare County bombing range in fairly brief sorties of around a hundred minutes, using practice bombs, or off-range sorties on north-westerly routes into the Appalachian Mountains to do TFR and radar navigation training over some more challenging terrain. Range 'blocks' required booking well in advance and the slots were usually taken by four-ship clients. Off-range flights required more planning, with WSOs tackling the programming of their weapons release patterns, radar offset locations, routes and IFF codes for their APX-101 system. In the air the WSO relied heavily on his tactical situation display (TSD)/moving map on the right-hand screen of the four at his disposal.

Mission preparation for an off-range sortie would take around three hours, often during the day before the flight. Suiting up for the crew involved donning the flame-resistant Nomex CWU-27/P flying suit and CWU-36/P overjacket. Overwater flights required a waterproof 'poopy suit' and self-inflating life preserver in place of the overjacket. On top of this went a g-suit with parachute harness. Fire-resistant GS/FRP Nomex gloves and a sweat-absorbing skull cap to go beneath the helmet completed the sartorial exercise, though the lightweight HGU-55 helmet, individually shaped for comfort and MBU-12/P oxygen mask needed carrying to the aircraft with the other essential support equipment about fifteen minutes before take-off.

Having completed the usual walk-around checks and climbed the ten feet to the cockpit to strap in and set up their cockpits the crew initiated engine start using the batteryless jet fuel starter (JFS). This was triggered by pulling a black handle on the pilot's lower front panel and powered up by hydraulic accumulators. The JFS could start either left or right engine first, though 'right first' is usual, disengaging when the second engine reached half speed. Power flowed from the JFS to the F100 engine when the pilot raised a finger-lift lever on the front of each throttle. As each engine fired up, its 'nodding' intake ramp sequenced automatically to the 'down' position while inlet temperature and rpm were monitored. Cockpit CRTs would then be switched on, BIT would then be

(Above) With a travel pod proudly bearing the inscription 'Seymour Johnson AFB, North Carolina' the 334th TFS *Eagles* CO's F-15E (89-0491) is towed out at London IAP, Ontario on 5 June 1995.
Norm Taylor

A bomb-laden 48th FW F-15E leaves Aviano AB on an *Allied Force* mission in 1999. USAF

run, the INS aligned, canopy lowered and air conditioning started. In the rear seat the WSO pre-flighted his cockpit, setting or checking radio frequencies, TACAN, EW and countermeasures switches, oxygen regulator and a series of circuit breakers. With checks of flying controls completed, including the speed brake, the Crew Chief disconnected his headset communication that was plugged into the fuel-flow/bleed air/ temperature BIT panel that hinged down beneath the left intake.

Despite its enormous external stores capacity the F-15E preserves the essentially curvaceous appeal of the Eagle species when seen from above. USAF

The F-15E could then be cleared to taxi out, powered along by the idle thrust of its engines. At the 'last chance' pit, its missile seeker head safety covers were pulled off, armament checks completed and a thorough scan would be made for any leaks of fuel or hydraulic fluids. Rolling on to the main runway the pair of Eagles took up position, probably with a second pair waiting 500ft behind them, the flight leader gave the 'wind up' signal with his finger and engines would be advanced to 80 per cent power, though 90 per cent was possible without tyre creep. At a nod from the leader, throttles were advanced to full power, a process unimpeded by detents on the throttle controls as afterburners cut in after brake release. With serrated tongues of flame, orange for the F100-220 engine, 'gas flame blue' for the -229, the aircraft quickly reached rotation speed that could be a little over 100kt for the F-15E. Lift-off occurred within about 1,200ft (366m) of runway at training sortie weights and

another nod from the flight signalled gear and flaps up before gear-door speed limits were reached at around 300kt. At 100ft (30m) altitude the duo held a 10 to 15 degree climb with afterburner out and a speed of about 350kt, aiming for a cruise altitude of 20,000ft (6,100m) at 325kt.

In a dire emergency at any time from engine start, the ACES II ejection seats could be fired to escape from the $50m aircraft. Three options were possible: the NORMAL setting allowed the frontseater to eject both occupants, with WSO first; SOLO fired one seat only and AFT INITIATE gave the WSO control over both seats. Although landing an F-15 from the rear cockpit was theoretically possible if the pilot was incapacitated, the high angle of attack on landing made forward visibility marginal from the rear seat making ejection a tempting alternative. Each seat-firing handle had a snap-down cover to prevent accidental firing and the seat had an added metal frame with a canopy

piercing spike to allow ejection through the canopy as a last resort.

During the cruise to the target area at medium altitude, the WSO would be occupied in updating the computer's mission data with new navigation inputs that would have been loaded from the planning computer back at base onto a 32k data transfer module (DTM). This cartridge was then slid into an input slot as part of the pre-flight, thereby programming the aircraft for its mission. Also he would be preparing to let the INS check the actual location, relative to the aircraft's position of the chosen radar offset points for use in the target approach phase, against the required offset points as they had been fed in by the WSO. Any adjustments would then be effected to make the two locations coincide exactly. Using the hand controller situated on the left of his 'work area' he could access the INS and put moving map data on one of the colour MFDs. The hand controller on the right side called up

FLIR, radar or weapons information. Between them the two controllers gave a range of eighteen control options and the data they summoned could be 'layered' on the MFDs so that a WSO could rapidly flick or scroll from option to option depending on the type of display or data he required at that moment. Additionally he would be alert to threats from the air or ground, relying on the TEWS and his own eyes. During high-g manoeuvres he could grab the grip bar ('sissy bar') across the top of his instrument panel to provide extra leverage for turning around to 'check six'.

The primary means of identifying the target would be the APG-70 returns, giving accuracy in the order of 10ft (3m) at 20mi (32km). Alternatively, the imagery provided by the AAQ-14 FLIR turret could be used with a similar degree of accuracy though it could be degraded by rain or fog. Its field of view would also be narrower than the FLIR in the AAQ-13 navigation pod. The targeting pod's laser could also be fired to measure a precise range to a set feature on the ground as a means of updating the INS. During the attack the laser could give 'boresight' ranging for the release of 'dumb' ordnance too. For training flights the laser could be 'turned down' to a low-intensity setting to prevent injury to those on the ground, but its use was generally

avoided except over barren range areas.

Using the various navigation updates the WSO would make his radar map of the target area using the APG-70's real beam radar (RBM) mode from about 25nm out. Because mapping cannot be done with the target at the aircraft's 12 o'clock position the pilot would angle the aircraft at about 35 degrees to the target giving the APG-70 an adequate degree of Doppler 'shift' to make an accurate map. From this a smaller, more detailed photo-quality map of the immediate target area was 'frozen' for targeting purposes and the radar could then revert to air-to-air mode in order to cope with fighter threats. Closing to the target, the WSO placed crosshairs over the selected impact point on the radar map and designated it with a click of a switch, moving to AAQ-14 FLIR for an image of the target that could be viewed at various magnifications. He would then put the pod into 'tracking' mode and operate its laser to give a final 'range to target', refining his aim point so that the target could be redesignated even more exactly, usually for PGMs. In the pilot's HUD, precise steering cues would appear, taking him to the weapons release point.

After bombs were 'pickled' off, the WSO's job was to keep the crosshairs on target in his targeting IR display and fire the laser again to provide the LGBs with

coded data that took them to impact point. Although F-15E crews normally opt to deliver ordnance from medium altitude the AAQ-14, in its later forms, can operate at altitudes up to 40,000ft (12,200m). Earlier variants were limited to 25,000ft (7,620m) by minor electrical arcing problems.

On daylight range practice the 4th TFW Eagles usually flew their target approaches at around 500kt in tactical spread (line abreast with about 6,000ft (1,830m) separation), pushing up to 550kt as the initial point (IP) approached.

Attack profiles would be adapted for the type of target and for the ordnance that was being delivered or simulated. Eagles practised dive, level and loft delivery of weapons, usually approaching and egressing the target at a set TFR altitude. Weapons release was sequenced by the aircraft's programmable armament control system (PACS) and its associated intervalometer. Release point was decided by the weapons computer, the crew's press on the pickle button serving only to tell the computer to release when it detected the correct parameters. For a range sortie, scoring of the drop would be done by a television optical scoring system (TOSS) and all the weapons release data were stored in the computer, ready for the WSO to retrieve them at the end of the sortie for the debrief.

(Left) Eerily lit by his HUD this Mud Hen pilot starts to run cockpit checks on his jet. USAF

An F-15 take-off is invariably a memorable sight and sound. This Mud Hen blasts off from Aviano with a GBU-28B/B 'Deep Throat' penetration weapon on its centreline rack. USAF

(Above) Pair o' Dice F-15Es lined up for a practice mission with concrete 'blue ballute' bombs ready for loading. Author's Collection

Two Seymour Johnson F-15Es, the nearer one loaded with twelve Mk 82 LDGPs. USAF

(Below) An AIM-9M and an SUU-20B/A practice bomb dispenser on an F-15E. The SUU-20 has its own intervalometer to select bomb release patterns and it can be adapted to fire rockets, though this function is not usually used on F-15s. Andy Evans

After a number of passes at the range the Eagle crews looked each others' aircraft over to check for hung ordnance, though PACS would indicate this condition too. On the return from the range slot pilots often handed over the aircraft to the WSO so that he could get in a little 'stick' time. Within 10mi (16km) of Seymour Johnson crews requested an approach to landing, reducing speed to 300kt to join the 'pattern', rolling out for final approach at 250kt and dropping undercarriage and flaps for touchdown at around 20 degrees aoa.

While the 4th TFW continued to establish the F-15E as an operational combat type other units began to absorb the batches of aircraft that Congress funded; thirty-six in each of Fiscal Years from FY 89 to FY 91, adding to the ninety-two already ordered up

(Above) Rocketeers F-15E 87-0198 with a pair of SUU20B/As underwing and the bombs' safety tags fluttering from them. USAF

The crew of F-15E 90-0262 disembark after an *Allied Force* mission. Crew names were erased from the panel below the cockpit during the campaign. USAF

(Left) As Luke AFB's role shifted towards F-16 training the base code changed to 'LF' (Luke Falcon), leaving the *Silver Eagles* to wind up Strike Eagle training and transfer the task to the 333rd FS at Seymour Johnson. API

(Below) F-15E 90-0246 of the 90th FS at Elmendorf AFB lines up for take-off with four AAMs and a pair of travel pods. API

(Above) A WSO's view of the UK from an F-15E at low altitude. Dev Basudev

(Below) Practice Mk82s occupy the CFT hardpoints on a *Rocketeers* F-15E as it cruises to a range session. USAF

(Top) Capt Mark 'Bones' Wetzel, a Flight Commander/WSO with the 334th FS Eagles, checks an AIM-9M on his aircraft before climbing aboard. Andy Evans

(Above) Desert Storm veteran Mark Wetzel discusses the mission plan with pilot Capt Freddy Buttrell (centre) and wingman Capt Carson Berry (right). Andy Evans

to FY 88 in Lots I to III. At Clark AFB in the Philippines the 90th TFS *Pair o' Dice*, 3rd TFW was scheduled to turn in its 'PN' coded F-4s in October 1990 and convert to the F-15E. A combination of political exigencies, hastened by the eruption of the volcanic Mount Pinatubo, obliged the Wing to leave the base and relocate at Elmendorf AFB, Alaska where the 21st TFW effectively became the 3rd TFW on 19 December 1991. The 90th TFS had been officially acquired by this Wing on 29 May 1990 and

In 1992 the 366th Wing included the 391st FS *Tigers* as its F-15E squadron and the 390th FS with F-15C/Ds in a Composite Wing at Mountain Home AFB. Boeing/McDonnell Douglas

proceeded with F-15E transition at Seymour Johnson AFB. The squadron's first F-15E (90-0233) was taken aboard at the end of September 1991.

Former F-4 crews joined with others from F-111s, A-10As and even F-15Cs as *Dicemen* in learning to ride the squadron's twenty F-15Es and adapting to the aircraft's advanced missionized cockpits. The standard practice on arrival at Elmendorf was to train up a new pilot with an experienced WSO, or vice versa, and then pair up trained crews who would tend to stay together in the squadron. Unlike their previous two-seat aircraft many of the cockpit routines in the F-15E could be shared or performed from either front or rear cockpit, requiring a type of teamwork that tended to break down the specialist roles to which two-seat crews had been accustomed. Like the F-15C squadrons at the Alaskan base the *Dicemen* trained for air-to-air as well as ordnance delivery. They could expect to launch at least one live missile during a tour with the squadron and drop live ordnance up to five times on range sorties or at exercises such as *Cope Thunder*, *Red Flag* or *Northern Edge*. Gun practice meant firing out the 450 rounds of M51 target practice 20mm, or the later PGU-27 rounds. Ammunition had to be reduced from the 940 rounds in the F-15A/C to accommodate elements of the AN/ALQ-135 internal countermeasures set. The original cylindrical

ammunition container was replaced by a smaller, box-like structure using a linkless feed system with a hydraulic drive for the M61A1 gun. The new installation required a bulge in the underfuselage panel directly below the ammunition box. Despite its reduced ammunition capacity, F-15E crews still rate the gun for air-to-air engagements. Col Mike Casey of the 48th FW explained:

You need the gun for close-in fighting. I've just shot my 'heater' [AIM-9] and it missed. I've got another heater, and that misses. Then I've got to use the gun. BVR missiles have a minimum range. Once you are inside that and out of AIM-9s your only option is to 'go gun'.

Despite the move to a colder climate the *Dicemen* retained their PACAF commitment with the 3rd Wing. In July 1992 they were part of a twelve-aircraft detachment that visited Luke AFB for the PACAF-originated Exercise *Tandem Thrust*. Nine from the 90th FS were at the September 1992 *Red Flag* and five returned to Nellis the following autumn for *Gunsmoke*. More recently, in addition to its regular deployments in support of *Deny Flight* and *Provide Comfort* in the wake of the Gulf War the squadron sent eighteen F-15Es to Kwang Ju AB in South Korea. This deployment, in May 1999 was intended to reaffirm the US commitment to preserving peace in the area and it required the 3rd Air

Expeditionary Wing to be established at Kwang Ju as the support organization.

F-15Es became part of the first USAF Composite Wing, the 366th Wg at Mountain Home AFB when it was established in March 1992. Alongside a squadron of JTIDS-equipped, late-production F-15Cs (the 390th FS), the 391st FS *Bold Tigers*, formerly an F-111 unit, transitioned to the E-model from February 1992 to operate with the 389th FS's F-16CS, 34th BS B-1B Lancers and the KC-135R tankers of the 22nd ARS. *Tigers* aircraft took part in the Wing's first overseas deployment to Egypt in 1993 for the three-week Operation *Bright Star* and flew with the Composite Wing in Canada for a 1995 exercise. Twenty-four Eagles flew with Egyptian and other USAF aircraft for *Bright Star* and the Exercise was repeated in 1996. Deployments to *Green Flag* and *Red Flag* events in 1994/95 involved eighteen Eagles, both C and E models, with a couple of F-15Ds included. Six F-15Es plus six F-15Cs and a number of F-16Cs attended Exercise *Northern Edge '94* in Alaska and a large deployment of twenty-one aircraft was readied for the abortive *Coalition Flag* exercise at Nellis in summer 1995. In that year the 391st became the only F-15E unit to be equipped with the AGM-65G IR Maverick missile.

F-15E had been designed with USAFE operations particularly in mind and the 48th FW *Liberty Wing* at RAF Lakenheath was the obvious Wing to take on the new Eagle. With the F-111F the 48th had amassed an impressive record of success and expertise in night interdiction and strike missions including combat over Libya and Iraq. With its final, digital *Pacer Strike* avionics updates and a well-tuned *Pave Tack* pod the F-111F was a hard act to follow – 'the ultimate PGM machine' in the view of Capt Dev Basudev. However, in transitioning from it to the F-15E he found the new aircraft 'superior in handling in all regimes except for low-level ride, where the F-111 was extremely stable and smooth'. Those who came to the F-15E with experience of *Pave Tack* found LANTIRN offered many advantages. Col Mike Casey flew *Pave Tack* on Seymour Johnson F-4Es and with the 3rd TFW at Clark AFB:

There was no comparison with what we have now with LANTIRN. The field of vision is much larger with the targeting pod. It has the ability to go to a narrow or wide field that we didn't have with *Pave Tack*. The imagery is much better since you can focus it and adjust all the shades.

Alaska-based Eagles have to operate in severe climatic conditions. F-15E 90-0250 was assigned to Capt Ian Thompson and WSO Capt Mark Houtzer. Andy Evans

In its defence, Dev Basudev observed that, 'the USAF didn't fund any improvements in the *Pave Tack* that would have given it the automatic hold point tracker/area tracker that LANTIRN has'.

Lakenheath accepted its first F-15E (90-0248, appropriately) on 21 February 1992 and it remained in use as the 'Wing' aircraft until late 1999 when it was replaced by 97-0218, one of five Block 61 attrition replacements. The aircraft flew as Duster 21 direct from St Louis with 48th FW CO Col Mike Guth in the rear seat though its departure had been delayed by a week due to equipment problems. Based F-111Fs had begun to return to the USA for use by the 27th FW and the last was away by 18 December by which time there were thirty-one F-15Es on strength with the 492nd and 494th Fighter Squadrons. The 493rd FS *Grim Reapers* disestablished at the end of 1992 and moved to the 27th FW only to re-establish at Lakenheath with F-15Cs in November 1994. Initially, it was planned to transfer the 22nd FS intact from Bitburg when the parent 36th FW closed down, or even to relocate the 32nd FS from Soesterberg. In practice, the 493rd FS nameplate reappeared and F-15C/Ds from Eglin AFB, led in by 86-0164 and 86-0182, began to arrive on 15 November 1994 with twenty-one on charge by the following May.

The two F-15E units reached IOC by the end of 1992, the 492nd FS *Bolars* (or *Bowlers*) on 20 April and the 494th FS *Panthers* on 13 August. The Lakenheath F-15 squadrons soon became some of the hardest-worked units in the USAF and that situation has remained ever since. In taking over from the F-111 they inherited the nuclear weapons mission that had been the Aardvark's basic *raison d'être* within NATO and that had made it a vital element in the Strategic Arms Limitation Talks (SALT). As their ultimate mission F-15Es would have carried the 3,000lb (1,360kg) B61 nuclear device and typically would have borne a pair of low-yield (5-20 kiloton) bombs, one per CFT, for toss or

Pre-flight preparation of F-15E 90-0494 of the 334th FS. Andy Evans

parachute-retarded delivery. With the collapse of the immediate Soviet threat this mission was removed from USAFE's tasking and the last nuclear weapons left Lakenheath in December 1996.

For conventional weapons delivery 48th FW crews trained for the HVA (high value asset) strike as a priority, honing their sophisticated attack systems for potential command and communications, airfield, bridge and other key targets that would have been tackled at night. Battlefield air interdiction (BAI) was also high on the menu. Crews were also trained for SEAD against hostile radar, missile and AAA installations and to a lesser extent close air support (CAS), though aircraft like the F-16 were more likely to take on these tasks. For SEAD, the F-15E was made compatible with the AGM-88A HARM anti-radiation missile but was unlikely to use it, this specialized 'Weasel' role having passed in USAFE to the F-16CJ-50s of the 52nd FW at Spangdahlem. In any case, as Capt Herman Shirg pointed out, 'It wouldn't make sense to take a deep penetration interdiction fighter as capable as the F-15E and make a Weasel out of it'. In the BAI or CAS roles conventional Mk 80 series bombs, SUU-30H cluster munitions dispensers or possibly AGM-65 Mavericks on LAU-88 triple-round launchers would be brought to bear upon armour and troop concentrations, supply chokepoints or stores dumps.

Lakenheath's 'Mud Hens' settled into the training routines established by the F-111 flyers, roaring through Scottish and Welsh low-level routes in all kinds of weather. In 1992 they even caught the last of the 'mass launch' *Hammer* Exercises (that USAFE mounted as a show of might for the Warpac satellite cameras) when the 48th launched to accompany twenty of Upper Heyford's F-111Es. However, the Lakenheath contingent amounted to eight aircraft rather than the squadron-sized performance of previous years. Training sorties with ordnance more typically took two or four F-15Es to ranges around The Wash, Wainfleet, Donna Nook, Holbeach or Tain in Scotland, depending on availability. They dropped BDU-33 practice bombs on some of these but actual 'pig iron' wasn't really necessary as the aircraft's computer can simulate drop parameters for all the ordnance in the F-15's armoury. On longer-range sorties the emphasis was on high-speed, low-level penetration, weaving through the valleys on TFR to a meticulously timed mission plan that would have

been established twenty-four hours in advance. Flights could be scheduled as air-to-air, air-to-ground or as attack sorties on which crews would have to fight through 'hostile' air opposition to reach their target. A detailed flight plan was composed about four hours before take-off using routes and waypoints downloaded from the computerized map projector in the squadron ops room onto the WSO's DTM cartridge. Absolutely accurate planning and timing were vital for the potentially hazardous terrain-following routes through training areas where other NATO jets would also be at work. The thoroughness of this procedure was reflected in the fact that, at the time of writing, the *Liberty Wing* had lost no F-15Es in flying accidents since the delivery of its first Eagle in 1992, despite many detachments to 'hot' combat situations from Italy and Turkey, *Red Flag* visits and the day-to-day risks of the UK's complex and crowded airways.

Mastery of the HOTAS cockpit is crucial to all F-15 training. As Mike Casey explained:

Guys go through the 'school house' of F-15 RTU and that's where they learn it. They do it with simulators and CBITS (computer based integrated training systems) and that's where they get used to HOTAS. Then they go out in the air for about eighty-five hours' flying time to get used to HOTAS, either for air-to-air or air-to-ground. It takes about 150 hours in the airplane before they feel really comfortable with it. Air-

to-air is the most challenging, with all its different missile envelopes and acquisition modes and they need to master these quickly or they're not going to make it through the programme.

Herman Shirg added:

It becomes a second-nature reflex action. Once you get it down, that's what makes it an air superiority system compared with some of the Soviet systems. If you go out there and do a lot of air-to-ground [the Kosovo crisis compelled F-15E units to do this for around six months] and then you get back to training for air-to-air you almost have to learn air-to-air again and get the memory back in there.

Among the other cockpit innovations many F-15E crews value the TSD (tactical situation display) in particular. To Mike Casey:

It's worth its weight in gold. Basically it gives you your entire scenario and it's a large SA [situational awareness] builder. Its circles and lines show an intel assessment of where the threats are. Other circles show the targets and IPs, or a confliction problem (there may be some bombs going off over there, so I avoid that). If you lock up a bad guy [on radar] he's going to be projected on the TSD as well as a red symbol. In the old days in the F-4 all we had was a bullseye map and the only SA was based on what was going on out there. Then you had to know where you were at that time and compute on that.

Like other Eagles, F-15Es inhabit hardened shelters whenever possible. 90th FS 90-0251 pokes its beak from the relative warmth of an Elmendorf HAS. Yellow floor-lines coincide with the Eagle's narrrow-track undercarriage for entry and exit from the HAS without damage. via A. Thornborough

Generally, the multifunction display (MFD) cockpit philosophy lightens the workload. For example, the aircraft's engine monitoring display system (EMDS) presents information on engine status and performance that can be called up on a single MFD whereas pilots of earlier jets would have had to monitor a dozen 'steam gauges' for the same data.

Further assistance to the F-15E crew as they 'fly the contours' at low altitude with a heavy load aboard comes from the third person in the cockpit; 'Bitchin' Betty', the recorded aural warning to the crew that they were overloading the aircraft with 'g'. If a 'g' overload approached:

F-15E 96-0202, the second of the 'E210' batch of attrition aircraft, over Wales on a training sortie. Dev Basudev

> … you get beeps. First a single-rate beeper, then a double-rate beeper, then Bitchin' Betty. By the time she comes on it's too late. It's easy to

A production Lot II F-15E, 87-0194 returns from another 550th FS training mission from Luke AFB. via A. Thornborough

'pull' through the warning beepers and get Betty right away. Overload can be more a function of airspeed than weight. As you approach anything over 0.92 Mach you have to be careful with the amount of 'g' you pull. It's all displayed in the cockpit; it will say, 'You're a 9g airplane right now', and as you increase your speed above 0.92, if you're fairly heavy, then you'll see the 'g' envelope shrink. It'll say, for example, 'You can only pull 7g now'.

At Lakenheath in late 1999 a typical training sortie occupied an eight-hour working day for an F-15E crew, including the briefing, stepping out to the aircraft, flying the sortie, debriefing the maintenance people after landing and then debriefing the other participants in the mission. Anticipating a

sortie that he was due to fly later that day Herman Shirg explained:

> We are the bandits for another two-ship on a low-level attack. We're going to attack them as they are attacking their target. It's also an upgrade ride for the flight leader in the other two-ship. We get together four hours prior to take-off time and break up duties on the mission plan in advance of the briefing. Two hours prior to take-off we brief it up for an hour. We then get into flying gear and step out to the jets. Today's mission will be about two hours long. We will then do the maintenance debrief and a 1.5 hour debrief on the lessons learned. This happens two or three times a week. To maintain currency you only need to fly about nine times a month, but last month I flew twenty-three times.

At that time the 48th FW were catching up on their training routines after returning from Kosovo operations and flying activity was at a high pitch. A consistently busy timetable has given the two F-15E squadrons at 'The Heath' many calls within NATO in addition to their regular commitments to bases in Italy and Turkey. In December 1994, twelve aircraft visited Sidi Slimane in Morocco for Exercise *African Eagle*, while twenty made the journey to Tyndall AFB over the following three months for WTDs and eighteen attended *Red Flag*. Later in 1995 nine Eagles flew to Davis Monthan for a pre-Exercise work-up before appearing at *Gunsmoke '95* at Nellis. Meanwhile, the CO's 'Boss Bird' 90-0248 flew to Waterloof AB, South Africa for an airshow. 1996 saw deployments of six or eight Eagles at a time to Tyndall AFB, to *Green Flag* via Hill AFB and to Zaragosa in Spain and Monte Real in Portugal. Meanwhile, five aircraft attended the RAF's Qualified Weapons Instructor Course at Leuchars and ten revisited Sidi Slimane for another *African Eagle* under 16th AF control, flying air-to-air missions with Moroccan AF Mirage F.1s and Northrop F-5s. Air-to-air over the usual North Sea ACMI range was denied them at that time after a ship collided with the range's main data collection tower, putting the range out of action for several weeks.

Lakenheath aircraft took part in *Maple Flag* in April 1997, visited Karup in Denmark for the 1997 Tactical Fighter Weapons Meet and Orland, Norway for Air Meet '97. Another NATO Tactics, Discussions and Procedures Update (TDPU) took four 492nd FS Eagles to Beauvechain, Belgium in October. Range practice on the Vlieland range and Germany's Polygone electronic training range was combined with three days of composite operations. Further detachments to work with RAF Tornado units came from the 494th FS in 1998 while *Red Flag* continued to provide essential combat simulation throughout.

One of the greatest pressures on the 48th FW and other F-15E units is still the relative scarcity of aircraft. Only seventeen attrition replacements were funded through FY 1996–98 (F-15E build numbers 210-226) with deliveries scheduled to begin in 1998 but delayed to allow deliveries to Saudi Arabia and Israel. The two

hundred F-15Es in service at the end of 1999 were fighting two conflicts simultaneously in the Gulf and the Balkans, providing training on the type and fulfilling the normal operational commitments of three USAF Wings. Despite unexpectedly low attrition (nine losses up to mid-2000 including two combat losses), the Eagle force is consistently stretched and the Air Force has needed more aircraft. The need to preserve funding for high-priority projects like F-22 and B-2A has meant that the need for less glamorous items like the 'Mud Hen' has been consistently repressed within defence budget requests. It has also cut into the possibility of the superior LANTIRN 2000 system and the F110 re-engine programme, recommended for the F-15 by USAFE CinC Gen John Jumper in 1998. The cancellation of Greece's F-15H order that would have had F110 engines, was a factor in stopping the USAF version from receiving this new power-plant. In 1999 only eighty-one F-15Es had even received the -229 version of the F100. Although new-build F-15Es at $48m each were less than half the projected cost of an F-22A in 1999 dollars, they were exactly a footnote in a defence budget even when only three units were ordered, as was the case in the FY98 and FY2000 Budgets. In the latter case an option on two more to be delivered late in 2002 was also agreed, though the real USAF request was for another twenty-four F-15Es.

For Boeing there was something of a cleft stick situation. After the company mergers of the 1990s, Boeing found itself with a one-

third stake in the F-22A, a project that was already threatened with cuts or protracted development. At the same time the company had an interest in preserving the F-15 production line at St Louis and hoped for extended export orders to justify more domestic orders for the USAF, without threatening funds for projects within its other divisions. There was constant pressure from Congressmen in Missouri and Illinois who believed that the St Louis line could close within a couple of years, risking up to 5,000 jobs at the McDonnell Douglas complex. As Senator Christopher Bond put it:

> We're going to have to depend on the F-15E for the next thirty years. If the line shuts down we're not going to be able to get the replacement planes we need because of attrition. Spare parts and other equipment needed to keep the plane flying will be extremely expensive and difficult to obtain.

At St Louis on 1 April 1999, Joe Felock and Guy Clayton gave F-15E 96-0200 its first flight. It was the USAF's first new Eagle since 1993 and ten of the new FY96/97 batch were delivered to Lakenheath between September and December 1999 allowing some of the original complement to return to the USA. In mid-2000, the Wing 'owned' eighty-one F-15C/E aircraft, including five at Warner Robins for PDM. However, as the Kosovo crisis had shown, those numbers could be depleted so quickly by deployments to forward bases that Eagles from other units had to be brought in to keep an F-15 presence in the UK.

F-15E 90-0250 surrounded by ground-support equipment. Andy Evans

CHAPTER SEVEN

Desert Eagles

A 336th TFS 'Strike Eagle' in April 1990 with a CBU load-out on its CFTs. Norm Taylor Collection

thorough review would demonstrate a combat record over the arid wastes of Iraq early in 1991 that would have made its Vietnam-era predecessors sore with envy. In a little over two months F-15C Eagles deployed to bases in Saudi Arabia and Turkey nullified the advanced combat aircraft of the Iraqi Air Force and took the F-15's record of air-to-air kills to ninety-one without loss. At the same time F-15Es were unleashed on a wide range of targets with outstanding accuracy and hitting power, sustaining only two losses against some of the most heavily defended objectives in the history of air warfare.

One of the main architects of this air action, Gen Chuck Horner also drew heavily on his own combat experience. As an F-105D pilot with the 333rd TFS *Lancers* during the Thunderchief squadrons' bloodiest ordeal over North Vietnam, he well understood the cost of politically inept application of air power. He saw also how the unsuitability of US training and equipment at the time enabled VPAF MiGs to destroy so many American fighters. His energetic development of USAF Aggressor training and support for the F-15 programme prepared him for eventual command of an F-15 Wing and in due course overall command of air operations during the 1991 Gulf War. It was in this capacity that he ordered Robert Russ, CO of Tactical Air Command to send 1st TFW F-15s and half the Wing's 6,000 personnel to Saudi Arabia as tensions rose in the run-up to that conflict.

Desert Shield

Col John 'Boomer' McBroom's *First Fighter Wing* was put on alert early in June 1990 as Saddam Hussein's aggressive stance towards his Kuwaiti neighbours became more apparent. During 6–8 August, the 27th TFS and 71st TFS deployed to Dhahran, Saudi Arabia, becoming the 1st TFW (Provisional) under the jurisdiction of the 14th Air Division (P). Operation *Desert Shield*, ordered by President George Bush was under way.

There was a certain irony in the naming of the project at the Tactical Fighter Weapons Center, Nellis AFB that led to the detailed specification for the F-15. Established to develop new air tactics and weapons and to

formulate requirements for a new air superiority fighter in the light of the South-East Asia experience the study was dubbed Project *Sand Dune*. Its contributors could hardly have foreseen that the product of their

Saddam Hussein was thereby given due warning that the USA was not, as he seemed to imagine, unconcerned by his invasion on 2 August of Kuwait, a nation that had financed his war with Iran and that he claimed was a part of Iraq. Twenty-four F-15Cs and three F-15Ds from the 71st TFS *Ironmen* were prepared for their transatlantic flight from 3 August, departing as four cells of six aircraft during the afternoon of 7 August on a numbing 14.5hr flight with nine in-flight refuellings. The frequency of top-ups was to ensure that aircraft could still make landfall if a refuelling session had to be missed through poor weather or mechanical problems. The aircraft also had to be capable of responding immediately to an airborne threat when they arrived at their Saudi base so fuel and weapons had to be ready.

By the time the first pair, led by Lt Col Howard Pope, smoked onto the baking Dhahran runway there was a well-founded belief that Saddam could advance into Saudi territory with the world's fourth largest army and grab oil reserves, holding the Western world effectively to ransom. An Alert facility was set up straight away enabling F-15s to be airborne with wheels in the wells within five minutes of the bell sounding. The following day Lt Col Don Kline led twenty-five F-15C/Ds from his 27th TFS *Fighting Eagles* by the same punishing route. Like the *Ironmen* before them each cell of aircraft flew CAP over the airfield on arrival until the next cell arrived

and then landed under the protection of the next CAP at the end of the longest-ranging fighter deployment ever made. Within thirty-eight hours of the initial Alert at Langley AFB all the Eagles were standing armed and ready in the purpose-built shelters at Dhahran.

The base was already protected by the Eagles of Number 13 Squadron, Royal Saudi AF and their presence meant that the base already had 'Eagle-friendly' maintenance facilities and groundcrew, greatly facilitating the deployment. Like their USAF visitors Saudi F-15s were controlled by E-3B/C Sentry AWACS aircraft on detachment from the 522nd AWACS Wing and the Saudi AF. The latter had regularly deployed up to four of their five aircraft on 18hr border-watching patrols and worked with their own F-15s, establishing effective routines into which Langley pilots could easily integrate. USAF E-3s had actually been based at Riyadh since the early 1980s keeping an eye on oil tanker movements in the Gulf and observing air activity during the Iran-Iraq War. Their crews were familiar with the area and had assimilated useful information on Iraqi AF combat tactics during that conflict. The electronic barrier formed by the E-3s in 1990 invariably deterred probing flights towards the Saudi border by Iraqi fighters. Fearful of interception by F-15Cs or the Tornado F.3s of 29 Sqn RSAF (and in due course those of 43 and 29 Sqn RAF) they turned home, denied the chance of a peek at the steadily

increasing Coalition force build-up in Saudi territory. *Desert Shield* also gave Coalition pilots the chance to test Iraqi air defences in the same way and the response times and radar frequency signatures were studied by 55th SRW RC-135s from Riyadh and stored for future reference. The burgeoning fighter force, supplied by waves of C-5 and C-141 transports, set up a virtually impenetrable aerial blockade of CAPs along Saudi Arabia's extensive border, establishing a pattern that would occupy countless tedious hours for F-15C pilots throughout the war. Flying interminable race-track orbits as two-ship sections (later as four-ships when the threat increased) the pilots would run a 20mi (32km) leg and then fly the return route in a figure-of-eight pattern returning to base after 3hr on station when the relief aircraft showed up. Many crews found themselves flying twice a day but they could at least be reassured that their presence was deterring an Iraqi advance against a capable but small Saudi army. While on CAP there was also the chance that an Iraqi pilot might press on towards the border, even after hearing an F-15 radar lock warning in his headset and try his luck with the CAP. With this rather vain hope in mind the Langley pilots kept their BFM skills honed with some practice between CAPs. It helped to mitigate the inevitable shock of climbing out of the aircraft on return from the mission and facing temperatures of up to 135°F (57°C) – a serious problem for flyers and aircraft alike.

Chiefs F-15E-45-MC 88-1686, assigned to Vietnam veteran Lt Col Steve 'Bald Eagle' Pingel, the 335th's popular Commander. The aircraft's scoreboard records 52 *Desert Storm* missions. Norm Taylor

The Opposition

In assessing their potential adversaries the USAF pilots regarded Iraq's recently acquired MiG-29s as the most capable fighters ranged against them. Although its BVR capability was known to be much poorer than the F-15's it was a formidable fighter in the sort of close combat that had cost so many US losses in Vietnam. However, among the squadrons of Mig-21, Sukhoi Su-7 and other fighters it was

(Top) **F-15E 88-1686, marked for the** *Chiefs* **CO, at Shaw AFB on 14 March 1991 on return from the Gulf.** Norm Taylor

(Above) **4th TFW Mud Hens settled on the specially constructed Al Kharj air base. For most of the war ninety per cent of their missions were by night.** USAF

On combat air patrol over arid terrain. Unusually, AIM-120s are carried on the inner missile rails rather than outboard, indicating a 'captive carry' that will not be fired. USAF

1st TFW F-15Cs bake in the sun at Dhahran. Two squadrons from the Langley Wing were based there from August 1990 until March 1991. USAF

known that the most experienced pilots were flying the Dassault Mirage F.1Es. Their aircraft had better avionics than the earlier Russian fighters and some were Exocet missile-capable. Pilots had been taught by French instructors at Orange, France and by Jordanian instructors, all of whom imparted a greater sense of initiative than the Soviet teachers who had trained Iraq's other aircrew in the standard, rigid, ground-control-dependent techniques of the Soviet air force. After 1985, Mirage instruction had been transferred to Iraq and a number of the Mirage pilots had chalked up more than 300 combat missions during the Iran/Iraq war, though their experience of air-to-air combat was still limited. Although the more centralized Soviet approach appealed to Saddam (who had already vetted all his pilots for their loyalty to the Ba'athist Party before training them), it did little to engender a true fighter-pilot ethos and the sheer lack of flying hours allowed to the Air Force further weakened their position. General Horner's understanding of these training techniques was vital to his formulation of plans to minimize the Iraqi AF threat. By destroying its command and control systems in the opening hours of the war he effectively paralyzed the Soviet-trained fighter units. He also knew that only a third of the pilots were qualified for night or all-weather flying because of their restricted training hours. The better-trained Mirage elite was singled out for attention by F-15C air superiority fighters and 1st TFW tactics rehearsed during *Desert Shield* were calculated to tackle the Mirages as a priority. DACT training with French AF Mirage F.1s helped. From 23 December, refugee Kuwaiti AF Mirage F.1CKs also began combined air-to-air training with F-15Cs.

On paper the Iraqi AF represented a formidable threat. Reacting, like other Air Forces to the effects of Israel's pre-emptive strikes on Arab airfields during the Six-Day War of 1967 Iraq had invested a fortune in hardening its airfields. Aircraft shelters were built to higher specifications than those of NATO forces, air assets were dispersed onto many large bases and command, control and communications (C3) facilities were heavily protected. A small number of Ilyushin Il-76 'Adnan 1' AEW aircraft were about to become operational, though these were among the first to seek refuge in Iran later in the war. Many older fighters such as MiG-19s, MiG-21s and

BAe Hunters were stored in underground shelters for short-notice reuse.

From the mid-1980s the majority of USAF through programmes like *Have Idea* and *Constant Peg* (using real Soviet fighters) had concentrated on tactics against the MiG-21 and MiG-23. The latter was seen as fairly easy prey but the MiG-21's small size and great agility still conferred advantages on it. However, it had no BVR capability and the F-15's excess thrust enabled it to turn inside a MiG-21 after a two-circle turning fight. No samples of the MiG-29 were available to offer authentic training but it was obviously a more worrying opponent, handled by experienced pilots. It was known to have pulse-Doppler radar with look-down, shoot-down capability for its excellent AA-10 Alamo missiles, IRST, VTAS-type helmet sighting and a better thrust/weight ratio than most US fighters. However, the fifty aircraft supplied to Iraq had only recently arrived and pilot training was incomplete. In any case it was assumed that Saddam would keep these fighters on a fairly tight rein to defend the area around Baghdad and his presidential palaces. Thus, while the technology often matched that of the Allied air forces the training did not. F-15 pilots had concentrated hard on air-to-air tactics in the 1980s while those in the Iraqi AF were allowed very limited flying hours and their initiative was stifled in an atmosphere of fear and repression.

Building the Force

Langley pilots, continuing their CAPs and air-to-air training, were not expecting an easy ride against the Iraqis if the situation went 'hot'. They continued to monitor Iraqi fighter activity, learning more through cat and mouse games about their ECM, radar ranges and signatures. Coming within 20mi (32km) of each other at times each side would occasionally fly right up to the border. Iraqi fighters crossed it a couple of times. In case they chose to go further into Saudi airspace effective base defence tactics, using simulated airfield attack packages, were included in the Eagle pilots' routines.

Soon after they had established themselves at Dhahran, a second F-15C element was deployed to King Faisal airbase, Tabuk. Col Richard Parsons led the 58th TFS *Gorillas* from Eglin's 33rd TFW on the long haul from Florida's 'Redneck Riviera' to the remote base in north-west Saudi

With canopy open to keep the cockpit temperature below melting point, 82-0046 from the 27th TFS was among the first USAF F-15Cs to arrive at the Saudi base. USAF

Arabia at the end of August 1990. There they operated alongside the RAF Tornado GR.1 detachment and RSAF F-5Es. Twenty-four Eagles arrived, including the 'Boss Bird'; 85-0118 *Gulf Spirit* and five others wearing special fin-tip decor for that year's *William Tell* Meet – cancelled shortly after they deployed. With nearly six years of experience on the F-15C the *Gorillas* were well prepared for combat under their Commander at Eglin, Lt Col Francis 'Paco' Geisler. He had pushed his troops to a high level of combat efficiency through many visits to *Red Flag*, *Green Flag* and 'Triple A' (all aspect adversary) Counter Tactics in which his crews had regularly faced extremely realistic MiG-type opposition. Having prepared his men so effectively Geisler's career took him to another posting just before the *Desert Shield* build-up commenced. However, even the most gung-ho of his pilots could not have expected that the forthcoming battle would make the unit the top-scorers with thirteen Iraqi aircraft destroyed. No less well-honed were the *Fighting Crows* (60th TFS) who followed them to Tabuk with experience of providing fighter cover from Puerto Rico for the 1983 Operation *Urgent Fury* in Grenada and for *Just Cause* in

Panama. For the latter Operation they had taken up CAP stations near Cuba to cover the large force of US troop-carrying aircraft. Fate decreed that the squadron would score only one Iraqi fighter, while pilots from the 59th TFS *Golden Pride*, who also deployed, would down two.

Next among the 120 F-15C/Ds from the five units to deploy to the Gulf were the twenty-four F-15Cs of Lt Col Randy Bigum's 53rd TFS *Tigers* from Bitburg, who took up position at Al Kharj with the 4th Composite Wing (Provisional). Another dozen of their aircraft were passed to the Saudis, the first six arriving at Dhahran on 20 September. Like other squadrons, the Tigers rotated some pilots and maintainers from the other Bitburg squadrons through Al Kharj, the 22nd TFS being their main source. Bitburg's other Eagle squadron, the 525th TFS was allowed to fly from Incirlik, Turkey providing an air superiority element for *Proven Force* air operations over the north of Iraq. Joining them there with the 7740th Composite Wing (P) was the 32nd TFS from Soesterberg, though the 525th could not be moved to Incirlik until December 1990 and Soesterberg Eagles did not deploy until 17 January 1991 on the threshold of war. Shortly before that they had returned to the 36th TFW several aircraft borrowed in October 1990 so that the 53rd TFS could work with a standard complement of FY84 jets. Spare parts and supplies were inevitably a problem as the logistic base was expanded. A shortage of F-15 drop tanks was officially declared to be a 'limiting factor in their operations' during September. Some 536 tanks were required for a 45-day period. In action, the 58th TFS alone dropped over ninety external tanks in the first three days of *Desert Storm*, usually as a prelude to engaging enemy aircraft or evading SAM threats. F-15C wheels were scarce for a time too and their usual 24-month overhaul limit had to be extended by six months. On the eve of *Desert Storm* sixteen of the 33rd TFW's F-15Cs were found to have cracks in the leading edges of their vertical stabilizers and repair kits were urgently ordered up.

Air (Force) Superiority?

With five F-15 squadrons in place the USAF had a powerful air superiority element that was calculated to match the anticipated Iraqi fighter hordes as war inexorably approached. Their role was

exclusively to deal with the air-to-air threat, a task that they could have shared with RAF Tornado F.3s and USN F-14A /A Plus Tomcats that were also dedicated air superiority types. DACT exercises were conducted between Dhahran F-15Cs and carrier-based Tomcats on 28 September as part of the preparations. However, Chuck Horner's air plan for the opening phases of the war placed the F-15 'blade' conspicuously at the leading edge of the massive Allied air armada. Since the air campaign was US Air Force-led it was logical to keep the Air Force's dedicated air superiority machines, the F-15s, in the areas where the most Iraqi air opposition was anticipated. The Tornado lacked the AN/ASW-27 data link that enabled F-14 and F-15 to interface effectively with AWACS and with each other, minimizing the possibility of a 'blue on blue' accident. They were therefore effectively excluded from Iraqi airspace and limits to CAPs over Kuwait, and AWACS or tanker CAP missions, though they occasionally had the chance to chase Iraqi fighters off returning strike packages.

The situation of the F-14 was rather more complex. In retrospect there are several possible explanations for the decision to give it 'second fiddle' status, the most

common theory being that it was the Air Force's turn to run the fighter operation since Navy Tomcat squadrons had grabbed all the headlines in their 1980s skirmishes with Libyan fighters. In Vietnam both Navy and Air Force had been given their own geographical 'Route Packs' of target areas over which they had control of air operations. Horner rejected that idea as 'stupid' for the Gulf operation and included USN fighters on some Air Force-led strikes. In all, twelve squadrons of F-14As and thirteen squadrons of F/A-18A/C Hornets were available aboard the carriers on station. Partly, the Tomcats were restricted by their own main role as Fleet defenders, flying CAPS for their own carriers and partly also by ongoing problems with their TF30 engines in the hot climatic conditions. The severe shortage of Coalition tactical recce aircraft also took out those Tomcats that could be equipped with the excellent TARPS reconnaissance pod. When Horner's staff planned the air campaign, the initial CAP duties inside Iraq and over the borders all went to F-15 units, several of which were at Tabuk, quite close to the Iraqi border. Navy aircraft were not allocated CAPs over hostile territory until the Iraqi fighter force was

F-15Cs 85-0105 and 85-0118, both marked as 33rd TFW Squadron aircraft, train with an RSAF F-5E during *Desert Shield*. USAF

virtually eliminated; a sore point for them at the time. When F-14s were allowed on strike escort duties or on occasional sweeps into enemy airspace the merest hint of emissions from their hugely powerful AN/AWG-9 radars sent any opponents scurrying away. The Tomcat force never had the chance to down anything more formidable than an Mi-8 helicopter while their F/A-18 deckmates managed to score a pair of F-7A (MiG-21) fighters with AIM-9s while conducting bombing missions with heavy bombing loads. Mainly, there was not enough enemy fighter activity even at the start of hostilities to require anything other than the F-15 force to contain it. Possibly too, the idea of Tomcats' long-range BVR Phoenix missiles being lobbed into the densely packed airspace over Iraq alarmed those in charge of the operation. If the campaign had been run differently it is quite conceivable that F-14s or F/A-18s used for air superiority might have scored just as many enemy aircraft as the F-15 force but the choice of F-15s for that task was obvious and logical.

An additional factor was the F-15C's unique NCTR (non-cooperative target recognition) technology. Although this 'black box' programme is still highly classified it is widely acknowledged that it was vital in establishing the F-15 as the primary fighter in the campaign. Essentially, it was a relatively foolproof way of avoiding 'blue on blue' casualties that were the nightmare of every air commander as the complex aerial ballet of *Desert Storm* took over the skies above Iraq. Using BVR missiles and relying on long-range radar returns to identify targets was theoretically possible given that AWACS controllers would have a comprehensive 'big picture' of the air battle and could say where the good and bad guys should be at any given moment. However, all previous experience reinforced the fact that visual identification (VID) was the only truly safe way of ensuring that a missile was sent against a genuine bandit rather than a 'friendly' who had lost the plot or a vital piece of IFF equipment. *Combat Tree*, tested in twelve *Triple Nickel* F-4Ds at Udorn, Thailand in 1972, had enabled the Phantom's APQ-109 radar to emit signals that made MiG IFF equipment 'squawk' its owner's identity and also provided a source for AIM-7 missiles to be launched against it at optimum BVR range. Electronic devices such as this were vulnerable to the rapid advances in ECM and could be defeated. A more positive way was needed for pilots to

Almost 'out of the frying pan and into the fire': an engine inspection takes this maintainer out of the sun for a while. USAF

F-15C 85-0103, marked for the Commander of the 33rd TFW that shot down sixteen Iraqi jets between 17 January and 7 February 1991. Norm Taylor

have a clear idea of the exact identity of their potential targets. Project *Musketeer* had shown the feasibility of checking the physical configuration of an unknown aircraft by counting the revolving blades of its engine's turbines via radar from directly ahead or astern of it. In the 1980s the enormous increases in miniaturized computing power made it possible to equip the APG-63 radar with a supporting memory bank of front and rear engine identities to compare with the specimen that it was seeing, thereby establishing the type and even the subtype of the 'bogie'. Obvious exclusions from the list were stealth types like the F-117A and B-2A where both ends of the engine compartment were hidden from radar. NCTR was tested and proven. When the F-15 MSIP programme began it was incorporated along with AIM-120 capability and another radar modification known as LPI (low probability of intercept). This facility reduced the power of the radar's emissions so that it could still pick up targets but without triggering hostile radar warning receivers. F-15Cs had begun to emerge from the MSIP-II line in June 1985 and when the Eagle was deployed to Saudi Arabia and Turkey the units with MSIP-II aircraft were chosen, including the MSIP F-15As of the 32nd TFS. The combination of NCTR and LPI, added to the aircraft's already formidable capabilities, was to be the death of the Iraqi fighter force during its brief resistance to the Allied air campaign.

Approaching Thunder

In the final weeks of 1990, US and Coalition air elements conducted a series of increasingly massive simulated air strikes to develop force coordination and rehearse the seemingly inevitable assault on Iraq. The USN had already begun these exercises in mid-September using up to sixty-three aircraft and RSAF Eagles as top cover. Similar F-15 escorts were provided for packages of sixteen USAF and RAF strikers on 28 September and in early October both RSAF and USAF F-15s covered coordination exercises involving

(typically) eight F-16Cs, four F-4G Wild Weasels and a pair of EF-111A Ravens. Canadian CF-18As were included after 10 October and by the end of that month the packages had increased to thirty-six aircraft, including pairs of F-117As and B-52Gs plus four F-15Es. Simulated night strikes on Saudi airfields were 'repelled' by based F-15Cs and Tornado F.3s. November saw a marked increase in the weight of these 'attacks'. The ominously named Exercise *Imminent Thunder*, begun on 15 November, initially scheduled nine combined strike and CAS packages totalling over 700 aircraft. In effect, it rehearsed the first three days of *Desert Storm* and on its completion on 21 November it had used over 1,000 aircraft flying 4,000 sorties. Exercise *Desert Force* from 5 to 7 December added another ten strike packages and included French aircraft. F-15Cs also continued their *Desert Triangle* feint attacks on the Iraqi border and maintained their CAPs (relieved only by in-cockpit musical entertainment) while Saddam's pilots put up 150–200 sorties daily, though in October there were no direct responses to Allied air movements along the border. Things livened up on 1 November when a couple of Mirages flew nine miles into Saudi airspace and were chased off by Eagles. A pair of MiG-23s attempted to

engage an RF-4C on a border recce flight and were similarly seen off. The Alert pad became a slick operation. On 29 November a single Iraqi fighter had barely got within ten miles of the Iraqi border when a four-ship of F-15Cs appeared and pushed it back. AWACS observation also gave insight into the night capability of the opposing fighters; for example on the night of 25 December thirty fighters from six bases were seen to be indulging in some rare practice ground-controlled intercepts.

Into the Barrel

At about midnight on 16 January 1991 efforts to find a diplomatic answer to the Gulf crisis were finally put aside. Eight AH-64 Apache helicopters penetrated Iraqi airspace undetected and destroyed radar sites west of Baghdad creating safe air corridors for strike packages. 37th TFW F-117A Nighthawks took off from Khamis Mushayt into a moonless night to spearhead that sequence of attacks, followed by waves of F-111F, F-15E and Tornado GR.1 strikers with their attendant SEAD and fighter elements. F-15 CAPS earlier that night had continued on the same three 'racetrack' patterns as previous nights to avoid alerting the defences. When the strike packages entered Iraq, though, they were fronted by a 'wall' of twenty F-15Cs, sweeping ahead in a line from the Jordanian border to Kuwait. Pushing into the Iraqi heartland they soon began to acquire radar targets at over 40mi (64km) range and were cleared to fire BVR when they had closed to 15mi (24km).

As F-117s went for the command and communication centres in the Baghdad area and F-111Fs bombed the French-built air defence network (KARI), Eagles of a different feather attacked Saddam's numerous fixed SCUD missile emplacements some of which had missiles poised for launch against Israel. Among the migrants to the Gulf in the Summer of 1990 were forty-eight F-15Es from the newly equipped 4th TFW. On Tuesday, 7 August 1990 the 336th TFS *Rocketeers* (commonly known as the *Rockets*) got their stand-by order. In anticipation of a deployment, absences were filled by crews from the 335th TFS and last-minute personal purchases were made including 9mm Beretta handguns for self-defence on the ground and inflatable rubber rings to soften the 15-hour non-stop flight on fur-lined, but firm ejection seats.

Fine, wind-borne sand was an insidious problem as it found its way into aircraft, requiring frequent wash-downs. USAF

With three external tanks, a pair of travel pods, four AIM-9 and two AIM-7s (a load-out that was only cleared for use a matter of hours prior to take-off) the *Rockets* began their transfer to Thumrait, Oman in heavy rain on 9 August.

Only a week previously the squadron had assumed that the 4th TFW's low state of readiness with its new aircraft would provide a degree of immunity to the call to battle. The *Rockets* were the only mission-ready F-15E unit at Seymour-Johnson, with the 335th TFS *Chiefs* less than half-way to that status. Some of the aircraft's equipment was still in the final stages of acceptance testing, including the TEWS. Its AN/AAQ-14 targeting pods were in extremely short supply and there were no film strips ready for the moving map display so that films from the similar F/A-18 unit had to be modified for use. GPS, so useful for this type of deployment, was still eight years away. Although Chuck Horner had specifically requested F-15Es for his Air Plan the aircraft was specifically limited to using only Mk 82 and Mk 84 bombs since no other ordnance had completed clearance trials on the aircraft.

The gruelling flight to Oman triggered a few minor faults in the F-15E's comparatively 'young' systems. Soon after take-off an aircraft suffered an engine flameout and could not be restarted. It had to turn back, as did the CO's aircraft when fuel started to leak from a wing tank. Fuel problems caused three other Mud Hens to divert to bases en route after defective cut-off valves in their wing pylon fuel lines caused their fuel systems to siphon fuel out of the wing tanks. The formation's KC-10As were kept fully occupied feeding the hungry Eagles to an extent that the smaller KC-135s would have been hard-pressed to match.

During their transit the *Rockets* were ordered to break for an overnight stay at Dhahran before flying on to the spartan Thumrait base. On arrival there was much to do in establishing tolerable living conditions and studying the weapons manuals to work out delivery parameters for the Rock-eye CBU that they would surely have to use if they were called in to deter another Iraqi armoured advance. Without targeting pods their role was likely to be 'dumb' bombing while they awaited a rushed delivery of a dozen AAQ-14s to be shared throughout the squadron. Their APG-70 radar could of course be employed for bombing but with the concomitant risk of revealing the aircraft's presence to Iraq's vast radar warning

Self-portrait of a 94th TFS pilot during a CAP mission. USAF

system. Blasted by the heat and denied effective communication with higher authority the Rockets sat out *Desert Shield* at their arid, wind-whipped base, 900mi (1,450km) south of the Saudi-Kuwait border, expecting at any moment a call to perform CAS sorties against Saddam's force of 2,000 tanks and artillery pieces as it rolled into Saudi Arabia. In this endeavour they expected big losses and it was small consolation to know that their airbase, unlike those in Saudi Arabia, was unlikely to be rapidly overrun by an enemy advance. An Alert facility was set up with aircraft 'cocked' for take-off around two minutes from engine start. Training was at first continued at a fairly low level. Apparently, the CO felt that his job would be on the line if one of the scarce aircraft was lost. In fact, the desert wastes of Oman offered unrestricted low-level training in the full range of attack modes, enabling newer crews to build experience. Air-to-air training was ruled out for safety reasons, denying some valuable initiation for crews who had come to the F-15E from non-fighter types. Despite the effectiveness of the F-15C 'albino' fighter shield there seemed no reason to assume that Mud Hens would not have to fight their way in and out of targets defended by the world's sixth largest air force.

Crews concentrated on running in below the radar to minimize detection times by the defenders. Emulating RAF Tornado GR.1 and Jaguar crews who were allowed to train down to 100ft (30m) altitude they frequently broke their '300ft (90m) minimum' rule, despite the risks from poor visibility and horizon definition in the windy, sand-bearing air conditions. Erosion of transparent surfaces on the aircraft was one consequence. Windshields became pitted and the 'windows' at the front of FLIR pods were sand-abraded. By the end of December twenty-one pods were within days of being unserviceable because video reception had been degraded through sand blasting.

The loss of F-15E 87-0203 and its crew on 30 September brought the safety issue to a head again. Maj Pete Hook and his WSO, Jim 'Boo Boo' Poulet were involved in a little unscheduled air-to-air practice with a Jaguar from an RAF unit with which Hook had done an exchange posting. From his altitude of around 15,000ft (4,500m) Maj Hook approached the Jaguar (that was at 100ft (30m)) head-on, rolled and reversed for a stern conversion intercept but misjudged his altitude in the dive. The F-15E with three heavy fuel tanks aboard, did not pull out in time. After a four-day suspension of flying the minimum altitude was raised to 500ft (150m). Gen Horner was convinced that the risks of low altitude outweighed the chances of evading hostile radar detection in any case. Under pressure from the commanders of the F-15E squadrons and Col Tom Lennon, managing the F-111F contingent at Taif, Horner relented but experience tended to demonstrate the wisdom of his original edict. After two combat losses at low altitude, F-15Es reverted to the medium altitude attack profiles that have become their standard.

While the *Rockets* pushed ahead with training under their new CO, Lt Col Steve 'Steep' Turner (who took over in October 1990) other Mud Hen units completed their transition and prepared to join the battle array. Lt Col Steve Pingel's 335th TFS *Chiefs* attained IOC on 1 October and were ready to deploy to Al Kharj, Saudi Arabia at the end of December. Seymour Johnson's last F-15E squadron, the 334th TFS *Eagles* didn't become fully operational until after the war, on 18 June 1991 and deployed to Saudi Arabia the following day to help maintain an uneasy peace. Al Kharj was a new airfield, built by *Red Horse* engineers using hardened clay with asphalt covering for runways and dispersals. After its completion on 16 November it enabled the *Rockets* to move closer to the action and they began to occupy the new base from 17 December, sharing it with Bitburg's 525th TFS F-15Cs (that flew in on 21 December) and a couple of ANG F-16 squadrons to make up the 4th Composite Wing (Provisional). Fuel for the thirsty Eagles was provided by the KC-10As of the 68th ARW and the *Rockets'* heavy equipment was shifted to Al Kharj (or 'Al's Garage') on a single C-5A sortie. Twenty-four *Chiefs* jets arrived over Christmas 1990, some of them containing crews with only around sixty hours on the type. Equipment shortages caused a temporary problem for the newcomers whose chaff-flare dispenser modules could not handle the available supplies of munitions.

The 'Strike Eagle' units featured prominently in the 600-page air tasking order (ATO) that was the master plan for a devastating assault on Iraq. While the light grey ('albino') F-15Cs were assigned CAPs for the strike forces, twenty-two 'dark grey' Mud Hens with accompanying SEAD EF-111As and F-4Gs were scheduled to attack airfield and SAM sites. *Rockets* crews, with the most experience of the area, occupied eighteen places in the attack formations with the other four going to *Chiefs* aircraft. The Wing's KC-10As were in big demand so fuel for the Mud Hens came from seven KC-135As, provided in radio silence with all lights extinguished.

Once the strike packages had passed through their safe corridors into enemy airspace the F-15Es divided into three-aircraft cells. One cell had to abort after two of its number reported systems problems. The others pressed on at 500ft (150m) altitude. Several fixed SCUD missile sites were hit, including one that had a missile elevated to the firing position. Link stations for the buried fibre-optic telecommunications link between Baghdad and Kuwait City were taken out and the huge H-2 airfield was on the target list. As the F-15E cells made their 45-minute flights to their targets, crews were amazed to see that Iraq had left all its lights on, including the runway lights at H-2. The element of surprise was short-lived and all aircraft encountered heavy AAA and SAM with several crews having to make violent manoeuvres or very low altitude egress flights to avoid the flak. Fighter opposition was slight. One F-15E crew was pursued by

a MiG-23 as they pulled away from H-2 but its radar lock was broken by chaff. Another crew almost scored the Mud Hen's first air-to-air kill when they fired an AIM-9 at a MiG-29. The missile failed to connect but its target attempted another interception at very low altitude and ran into the ground. Another MiG-29 tried to intervene but F-15E crews saw it explode and concluded that it had been hit by a stray missile from a MiG.

Attacks on well-defended sites, particularly those with the very efficient Roland SAM had to be made from medium altitude. In these cases ordnance was limited to Mk 82 LDGP as the Mk 20 Rockeye's 'scatter pattern' would have been ineffectively wide from altitudes above 8,000–10,000ft (2,400–3,000m). Against SA-2 and SA-3 missiles the F-15Es were forced to adopt defensive manoeuvres that had changed little since American pilots first learned to duel with the missiles over Vietnam. If SEAD couldn't neutralize the problem and a hit was imminent pilots learned to wait until about five seconds from missile impact and then performed a rapid, diving barrel roll to avoid the SAM. During the first strikes on fixed SCUD sites the *Rockets* crews came under heavy SAM attack and several aircraft were forced to clean off their ordnance in order to manoeuvre (in one case to 10.5g). A further complication was that the aircraft's RWR wasn't always programmed to the frequencies used by the missiles and their radars.

Horner's policy was to remove a substantial part of Saddam's fighter force by destroying its command and control networks, damaging its airfields and shooting down as many planes as possible. The opening movements of the ATO (dubbed 'Poobah's Party') included a series of Tomahawk and F-117A attacks on strategic targets in Baghdad, followed by waves of BQM-74 drones that brought up the Iraqis' numerous air defence radars. These were then systematically decimated by a deluge of AGM-88 HARM missiles from US SEAD aircraft, homing onto their radar transmissions. After that, the radar operators were reluctant to activate their sets, effectively blinding much of the defence network. As a result there was relatively effective radar-guided SAM and AAA opposition to F-15E attacks after 18 January. This also enabled crews to use their preferred medium-altitude attack profiles in greater safety. At lower altitudes the threat from optically-guided SAMs and

AAA was murderous, as a 355th TFS crew proved on the second day of the conflict.

Six groups of F-15Es were targeted against oil storage and electricity generating facilities near Basrah early on 18 January. Attacking at 500ft (150m) from approaches over the Hawr al Hammar swamps to avoid SAM installations, the Eagles were fired on by numerous gun positions. Just after F-15E 88-1689 *Thunderbird* 6 called that it had bombed its target contact was lost. Its crew, Maj Tom E. 'Teek' Koritz (the dual-rated flight surgeon) and WSO Lt Col Donnie R. Holland, both of them senior and respected squadron members, were lost and their remains were returned after the war. Possibly the glare of the flames from previous bombing of the oil tanks blinded the crew to the ZSU-23-4 AAA shells coming their way, but at their altitude they had little chance of evasion in any case and may have hit the ground.

The First Six

For the F-15C units Night 1 yielded six Iraqi fighter kills; three MiG-29s and three Mirage F.1EQs. The high-altitude wall of five F-15C four-ships from the 58th TFS, 36th TFW and 1st TFW that swept across Iraq was anticipating serious opposition from Saddam's MiG-29 and Mirage pilots. Some crews would have been aware of Gen Charles L. Donnelly's estimate that there would be a hundred Allied losses in the first ten days or 20,000 sorties. There was also the strong possibility of attempted interceptions of the crucial E-3C AWACS high-value assets (HVAs) by MiG-25s, approaching from 70,000ft (21,330m) at up to 1,400kt. With thirty packages of air-to-ground aircraft and two of recce types the Eagles were extremely busy. The 58th TFS put up two four-ships; *Citgo* and *Pennzoil*, forming the western end of the 'wall'. *Pennzoil* was led by Capt Rick 'Kluso' Tollini with Capt Larry 'Cherry' Pitts as his wingman, Capt John 'J.B.' Kelk (a veteran of Bitburg's 525th TFS) as Number 3 and Capt Steve 'Willie' Williams in the Number 4 slot. Both Tollini and Kelk had been among the four 58th TFS pilots picked as air-to-air mission commanders alongside Capt Rob 'Cheese' Graeter and Capt Chuck Magill, a USMC F/A-18 exchange pilot from VMFA-531 *Gray Ghosts*. Graeter led the *Citgo* four-ship at the extreme western end with Lt Scott Maw on his wing. The eight *Gorillas* jets took off at 0030Z, tanking at 0200Z and were over the Iraqi border at 0300Z. As they were completing business with their tanker *Pennzoil* leader received an AWACS message that F-15Es attacking SCUD sites at H-2 airfield were being pursued by MiG-29s. In fact the F-15Cs had been scheduled to run in a little later than the Mud Hens in the hope that the strike force would draw out some Iraqi fighters. With the F-15Es and F-117As well out of their target areas the 'albino' birds would have a clear sky for BVR missile shots and avoid Chuck Horner's greatest fear, a blue-on-blue loss in the overcrowded airspace.

The AWACS controller's anxiety for the 'Strike Eagles' persuaded Tollini to push north from his tanker a little sooner than planned and he took his four-ship to 30,000ft (9,140m). They were confronted with around sixty aircraft at lower altitudes all heading for the border and safety. Sorting out friend from foe on their Mode 4 IFF took a little while but it was clear that two groups of bandits were presenting a problem for the egressing F-15Es; one north of the Mudaysis forward airstrip and another nearer to Baghdad. Kelk and Williams were detached to deal with the second threat and they picked up MiGs at 25mi (40km) but Kelk was unable to get AWACS confirmation of the targets' 'bandit' status due to crowded comms channels, despite being unable to get a friendly IFF signal from them himself. One of the MiGs then locked up 'J.B.'s' Eagle at 7,000ft (2,134m) and 35mi (56km) range. Kelk pulled hard away from the MiG, dispensing chaff to defeat a possible Atoll shot, but he released an AIM-7M at the bogie before beginning

this evasion tactic. Tollini, following Kelk's missile visually, attempted to release chaff himself but pressed the 'flares' option instead, creating an interesting visual diversion. However, like Kelk he was able to see the Sparrow missile explode on a MiG-29 at about 10mi (16km) range. In fact, Kelk didn't realize at first that it was his missile as an armament panel fault meant that its release hadn't been indicated in his cockpit. Later, when all the data were amassed it was realized that this was the first kill of the war.

'Cheese' Graeter's *Citgo* four-ship meanwhile blazed on towards the Mudaysis base where they arrived just as the alert flight of three Mirage F.1EQs was taking off to join in the pursuit of the fleeing F-15E elements. Turning in to follow the Mirages as they banked left away from Mudaysis's runway Capt Graeter locked up the first aircraft, switched to the second and then 'spiked' the first on his radar again. He fired an AIM-7M inside the 10mi (16km) range when the Mirage passed through 4,000ft (1,220m) altitude and then turned hard in case a retaliatory missile had been aimed his way by one of the other Mirages. Scott Maw had meanwhile acquired the third Mirage as it cleared the base. Graeter saw his missile disintegrate his target at 7,000ft (2,130m) and he also watched the second Mirage explode on the ground to the south-west of him. It seems that its pilot became disorientated by the loss of the lead aircraft and flew into the ground in his anxiety to escape the *Citgo* F-15s. at very low level the third Mirage got away and Capt Graeter regrouped his foursome and returned to the tanker.

At the eastern end of the 'wall' was a 71st TFS four-ship led by Capt Steve Tate in F-15C 83-0017 *Quaker 1*. Their assignment was to CAP the airfield at Al Jawah with a high-altitude pair and another two aircraft at lower altitude to catch bandits as they took off. Tate and his wingman, Bo Merlack took the low orbit. Soon after their arrival AWACS gave them a single contact and the 'low' CAP blew off their external tanks to engage it, heading southeast. Luckily, the bogie transmitted a friendly IFF signature revealing itself as a Taif F-111F that had become separated from the strike force. A second bogie approached the CAP from the east at 8,000ft (2,440m) and Tate confirmed it as a Mirage F.1EQ and launched an AIM-7M at around 12 nm range. The Iraqi fighter fragmented in a huge blossom of fire. It was to be the 1st TFW's only MiG kill of the war. Tate's *Quaker* section completed the CAP in the hostile, flak-filled skies around Baghdad before heading for the tanker.

Good fortune stayed with the 58th TFS later on the 17th during the first daylight strike into Iraq. Capt Chuck 'Sly' Magill led *Union* flight among sixteen F-15Cs from the Eglin and Langley Wings, escorting a strike package of forty-six aircraft against Al Taqaddum and Al Assad airfields. Magill and his wingman 1st Lt Mark 'Nips' Arriola, both on their first combat mission, left the tanker and crossed into Iraq at 30,000ft (9,140m), receiving AWACS warning of two MiG-29s orbiting low to the south of the airfields. The eight *Union* Eagles forged on, ahead of the strike package to test the Iraqi CAP. The IAF's poor performance during darkness was

The F-15C in which Capt Steven W. Tate destroyed an Iraqi Mirage F.1EQ on 17 January 1991. He fired an AIM-7M at 12nm from the target, hitting it at 4nm. via P. Smith

assumed to be through lack of night intercept training but the Eagle drivers expected a much stronger performance by daylight. If necessary they were prepared to hold back the F-16 bombers until the MiGs had been defeated, calling in reinforcements if required.

Magill had the MiGs on his radar at 60mi (96km) but was also manoeuvring to avoid heavy SAM and AAA as his F-15Cs winged north. At 40mi (64km) it was clear that there were no other MiGs extant so he released the second (*Pennzoil*) four-ship led by 'Kluso' Tollini to check Al Assad airfield to the north-west. SA-2 indications on the F-15s' RHAW and a sighting of smoke from a SAM launch caused the Eagles to shed their wing-tanks and make a 10,000ft (3,050m) dive to port, pushing out chaff. Intent on their intercept the Eagles had flown directly over an SA-2 site, but they maintained contact with the MiGs by periodically 'sniffing' with their radars. The MiGs increased speed from their leisurely 370kt CAP pattern, headed north at 500kt, but at 20mi (32km) turned back towards the incoming Eagles. Magill (in F-15C 85-0107) and Capt Rhory Draeger, his Number 3 in 85-0108, each locked up a MiG while their wingmen directed their radars behind the bogies to check for other lurking bandits inside the radar plot. They expected the Fulcrums to fire first but it transpired that the Iraqis were intent on intercepting some USN F-14As to the west of the Eagles instead. Magill and Draeger both fired AIM-7Ms and Magill shot another when his first seemed to dive below its intended trajectory. At seven miles the Eagle pilots were able to make a visual ID of the blue-grey MiGs and at 2mi (3km) they saw all three of their Sparrows slam into the pair of Fulcrums. Flying through the 'merge' with their shattered targets to check for others behind them the two pilots took more SA-2s and beat them with chaff and hard manoeuvring, though this meant that both of the fuel-hungry Eagles had to shed their centreline tanks. Magill instantly got a 'zero fuel' indication (that turned out to be an electrical mis-cue) when he punched his off and he headed straight for a tanker 180mi (290km) away. On return to Tabuk the two MiG killers permitted themselves an illicit aileron roll display to the many ground troops who were waiting to welcome them.

Two more Fulcrums were added to the 58th's scoreboard on 19 January. Capt Craig 'Mole' Underhill originated from Texas A&M, *alma mater* of several Vietnam-era MiG-killers and had enjoyed a quieter existence driving C-130 transports before joining the 33rd TFW. On the morning of 19 January Underhill's four-ship was led by Capt Caesar 'Rico' Rodriguez's and flying HVA CAP for the AWACS and tankers, plus cover for the egress of a forty-strong F-16 strike. While Mike Fisher and Pat Moylan (Rodriguez' Numbers 3 and 4) went to the KC-10A to refuel, AWACS called that there were three groups of bandits in the area of the strike package, two of which were being engaged by Tollini's flight. 'Rico' and 'Mole' went in pursuit of the third group, a pair of MiG-29s which was threatening the F-16s as they ran for the border. At 30mi (48km) the Fulcrums turned back towards their base, chased by the F-15s and it soon became clear that they would land before being caught. Rodriguez turned back but immediately received another contact via AWACS in a position some thirteen miles south of them and closing on the Americans. Underhill picked them up on radar at around 12,000ft (3,650m) while Rodriguez was too close to detect them on his screen. AWACS confirmed the contacts as hostile (though there was a bad moment when Underhill got a spurious 'friendly' IFF signal) and Craig Underhill (in 85-0122) released an AIM-7M, saw a fireball and heard 'Rico' call 'Splash One'. Closing on the second contact Underhill was looking into the sun and could not get a clear VID but, alarmed by the supposedly friendly IFF signal he had received he asked Rodriguez (flying 84-0114) to make the identification of the bogie. As the aircraft pulled towards Underhill, 'Rico' was able to confirm it as a MiG-29 and was supported in this by a second AWACS controller. He followed the MiG down as it made a steep descent for a split-S manoeuvre, begun at only 2,000ft (610m). As the Fulcrum pilot neared the bottom of his manoeuvre he realized he was very low for a successful pull-out and punched off his wing-tanks. It was not enough to add the crucial few degrees and the MiG became a streak of fire across the desert floor. Critically short of fuel the Eagles found a Saudi tanker as their wingmen covered their retreat in case the other pair of MiG-29s that had initially turned back towards the Eagles, chose to make something of it. After the mission it was established that the confusion over a 'friendly' IFF was another inter-service coordination difficulty between AWACS and USN aircraft. The MiG-29s had been interested in an unannounced Navy strike package and the IFF signal probably originated from an A-7 Corsair. Rodriguez was credited with the second MiG on the basis that he had manoeuvred it into the ground. The importance of visual ID was underlined on Night One when a 1st TFW pilot, Capt Drummond, was ordered by AWACS to pursue a fast mover at 1,000ft (305m) and then cleared to fire at it. Unable to get final target ID from AWACS the Eagle pilot dived from high altitude to follow the 'bogie' and made his own visual identification – of a Saudi Tornado GR.1.

Jon Kelk led another dawn escort on 19 January with a *Citgo* four-ship accompanying a large 'gorilla' package of Aardvarks and F-16Cs that was weather-aborted. Very soon after their return to base they were rescheduled as SCUD-hunter CAP between Mudaysis and H-2 airfields. Lead passed to the moustachioed 'Kluso' Tollini with Capt Larry 'Cherry' Pitts as his wingman, Kelk as *Citgo* 3 and Steve Williams as Number 4. Bandits appeared on the AWACS screens following a big Navy strike out of the Baghdad area. At 30mi (48km) range these MiGs retreated north but a second group, at much lower altitude was detected heading for the Eagle CAP. While Tollini and Pitts were reassigned to another CAP, 'Kluso' and Kelk kept the swerving 'low runners' in their radar view and *Citgo* flight dropped to lower altitude to engage. Pitts finally got within range of the target that turned out to be a MiG-25 Foxbat, travelling supersonic at 500ft (150m) and attempting to turn across the Eagle at 90 degrees in a beam manoeuvre to break Pitts's radar lock. It took two AIM-7Ms and two AIM-9Ls from F-15C 85-0099 before the MiG pilot was forced to take to his ejection seat. Pitts AIM-9s were decoyed by flares and his first AIM-7 failed to detonate. His last Sparrow finally despatched the MiG though an AIM-9 from Tollini also exploded in the fireball. Tollini had the Foxbat's wingman in sight but once again the need for visual ID proved crucial since he was looking at an aircraft that at certain angles could have been an F-14 or F-15. However, a quick radio check with neighbouring 'friendlies' revealed that only one was in afterburner: his MiG target. He launched an AIM-9L, then an AIM-7M from F-15C 85-0101 and the big Foxbat fell apart.

Two more Mirage F.1EQs fell on the 19th, this time to Bitburg's 525th TFS when Capt

Capt Rory R. Draeger was flying this 33rd TFW Eagle (85-0119) when he scored his second MiG on 26 January 1991. Ahead of its windshield is an ALQ-135B antenna, repeated in a corresponding position under the nose. Norm Taylor

F-15C 79-0078, the Eagle in which Capt Thomas N. Dietz shot down a pair of MiG-21s with AIM-9Ls, is seen here in September 1992 with a different paint-job. Jim Rotramel

David S. Prather (F-15C 79-0069) and Lt David G. Sveden (79-0021) each destroyed one with an AIM-7M while on a CAP to protect a *Proven Force* F-111E strike on chemical and ammunition bunkers near Kirkuk and Qayyarah. The Mirages attempted to intercept the Aardvark formation at medium altitude.

In three days Allied fighters had achieved air superiority. After that, the Iraqi fighter squadrons chose not to appear again until 24 January when the Mirage units attempted to fly five aircraft out towards Coalition ships off Saudi Arabia. This was a dangerous move because a number of the Mirages were known to have Exocet anti-shipping missile capability. This time the interception duty went to Number 13 Sqn of the RSAF and Capt Ayehid Salah al-Shamrani in F-15C 80-0068 was guided in by AWACS towards two pairs of Mirages from 80mi (130km) out. He destroyed both fighters rapidly with

Sidewinders and the other Mirages turned back to safety and eventual escape to Iran.

By 26 January the Iraqi Air Force was on the run. Pilots were beginning to fly for sanctuary in Iran, which had promised to 'look after' Iraqi aircraft until after the war (and was still keeping that promise ten years later). Other fighters began to transfer from base to base in an attempt to avoid the systematic destruction of aircraft in their expensive hardened shelters by PGMs from F-111Fs and F-117As. Eagle CAPs began to block the escapees and catch those who sought to move base within Iraq. Capt Tony 'Kimo' Schiavi was in a four-ship HVA CAP on the 26th around airfields near the Jordanian border. As he and flight leader Capt Rory 'Hoser' Draeger, flying 85-0119, came off the tanker they received an AWACS alert that four MiG-23 Floggers were departing from H-2 airfield and flying north-east, apparently towards another base near Baghdad. Draeger got permission to take his entire four-ship (including 'Rico' Rodriguez and Capt Bruce Till who were due for a tanker top-up) in pursuit. This began with the bandits over 100mi (160km) ahead and eventually closed to less than 80mi (130km) but the Iraqis were clearly going to make it to the SAM protection ring around Baghdad. At the point of turning back, Draeger got another AWACS call that four more MiG-23s had departed H-2 on the same heading. Taking a chance that the original quartet could conceivably reverse and sandwich his *Chevron* flight between eight MiGs Draeger decided to run an intercept on the second group that was sprinting along 'in the weeds'. From 25,000ft (7,620m) the F-15Cs' radars were able to see the MiGs in search mode at 80mi (130km). As the Eagles closed on the MiG formation one of them turned back to base, presumably with a mechanical problem. Draeger allocated targets from the remaining trio to each F-15 pilot, ordered wing tanks to be jettisoned and took his flight down at Mach 1.2 for a radar lock on the bandits at 20mi (32km). Draeger launched an AIM-7M as soon as the lead MiG was spiked on his radar but the missile fell away with motor failure. He immediately launched a second and 'Kimo' Schiavi fired at the Number 2 MiG from his Eagle (85-0104). Bruce Till, targeting the third bandit also had a misfired Sparrow so Rodriguez, sharing the same target, fired a couple of seconds before Till got his second missile off. Diving through a gap in the overcast the pilots saw Capt Draeger's missile make a fireball around the lead MiG.

Although it appeared to fly through the explosion, its fuel tanks had been ruptured by the warhead and it soon dissolved into flame and hit the ground. The other pair of Floggers began hard turns into the Eagles but Schaivi's missile was already eating up the distance behind the Number two aircraft and destroyed it as it turned. 'Rico's' missile got to the third MiG fractionally before Till's and it too splashed into the desert as his second victim, ending the seven-second engagement. Four 'bingo fuel' Eagles went in search of a tanker, announcing their three kills to the AWACS controller as they departed.

With Allied air supremacy achieved the Iraqi Air Force had few choices left. It could either hide in its remaining hardened shelters or underground stores or remove itself from the area. Many chose the latter. Although Allied war planners had anticipated an exodus of aircraft to friendly Jordan and established BARCAPs to prevent this the Iraqis had already negotiated safe passage to Iran. Three BARCAPs were set up on the Iran/Iraq border instead and a steady trickle of Iraqi fighters awaited their moment for any gaps in this barrier, caused by late or unavailable Allied fighters, before trying their luck. Capt Jay T. 'Op' Denney and Capt Ben 'Coma' Powell of the 53rd TFS each caught a pair of escapees on 27

January. Denney's two fleeing Floggers each succumbed to an AIM-9L and Powell caught another MiG-23 and a Mirage F.1EQ with AIM-7Ms. Capt Don 'Muddy' Watrous followed up with a further MiG-23 the next day, adding a third kill to the 525th's list. Watrous was actually 'on loan' from the 32nd TFS and in a four-ship BAR-CAP (*Bite 1-4*) that was given two bogies by AWACS. He and his wingman dived on a pair of MiGs that broke from a larger formation and *Bite 03* went off after the others. The MiG formation was already approaching the Iranian border so Don Watrous cleaned off his tanks to catch up with them and fired two AIM-7Ms, causing the lead MiG to dive and hit the ground. The others just made it over the border. 'Muddy' Watrous found himself a tanker, whose 'boomer' drew his attention to the fact that the Eagle had somehow lost over 2ft (60cm) off its port wing during the high-speed chase. A further kill for the 525th TFS came on 2 February when Capt Greg Masters in F-15C 79-0078 destroyed an Il-76 transport with an AIM-7M.

Denied the chance to defeat the enemy in the strenuous air combat that some pilots had expected, the F-15 squadrons vied to be selected for the border CAP sectors (named after girls: *Carol, Cindy, Emily,* and so on) and hoped to rack up enough kills for individual pilots to become the first USAF aces since 1972. The 53rd TFS

often landed the *Cindy* CAP over airfields nearer Baghdad, increasing its chances of 'trade' during seven-hour CAPs by four-ships. Pairs of fighters alternated on the tankers that had to hold station quite close to the Iranian border. The squadron was divided into 'day' and 'night' sections and ran shifts to man the CAP stations. Occasionally the enemy still fought back. Two 53rd TFS pilots on a 30 January CAP were caught by a pair of MiG-25s making a very high-speed interception. Both sets of fighters launched missiles and all were evaded. The F-15s then turned in behind the Foxbats for another shot and Capt Thomas Dietz had no less than three successive AIM-7 misfires while his leader fired one that had a guidance failure. The other two CAP Eagles, led by the Commanding Officer, hurried back from their tanker and gave chase, catching the Foxbats as they prepared to land at Al Taqaddum. Four more AIM-7Ms were fired but still the MiGs managed to land unscathed.

Other pilots occasionally encountered Iraqi fighters in other sectors. Capt David 'Logger' Rose (another Texas A&M product) of the 60th TFS picked up a MiG-23 near the north-eastern border during a BARCAP, making radar contact at 60mi (96km). NCTR returns indicated the contact was hostile but confusion led to Rose being vectored onto a four-ship from Bitburg that had just entered the arena. Reacquiring his original radar trace he swung in behind a pair of MiG-23s at very low altitude and destroyed one with a Sparrow. His wingman, Capt Kevin Gallagher and another Bitburg Eagle went for the other Flogger but it managed to lose them at ultra-low altitude.

In early February the MiG exodus increased, probably spurred by the news that Saddam Hussein was executing senior Air Force personnel for their 'failure' to stop the Allied air armada. Tom 'Vegas' Dietz and Lt Robert 'Digs' Hehemann were CAPping again on 6 February when AWACS guided them to a pair of Su-25 Frogfoot attack aircraft and two MiG-21s, all high-tailing it for Iran. Hehemann disposed of the Su-25s and Dietz the MiGs, all with AIM-9Ls. Both pilots went on to add a third kill in air action after the cease-fire but Dietz's kill had been the third for his F-15C, 79-0078.

Tuesday, 7 February was the last day on which a 'mass escape' to Iran was attempted. BARCAPs had been re-established on 5 February after relaxation earlier in that

The 33rd TFW had a 'Gulf Spirit' F-15C for each of its three squadrons. This one, 85-0118, was flown by the Commander, Col Rick N. Parsons before the Wing deployed to Tabuk. Col Parsons shot down an Su-22 during the war. A. Thornborough

month when escape flights seemed to have stopped after a total of 118 aircraft had been tracked heading for the escape routes. Chuck Horner had decided to give his overworked Eagle drivers a break, particularly on the night shift, though the absence of BARCAPs caused a sudden upsurge in runs for the border. He also reasoned that Iraqi 'runners' were no longer a threat to the air effort in any case. Some had crashed just short of the border, or in Iran from fuel shortage. On the 7th Col Rick Parsons, 33rd TFW CO and Capt Tony Murphy were vectored onto a flight of Su-17s. Murphy got two and Col Parsons a third, all with AIM-7Ms. On the same day Maj Randy W. May of the 525th TFS took out an Mi-24 Hind helicopter gunship using a pair of Sparrows. Another helicopter was shared by Capt Steve Dingee (79-0048) and Capt Mark McKenzie (80-0012) from the 525th TFS. Of the twelve Iraqi border-runners that day three were shot down and AWACS traces indicated that six others crashed just over the Iranian border, presumably after running out of fuel.

Scud Busters

Iraq's one military achievement during *Desert Storm* was its persistent Scud missile campaign. Saddam Hussein's ability to launch upgraded Soviet SS-1C Scud-B ballistic missiles, known as 'Al Hussein' and 'Al Abbas', had been well understood before the conflict opened. Originally acquired from Libya the missiles had been modified at the al Falluja factory near Baghdad, with German assistance, to increase their range from 168mi (270km) to 373mi (600km). their original purpose had been to attack Teheran during the Iran–Iraq War but the modifications had severely impaired their accuracy and the extra fuel space meant that the warhead was reduced to 420lb (190kg). However, they could reach targets in Saudi Arabia and, more crucially, in Israel. Launched from purpose-built Al Waleed TEL (transport/erector/launcher) vehicles built under SAAB/Scania licence, or Soviet MEL (mobile erector/launcher) trucks they could be moved around at night and launched with little preparation once they had been fuelled. Launch vehicles could then be hidden in buildings or camouflaged locations during daylight. The Allies' greatest fear was that Saddam would carry

Of the fifty missions chalked up on this F-15E many were 'Scud-hunts'. Andy Evans

out his threat to pack Scud warheads with chemical or biological warfare substances. Scuds were therefore taken very seriously even before they started to fall on Israel. Fixed Scud sites were attacked as a priority on Night 1 and there was a separate Scud targeting section at General Schwarzkopf's Riyadh HQ that processed all details of storage, fuel supply and potential sites for the weapons. Their main fuel supply centre at Latifiyah was eliminated on Day 2, as was the factory for their rocket motors. However, Gen Horner made clear that the mobile Scuds would continue to provide a threat and their elusive nature made it hard for him to promise that they could be removed completely. Unexpectedly poor weather and a lack of tactical and strategic (particularly the SR-71A) reconnaissance assets made it still harder to locate the TELs and MELs. From night 1 up to 25 January at least five were launched each night and from Day 2 the 'Great Scud Hunt' began.

Horner's main strategy was to devote half of his F-15E force to the hunt. Once they had wiped out the fixed sites, flights of four Eagles were placed in orbits over likely Scud launch target boxes in the hope that they could catch launch vehicles in transit at night or actually launching weapons. The ongoing SCUDCAP was a hugely time-consuming diversion of F-15E interdiction capability but the political consequences of Israel entering the war in retaliation for missiles hitting

its territory would have been the possible dissolution of the Arab alliance against Iraq. Soon after the first missiles did hit Israel a retaliatory force of IDF/AF F-16s and F-15s was launched towards Iraq and was only recalled at the last moment after some frantic diplomacy and an assurance that a huge air effort would be devoted to tackling the problem. The SCUDCAP had to be draconian: any long vehicles that resembled TELs on radar or FLIR were open to attack at night and a number of petrol tanker or cargo lorries that braved the highways at night may well have appeared as 'probable kills' in the statistics.

From 1 February F-16Cs and A-6Es joined the hunt and A-10A 'Warthogs' had already started anti-Scud operations from the forward airstrip at Al Jouf ('Cajun West') from the day that Scud launches against Israel began. TELs had to use road or roadside launch locations, principally on the 320mi (515km) Baghdad to Amman highway, so the patrols concentrated on trying to catch launchers as they fuelled up missiles and launched them before hiding in the hundreds of drainage culverts under the roadway. Long Bedouin tents were also used as daytime camouflage. Of the available aircraft only the F-15E had adequate radar resolution to identify the vehicles at night, though its chances of locating them still remained rather low and confirmed strikes remained elusive throughout the war. A-10 pilots had to use binoculars by day or peer through the narrow 'eye' of their IR Maverick missiles at night, using them as primitive FLIR devices to acquire targets on a tiny 4in (10cm) TV monitor. However, they did hit a number of missiles and their kills were not confined to Scuds: after 'Warthogs' shot down two helicopters their CO called the 1st TFW that had only one kill, and offered to provide top cover for their F-15Cs!

Gen Buster Glosson was so determined to eliminate the Scud, with its largely political destructive power that he was prepared to throw the bulk of Allied air power into a sustained 72hr effort to destroy any building, tunnel or culvert that might hide Scud activity. Fortunately for the Bedouin and the Jordanian tanker drivers the plan was shelved. However, the fact remained that the numbers of missiles and launchers supplied to Iraq had been seriously underestimated and containing the problem required a massive effort, particularly by the 335th TFS that diverted its F-15Es from the deep interdiction missions for which they had been intended. An alternative plan that came into effect from 13 February was for SCUDCAP Eagles to orbit the suspected launch areas until reaching 'bingo' fuel. They then expended one bomb or CBU on each of the known 383 culverts. An earlier variation was for SCUDCAP Eagles to drop a Mk 82 every 10–15min, with no particular target, in the hope that the explosions would deter missile crews from setting up a launch. The effects were hard to assess but the tactic may have restricted Scud activity beneath low cloud, a favourite camouflage for the missile crews.

The SCUDCAP had two other sources of support. SAS and US Delta Special Operations teams were inserted near to suspected launch areas and they guided Eagles to their targets using simple hand-held aircrew rescue radios. Sometimes these locations were established in connection with relatively infrequent satellite imagery that gave a rough 'plot', though the hotspots registered by the satellite when a launch took place sometimes turned out to be caused by other explosions, particularly B-52G strikes. RAF Tornado GR.1As with IR reconnaissance equipment also assisted. The most sophisticated technology was offered by Grumman with its loan of the two prototype E-8A Joint Surveillance Target Attack Radar System (J-STARS) aircraft, 86-0416 and 86-0417. Using synthetic aperture radar they could see up to 100mi (160km) into Iraq and detect moving

targets with sensors in their under-fuselage 'canoes' housing the Norden multi-mode sideways-looking radar in several pulse Doppler modes; either 'wide' or 'small sector' (close-up). Its moving target indication was sensitive enough to distinguish between tracked vehicles and those with wheels, and to filter out cars from military vehicles. Operated from Riyadh by the Provisional 4411th J-STARS Squadron the two aircraft were still at a relatively early stage of development: the USAF's production-model E-8C did not achieve IOC with its 93rd Air Control Wing operator until November 1997 and thirteen were eventually ordered. Its radar systems and data-link worked particularly well with the F-15E's APG-70 in synthetic

aperture mode and targeting data could be passed to the SCUDCAP 'Mud Hens' for speedy action. E-8As flew sorties of up to twelve hours per night, totalling 535 hours during the war. However, their targeting data were usually presented to the F-15E crew as target coordinates for an area up to 5sq mi (13sq km) and this still required the Eagle crew to do a lot of FLIR searching to refine the target area.

Scud hunting proved to be a frustrating experience. Many A-10 crews flew over twenty missions without seeing any activity at all. F-15E crews reported kills or 'probables' on many nights (three Scuds and launchers as a result of forty-nine missions on the night of 10 February, for example) but confirmation was always difficult and

Two kill markings on 84-0019 record the destruction of a pair of Iraqi Su-25s on 9 February by Lt Robert 'Gigs' Hehemann, who later added a PC-9 trainer to his score in F-15C 84-0015. Author's Collection

'Gigs' Hehemanns's F-15C with its two kill-markings. Author's Collection

post-war analysis dismissed most of these claims. Sometimes the results were spectacular. Missions on 17 and 23 February resulted in huge secondary explosions. On the second of these, ninety sorties were flown and secondary explosions lasted over three minutes. Sadly, these were probably not from Scuds that could only be fuelled very shortly before launch. Post-war many of the Scud kill claims were discounted and launches continued throughout the war, albeit at a reduced rate. From five per day early on (by 7 February twenty-nine had been launched against Israel and a similar number against Saudi Arabia), the total was reduced to one per day by the end of the month. The introduction of the Patriot anti-missile system may also have reduced the severity of the threat. Scud patrol sometimes produced some bizarre results. One F-15E crew apparently bombed on a strong infrared signature from their LANTIRN only to discover that the heat originated from a flock of sheep rather than an active Scud site. In all, eighty-eight missiles were launched and the most damaging strike was the chance hit on US barracks at Dhahran on 25 February that killed twenty-eight soldiers, the largest loss of American lives in any incident during the war.

Against fixed Scud sites the F-15E's radar was particularly useful as it was uniquely capable of distinguishing the radar signature of the metal railings used around the sites. On SCUDCAP pairs of F-15Es often used 'buddy-lasing' techniques: one aircraft carried the LANTIRN targeting pod while the other toted a dozen Mk 82 bombs. Once the 422nd TES had cleared LGBs for use on the F-15E that had gone to war cleared only for Mk 82 and Mk 84, the range of options opened up. Some of the LGB clearance trials stateside had to be done using only computer simulation because of the shortage of real LANTIRN targeting pods. When the *Chiefs* deployed they had only one serviceable pod and had to borrow others from test and training units, but there was no time to train crews or maintainers in their use. However, the Squadron's first LGB mission against a communications centre on the Kuwait border resulted in four 'shacks' (direct hits) with four bombs. In some cases crews got their first direct experience of using the pod during a mission, having skipped the four check rides they should have received back home. This new capability brought a change in ordnance load-outs. Lead SCUDCAP Eagles carried four GBU-10C/B LGBs on the front or rear lower CFT pylons plus LANTIRN pods and AIM-9Ms with 600gal (2,728l) wing-tanks.

Also with two Iraqi flag markings below its name panel is 84-0027 of the 53rd TFS after its return to Bitburg. Capt Ben Powell used AIM-7Ms to shoot down a Mirage F.1EQ and a MiG-23 on 27 January 1991. Jim Rotramel

Seymour Johnson F-15Es await the night at Al Kharj as another airlift of supplies arrives. USAF

The wingmen usually loaded six CBU-87/B CEM cluster bombs, particularly against targets sheltering under culverts, or the standard twelve Mk 82s.

Attacks on suspected Scud launchers were necessarily mounted at very short notice and they sometimes took F-15E crews into heavy defensive fire without SEAD support. Some of their targets were fixed Scud sites in the Baghdad region. In a repeat attack on the heavily defended Al Quaim ('Sam's Town') sites, where Scud pads had been hit the previous night, the second F-15E loss occurred on 19 January. Col David Eberly, the 4th TFW DO and his

attack from 20,000ft (6,100m), diving to lower altitude to release CBU that had been rapidly uploaded in place of Mk 82s when their mission had been changed. Eberly's aircraft, *Corvette 3*, evaded two SA-2s by using chaff but a third exploded beneath their SJ-coded 88-1692 at 21,000ft (6,400m). Col Eberly was wounded in the neck but managed to command-eject himself and Tom Griffith before losing consciousness. Both men landed near the blazing wreck of their aircraft and dangerously close to the target defence positions that had shot them down. Maj Griffith, with a wounded leg managed to get some distance away and raised Eberly

an F-15C overhead and its pilot relayed their location. During the next day they listened to the successful rescue of F-14A TARPS pilot Lt Devon Jones near Mudaysis. RESCAPped by F-15Cs the USN crew were picked up on the second attempt by MH-53 helicopters with F-16, A-10 and F-15 support. The first effort had been abandoned when it was found that the crew's location was 30mi (48km) away from their reported position. In Eberly's case the official line was that there had been no accurate report of their situation after an initial, possible voice contact with the crew. Finally, running short of water, they used Col Eberly's parachute to make 'Arab costumes' and resumed their journey west the following night. En route they raised another F-15C on the radio but after an initial reassuring contact they heard no more. Finally, as they approached the Syrian border their overwhelming thirst drove them to investigate a silent building. Inopportunely, they had chosen a guard post full of troops and they were immediately captured. In fact, had they gone further they would have walked into a minefield. Both men were released after 43 days in captivity having survived hits by Allied LGBS on the building in which they were incarcerated.

Potentially even more hazardous for the F-15E contingent was Operation *Pacific Wind*, a *Delta* Force mission that was planned to rescue US diplomats detained in Kuwait City after the Iraqi invasion. This plan included pin-point strikes by eighteen F-15Es against the heavy air defences to prepare a helicopter landing zone. Although the mission was carefully rehearsed at Hurlburt Field it was not required as the diplomats were subsequently released. The *Rockets* did provide assistance to a *Delta* operation in a rather more unorthodox manner on 14 February. A Special Forces recce team that had been inserted to locate mobile Scuds was detected by the Iraqis and three troop-carrying helicopters closed in to capture the team. Capt Tim 'T.B.' Bennett and Capt Dan 'Chewie' Bakke in F-15E 89-0487 were on SCUDCAP as *Packard 4-1* and were called down by AWACS with direct orders to stop the helicopters. Bakke got a radar return from their rotors at around 50mi (80km) and an AAQ-14 image at 14mi (22km). He released a GBU-10 LGB at 6mi (9km) and tracked it, but its helicopter target took off and climbed to 1,000ft (300m). Bakke continued to designate for the bomb and scored the F-15E's first air-to-air kill and

LGBs were cleared for the F-15E as rapidly as possible in compatibility tests in the USA. A Nellis 'Strike Eagle' releases four GBU-27/Bs on test and their switchblade fins deploy. USAF

WSO, Maj Tom Griffith were rescheduled at short notice for the mission and the resulting changes in the ATO had the knock-on effect of making the F-4G and EF-111A support jets late. The ten *Rockets* aircraft, led by Lt Col 'Scottie' Scott elected to press on as they were to be followed half an hour later by a 336th TFS group at 2230Z. In fact, their EF-111As turned back after being approached by a MiG-25 and the F-4Gs were accidentally cancelled through a misunderstanding. The Eagles began their

on his survival radio. Meeting up in the dark, the two men headed west in the hope of reaching the Syrian border or a safe pick-up area for the SAR effort that they assumed would be activated on their behalf. Before sunrise they were able to hide among boulders on a hill-top, where they spent the day trying to contact other aircraft and provide coordinates for the rescuers. Three CSAR sorties were flown south of their location to search for them but it was nightfall before they were able to make fleeting contact with

(Top) F-15Cs strut out for a *Desert Storm* mission. USAF   *(Above)* The aircraft may be digital but they still require muscle to keep them capable. USAF

the first aerial destruction of a helicopter with an LGB. Meanwhile, Capt Greg Johnson and Lt. Karl von Luhrte in *Packard 4-2* used their load of Mk 82s to remove ground troops who appeared to be advancing on the *Delta* patrol. Both aircraft set up

for AIM-9 attacks on the remaining helicopters but this was frustrated by delays in getting reassurance that they were not, in fact, the Special Forces helicopters that were also in the area but unscheduled. By the time clearance was received the Eagles

were at bingo fuel. The Iraqis escaped, as did the *Delta* team, though *Packard* flight nearly didn't. They were almost hit by a high-altitude Mk 82 drop from another flight of F-15Es that had been called in to 'sanitize' the area.

While the 335th TFS kept up the pressure on the Scuds by night the *Chiefs* continued to fly deep interdiction missions with F-117A and F-111F units. Many of these were against Iraq's vast and numerous airfields, most of which required successive re-attacks. Targets were divided up by WSOs into areas known as 'dimpies' (DMPI - desired mean point of impact) so that CBU could be distributed across an airfield for maximum long-term disruption. Delayed explosion of anti-personnel ordnance could then deter runway repairs or maintenance work. Despite fearsome defensive fire these attacks steadily eroded what remained of Saddam's massive air power. In one raid eighteen MiG, Sukhoi and Mirage fighters were destroyed by LGBs in their hiding place close to an ancient religious shrine that was undamaged. Large strike packages including over thirty F-15s flew against SAM and AAA sites in western Iraq and a couple of missions took F-15Es on the

(Top) Checks and adjustments to an AIM-7M. Its replacement by the AIM-120 leaves many Sparrows to be used up in training. USAF

(Above) Like other Allied strike aircraft the F-15E relied heavily on SEAD support from F-4G Wild Weasels and EF-111As. This Raven (66-049) is from the 390th ECS at Mountain Home, which converted to the F-15C/D a year after *Desert Storm*. USAF.

(Above) A meaningful look from this F-15C pilot possibly connects with another long and unrewarding CAP mission. Some of these flights were extended beyond eight hours, a long time on a hard seat. USAF

(Left) Thumbs up from the WSO of a Strike Eagle as a refuelling is completed. USAF

Groundcrew discuss the status of an F-15C as it is turned around for a combat mission. USAF

famous 'Winnebago Hunt'; an attempt to catch Saddam in one of his mobile trailer command posts. One of these was demolished by an F-15E and another by an F-111F, though the Coalition's resolve to target Saddam Hussein was weakened by lack of information on his precise whereabouts and reluctance to remove a Head of State in that way. Instead, the grinding attrition of his military power-base continued. Through the medium of the Chiefs' FLIR imagery it also provided the world's TV networks with some of its most spectacular video imagery of pin-point LGB attacks, a powerful morale-booster back home. The squadron's own 'Greatest Hits' video contained rather less TV-friendly imagery in which it was possible, for example, to see Iraqi personnel running from an impending attack and becoming 'whiter' in the thermal imagery as their running speed made them heat up.

Plinking Eagles

From 11 February, when F-15Es were officially cleared to carry the GBU-10 LGB, the 4th TFW (P) began to fly 'tank plinking' missions against the phalanxes of armour and artillery emplaced in Kuwait and neighbouring areas of Iraq. Pioneered by F-111F crews, the tactic used two F-15Es, one to designate a target with AAQ-14 and the other as 'bomber', loaded with Paveway II ordnance. FLIR was able to detect the small temperature differentials between cool sand and the residual heat in metal vehicles. On the first F-15E plinking mission Maj Larry Coleman and his wingman eliminated sixteen targets with sixteen GBU-10s, bombing from 20,000ft (6,100m). Although some of the tank and artillery pieces may have been hit in previous strikes (FLIR could not unfailingly spot undamaged vehicles) these attacks steadily reduced the carefully prepared armoured defences and demoralized Iraqi troops. This in turn prepared the battlefield for an Allied advance that was calculated to begin when around a half of the Iraqi armoured force had been destroyed. Eagles and F-111Fs were also able to carry out this attrition at a time when most other aircraft were grounded by repeatedly poor weather and availability.

When the land war began and Coalition forces re-entered Kuwait the two F-15E squadrons, like other air assets were allocated 'kill boxes' of enemy artillery and troop concentrations. In poor weather they flew low-altitude missions against Iraqi convoys retreating from Kuwait City, often with J-STARS guidance and CBU ordnance. Low cloud often forced them to attack from around 3,000ft (900m), putting them well within range of the enemy's still-formidable AAA and MANPAD (particularly SA-8 missiles) defences. Where possible, the classic convoy attack method was used: hitting the first and last vehicles and trapping the rest for later attack. In their desperation to escape many vehicles just ran off the road into the desert. By 20 February 89 per cent of sorties were targeted on Republican Guard and other Iraqi troops and eight days later offensive air operations ceased at 0500Z, though F-15E anti-Scud patrols continued. The Mud Hen squadrons had completed 7,700 combat hours with each squadron flying around 1,200 missions many of them included among the 1,468 anti-Scud sorties flown by Allied aircraft. One F-15E (87-0200) had fifty-four missions to its credit, only two short of the 'high time' F-111F.

For the 'albino' Eagles combat activity extended into March 1991 after the cease-fire and the establishment of no-fly zones covering large areas of north and south Iraq. Two Su-20s were detected by AWACS on 20 March breaking the 'no flying by fixed-wing aircraft' rule and one was downed by Capt John T. Donski (22nd TFS) with an AIM-9M from F-15C 84-0014. Capt Tom Dietz and his wingman Bob Hehemann were back in action on 22 March. Dietz (in 84-0010 again) fired an AIM-9M at an Su-22, destroying it, while Hehemann (85-0015) pointed his aircraft at a Pilatus PC-9 trainer that was in breach of the rules. Seeing an F-15C smoking in towards him persuaded the Iraqi pilot to bale out immediately.

By that date the 120 F-15Cs that had deployed to the battle area had flown over 5,900 sorties, maintaining a 94 per cent mission-capable rate. Against the larger, well-equipped Iraqi Air Force they had scored thirty-seven kills (including two by a Saudi pilot and one by an F-15E) without loss. Thirty-two of the Iraqi losses were high-performance jets including five MiG-29s and two MiG-25s. Twenty-four kills were with the AIM-7M that proved to be immeasurably more reliable and effective than its Vietnam-era record might have suggested. Shorter range engagements with the AIM-9M Sidewinder accounted for only nine kills and the gun was not required at all. AIM-120s were supplied and many 'captive carries' were loaded onto F-15Cs to test the missile's acquisition capability, but none was fired in anger. *Desert Storm* took the Eagle's proud record of air combat victories to ninety-one without loss.

The 52nd FW joined *Northern Watch* after *Desert Storm* and the 53rd FS reappeared in the region as part of the Spangdahlem Wing once Bitburg, its former home, had closed down. This was the squadron's 1997 Tiger scheme on F-15C 84-0001. Author's Collection

CHAPTER EIGHT

Eagle Police

Watchful Eagles

Although the cessation of hostilities at the end of February 1991 left Saddam Hussein's forces severely depleted he remained in power and soon began to punish those sections of his population that had shown opposition to his rule in the latter stages of the war. The Kurds in the North came under attack as did sections of the Shi'ite population in southern Iraq. In 1991 the Turkish Government permitted forty-eight 'foreign' aircraft on its territory to carry out Operation *Provide Comfort* for the protection of the Kurds. A six-month extension was granted in December 1993 by which time fifty-three US, British and French aircraft were usually based at Incirlik. Further extensions continued the Operation up to the end of 1996 when it was replaced by Operation *Northern Watch* (ONW) with broadly similar aims. For the south of the country Operation *Southern Watch* (OSW) began on 27 August 1992 to enforce a no-fly zone below 32 deg. N. Aircraft to implement this exclusion zone came mainly from Dhahran and from USN carriers.

In all these policing actions the USAF F-15 force was heavily involved. Abusing a condition of General Schwarzkopf's 'no fly' rule that allowed helicopter flights in the exclusion zones for civilian supply purposes, Saddam Hussein began to use gunship helicopters against the Kurds very soon after the ceasefire. F-15 pilots had to hold their fire and witness a number of these attacks on civilians without the political authorization to intervene. Some bent the rules and buzzed the gunships until this practice was also banned. Occasionally, Iraqi fixed-wing units challenged the no-fly rule too, beginning in December 1992 when two Floggers were shot down by F-16Cs. This encounter marked the combat debut of the AIM-120A AMRAAM and the demise of a MiG that had crossed the 32nd parallel an hour previously and retreated after being challenged by an F-15C. On 27 December a MiG-25 harassed a 4th Wing F-15E that escaped. Ninety minutes later another

F-15E 91-0601 was one of nine extra F-15Es funded by the transfer of USAFE Eagles to Saudi Arabia for *Desert Storm*. USAF

Foxbat entered the area and it was shot down by a 33rd FW F-15C. Another of Saddam's remaining handful of Foxbats attempted to challenge a 9th RW U-2R on 2 January 1993 and it was seen off by Eglin F-15Cs. Despite losing over 240 aircraft to Allied attacks and another 100 defectors to Iran the Iraqi Air Force still posed a threat.

The continued presence of SAM sites below the 32nd parallel was another obstacle to Allied monitoring flights and the Iraqis were told to remove their missiles by 6 January 1993. Their failure to do so caused President Bush to order attacks on SAM sites and their related command and control centres around Basrah and Nasiriyah on 13 January. In a concentrated half-hour night attack led by 4th FW F-15Es with F-117As, A-6Es, F/A-18s and Tornado GR.1s, with cover from ten 33rd FW F-15Cs, the 'Mud Hens' scored 80 per cent

hits on their targets (SA-3 Goa sites and radars) although the other strikers were less effective. Further attacks on radar sites took place on 18 January with twenty-nine aircraft, led once again by ten Seymour Johnson F-15Es. One of the CAP F-15Cs was vectored towards an intruding MiG-25, released an AIM-120A at 25mi (40km) and followed up with an AIM-7M. The available evidence suggested that the MiG escaped. Further strike packages hit AAA and radar sites until 20 January since there was clearly no intention on the Iraqi side to take away their air defence installations. Using an old-established tactic, Iraqi fighters entered the no-fly zone and attempted to 'drag' F-15Cs across SAM sites to make targets of them. The general lack of Iraqi air opposition left the 'albino' Eagles with little to do in any case. About five MiG-25s remained in service, but in various stages of unserviceability, and only nine MiG-29s, one of which crashed when its pilot was attempting to defect. Over thirty Mirage F.1s and thirty-four Sukhois had shifted to Iranian ownership.

Similar airstrikes on SAM and AAA locations in the Northern air exclusion zone (AEZ) began on 14 January 1992 but much of the Eagles' time was occupied in flying escort for reconnaissance flights by US and British aircraft. After Bitburg's *Desert Storm* contingent returned to Germany on 22 June 1991 (and the 525th FS was inactivated in May 1992) the Incirlik Detachment was taken on by a variety of other units for *Provide Comfort*. Soesterberg's 32nd FS deployed eight F-15A MSIPs to the base on 3 December 1992, relieving an 81st FW contingent. They began CAP missions the following day, led by CO Lt Col Doug Didly. Flying CAPs that lasted up to four hours, they amassed 753 sorties in the 165 days up to their return on 12 May 1993. Six months later F-15 operations ceased at the Dutch base but other units were progressively involved in the *Provide Comfort* schedules, including ANG squadrons. Three F-15As from the 199th FS, Hawaii ANG accompanied three from the 122nd FS, Lousiana ANG to Incirlik for a 90-day TDY from 12 December 1994 and returned with their MSIP F-15As in January 1996. The HANGmen provided personnel for the first half of the 1994 duty and the 122nd for the second part, giving the resident USAFE units a Christmas break. It was the first time the Hawaii squadron had deployed abroad since it sent some of its pilots to Vietnam in the 1960s. F-16 units provided relief for the Eagle squadrons on the *Provide Comfort* rota, particularly for the less numerous F-15E providers. One of the latter, the 3rd Wing sent six F-15Cs from its 54th FS to Incirlik from 13 April 1995 until July rather than F-15Es. Since then the *Northern Watch* schedule has drawn in units from as far afield as Kadena. In September 1999 F-15Cs and an E-3A from the 18th Wing deployed to Incirlik via Moron, Spain while a 44th FS detachment arrived at Al Kharj in May 1998 for six weeks during a period of heightened tension with Iraq. The ANG continued to participate in the policing action. Six *Redhawks* Eagles from the 123rd FS, Oregon ANG were at Incirlik in a deployment up to mid-April 1998.

At Dhahran a similar succession of units manned the 'no fly' patrols. Having led the 71st FS contingent back to Langley on

Armourers load a GBU-28B/B (Number 003) on an F-15E's centreline pylon. Known as 'Deep Throat' in the Gulf War these weapons used the BLU-109/B penetrator warhead and resulted from a fast-moving cooperative effort by Texas Instruments and Lockheed in January–February 1991. During *Allied Force* GBU-28 was used to attack underground aircraft storage in Serbia. USAF

8 March 1991 with MiG killer Steve Tate in the formation, Col John McBroom was soon involved in organizing a 1st TFW deployment. Its first detachment, under the 4404th Wing, included twelve aircraft that began a six-month return to Dhahran on 16 June 1992, replacing the 60th FS from Eglin. They, in turn, were replaced by the 9th TFS, 49th TFW that had taken over from the 36th TFW in June 1991. The 9th FS then de-activated shortly after returning to Holloman AFB, ending the Wing's Eagle operations. Thereafter, as the USAF 'drawdown' reduced the number of available units, the 1st and 33rd Wings rotated their squadrons alternately through 1993 to 1996, sending between eight and twelve aircraft at a time. From January 1996 the Eglin deployment packages increased in size with eighteen 59th FS aircraft flying to Dhahran in January 1996 and eighteen from the 58th FS replacing them in mid-April. By 1997 the Quadrennial Defence Review had inactivated the 59th FS leaving the 58th and 60th Squadrons to carry the burden.

With the passing of the 36th FW its last squadron, the 53rd FS *Tigers* transferred to the 52nd FW at Spangdahlem on 25 February 1994. It flew a mixture of FY79 and FY84 F-15Cs, some of which had spent their entire careers with USAFE units. A year later the squadron appeared on the Incirlik rota, replacing two ANG units. However, its new role as Alert squadron for the NATO Central Region restricted its ability to deploy to the Gulf. A compensation (if any was sought) was the selection of the squadron to fly the first sorties by USAF fighters in the newly unrestricted airspace of Eastern Germany in January 1995. The other CONUS F-15C deployer has been the 366th Wing that supplied a six-aircraft *Provide Comfort* detachment in October 1996 and eighteen jets to Al Kharj in April 1997 for *Southern Watch*. The 4404th Wing (P) that was formed at Al Kharj (Prince Sultan AB), moving to Dhahran in June 1992, returned to Al Kharj to manage detachments to the base by F-15C and F-15E units.

Among these was the 366th wing, but this time its 391st FS with 'Mud Hens', eighteen of which proved their 'fighter' credibility by taking over the *Southern Watch* in March 1997. Prior to that, F-15E detachments to Dhahran by the 4th Wing had continued at a steady rate since *Desert Storm*. The Wing's squadrons each rotated twelve aircraft (reduced to nine in March 1994) with the 336th FS replacing the 334th on 27 December 1991 and the 335th taking over in June 1992. Transit flights were usually via Torrejon until the base was closed to USAF operations in mid-1992. In times of increased tension the size of the deployments could easily be increased. For example, in October 1994 when Saddam Hussein began to concentrate his troops near the Kuwaiti border, the 4th FW was tasked with providing thirty-six F-15Es, if required, for Operation *Vigilant Warrior*. Throughout 1995 and 1996 the Wing reverted to an eighteen-aircraft presence at Dhahran. With eighty-five F-15Es on strength in mid-1999 the Wing continued to supply detachments, including a 336th FS contingent to Incirlik in April and May 1999 to relieve the 48th FW on *Northern Watch*. In this capacity the F-15Es were ready for air combat just like their light grey namesakes and ACM was a major part of their training. This led to the extraordinary escape of Capt Brian Udell from F-15E 89-0504 following HUD failure and control loss over the Atlantic during ACM practice. Udell ejected in a vertical dive at 780mph (1,255km/h) and survived, although his WSO failed to escape.

Lakenheath's F-15Es began to visit Incirlik soon after the 493rd FS became operational on 1 July 1993. Nine aircraft flew to the Turkish base on 2 August and soon saw action, making a retaliatory strike on an SA-3 Goa site near Mosul on 19 August. A replacement detachment was sent in February 1994 while the 493rd FS provided F-15Cs for the same duty on 27 June 1994. In July and August 1995 the 48th FW was supplying six F-15Cs and twelve F-15Es for *Provide Comfort*, a pattern that continued into 1996. Throughout the deployment, pairs of aircraft were rotated back to Lakenheath for Phase maintenance or to even out the airframe hours on the Wing's complement. The additional demands of the Balkans crisis from 1993 onwards made this pattern of operations far more complex, but the *Northern Watch* had to be sustained and daily flights continued over Northern Iraq.

It was on one of these flights that two US Army UH-60A Blackhawks (87-26000 and 88-26060) with twenty-six UN diplomatic and military personnel aboard were destroyed in an extraordinary accident involving 53rd FS F-15Cs. E-3B AWACS controllers had detected what they took to be a pair of Mi-24 Hinds attacking a Kurdish settlement near Irbil in the northern air exclusion zone. The Bitburg squadron had arrived on a *Provide Comfort* TDY from 25 February 1994 and two of its pilots, the CO and a captain as *Tiger* flight, acquired the two helicopters at 40 nm. The junior officer (flying lead position) elected to set up an AIM-120 AMRAAM BVR attack having been cleared to do so. However, the F-15s did approach to visual range and made a single pass at the helicopters at 450kt in which the captain made an uncertain visual ID that was unfortunately accepted by the Commanding Officer and AWACS controllers as confirmation of the helicopters' hostile status as Hind-Ds. The Eagle pilots later stated that they had found visual ID difficult because of sun glare, preventing them from seeing the US flags painted on the UH-60s. They also relied strongly on the fact that they could not obtain the correct IFF responses from the helicopters' on their Mode 1 IFF interrogator channel. Probably the Blackhawks were still using IFF codes designed for use over Turkey but it was also suggested that their IFF equipment may have been turned off because of overheating. In any case, after a single VID pass the lead F-15C (84-0025) fired an AIM-120 at the leading helicopter from 4nm range and his wingman (79-0025) fired an AIM-9M at the second machine. Both were destroyed. Clearly the tragic incident raised crucial issues concerning over-reliance on IFF, visual recognition training and effective coordination with AWACS controllers as well as the correct observance of procedures for such an engagement. In mitigation, it was the only confirmed occasion on which incorrect visual ID by fighter crews led to such a loss although the potential for occurrences of this kind was always present. During *Desert Storm*, however, it is possible that the loss of EF-111A 66-0023 and its crew may have resulted in part from over-zealous pursuit by an F-15C pilot who had been unable to get an accurate ID on the aircraft. The Raven crew may also have overreacted, hitting the ground as they manoeuvred to evade the fighter. After the Blackhawk affair the rules were tightened considerably.

Fox, Focus and Strike

On various other occasions during the 1990s the Iraqi leader tested the resolve of the remaining members of the Coalition (principally the USA and Britain) by massing his troops on the Kuwait border. The response was always rapid. Operation *Vigilant Warrior* took 100,000 US troops by airlift to the Middle East after one of these belligerent displays. Among the 200 CONUS-based combat aircraft that were prepared for deployment were forty-two F-15Cs, mainly from the 1st FW. Only a small number of the initial twenty-seven had actually flown to Dhahran when Saddam Hussein backed down and removed his troops. The thirty-six Seymour Johnson F-15Es intended for the Operation were held back but the 1st FW returned to Alert status in September 1996 when Operation *Desert Focus* was mounted to deter the Iraqi dictator once again. Throughout 1996 Allied reconnaissance aircraft, including RAF Harrier GR.7s and French Jaguars continued overflights, with F-15Cs flying ahead to sweep the area for signs of aerial opposition while EF-111As checked for electronic emissions.

In 1997–98 the priorities shifted to providing responses to Saddam's intransigence over allowing UN Special Commission (UNSCOM) weapons inspection teams to visit sites suspected of harbouring nuclear or chemical and biological weapons materials. In February 1998 the resultant tension took the largest US force reinforcement since 1991 to the area. Six F-15Cs were already at Incirlik for ONW and another thirty at Al Kharj. Additional F-117As, F-16CJ SEAD fighters, B-1Bs and B-52Hs were deployed to the area for potential attacks with F-15C cover. The Operation's ominous title, *Desert Thunder*, may have helped to persuade the Iraqi leader to comply with the UN edicts. Remaining in the area the F-16CJs were called in to remove a number of anti-aircraft radar and missile sites in Operation *Desert Strike*. A larger-scale assault called *Desert Viper* was called off when its strike packages were minutes from the Iraqi border, but by 17 December 1998 renewed tension brought a stronger reaction in Operation *Desert Fox*. Political considerations ruled out the use of F-15s on this occasion (see *On Northern Watch*) so USN carrier aircraft, USAF B-1B Lancers and B-52Hs with Tomahawk missiles and RAF Tornado GR.1s destroyed a number of key strategic targets in Iraq. On this occasion much of the early fighter cover was provided by USN Tomcats. LANTIRN-equipped F-14B 'Bombcats' with GBU-12, GBU-16 and GBU-24 LGBs flew strikes to support USN BGM-109 Tomahawks in the first phase of attacks. In all, over a hundred targets were hit. International opinion prevented the Operation from continuing long enough to deter Saddam Hussein from further provocation and the UNSCOM inspection effort had to be ended in 1999.

Quick-reaction attacks in response to Iraqi challenges to ONW and OSW overflights have continued, particularly after Iraq claimed that it no longer recognized the no-fly zones and would fire on any aircraft within its airspace. SA-3 missiles were fired at three ONW aircraft on 28 December 1998 over Mosul and their site was hit in a DEAD (destruction of enemy air defences) attack by F-15Es with PGMs

and F-16CJs with HARMs. This was the first of sixty-one strikes by US and British aircraft in the next five months. F-15Es were involved in at least thirty-six of these, either as sole strike aircraft or in conjunction with F-16CJ and EA-6B specialists. USN and RAF Tornado GR.1s shared some of the missions with the 'Mud Hens' from the 4th or 48th FWs. The majority of targets were SA-2, SA-3 or SA-6 sites and radars but AAA sites and communications hubs were also struck. F-15Es used GBU-12, though GBU-15 and GBU-24 were occasionally required for specific hard targets such as bunkers. The AGM-130 (a powered version of the GBU-15) was used for the first time also. All missions were conducted without loss or damage to the aircraft though not all were trouble-free. In one attack F-15Es inadvertently hit pumping stations that were taking oil legitimately from Iraq to

Turkey, thereby precipitating friction with the host country for ONW operations. Iraq's few remaining MiG-25s continued to offer sporadic opposition. On 5 January 1999 two F-15s were locked up on a Foxbat's radar as it attempted a dash interception. Three AIM-120As and an AIM-7M were fired BVR at the MiGs that turned away, though shortly afterwards two Phoenix missiles were launched by F-14Ds against a pair of MiG-25s, making the combat debut for that missile. In all cases the missiles inexplicably failed to make contact. More frequent resistance to the overflights has come from Iraq's AAA batteries that are usually mobile, hard to detect and frequently located next to civilian buildings.

Although these SEAD and DEAD activities have caused steady attrition of Iraq's integrated air defence system (IADS) to the point where, for example, few of the older SA-2 and SA-3 missiles remain, the Iraqi President has usually managed to portray them as examples of 'US aggression' against his country while at the same time challenging these UN-sanctioned monitoring flights. Nevertheless, in 1999 over 10,000 sorties were flown over Iraq and by September 2000 over 480 targets had been struck, though not all were in the 'no-fly' zones. They included 139 AAA installations and 13 SAM erector/launchers. The other targets were mainly radar and IADS communication elements. Brig Gen David Deptula, one of the principal planners of the Desert Storm air campaign, was in command of ONW at the time and he was able to report a 100 per cent mission accomplishment rate for 1998 to mid-1999. Some of those mission rosters included himself in an F-15C.

There was an upsurge in these activities in August 1999 with the majority of the strikes aimed at SAM sites. In many cases these were launched unguided to protect their radar installations from detection. Supporting F-15Es on the Southern watch in mid-1999 were the F-15C/Ds of the 27th and 94th FS, some carrying rare examples of F-15 nose-art. RAF Tornado F.3s and ANG F-16Cs are also frequent residents at al Kharj and SEAD comes as usual from F-16CJs and EA-6B Prowlers with joint USAF/USN crews. These patrols continued through 2000, albeit with less to hit as the Iraqi IADS was ground down and airfields in the exclusion zones were progressively abandoned. Partly, this was to deter further defections to Iran but mainly so that Saddam Hussein could concentrate his remaining air force units around Baghdad.

On Northern Watch

By Captain Mike 'Starbaby' Pietrucha, USAF

We had been grounded during *Desert Fox* . There were concerns about 'offensive' operations being conducted from Turkey. Since the USAF was unable to conduct combat operations from Saudi Arabia either, most attacks were made by cruise missiles, aircraft based in Bahrain and the US Navy. Due to the increased risk to aviators, all ONW aircraft were grounded for the duration of the strikes. Worse yet (from our standpoint), we didn't fly for another week. This had the unfortunate effect of denying us the tactical recce that we needed to get a really good picture of the threat array. Finally, we got to fly in the North [over Iraq] again, but the new defence array was mobile and the thickest I'd ever seen in over 100 missions.

We had a plan and were a little more keyed up than normal. The weather wasn't optimal, with a thin deck at 20,000ft covering two-thirds of the area. It scattered out as time went on and the F-16CJs went into the threat array to test the waters. As they were exiting, those waters heated up. We (*Coors 1*, the F-15E lead) were established in a CAP north of the town of Irbil. *Bud* flight was in the west, north of Saddam Dam, also looking for the rarely present Iraqi fighter. *Bud 02* and *Coors 01* got simultaneous SA-3 missile launch warning on the RWR. The radio calls stepped on each other and who you heard depended on who you were closer to. No matter, they both said the same thing: we were defensive and manoeuvring. We ran east through the Mach and *Bud* executed a defensive manoeuvre and jettisoned tanks. Somebody called that there were two missiles in the air, but the radio chatter was both excited and confusing. We were tail-on and out of range and didn't see the missile at all, but saw the contrails and self-destruct puffs well above us. We got clear and our wingman, who had not been targeted, told us which site had fired. While [we were] looking at the location the SAM fired a third

shot. (It was the booster exhaust from this third shot that was captured on tape and released to the Press.)

We gathered the two F-15E elements and requested clearance to attack. BGen Deptula, the Combined Task Force Commander, was standing by on the radio; clearance took 45 seconds. We executed an attack plan that we had developed the previous year, using old F-4G [Wild Weasel] tactics. The F-16s provided cover with HARMs while the EA-6Bs jammed every radar in sight to deny the enemy a clear picture. Even so we felt a little exposed. My RWR scope is programmed right next to my target pod and I had one eyeball for each one on the way in. My pilot, Lt Col Larry 'Bat' Cross, S-turned the whole way in, making a firing solution more difficult.

Attacking a SAM site with free-fall ordnance is like bringing a knife to the OK Corral. The SA-3 site has more missiles than we have bombs, with triple our bomb range and triple our bomb speed. 'Fast' is merely an academic consideration until the missile leaves the rail, and then it is damned fast. To complicate matters, there was an SA-2 site standing overwatch over the SA-3, but he could only go after one of us at a time and there were four F-15Es on the attack. We ran in and let go with both GBU-12s and checked off. We lased the *Low Blow* target tracking radar and both weapons scored direct hits, followed one second later by both bombs from *Bud 02*. Bud didn't have a target ID and (correctly) went through dry. *Coors 02* hit the control van with two weapons. There was probably severe collateral damage to the missiles and other equipment, but the *Low Blow* was completely obliterated. We egressed, completed a roll call and returned to base. The adrenaline wore off and I stopped shaking at about the time we crossed into Turkey. BGen Deptula met the crews at the jet to congratulate us. As part of the ADVON I got to pick the callsigns. We used the F-4G callsigns from *Desert Storm*: domestic beers only!

Denying Flight

While operations in the Gulf continued a new demand was made of the USAF Eagle force. Years of political strife in the disintegrating country of Yugoslavia had required a UN peace-keeping contingent to supervise the 1992 cease-fire between the Serbian state and the newly independent Croatia, but an associated conflict in Bosnia-Herzegovina needed United Nations Protection Force (UNPROFOR) troops to deploy to Bosnia, with protective air cover. The situation deteriorated so rapidly that by 12 April 1993 a ban was enforced on military flights in Bosnia-Herzegovina airspace following the bombing of a Muslim village near Srebrenica by Serb An-2 Colts on 15 March. This *Deny Flight* ban reinforced an earlier closure of the airspace from 9 October 1992 that had been repeatedly violated. NATO E-3 AWACS aircraft began Operation *Sky Monitor* on 16 October.

Initially, the air operation involved creating an air bridge to supply the besieged city of Sarajevo in the Summer of 1992 and several of the aircraft involved took ground fire. Fighters from the carriers USS *J.F. Kennedy* and USS *Theodore Roosevelt* flew CAPs over *Provide Promise* supply drops in the area and CAPs by land-based fighters commenced on 12 April 1993 under NATO's 5th Tactical Air Force (5 ATAF) from its base at Vincenza in Italy.

An FY90 F-15E lifts off from Aviano AB with a pair of AGM-130s, four AIM-9s and two AIM-120As en route for a target in the former Yugoslavia. USAF

CAP sorties usually lasted up to five hours with an hour in transit each way and a refuelling after the first two hours. Race-track patterns were flown over two stations; one in the north covering the Banja Luka/Tuzla region and a second patrol over Mostar and Sarajevo. Aviano AB, where 48th FW F-15Es had sometimes deputized for the resident 31st FW F-16Cs when they were at *Red Flag*, became home to a dozen F-15Cs, including MiG-killer 84-0019, from the 53rd FS (the first of their kind to fly from the base) while Dutch F-16s, RAF Tornado F.3s and French Mirage 2000Cs arrived at other Italian bases. Radar contacts in the CAP areas were first made on 24 April but F-16s were unable to intercept before the traces were lost.

Within the former Yugoslav state there were substantial numbers of effective combat aircraft in the possession of all the factions apart from the Bosnian Muslims, including MiG-29s for the defence of Belgrade, MiG-21s, ex-Iraqi MiG-23s and indigenous J-21 Jastrebs and J-22 Galebs. Like the Iraqi pilots encountered in *Desert Storm* the Yugoslav fighter crews had been trained in Russian disciplines. Capt Lawrence Pravacek observed:

> It seemed to us that they had used a lot of old Soviet-type theories. They relied a lot on their GCI command and control and we kind of liked that because once you've taken their command and control out they're flying around a lot more blind. We're used to doing a lot more of it on our own so it worked to our advantage.

A favourite Soviet-style trick from Vietnam days was to 'hide' a third fighter in a two-ship flight by placing it close to one of the other two. At close range it would then emerge from the radar plot to surprise an opposing pair of fighters with a new threat. However, as Col Mike Casey pointed out: 'Even if we only had the two on radar and fired BVR so that they blew up, the third guy close to one of them is going to blow up too.'

Anti-aircraft defences included a wide spectrum of SA-3, SA-6, SA-7 and SA-9 missiles with comprehensive radar and

Ten bomb-score mission marks, kill-markings for a radar site, an AAA site and a SAM launcher are stencilled on the nose of this 492nd FS Eagle. USAF

optically aimed AAA. Before the air exclusion zone was established, over seventy-five aircraft had been shot down since the civil war began in 1991. If air combat with NATO aircraft was to occur it was anticipated that it would be against small, low-flying targets over difficult terrain. VID would be needed and this would bring Allied fighters within range of intensive AAA and MANPAD fire. When F-15C pilots arrived

they found that aircraft fitted with the telescopic rifle sight conferred a slight advantage. A more intractable problem was that AWACS orbits outside hostile airspace made it difficult for them to detect low-flyers in the mountainous terrain. Low-flying, terrain-hugging helicopters presented special problems, though the Bitburg Eagles did encounter two ammunition-filled Serb Gazelle helicopters in the AEZ on 1 May,

forcing one to land and the other to leave the area. Some Serb helicopters adopted the white paint of UNPROFOR aircraft to frustrate attempts at aerial VID.

In a curious reprise of *Desert Storm* the Serbs threatened to use Scud missiles against NATO bases in Italy and the possibility of letting the *Chiefs'* F-15E Scud-hunters loose on them was explored. Attack aircraft, including RAF Jaguars and USAF A-10As were moved to Italy in July 1993 for Operation *Disciplined Guard* – the protection of UN 'blue helmets' on the ground. The Bitburg F-15C detachments were relieved in July by 23rd FS F-16Cs that month after flying 660 sorties for Operation *Deny Flight*. They took over patrol of the air corridors across Bosnia and were succeeded in February 1994 by the 526th FS that lost one F-16C after engine failure over Porec. By then the F-16Cs were being armed with a pair of Mk 84 bombs in case attacks on AAA sites were required. Strikes did not occur until 10 April when Serbian ground positions were hit in Operation *Blue Sword*. F-16Cs bombed Serb tanks that were shelling Gorazde and thereby performed the first ground-attack mission in NATO's history. This followed the first-ever NATO offensive action on 28 February when Aviano F-16Cs destroyed four Serb Galeb light attack aircraft from Udbina air base after they bombed a munitions factory in breach of *Deny Flight*. In a second strike in support of ground troops on 16 April Lt Nick Richardson's Sea Harrier FRS.1 became the first NATO casualty. This raising of the stakes had already brought increased air deployments to 5ATAF including eight F-15Es from the 492nd FS *Bolars* in February 1994. They and their 494th FS successors remained at Aviano for about twelve months.

By November 1994 the situation had worsened. Serbian J-22 Orao attack aircraft dropped napalm and CBU within the UN safe area around Bihac as a reprisal for Bosnian Army attacks. A second attack that occurred the following day triggered a UN Security Council decision to attack Serbian targets within Croatia, particularly Udbina airfield where the Oraos were based. Eight 492nd FS F-15Es with GBU-12s were among thirty aircraft involved. The Eagles concentrated on SA-6 sites and runway cratering with F/A-18Ds HARM-shooters from VMFA(AW)-332 in support. A further NATO strike followed on 24 December after two Sea Harriers were fired on by

AIM-120 AMRAAM was the primary air-to-air weapon for all F-15 crews in *Allied Force*. The walk-around check required a moment to ensure that the missiles were correctly hung. USAF

Patches for the 493rd FS and for *Deny Flight*.

an SA-2 battery. Four Lakenheath F-15Es hit a pair of SA-2 sites at Bosanka Krupa and Dvor after they had locked onto NATO aircraft en route to destroy the missile battery at Otoka that had fired on the Royal Navy aircraft. However, although the Serbs expected further large-scale strikes these were put on hold when it was clear that they were only hardening Serb attitudes. Despite this there had to be a response to the Serbs' continued shelling of Sarajevo and a thirty-aircraft package including F-15Es was launched on 25 November. Under the elaborate NATO rules of engagement these aircraft were turned back because the Serb tanks stopped firing before the aircraft arrived over the target area. The same rules of engagement made effective action by CAP fighters very difficult since responses to hostile action or enemy aircraft required permission from a NATO General via UNPROFOR HQ to the pilot concerned. F-15E patrols continued in the SEAD role to provide a more instant reaction to any ground-fire against reconnaissance flights. No further bombing took place until 25 May 1995 when six F-16Cs hit a Bosnian Serb ammunition dump near Pale, but further attacks were halted after the Serbs took ninety UN personnel hostage. Demonstrating that their SAM

defences were still formidable the Serbs fired two SA-6 missiles at a pair of Aviano F-16Cs, downing one with Capt Scott O'Grady aboard.

28 August 1995 brought a much more severe response from NATO when a Serb mortar attack on Sarajevo market place killed thirty-eight civilians. Within a day 5ATAF aircraft commanded by Maj Gen Hal Hornburg, former Commander of an F-15E Wing during *Desert Storm*, received detailed 'frags' for punitive airstrikes in Operation *Deliberate Force* on 30 August. Five strike packages hit Serb armour and supplies around Sarajevo and three more followed on the 31st. The 494th FS F-15Es were the prime strikers although only eight were available. The bulk of the strikes went to forty-eight Aviano F-16Cs. Since the Bosnian Serb leadership showed no greater willingness to negotiate a peace more widespread strikes commenced on 5 September. F-15Es again hit air defence sites and armour, using GBU-10 and GBU-12 LGBS. Nine GBU-15 electro-optical guide bombs were also used for the first time on 9 September against air defence targets around Banja Luka. Five daily packages were launched over the following five days hitting mainly ammunition stores, EW sites and communications bunkers. Medium-altitude attacks were made, using the extremely effective SEAD provided by EF-111As and HARM-equipped F-16CJs. When the last of 750 strike missions were flown on 13 September fifty-six targets had been hit. F-15Es were the only Eagles involved since there was no F-15C detachment in Italy and little need for dedicated air superiority fighters on this occasion.

Air operations, particularly with LGBs were hampered by poor weather and finally suspended when the Serbian Gen Mladic decided to pull back from Sarajevo, the last 'safe' area, and a cease-fire was declared. Air exclusion flights continued over western Serbia and further LGB strikes were made on 9 October to rescue some UN peacekeepers. Without their heavy weapons the Serbs were soon expelled from large areas of Bosnia and they signed the Dayton Peace Agreement that allowed 40,000 NATO troops to deploy to Bosnia as a peace implementation force (IFOR) under Operation *Endeavour*. F-15Es that had flown over a hundred sorties, remained in place at Aviano with the 7490th (Provisional) Wing to help deter further aggression by any of the factions involved. Their use, with other air power, had at last forced the

For ground crew, arming and maintaining the Eagle force went on around the clock and in all weathers. USAF

A PGM-laden Mud Hen leaves a trail of shimmering heat as it thunders down Aviano's runway. USAF

493rd FS *Reapers* F-15Cs took on the Yugoslav Air Force during *Allied Force*, achieving air superiority in a very short time. Author's Collection

Bosnian Serb government to view NATO's resolve more seriously. However, the defiant statements by Serbian leaders Mladic and Karadzic left little doubt that their nationalism was far from being a defeated cause.

Allied Force

Calls for renewed air strikes in response to Serbian repression in Kosovo began in mid-1998 and NATO was at several points on the verge of issuing an ultimatum to President Milosevic to remove his forces from the threatened areas. By October it was clear that NATO's warnings were once again being ignored and a renewed build-up of forces began with the arrival of six B-52Hs in the UK on 10 October. Among other movements, fifteen F-15Cs of the 493rd FS were flown to the forward location at Aviano. Three years after NATO's first air strikes in Bosnia the air elements that had been continuing patrols over the area were substantially increased and organized into four Aerospace Expeditionary Wings (AEWs) on 11 October 1998. At the same time the NATO Commander, Gen Wesley Clark was authorized to initiate a five-stage aerial bombardment to end the Serb offensive, preceded by *Phase Zero*, a period of intensive reconnaissance and 'deterrent' overflights. Several extended deadlines later, Milosevic began to remove his troops and armour on 26 October, with NATO verification teams emplaced to monitor the situation under Operation *Eagle Eye*. Serbian forces recommenced attacks on civilians in January 1999 bringing renewed

Full power on the F100-229s hauls another load of CBU, fuel and missiles off the concrete for another *Allied Force* mission. USAF

threats of air action and an increase in the available air power to 430 aircraft, mainly at Italian bases and on 48 hours' standby. Negotiations at Rambouillet, France reached a tentative peace agreement on 23 February, though it was backed by a further force expansion including twelve F-117As, F-15Es from the 492nd FS and a new B-52H deployment. At Aviano the F-117As took over the HAS accommodation, displacing the F-15C contingent to Cervia. The Eagles were controlled by the 16th AEW that also included the B-52Hs, U-2S spyplanes and KC-135 tankers. For his part, President Milosevic massed 4,500 of his troops on the Kosovan border, while the Kosovo Albanians maintained that a military solution was inevitable. Diplomatic efforts to establish a lasting peace were exhausted by 24 March and NATO air action began after its peace-keepers had been evacuated.

F-15 assets had been increased to eighteen F-15Cs at Cervia, drawn from the 493rd FS and operating as the 493rd Air Expeditionary Fighter Squadron of the 501st Expeditionary Operating Group. Twelve aircraft arrived on 21 February and another six later in the month. At Aviano a core of six 494th FS F-15Es led by Col Warren Henderson had arrived in December 1998 to allow the based 492nd FS aircraft to commit to ONW. By March the base housed twenty-six F-15Es among 173 aircraft, with many crews living in a 'tent city'. Most of these Eagles arrived on 22 February. The base soon became rather crowded as Col Casey recalled:

Instead of parking our airplanes in the shelters we were parking them anywhere we could. We had twenty people working in one small room, constantly on top of each other, with briefings and de-briefings going on in the same room. As a working environment it wasn't the optimum way to go to war, but with the weather and the food, we couldn't complain!

Following CALCM launches by B-52Hs that initiated Operation *Noble Anvil* (the

Paveway II series weapons were still in the US inventory in 1999, having been in combat use since October 1983. USAF

US part of Operation *Allied Force*) F-15Es were prominent in the first night of bombing; 24–25 March 1999. They were among seventy aircraft launched from the 31st AEW at Aviano and other bases against forty targets in Yugoslavia. Facing them were around fourteen MiG-29s, over seventy MiG-21s and a formidable array of SAMs including sixty SA-6 Gainful units and numerous mobile SA-9 Gaskin and SA-13 Gopher systems plus a worrying number of SA-7 and SA-14/-16/-18 MANPADS that dictated a 15,000ft (4,570m) ceiling for any NATO aircraft without a missile approach warning system. To increase the hazards for strike aircraft, forced on occasion to lower altitudes by poor weather, there were huge numbers of 20mm, 30mm and 57mm AAA batteries.

Ahead of the strike force went the F-15C OCA 'sweepers', performing a standard F-15 tactic. As Eagle pilot Lawrence

Pravacek pointed out, 'We like to be out in front of everybody. We have the biggest radar and the best missiles and we want to make sure that we are getting our job done fast so that everybody else can get their job done.' F-15E planning concentrated on enemy air defence targets from Night 1 using warloads averaging 6,000lb (2,700kg), but the target list widened and Eagles shared in attacking over 150 targets struck in the first seventeen days of the war, including the destruction of half Yugoslavia's fuel supplies. Later in the conflict F-15Es carried CBU as they joined the search-and-destroy campaign against well-hidden Serb armour and troops in Kosovo. As SEAD attackers they worked with F-16CJs, hitting SAM sites with LGBs and often using the tactics for DEAD developed over Iraq, though much of the Yugoslav IADS remained intact throughout the conflict.

Like other NATO strikers, the F-15Es' sensors were hampered by continued bad weather and poor visibility on many nights. Even so, their unique capabilities fitted them for a number of specialist missions including the dropping of a 4,700lb (2,130kg) GBU-28/B 'bunker buster' with BLU-113 warhead on a tunnel-accessed underground hangar at Pristina airfield on 29 April. Pioneered by the 48th TFW's F-111Fs in *Desert Storm*, this weapon could penetrate over 100ft (30m) into the terrain before exploding. On this occasion at least a dozen stored MiG-21s survived and flew out of the airfield later. BLU-28/B required specialist handling and loading and the weapon was flown into Aviano specially for this mission. Five BLU-116B Advanced Unitary Penetrator weapons were also flown to Italy and may have been issued to the F-15E unit.

In a conflict where at least 90 per cent of the Allied ordnance dropped was precision-guided, the 26 F-15Es were clearly at an advantage and their unique ability to carry the GBU-15 and AGM-130 stand-off weapons increased the aircraft's hitting power considerably. AGM-130 could use

Having started its combat career with a very limited menu of ordnance the F-15E is now fully capable of handling the current range of tactical munitions and this is a selection of the weapons most typically hung beneath the aircraft during the conflicts of the 1990s.

Low Drag General Purpose Bombs (LDGP)
Mk 82 (500lb (227kg)) Cast steel case with 192lb (87kg) of H6, Minol 2 or Tritonal explosive.

Mk 84 (2,000lb (907kg)) Cast steel case with 945lb (429kg) of H6, Minol 2 or Tritonal explosive.

These free-fall 'dumb' bombs can be fitted with various fuses, the most common being FMU-54 or M904 impact fuses or FMU-26, -72 or -139 delay fuses or the FMU-113 proximity fuse that detonates the bomb above ground level for maximum blast effect. The AIR (Air Inflatable Retard) versions in common use have the Goodyear 'ballute' (balloon/parachute) retarding tail unit to slow the bomb and allow the aircraft to escape its blast at low altitude. This replaces the previous mechanical Snakeye retarding system. For the Mk 82 the BSU-49/B (weight 56lb (25kg)) is fitted and for the Mk 84 the BSU-50/B (96lb (43.5kg))

Mounting Six Mk 82s can be hung on each CFT plus wing or centreline loads using Multiple Ejection Racks (MERs) to a total of about 26 bombs. The usual load for BAI missions would be twelve. With the Mk 84, two can be carried per CFT (lower racks only) and one per wing or centreline pylon.

Precision Guided Munitions (PGMs)
Paveway II Series. GBU-12 B/B (500lb (227kg)), GBU-10C/B (2,000lb (907kg)), Paveway III BGU-24/B (2000lb (907kg)).

The Paveway II bombs use a simpler, cheaper version of the Texas Instruments laser homing kit fitted to 1970s Paveway I weapons and a folding cruciform 'wing' group for added range and manoeuvrability. The free-gimballing laser seeker on the nose of the bomb (a Mk82 or Mk84) is aligned to the target by the ring 'tail' at the rear of the seeker unit, using the velocity vector of the bomb as it falls. The seeker head 'lens' is split into four quadrants that detect reflected laser energy fired at the target. A small computer housed in the section between the seeker and the forward fins compares the energy received by each quadrant and sends common signals to solenoids in the tail control fins, fitted to the rear of the Mk82/84 'core'. The bomb is then guided so that the angle of the seeker's line of sight equals the velocity vector of the bomb (that is, each seeker quadrant is receiving precisely identical energy radiation levels). GBU-12B/B was the main tank 'plinker' in *Desert Storm*. Up to eight could be carried on the CFT pylons.

Paveway III (from 1987) uses low-level guidance for release at low altitude and/or poor weather and high threat areas. It can also be released at higher altitudes and dropped at steeper angles of up to 60 degrees. A more advanced microprocessor allows off-axis drops in low visibilty. Its advanced digital autopilot (using a BAe Dart gyro) and mid-course correction guidance are combined with larger, high-lift folding guidance fins. Laser designating of the target can be delayed until the weapon is part-way to its target and the process of aligning the bomb to its target at lower altitudes is more rapid due to improved manoeuvrability. The bomb offers many advantages, though at higher cost, for more challenging battlefield conditions. GBU-24B uses the Mk 84 warhead for a wider blast effect while GBU-24A/B is based on the BLU-109/B 'Improved 2000lb' (I-2000) 14.5x95in warhead with inch-thick, one-piece, high-grade forged steel case. It is designed to penetrate targets before the tail-mounted fuse triggers detonation that can be delayed. It is designed for use against hardened shelters, bunkers and other hard targets such as bridges. Usually, four are carried. In uncertain weather or visibility F-15Es could carry a mixed load of GBU-10, GBU-24 and Mk 84.

For deeper penetration of underground bunkers or storage sites the GBU-28/B 4,700lb (2,132kg) 'Deep Throat' LGB has occasionally been used after pioneering combat drops from F-111Fs. Based on surplus 8in gun barrels reamed out to 2in the 18.75ft (5.7m) long

weapon uses a GBU-27A/B guidance kit to direct its 650lb (295kg) of Tritonal explosive to the target, where it penetrates up to 100ft (30m) before detonation. In tests it rammed through 25ft (7.6m) of solid concrete. GBU-28/Bs are 'built to order' for special missions.

Cluster Bomb Units (CBU)
This category includes a vast array of sub-munitions and dispensers but F-15Es have most commonly carried CBU-87/B CEM, CBU-89/B Gator or CBU-59/B (Mk 20 Rockeye).

CBU-87/B Combined Effects Munitions (CEM) and CBU-89 both use the same SUU-65/B Tactical Munitions Dispenser (TMD).

CBU-59/B uses the Mk 7 dispenser that can also be configured as CBU-59 APAM (anti-personnel, anti-material) or CBU-78 Gator (anti-tank). CBU-87/B was designed to replace this Rockeye series. It employs the BLU-97/B sub-munition, 202 of which are included. On release from the jet the unit's fins spin it up at up to 2,500rpm about its central axis so that when its time or proximity fuse commands it to split open like a seed-pod it will scatter the sub-munitions allowing all 202 to fall and explode in a set pattern. Each sub-munition contains a hollow charge, anti-tank warhead inside a fragmenting anti-personnel outer case and an incendiary zircon disc. One can cripple a vehicle or parked aircraft at

Lakenheath F-15Es armed with GBU-24/B LGBs, based on the Mk 84 bomb with a BSU-84/B tail (airfoil) group and a WGU-39/B guidance group. USAF

up to 250ft (76m). CBU-87/B can be dropped at speeds up to 800mph (1,287km/h) and as low as 200ft (70m). On the F-15E it can be carried in the same loading patterns as Mk 82 LDGPs, though it weighs 950lb (430kg).

CBU-98/B was another multi-service project, with the USAF as project leader. It contains 72 BLU-91/B Gator anti-tank minelets and 22 BLU-92/B Gator anti-personnel bomblets (Gator is a project code-name in a series that has included Grasshopper, Bigeye, Dragontooth, Rockeye, and so on). It is employed similarly to CBU-87 but is lighter at 700lb (317kg). Mk 20 Rockeye is a long-established USN-initiated weapon. Typically, the CBU-59/B version contains 717 PLU-77/B anti-tank bomblets, each with a shaped charge/fragmentation warhead.

Guided Bomb Units (GBU-15 and AGM-130)
Based on the Mk 84, this Rockwell-designed weapon uses the WGU-10/B imaging infrared (IIR) or DSU-27A/B (daylight only) TV imaging seekers designed for the Hughes AGM-65 Maverick missile. Evolved from the 1960s HOBOS (HOming BOmb System) series the 154in (3.9m) long weapon has cruciform tail fins of 59in (150cm) span that enable it to be steered in a glide for up to 15–20mi (24–32km) to its target from high altitude. It can be locked onto its target pre-launch or during its flight, with data provided by an AN/AXQ-14 data-link pod carried usually on the aircraft centreline. It is tossed or dropped in a trajectory that heads it generally towards its target and the WSO then steers it using a toggle joystick and a visual image from the weapon's IIR or TV (EO) seeker that is presented on his MFD. About seventy-five GBU-15(V)-1/Bs were

launched from F-111Fs in *Desert Storm* and the weapon then passed to the F-15E as sole user. Since it is essentially a night bird the 'Mud Hen' favours the IR GBU-15(V)2/B version. Raytheon added a GPS system to the GBU-15 conferring an all-weather capability. As the EGBU-15 (enhanced guided bomb unit) the weapon entered service with the 48th FW at the end of 1999 and up to 1,300 GBU-15s were scheduled to receive the GPS upgrade. By August 2000 over 100 had been processed following completion of Phase II tests at Eglin AFB.

AGM-130A is an enhancement of the GBU-15 using a bolt-on 480lb (218kg) Hercules rocket motor to increase its direct stand-off range to 15nm at altitude. Used in a similar way to GBU-15 it enables attacks on heavily defended targets at low altitude. It can either be locked on target before launch or launched and left while the WSO searches out the target during the bomb's 'flight' towards its target. At a predetermined altitude the bomb then fires up its motor 30sec after launch and heads for the target that the WSO will by then have locked with its IIR seeker. It resembles the GBU-15 but with bigger canards, smaller tail surfaces and a rounder body. AGM-130C uses the BLU-109/B I-2000 in place of the Mk 84.

AGM-65 Maverick TV/IR missiles can also be carried on LAU-88 triple launchers under-wing for closer range BAI or CAS missions if required.

The last resort weapon is the **B61 Mod 4** (or later) tactical nuclear weapon. Up to five could be attached though the usual load would be two on the lower CFT pylons. This 750lb (340kg) weapon can be parachute-retarded and yield can range from 10 to 500 kilotons. The BDU-36/-38/-39E are equivalent training shapes while 'dumb' bombs are simulated by the 25lb (11kg) **BDU-33** 'blue bomb in a six-round SUU-20 carrier.

F-15Es are seldom seen without **AIM-9M, AIM-7M or AIM-120A** in addition to other external munitions, plus the M61 gun internally.

On ONW/OSW, F-15Es have carried AGM-130 plus four GBU-12 and AIM-9/AIM-120 in mixed loads, while other load-outs include a GBU-10 with four GBU-12s and AAMs. AGM-130 can reduce collateral damage through precise targeting and provide instant BDA (bomb damage assessment).

Other more recent weapons systems such as GBU-31 Joint Direct Attack Munition (JDAM) that uses the Mk 84 with a GPS-aided guidance kit; the AGM-154A/B Joint Stand-Off Weapon (JSOW) and AGM-158A Joint Air-to-Surface Strike Missile (JASSM) – a stealthy 2,000lb (900kg) stand-off weapon – would further enhance F-15E's capability. The AGM-154C is Mk 82-based with IIR guidance, while other versions use BLU-97/B sub-munitions among other warheads. At present, the funding and development of these weapons is directed mainly at extending the conventional bombing capability of the B-1B Lancer and B-2A Spirit but F-15Es may use them as well as a new generation of Wind Corrected Munitions Dispensers (WCMDs) that will enable more accurate delivery of CBU. With shrinking budgets and an emphasis on developing new weapons for the F-22A the F-15E will probably be hung with 1990s ordnance for much of the remainder of its career.

(Top) **AGM-130 is essentially a GBU-15I guided bomb with a Hercules rocket motor to increase its glide range to over 16mi.** Rockwell International

(Above) **AGM-130A on test beneath a camera-equipped 'AD' coded F-15E.** Rockwell International

(Left) **A 492nd FS Eagle (91-0310) with Paveway LGBs, AIM-7M, AIM-9M and AIM-120 missiles photographed from another F-15E.** Dev Basudev

either a TV or IR seeker head and it had entered combat in 1999 when a 48th FW F-15E launched one at an Iraqi radar site on ONW. On that occasion the weapon went off course and hit a residential area near Basrah. In *Allied Force* F-15Es with AGM-130 destroyed at least two MiGs on the ground on 17 May at Batajnica. One, a MiG-29, took a direct hit in the cockpit area while it was parked under cover on a road. Earlier, on 11 May, five MiG-21s were torched by F-15Es including one under camouflage net that was eliminated by an AGM-130. Two other MiG-21s were bombed on a roadway at Novi Sad on the same day and a MiG-29 was destroyed with CBU on the main runway at Batajnica airfield. Although these did not count as official 'MiG kills' the F-15E could have coped perfectly well with airborne MiGs during attack missions, or vice versa, and AIM-120 or AIM-9 missiles were carried on virtually all missions especially the CAPs flown by F-15Es over Bosnia and Macedonia in *Allied Force*. As Herman Shirg explained, 'With the AGM-130 it is possible to launch the missile during an air-to air engagement. It will guide itself most of the way in, using GPS.' Whereas the GBU-15 was used very successfully during the 1995 strikes on Bihac, Bosnia the IR AGM-130 was the primary stand-off weapon in Kosovo. With the demise of the F-111F, the

'Mud Hen' was the only aircraft qualified to carry the GBU-15 and its powered AGM-130 derivative. Most of the improvements to the F-15E since it entered service have been due to advanced new weapons such as AGM-130 and the resultant cockpit updates and revised tactics.

Aviano's hard-pressed twenty-six F-15Es could have been reinforced by eighteen 4th FW aircraft that were doing a turn of *Northern Watch* at Balikesir in Turkey, but they were not required. Further F-15E deployments from the USA were also announced as the screws were turned on President Milosevic: another thirty-six were promised on 6 May with additional deployments to Turkey on beginning on 29 May, but the Lakenheath aircraft were able to fulfil the requirements of *Allied Force* unaided.

Throughout the war their sortie rate was to some extent governed by the weather but also by politics. At various points, peace negotiations seemed imminent and the air war was paused, only to recommence when talks stalled. On 8 June 222 strike and 65 SEAD sorties were flown during one of these surges, with 130 sorties the following night just before an agreement was signed to cease air action. The bombing effort had taken far longer than the three-day period that Lt Gen Mike Short, Commander of the Allied Air Forces, had originally assumed. Senior US

commanders later realized that this was in part due to spying within the NATO high command that had allowed the Serbs access to the overall Operations Plan and daily ATOs. They were therefore able to hide or move the mobile elements of their IADS from 'Eagle eyes' and destruction of the systems was never fully achieved.

Tact and Tactics

For Lakenheath's F-15E crews *Allied Force* was an opportunity to prove the validity of their hard training regime and to refine effective combat techniques, including cockpit coordination. Col Casey:

> All crews have an idea of the two-person crew concept and they know when to do something or not, when to talk and not to talk. Before the war, in a training environment, no two guys flew together every day. They switched all the time so you never knew who you were going to fly with. During the war we crewed everybody up and left these crews the same as long as we could. Then the routines were even more engraved with individual personalities. You know when the guy in the back (or front) is busy, when to shut up and when to make an input.

Herman Shirg added, 'During the war there was no duplication of effort – each crewman knew what the other was doing.' Over Kosovo the chances of air-to-air engagements were much reduced after the first two days, but the two-man crew meant that opposing fighters could be dealt with more quickly if they did show up and a sudden change of plan was required. Col Casey:

> If the cockpit is in air-to-ground mode and an air-to-air threat appears the thoughts go through your mind, 'Is this guy in position to kill me before I get bombs on target, or is he in a position to kill me – period? Will it happen post-target or during weapons delivery? If he is going to get me or my wingman prior to weapons delivery, now is the time to commit. Forget about dropping the bombs. Go kill him first.' That decision matrix passes through your mind, based on [classified] range parameters. You have those numbers firmly engraved on your brain and there will be a time when you need to make that decision. Probably it is up to the front-seater to decide since the WSO is concentrating on getting bombs on target.

Electronics technicians swing open the beaky radome of an F-15E to tweak its APG-70 radar. USAF

As in *Desert Storm* the issue of IFF in air combat was crucial and once again the need for visual ID had to be allowed for in an uncertain situation. As Col Casey explained,

That could easily have happened during the Kosovo war because if we weren't getting what we needed from AWACS, or whoever, to prosecute an attack the decision-making fell to the cockpit. The question arose as to whether you were confident that this guy was indeed hostile and that you've met all the ROE constraints etc. before you let the missile go? If you're not confident you're going to have to do a visual fight with him. Hopefully, you'll be able to ID him and let her rip rather than get into a turning fight and go heater [AIM-9] or gun the guy. It's possible, even with today's BVR capability, because of the rules, restraints and politics. A lot of the time the rule is 'eyeball' and not necessarily electronic imagery in the cockpit.

Air-to air certainly remained high on the agenda for *Liberty Wing* F-15E crews in *Allied Force*. Escorts for strike aircraft, including B-2A Spirits, were always required. Many hours were spent on 'HVACAP' by 'Mud Hens' as well as F-15Cs. The number of CAPs depended on the nature of the HVA and its orbit. If it was a tanker, two CAPs were adequate but,

If a guy's in a huge orbit in an intelligence-gathering mode then you're going to need three CAPs – six aircraft total. If you are able to do creative things like we did in the war and put a refuelling CAP and an ELINT CAP in the same pattern that economizes on our air assets and we could get all that done with six F-15s – if you have air superiority.

For Herman Shirg, air-to-air came second only to interdiction in training, but above close air support (CAS). If the MiGs did challenge, F-15E crews would aim to take them out at long range as they approached. As Col Casey commented:

Missiles love closure. Head-on is good. We'd employ AMRAAMs first, then AIM-7, then AIM-9, then gun. If none of that works out and the threat has a better 'knife-fighting' capability or can out-turn you may consider wanting to 'blow through' if your missiles fail to hit. Then you could turn back when you had got some separation or go and fight him head on again, then blow through a second time. The MiG-29 is probably the only thing that can knife-fight with us but I think that our pilots can out-BFM [basic fighter manoeuvre] any of theirs, based on training statistics.

(Top) The crew's walk-around checks include a look at the GBU-27/B hung on their F-15E. USAF

(Above) F-15E 91-0325 from the 494th FS takes GBU-24B Paveway II, AIM-9M and AMRAAMs aloft. With a lighter load, lift-off is at around 160kt and 185 for heavier jets, with 10–13 degrees angle of attack. A combat-load take-off requires up to 5,000ft (1,520m) of runway, reducing to 1,500ft (455m) or less for an 'airshow' performance. USAF

On long CAPs the basic human limitations were constantly in mind, despite the thoughtful provision of in-cockpit 'piddle packs' that could actually present:

> the biggest challenge: how to relieve yourself on a long flight. In the Kosovo war some guys flew nine-hour CAPs. Replacement CAPs were delayed. Sometimes you'd go in there, do your

shifted to nights because they're having more fun', while guys on nights would say, 'I want to go back to days because I want to see the sun sometimes'. People shifted around a bit but mostly stayed on the same shift for two weeks. Some said the hardest shift was from two hours before sunrise until three or four hours after it because you came into work at midnight and were there until noon, so your whole body clock was off. Also, you

likely drop would be two in a salvo within a nano-second of each other.' Weapons release altitudes were critical:

> For us the most difficult environment is low altitude but we did a large majority of our training at low altitude. If you can do that you can do the rest. We trained for the most difficult war. We take each situation and think of the most difficult way to employ the airplane at the time.

Mike Casey seconded the medium-altitude option,

> Low altitude is much more challenging. The odds on getting a golden BB from AAA are much higher. Our target acquisition capability and our ability to get weapons on target are much better at medium altitude. Low altitude would be better for a CAS environment, to see the target better, but the F-15E would not do CAS at night anyway. We have to be prepared to employ the F-15E in a CAS environment if we have attrited everything else, but it's not the bread and butter for the F-15E.

Landing gear is raised before 250kt followed by flaps as the aircraft climbs at around 340kt. With afterburner out, fuel consumption drops to about a quarter of the 90,000lb (40,824kg) per hour needed for a full 'burner take-off. USAF

mission, drop your bombs, then on the way back to Aviano they'd divert you to a CAP to make up for guys who didn't show up or who had to leave because of crew rest requirements. You never knew how long you'd be airborne.

A few pilots were actually on CAPs extended to ten hours.

F-15C pilots had day and night shifts to cover. Capt Pravacek explained:

> We had guys assigned to nights but it always seemed that there was more action going on with the other shift, so guys would say, 'I want to be

had to stare at the sun as it came up over the horizon while you were on the tanker.

Although CAS may have been third on the priority list plenty was flown in Kosovo. Herman Shirg: 'We did CAS sorties every day in the second half of the war using mixed loads of CBU, dumb bombs and LGBs.' Weapons were loaded on the BRU-46 rack when mounted on CFTs or on the very similar BRU-47 when suspended from wing pylons. When LGBs were carried it was, 'theoretically possible to drop and guide four at once, but the most

Albino Action

The responsibility for achieving air superiority over Kosovo rested with the 493rd FS and its eighteen F-15Cs. In the autumn of 1998 the 493rd deployed to the Italian naval base of Cervia, home of the 5th Stormo's F-104S A-Ms, as the nucleus of the AEF concept. It set up operations in what was essentially a bare-base environment, using pilots from Lakenheath and some from Spangdahlem, integrated into the same command structure. After a month at Cervia the Yugoslav situation cooled and the force was recalled. The *Grim Reapers* returned for *Allied Force* as the 493rd EFS and were heavily involved in making the first air superiority flights on Night One (24/25 March). The JRV (Yugoslav Air Force) MiG-29 unit, 127 Sqn *Knights* of the 204th Aviation Brigade, rose to meet them with at least twelve of its fourteen Fulcrums. Although one of them (probably Lt Col Nikolic) managed to launch an AA-8 Aphid AAM at Allied fighters, three of his squadron failed to return. The first fell to SEAD escort F-16AM J-063 of 322 Sqn R. Netherlands AF under RAF E-3D Sentry control and two from a formation of four to the *Grim Reapers*. One MiG, reportedly piloted by Lt Col Nebojsa Nikolic, was shot down (probably by Capt Mike 'Dozer' Shower) while still climbing out of its

Batajnica base that was under cruise missile attack, to meet the strike force. One of the other two Fulcrums probably came from the forward airfield at Pristina and the second of these (reportedly from Batajnica) fell to the Dutch pilot while the first was credited to *Desert Storm* MiG killer 'Rico' Rodriguez.

Capt Shower's F-15C (86-0159) was leading one of the escorts for the first two strike packages of two B-2As and ten F-117As hitting southern Serbia and the Belgrade area. 'Dozer' was in the second of these with F-16CJ support. He was accustomed to ONW missions but the sight of Belgrade with all its lights still on and an AWACS call that a MiG-29 had been shot

down by the other strike package's escort galvanized his attention in a wholly new situation for him. Also unfamiliar was the responsibility for protecting a formation of 'Stealth Fighters' that was, to him, invisible on radar or to the eye on that clear but relatively moonless night. Reporting that 'his' MiG, detected on their third CAP orbit, constituted a serious threat he received permission to fire and launched a pair of AIM-120As, probably those that Nikolic claims to have evaded by hard manoeuvring and the use of dispensable ECM. The AMRAAMs passed above an F-117A, warning its pilot of the engagement. Shower closed to 6mi (9.6km) and fired

another missile that hit the Fulcrum as it passed about 7,000ft (2,130m) from the F-117A. The MiG's cockpit filled with smoke, the plane became uncontrollable and fell to earth about 25mi (40km) from Batajnica. Nikolic ejected at 6,000ft (1,830m). Shower's flight immediately turned their attention to another MiG-29 that had lifted off from Batajnica and only eleven minutes into his mission he was in a position to make a second kill. 'Here he is in the [radar] beam', reported Capt Shower, 'and I knew he was a bad guy but we couldn't get a full ID on him. We were lacking one piece of information. There was no doubt, but I couldn't shoot.' The

(*Above*) 'Blue' squadron's 91-0326 returns from a training sortie. Author's Collection

A Paveway II LGB, with its BSU-84/B airfoil group and hardback adapter installed, awaits a WGU-12B or WGU-39/B guidance sensor group on its front end. USAF

MiG continued on its northerly course, returning to a southerly heading shortly afterwards, but Shower was by now more concerned about three other MiG calls in an area south of Belgrade. The Eagles went after them, passing over Belgrade and avoiding its SAM rings, but found nothing. By now the 'escaped' MiG-29 was in a position for Shower to have another go at it and he turned back into it, achieving a lock-on and a hostile ID. At 5mi (8km) he fired a single missile that missed, but the closure rate prevented him from reversing and getting on its tail to fire again. Despite making a third radar lock on the Fulcrum it retreated into the comparative safety of the Belgrade IADS and Mike Shower decided it was time to head home before the good luck conferred by the Squadron's 'Grim Reaper ball' (lucky baseball given to him to take on the mission) ran out. He later received the Air Force Cross for his efforts.

Meanwhile, the southern package's F-15Cs, flying OCA in the Pristina area, had also been threatened by MiG-29s and one was locked by 'Rico' Rodriguez who passed the contact to his wingman (call sign 'Wild Bill') who was on his first combat mission. There was some ID uncertainty once again as the AWACS controllers sorted out some coordination problems and finally gave clearance to engage. Rodriguez took the shot and the MiG-29 exploded in an orange fireball that lit up the night sky and reflected off the western mountains. Of the Pristina-based pilots shot down that night the Serb authorities reported that one, a junior pilot named Capt Zoran Radsavljevic, was shot down and killed though this may have been the pilot of a MiG-21 that was lost, though not claimed by Allied pilots. The other, an experienced Lt Col named Dragan Ilic ejected when his aircraft was hit

(Above) 'Albino' wing tanks were borrowed for this mission. USAF

(Below) There's a look of grim concentration on the face of this jammer driver as he carefully edges a Mk82 LDGP into position on a CFT station without damaging the targeting pod. USAF

in the engines, probably by Rodriguez's missile, and exploded into a fireball seconds after his RWR gave him warning of a hostile contact. The pilot of the other Fulcrum (according to Belgrade's announcement) ejected and may well have been Maj Iljo Arizanov. His aircraft was hit in the rear fuselage and entered an uncontrollable spiral dive on fire. Arizanov ejected and returned to Pristina airfield after narrowly avoiding capture by the Kosovo Liberation Army (KLA).

After the destruction of three other MiG-29s at Batajnica by Dutch F-16s with LGBs on 7 June and another loss to a 'friendly' SA-11 missile (killing the pilot, Col Milenko Obradovic) the Knights were virtually eliminated as a fighting force. Three other Fulcrums were destroyed in the air, two by F-15Cs and one by a 78th FS F-16CJ (91-0353) on 4 May, killing the pilot. The F-15C kills both occurred on 26 March during a *Grim Reapers' Deny Flight* DCA over Bosnia. Two MiG-29s were detected by AWACS heading for Bosnian airspace for reasons that remain unclear, though it was thought that they might have been attempting to attack an AWACS. At 1602Z the two Eagles that were on CAP over Tuzla in the eastern part of Bosnia-Herzegovina to protect SFOR troops, had been in the air since 1400Z including an hour on CAP and a refuelling session. As their orbit took them towards the Yugoslav border the pilot of F-15C 86-0156, a 493rd FS Captain with the callsign 'Claw', picked up a radar contact at 37nm heading towards the Bosnian border at over 600kt. AWACS had not picked up the trace. Claw's wingman, a Capt 'Boomer' M (by this stage in the war aircrew preferred to remain anonymous after 'reprisal' threats against a B-52 crew's relatives) flying 84-0014 'Dirk 2' also had a radar contact. Without an official ID and clearance to engage, and lacking permission to cross into Serbian airspace the two *Reapers* aircraft waited, assuming the 'bogies' would turn away to the east and return to base. Claw alerted the southern CAP F-15Cs over Sarajevo in case the MiGs tried to cross nearer their position and reported the contact once again to AWACS by radio. *Dirk* flight continued their orbit to the west and then turned

back 'hot' towards the contact that was by now heading west directly at them. By now AWACS was seeing the contact too. Claw checked his IFF but got no friendly squawk in return so he requested clearance to engage, using the relevant code word. This took quite a while for the AWACS controllers to acknowledge. Both pilots were confident of the contact's identity as a MiG-29, as indicated on their IFF/NCTR systems. With the threat heading directly at them inside 30mi (48km) they decided to bypass the AWACS clearance and go for it. Claw, in *Dirk 1*, broke lock to search behind the target in the usual way in a 120 degree sweep and 40nm scope on his radar.

A *Reapers* F-15C awaits the signal to move to the active runway.
Author's Collection

As the target turned slightly north-west the *Reapers* banked left to a north-east heading to cut it off. Claw's aircraft was positioned aft of Boomer's in so doing and he 'stroked it up' to full afterburner in order to resume a line-abreast configuration, calling 'Combat 1, arm hot' as he did so. In response, Boomer jettisoned his wing-tanks and Claw followed, blowing off his tanks at supersonic speed. He checked his stabilators to make sure the tumbling tanks hadn't damaged them and stayed in 'search' mode a little longer on his radar, though the urge to go back to 'single target track' against the MiG was strong. At that point AWACS had found the contacts and reported that there were two in trail formation. At 20nm Boomer, as primary 'shooter', got permission to fire and called 'Fox 3' as he fired an AIM-120 at one of the 127 Sqn MiGs. Claw locked onto the lead Fulcrum at 17nm and pressed the pickle button. After a seemingly endless delay (a second or so in reality) the

AMRAAM launched with a roar that Claw felt and heard in the cockpit, and flames that were visible in his HUD. Normally, the only detectable noise in the cockpit is the rush of the airstream, audible only if the helmet is removed. Pressing the pickle button for another three seconds he released a second missile. As the three AMRAAMs dashed towards their targets the MiGs began a descending turn to the south-west. At 10nm Claw had the presence of mind to check his RWR to ensure that there were no other threats to reckon with. Both pilots then rolled inverted from 30,000ft (9,150m) and began to descend, keeping their HUDs on the area of sky in which they expected to see the MiGs as they closed to 7nm. Claw spotted the trail aircraft against a cloud background, still turning south-west and tried to set up an AIM-9M shot, but couldn't get a missile tone. Seconds later he saw the lead MiG suddenly explode in a trail of glowing flame, followed immediately by another flash as the trail aircraft was wiped out by an AIM-120. Although, in the excitement of the moment neither pilot saw parachutes both Serb pilots were reported to have ejected and their aircraft hit the ground (in one case at a very flat angle so that it appeared to have been squashed by a giant foot) near Bijeljina in northern Bosnia.

Dirk flight continued its CAP after this five-minute engagement and Claw switched to autoguns and full afterburner to 'sanitize' the area in case of further 'bandits'. A combination of bad radar locks and false calls from the AWACS (one of whose 'hostile' contacts turned out to be travelling at 80kt on the ground) caused the pair to commit and 'arm hot' on three further occasions for imaginary MiGs before they could return to Cervia. There they received a heroic welcome: 'The taxi-back to the chocks was like having a bunch of kids following an ice-cream truck!' Both aircraft received 'kill markings'. In 84-0014's case it was an addition to the Iraqi kill mark for the Su-22 shot down on 20 March 1991 with Capt Doneski at its controls. Subsequent analysis of the combat attributed both kills to Claw's 86-0156 instead. However, to Claw the engagement remained a team effort.

F-15C CAPs continued through the 80-day war. They covered the CSAR effort to rescue the pilot of the F-117A that was lost on 27 March. There were no more air-to-air engagements for Eagle crews thereafter and the beaten JRV fighter force concentrated on hiding and protecting its remaining assets from then on. The 4 May kill by an F-16CJ was the sixth and final kill, though NATO claimed that by 11 June ninety-six other JRV aircraft had been destroyed on the ground.

The F-15's powerful radar was a vital tool in all the engagements and pilots generally eschewed its more subtle uses, such as 'sniff' mode (giving a quick search sweep ahead without betraying the Eagle's position). Col Casey, for one, dismissed this tactic:

There are so many electrons in the air during a war that they're not going to know who's coming from where. In Kosovo, before we even crossed the fence the EA-6Bs and everybody else were just putting 'trons all over the place. How were they ever going to tell who was doing what? If you want to do 'sniff' you may as well go standby on the radar.

Light, Lean and Lethal

The Kosovo crisis posed the first practical test for the USAF's AEF concept and gave an opportunity to show whether the much-reduced air force of the late 1990s could still fulfil its obligation to maintain a credible presence over Iraq as well as fighting *Allied Force*. The F-15 units were particularly hard-pressed in this endeavour. As the lead Wing in USAFE for the AEF idea the 48th FW had to deploy a lot of its leadership overseas for *Allied Force*. In return it could import F-15 strength from elsewhere. On 14 April 1999 six F-15Cs from the 54th FS at Elmendorf AFB (including Draeger's MiG-killer, 85-0108) appeared at Lakenheath to compensate for some of the absent *Reapers*. Most of its pilots headed on south. Col Casey:

The Alaska guys went on to Cervia to allow the 493rd Instructor Pilots to stay here and continue the upgrade of new pilots. They left their jets at Lakenheath with about 200 maintainers. That was a big help.

The six visitors returned to Elmendorf on 29 June via Langley and the resident squadrons began to reconstruct their training routines as they completed their return from Italy. Throughout that summer the Suffolk skies were full of the thunder of departing four-ships of Eagles as the squadrons built up their training hours. There were a few adjustments to be made; 'In the war we were just so loaded down with weapons that we got used to those long take-offs for months and months. We came back here into a training environment and, whoops! Airborne already!' Although military power take-offs are possible, use of afterburner is routine for safety. Noise abatement isn't really a problem at the base. On Runway 24 a right turn after take-off avoids offending the locals. Aircraft equipped with the Dash 229 engines are particularly nimble on take-off. Col Casey flew the -220 powered F-15E at Luke. 'Then I came here and flew the -229. Wow! Incredible.'

Eagle at dawn. A Cervia-based F-15C with a CAP load-out of three tanks and eight missiles. USAF

Eagle Keepers

Despite the pressure on space at the Italian bases (there were six different aircraft types at Cervia alone) the aircrew had experienced a well-coordinated operation on the whole, with a Central Planning Cell at Aviano containing representatives of the various nations involved. For the maintainers at the F-15 bases the goal of attaining near-perfect aircraft availability was assisted by a very efficient spares pipeline. Mike Casey:

> Since the end of the Cold War the idea of keeping the F-15 fleet's spare parts at 100 per cent has gone by the wayside purely because of monetary concerns. But when a war kicks off it's amazing what magically happens with spare parts. They come out of the woodwork from all over the world.

Allied Force kept the maintainers at Cervia on 12-hour shifts as the Eagles accumulated hours in the air averaging a hundred a week. 48th FW Phase Maintenance boss Betttig explained:

> That's a lot of hours real quick, so back at Lakenheath we set up our usual three maintenance docks, one for F-15C/Ds and two for E models, but we ended up with seven docks and we 'phased' up to seven airplanes a week. Airplanes were sent back from Italy when they reached the required hours and we did 62 Phases in 85 days. An average Phase dock runs 33–34 per year.

Phase inspections are done at 200hr flight-time (Phase 1) with Phase 2 at 400hr and 3 at 600, up to a maximum of 1,200hr. At that stage a more thorough Periodic check is made and by 2,400hr a full programme depot maintenance (PDM) inspection is necessary. This requires four to six months' work at the Air Logistics Center in the USA, 'wings off, the lot'. Each 200hr Phase normally takes a five-day inspection requiring up to thirty access panels to be 'pulled', with another twenty for a Phase 2. At 1,200hr intake ramps, speedbrakes and other components will be removed. 'They did a few contingency Phases on F-15C/Ds at Cervia – about fifteen. Those aircraft had really got behind on maintenance – they were real hurtin'.'

Generally, the 'fixers' have found the Eagle to be a fairly straightforward bird to upkeep. Some F-15Cs were beginning to show a few cracks towards the end of the 1990s, with vertical stabilizer-tip 'bullet'

(Above) CBU was the 'load of the day' for this *Allied Force* mission. In the background one of the hard-working force of EA-6B SEAD aircraft trundles out to support another strike package. USAF

91-0324, loaded and ready with Paveway IIIs and AAMs. USAF

Eagles and Raptors

Allied Force showed that air power could apparently resolve some political crises without appreciable loss to the 'police' force. As Gen Short judged,

> In Operation *Deliberate Force* we bombed Bosnia for six weeks and brought the Serbs to the table with no loss of American lives (or airplanes). Now we've done it again. We bombed for 78 days, lost two airplanes and no-one died in combat.

Some 12,500 combat sorties were flown and up to 700 SAMs were fired at Allied aircraft with only two losses. For the USAF, the Kosovo experience was seen as justification for its priority fighter programme, the F-22A Raptor that will survive a new generation of surface-to-air weapons better than the F-15.

The F-15 has been the undisputed champion in air superiority for a quarter of a century but it has been increasingly challenged technically by a new generation of fighters from the former Soviet Union. While it has largely maintained parity, through improved engines, missiles and radar, with MiG-29 and Su-27 variants, aircraft like the Su-34 and the thrust vectoring Su-37 have compelled the USAF to push ahead with a replacement. The F-15C is, in any case, an ageing design and the demands of the Balkans and Iraq conflicts have piled on the airframe hours. The first F-15 to hit 6,000hr (78-0518) did so with Kadena's 44th FS after twenty years' service with that unit. There are many other Eagles close behind and the entire F-15A/C fleet will be nearing the end of its fatigue life by 2004. As the USAF's primary strike/interdictor the F-15E has also been hard-worked; some aircraft were already nearing 4,000hr by the end of 2000. Funds have been secured for small batches of attrition replacement and supplementary aircraft; six each for FY96 and 97, three from FY98 and three in FY00. The addition of ten more (airframes E227 to E236) for delivery between May 2002 and mid-2004, bringing the total USAF buy to 237, was partly to reopen the production line in the hope of attracting more export orders and in part a result of fund-stretching delays in the F-22A Raptor programme. The new-build F-15Es will have the additional advantage of updated data processors, digital mapping, expanded LGB capability and a new integrated GPS.

Although the F-22 has been a top priority in USAF funding for many years (at the expense of radical updates to the F-15) only four have been manufactured in the decade since its first flight and their testing will continue until the type finally enters service in FY2005–06. The second YF-22 will have been in the USAF Museum for seven years by then! The USAF hopes to replace all 292 of its current F-15Cs one-for-one with Raptors, with the final delivery in 2013, plus an attrition/R&D quota to take the order up to its 1999 estimate of 339

Edwards-based F-15s from the 412th Test Wing assist in the work of the F-22A CTF.
USAF

with internal weapons carriage, the first true glass cockpit (resembling a personal TV lounge), twice the F-15's combat radius on internal fuel, double its sortie rate and half the maintenance requirements. Its 'air dominance' job description implies that the F-22 must achieve destruction of the opposing fighter force in around a quarter of the time that a 1999-era F-15 fighter component would take. Its 'first look, first shoot, first kill' philosophy relies on an

units. However, in addition to the basic 'air dominance' variant it also hopes to replace the F-15E and F-117A with the F-22 'Block 10' variant that would have strike capability including GBU-32 J-DAM or new, miniature smart weapons and run to a HARM-shooting SEAD version. Currently the 'wish list' includes at least 200 more Raptors for these roles in the decade from 2010. In the F-22 the USAF will have a stealthy, thrust-vectoring force multiplier

airframe structure, engines and avionics that are far ahead of the F-15's. Despite a price tag of about $100m per copy it is likely to be cheaper and easier to operate than the Eagle. Although most F-15 pilots are devoted to their current machines their reaction to the F-22 tends to be, 'We want it now.' Even so, they fully acknowledge that McDonnell Douglas's extraordinary 'God's jet' will be a particularly hard act to follow.

CHAPTER NINE

Eagle Reflections

A Rhino WSO Recalls the F-15

I was privileged to serve as a USAF F-4 Weapon System Operator (WSO) for eleven years from 1972–83, with operational flying experience in the US, Europe, and the Pacific. During that time I either flew in company with, or flew against, many different types of aircraft. Some were new, some were old. Some you'd give almost anything to get aboard, and others you hoped you never had to. Each aircraft made its mark in my 'aviation memory', but none made quite the lasting impression that the F-15 Eagle did. Following are recollections and personal observations from my intermittent encounters with the Eagle over the past 25 years.

First Sighting

I saw my first F-15 at Edwards AFB in the mid-1970s. A group of aviators from the 49TFW at Holloman were flown out to see the new aircraft in flight test at Edwards,

Holloman F-15As start engines after a storm.
via Ron Thurlow

with the F-15, F-16 and F-17 as the primary objectives. Like everyone else, I was struck with the huge size of the aircraft and the fact that its empty weight was less than an F-4! The ability to accelerate going straight up also made a big impression on us, since we were used to going 'down' to conserve or gain energy during combat. This was also the time when they were making the change from 'square' to 'cut back' wingtips. Our host told us how they just

took a power saw and zipped off the wingtips to the new configuration. It seemed pretty crude considering the otherwise sophisticated program they were running, but apparently it worked. As an aside, the F-16/F-17 flyoff was still in progress and naturally we wanted to know which aircraft was best. The pilot giving us the tour said that everyone who flew the two aircraft definitely favored one type over the other, but he wouldn't say which one that was.

First Encounter – Europe

Our F-4 wing at Holloman deployed to Europe each fall under the *Crested Cap* program, which basically meant based in the US but dedicated to USAFE. During the deployment one of our flights encountered a pair of F-15s near Bitburg and slipped into their six o'clock position unobserved. Remember, the F-15 was the 'super plane' of the day, and everyone was anxious to see one in flight. To be camped behind a pair of them in AIM-9 firing parameters was even better. Unfortunately the thrill didn't last too long and our F-4 crews got a firsthand demonstration of the aerodynamic capability of the new fighter. When the F-15s discovered the F-4s behind them they pitched up into a tight 'square loop' that quickly brought them into firing position behind the F-4s. The tables had been turned in a matter of seconds! I remember the flight lead recounting how fast they had gone from being the 'shooter' to being the 'shootee'. We all got a big laugh listening to his story in the crew lounge. Those initial Eagle drivers were highly experienced and flew the plane very well. Later the odds were evened out a bit as the experience level dropped, but in the early days, a quick shot followed by a solid separation was the best way for an F-4 to fight the F-15.

Kadena Eagles

The F-15 arrived in PACAF during the time I was flying F-4Es out of Clark AB in the Philippines, and we would often see them during our local *Cope Thunder* exercises and again during the annual *Team Spirit* war games in Korea. My biggest impression from those days was that the Kadena Eagle drivers seemed to do a lot of 'show boating'. Of course they did have the newest F-15C models, and they were flying the best air superiority fighter in the world, so maybe they had some cause to feel a little frisky. Whatever the reason, you didn't have to be around F-15 pilots long to learn why they were called 'Ego Drivers'. In those days PACAF was big into 'train like you fight' and that included what we called tactical departures and arrivals. The objective was to get into a tactical formation as quickly as possible after takeoff. The reverse was true for the recovery – you maintained a tactical formation right up until the break for landing. The normal

departure routine was to make a formation takeoff and then perform a 'tactical split' to assume a spread formation. When the F-15s were in town for their first *Cope Thunder* exercise, they performed the lowest and 'showiest' tac splits I've ever seen. Imagine two F-15s within a wingspan of the ground, rolling into a 90 degree bank and pulling a 45 degree turn right after liftoff. The first time you see that big wing planform that low to the ground it really gets your attention. I expected one day an F-15 would go cartwheeling across the field from dragging a wingtip, but it never happened. It made for a pretty good airshow though.

One of the more interesting events that happened while I was at Clark was the 'Bear' bomber intercepts made by the F-15s from Kadena. The Soviets started snooping around off the coast of Luzon, probably testing the air defenses and looking for ballistic missile submarines. Whatever the reason for their sudden interest, the challenge was not going to go unanswered. The 3TFW was tasked for the first couple of intercept attempts with their F-4s – supported by tankers – but missed the bombers. It was a tough proposition, trying to be in the right spot at the right time – using projected track data from stations further up the Pacific rim. I believe one time the F-4s were on the tanker getting gas when the bombers slipped by. And once they are past you out in the vast

Pacific, the game is over. At any rate, one day we came to work and there were a couple of F-15s parked in the old ADC alert barns at the end of the runway. The buildings were seldom used since the F-102s left a decade earlier, so everyone knew something was up. Sure enough, the Eagles soon went 'Bear hunting' and were successful on their first try. You may recall a widely published photo of a 'ZZ' coded F-15 flying alongside a Bear bomber – it was taken during one of those encounters.

My squadron deployed to Osan AB for *Team Spirit* one year and we did some target work for the F-15s on one of our 'weather days'. Most of the exercise schedule was canceled and we had to fly alternate missions for flying time. Our flight was tasked to do intercept training with some F-15s flying out of a base in southern Korea. The weather was solid clouds all the way up to 30,000ft, (9,150m) which we climbed above to get in the clear for our intercepts. Now a slat/TISEO F-4E is a heavy aircraft to begin with, and with all the other add-ons like two external tanks, ECM pod, AGM-65 Maverick, AIM-9 rails and missile, and centerline MER, we were real drag pigs. We let the F-15s use us for targets for a couple of runs, and then decided to go back down in the murk and do something more worthwhile for our own proficiency. The interesting thing was seeing how the F-15s literally flitted around us while we

An F-15C on the knife-edge. T. Shia

An 18th TFW F-15C at Clark AFB for Exercise *Cope Thunder*, May 1980. Ron Thurlow

struggled to maintain altitude and perform minimum evasive maneuvers. The Eagles were clearly in their element at that altitude. Equally impressive was their return profile at the end of the mission. Their base was a long way down the peninsula and they had to go high to conserve gas. The last we saw of them, they were up at 50,000ft (15,240m) headed south. Pretty impressive to a bunch of Rhino crews trying to maintain altitude at 30,000ft.

The View from Seymour Johnson

In the early 1980s I was flying F-4Es out of Seymour Johnson AFB, NC. We were primarily an air-to-ground unit, tasked with conventional bombing and nuclear strike missions for the European theatre. We also maintained specific taskings for AGM-65 Maverick and later the PAVE TACK pod and the GBU-15 glide bomb. We also did proficiency missions in air intercept and air superiority. To say that the F-4 was a multi-role fighter was a gross understatement, and it is a tribute to the flight crews, maintenance personnel, and the aircraft itself that we were able to accomplish all

our missions without fail. One of our periodic training events were air combat sorties against the F-15s out of Langley. Far from being intimidated by the mighty Eagle, we looked forward to these encounters as a chance to hone our air combat tactics and perhaps have an opportunity to get some gun camera film of the big birds.

The F-15 had somewhat better weapons than we did, with the longer range F-model of the Sparrow and the all-aspect 'Lima' version of the AIM-9. Basically we could trade face shots with the Eagle and felt the 'heat' shots were a draw due to our two-man lookout advantage and the ALE-40 flare capability. The F-15 pulse Doppler radar was superior to ours, especially in presenting a clean picture when looking down against ground clutter. However, a good WSO could do the same thing in the F-4 – it just took a lot of concentration on the radar and some good scope tuning ability. From 15,000ft we could easily pick out an aircraft down at 1,000ft AGL, then take either a radar or a TISEO lock on it. Plus, the F-4 had the advantage of a person who could concentrate solely on the radar for maximum range contacts, direct an optimum attack profile, and watch for enemy countermoves. That's harder to do in a single seat

aircraft, where you have to fly your own airplane, keep an eye on your wingman, and conduct your own visual search. Often the outcome of our F-4 / F-15 engagements came down to a matter of equipment status and experience level of the crews involved. Flying against Langley F-15s in the early 1980s was by no means an automatic death sentence, and it sure was good training. Many times the mission would end in a 'draw' – they would clearly win one engagement, we would win the other.

One of our favorite tactics against the F-15 in a clear air environment was to use the F-4s TISEO system to make a 'radar silent' run at the F-15s, while watching their tactics 'visually' with the 10× TV camera. You could take a quick radar lock on the F-15, slave the TISEO camera to the target and get an optical lock, then break radar lock to deny him RHAW data on your position and systems status. From that point you could watch for tactical splits or altitude changes and call out a warning to the flight. TISEO was an excellent aid in providing that last vital piece of 'situational awareness' that could be crucial to the outcome of a fight. The lack of a similar TV identification system on the F-15 always puzzled me. Granted, the

'Eagle Eye' rifle scope installation was an inexpensive and perhaps adequate solution to the visual ID problem for the F-15, but the thought of an Eagle pilot leaning forward to peer through his little telescope with enemy aircraft in the area left me a little cold. To me, it was akin to bending over to pick up a bar of soap in a prison shower – you become very vulnerable to attack in your 6 o'clock position. And that might not be the smartest way to be when you're the biggest target in the sky.

I especially remember one flight when my AC got a great guns tracking shot on an F-15 going 'over the top' at about 150 knots. It was a pretty maneuver by the Eagle, but not the smartest thing to do with a slatted F-4 camped at your six o'clock. Later, after the flight debrief, the F-15 flight leader told us the pilot we shot was a young lieutenant who had learned a valuable lesson that day. It's the same old story – you can have the most technically and aerodynamically superior aircraft ever built, but the mission outcome is still going to depend largely on the experience level of the person holding the stick. If good enemy tactics or internal systems problems cause your radar to break lock, or you lose mutual support because you've lost sight of your wingman, you're at the mercy of the team that has you in sight. And today, losing situational awareness 'electronically' can have the same result as losing a visual on your wingman or your enemy. That's one thing about air combat that hasn't changed, and that's why training is always going to be the key factor to success in the air-to-air arena.

Another thing I recall vividly from those F-15 dogfights – the way the F-15's nose could come to threaten you so quickly in a close-in fight. The aerodynamic capability of that aircraft was amazing compared to what we were used to. You'd see him across the circle canopy to canopy, and that plane looked like it would just pivot to point right at you. The first time I saw that – the way his nose rotated to us so smoothly and so fast – I just thought 'wow, we're in deep trouble now!!' The F-4 nose pointing process was a little slower, and once you got that F-4 'picture' in your head it could be fatal to apply the perception to other aircraft types you might be fighting. Which is another reason to train with dissimilar aircraft – so you have those 'gee whiz' surprises in training, not in actual combat when it can kill you. Of course, the pilots who could best talk about F-15 air combat capability were the F-5E Aggressors, since they

spent a majority of their time in direct support of the Eagle units around the world. An experienced Aggressor could really give an F-15 a workout, and could probably give the most objective assessment of what the real capability of an individual F-15 pilot, or an entire F-15 unit, was.

The most impressive F-15 takeoffs I ever saw were during a squadron deployment to Karup, Denmark in the fall of 1982. Towards the end of the deployment, as the exercise schedule eased up a bit, we had an opportunity to exchange a few back seat rides with other NATO units. My squadron did some work with the resident Drakens, and an F-15 unit based at Aalborg came down and gave a couple of our guys rides in their mighty Eagles. The local weather condition at the time of takeoff contributed greatly to the overall visual effect of their departure. In northern Europe during the fall you have days where individual rain showers march across the land, one after another. It pours and blows for 15 minutes, then the sun shines for a half hour until the next storm comes through – all day long. Just prior to the F-15 takeoff a large storm cell had passed the field, leaving a towering wall of dark clouds off the departure end of the runway. Meantime the sun had come out, so when the F-15s took off they did so illuminated in full sunshine, climbing vertically against that background of dark clouds. Also keep in mind that for three weeks we had been watching F-4s and Drakens make relatively flat departures, staying low against the horizon as they headed out on their missions. To see those two Eagles go thundering almost straight up, looking more like rockets being launched, was something I'll never forget. It was thrilling to watch, and it made you feel more than a little proud too.

HQ TAC / Langley

One of the side benefits of working at TAC Headquarters at Langley AFB was the free airshow put on by the 'East Coast F-15 demo pilot' once each week during the airshow season (his practice sessions). We could watch the entire routine from our office windows, and a large percentage of the TAC staff did just that. Most of them longing, no doubt, to trade their current fate of background papers, staff summary sheets, and decision briefings for a chance to get back in the cockpit. My favorite maneuver was always the triple

Immelman – an excellent demonstration of the excess power and vertical maneuvering ability of the F-15. You could Immelman an F-4 right after takeoff too, but I don't think you'd get very far into a second maneuver, let alone a third. The F-15 made it look easy, like it could just keep doing them until it was completely out of sight. I often wondered what the performance of that Edwards F-15 re-engined with the big 29,000lb (13,154kg) GE engines must have been like. It probably bordered on being scary!! Then again, I suppose you can never have too much power in a fighter aircraft. Hmm, I wonder if the F-22 engines will fit in the F-15?

Finally, a Ride

In 1991 I had the good fortune to fly on an F-15 training mission with the Louisiana ANG at NAS New Orleans. The mission was a 2 v 2 against some ANG F-16s. I flew with a highly experienced and disciplined fighter pilot, in a plane which I knew was maintained in near-perfect condition by a team of proud maintenance professionals. It was a chance to enjoy one last ride in a fighter, plus see how the F-15 itself performed, and was flown. The following were my major impressions. First, the F-15 is a huge airplane. It's big to walk around, and a long way up to the cockpit when you 'saddle up'. And that wing area! It's immediately apparent why F-15s are called 'tennis courts'. Second was the excellent visibility afforded by seat positioning and that big canopy. The view looking down and behind the aircraft is exceptional, allowing unrestricted visual lookout in all quadrants. Third was the high level of thrust available to the pilot. We made a military power takeoff to save gas and only used the afterburners during the systems check and again in the fight. To me, a mil power F-15 performed like an F-4 in full burner, and an F-15 in full burner – well, it's pretty impressive. And although the tremendous fuel flow at max AB won't let you fly around all day at that energy level, the power is nice to have when you need it. By far the biggest surprise to me was the amount of 'heads down' time devoted to looking at the radar scope – both during the intercept phase of the fight and once we were engaged. We lost sight of our leader at one point and tried using IFF and air-to-air TACAN to get back together, which meant even more time looking inside the cockpit. It made me uncomfortable from the twin perspectives of mid-air potential and getting hosed by an unseen adversary. And it reinforced my belief (admittedly biased) that no single seat airplane that big has any business stooging around in a multi-bogey dogfight. If that's the way we intend to fight with our 'Battlestar Galactica' air superiority fighters, then I suggest we replace that little radar display in the F-15A with a wide-screen video monitor, 25-inches minimum. That way the pilot can tell at a glance what's going on electronically, instead of having to peer intently at that little screen currently in the plane. I'm serious! Last but not least, I did get some stick time on the way home – formation flying and easy maneuvering. I'm no test pilot, but to me the F-15 felt similar to an F-4, but

A Final Perspective

It took me a long time to warm up to the F-15, but after 25 years I have to admit that it's a pretty good plane, and I have even come to like the looks of it. Maybe it's because it is so big, because it has two engines, and now, even two seats. Most of all, I think it's because the F-15 remains exactly what it was promised to be when it first flew so long ago – the world's premier air superiority fighter. The mechanics of attaining air superiority has changed considerably over the past three decades, especially in the area of close-in 'dogfighting'. We've gone from needing highly skilled pilots to maneuver for a six o'clock heat shot to a 'point and shoot' scenario (AIM-

providing 'arms length' airspace dominance which allows us to quickly (and safely) destroy and demoralize offensive enemy air forces. It also enables you to protect your own high-value forces while preserving valuable air-to-air assets through low attrition rates. The F-15E has also established itself as a versatile 'heavy hauler' in replacing the F-111. What the 'Dirt Eagle' lacks in range compared to the Aardvark is more than compensated for by the mission flexibility afforded by its multi-role capabilities. Consider a typical combat load being carried by F-15Es patrolling the Middle East today – a 2,000lb AGM-130 guided bomb, a guidance pod, four GBU-12 500lb LGBs, two AMRAAMs, and two AIM-9Ms. Plus the

F-15C 81-0030 of the 94th TFS at Shaw AFB, 13 March 1980. Norm Taylor

with a lot more power. It was a smooth and stable platform for formation flying, and the pitch rate felt good, but to me it still seemed like a hand full of airplane. It certainly did not have the same light feel as say, an F-5. But hey, the F-15 is a big airplane and that's the way big airplanes fly. Twenty-five tons of thrust and a huge wing just happen to make it surprisingly agile for its size. We did a couple of ferocious closed patterns upon arrival back at the field, and finished with the minimum-speed, 'hold the nose up until it drops' demo on landing rollout. Overall the flight provided a unique insight into the capability of one of the great aircraft in USAF history, and was for me, personally, a nice ending to my career in fighters.

9L) where even the most novice aviators can be deadly adversaries. Today, the helmet mounted sights and highly agile missiles have taken us one step further to a 'look and shoot' situation. The increasing lethality of the visual fight has pushed the air superiority strategy strongly back into the realm of Beyond Visual Range engagements, an arena where the F-15C excels. It has a powerful long range radar, modern avionics with massive computing power, and the ability to carry a heavy load of the most capable air-to-air missiles in history. Back that up with AWACS for long range lookout and battle management, then add a highly trained and well-motivated pilot. The result is an unmatched capability for

ability to carry that load at 200ft AGL at night if necessary, and deliver laser-guided weapons using the LANTIRN nav/attack system. If an air force could only afford one aircraft type, the multi-role F-15E with its unequalled abilities in both arenas, would be the clear choice. That's a pretty good testament to what a truly great aircraft the F-15 has turned out to be. The Eagle has excelled at every mission over the past 25 years, been one of the best investments ever made by the American taxpayer, and has proven an able successor to the fabled F-4 Phantom. You couldn't ask for more than that.

Ron Thurlow, Col, USAF (Ret.)

F-15 Statistics

DIMENSIONS

All Variants

Wingspan:	42.81ft (13m)	Length:	63.75ft (19.4m)	
Height:	18.46ft (5.6m)	Tailplane span:	28.25ft (8.6m)	
Wheel track:	9ft (2.7m)	Wing area:	608 sq ft (56.5sq m)	
Tailplane area:	111.3 sq ft (10.3sq m)	Fin area:	105.28 sq ft (9.8sq m)	
Aileron area:	26.48 sq ft (2.46sq m)			

Weights (lb):		F-15A	F-15B	F-15C*	F-15D	F-15E**
	Empty:	26,500 (12,020kg)	27,300 (12,383kg)	28,200 (12,792kg)	28,800 (13,064kg)	31,800 (14,425kg)
	Max. t.o.:	56,000 (25,402kg)	56,000 (25,402kg)	68,470 (31,058kg)	68,470 (31,058kg)	81,000 (36,742kg)
Internal fuel:	1,759gall (7,996l)		1,759gall (7,996l)	2,070gall (9,408l)	2,019gall (9,178l)	2,727gall (12,397l)

* F-15J similar

**F-15I/S/U similar

PERFORMANCE

F-15C

Max. speed (sea level):	Mach 1.2
Max speed (40,000ft/12,200m):	Mach 2.5
Approach:	125kt
Service ceiling:	60,040ft (18,300m)
Ferry range (with CFTs):	3,570mi (5,744km)
Max endurance:	(with CFTs) 5hr 15min
	(with in-flight refuelling) 15hr
Take-off run (typical):	900ft (274m)
Max. wing loading:	111.8lb per sq ft
Design g limits:	+9 to –3g

F-15E

Max. speed (40,000ft/12,200m):	Mach 2.5
Max. range:	2,762mi (4,444km)
Combat radius:	790mi (1,271km)
Max. weapon load:	24,500lb (11,110kg)

Capt 'Hoser' Draeger's MiG killer F-15C-40-MC 85-0119, which shot down an Iraqi MiG-23 on 26 June 1991. Norm Taylor

F-15 Production

MODEL	SERIALS	LOCATION
F-15A-1-MC	71-0280	Cat 1 Test, stores, handling. Pres., Lackland AFB.
F-15A-1-MC	71-0281	Cat.1 Test, engines.To NASA. Pres., Langley AFB.
F-15A-2-MC	71-0282	Cat 1 Test, avionics, radar, AECS. At Robins AFB.
F-15A-2-MC	71-0283	Cat 1 Test, structure. To MDC.
F-15A-2-MC	71-0284	Cat 1 Test, weapons. To USAF as instructional airframe.
F-15A-3-MC	71-0285	Cat 1 Test, weapons, avionics. To MDC.
F 15A-3-MC	71-0286	Cat 1 Test, armament, fuel. Pres., Chanute Museum.
F-15A-4-MC	71-0287	Cat 1 Test, spin. To NASA/DFRC. Stored, Edwards AFB.
F-15A-4-MC	71-0288	Cat 1 Test, airframe/engine.
F-15A-4-MC	71-0289	Cat 1 Test, avionics/APG-63. To MDC.
TF-15A-3-MC	71-0290	Cat 1 Test, chase a/c, S/MTD, NF-15B ACTIVE, NASA.
TF-15A-3-MC	71-0291	Cat 1 Test, MDC demo, Strike Eagle, Peep Eagle demo.
F-15A-5-MC	72-0113	Cat II Test, radiation tests Rome ADC, MASDC.
F-15A-5-MC	72-0114	Cat II Test, ECM. To Israel, 1992.
F-15A-5-MC	72-0115	Cat II Test, To Sheppard AFB as GIA.
F-15A-5-MC	72-0116	Cat II Test, climatic/operational. To Israel (*Peace Fox I*).
F-15A-6-MC	72-0117	Cat II Test (spare a/c). To Israel (*Peace Fox I*).
F-15A-6-MC	72-0118	Cat II Test, operational. To Israel (*Peace Fox I*).
F-15A-6-MC	72-0119	Cat II Test/Streak Eagle. To USAF Museum.
F-15A-6-MC	72-0120	Cat II Test (spare a/c). To Israel (*Peace Fox I* attrition a/c).
F-15A-7-MC	73-0085–0089 (5)	
F-15A-8-MC	73-0090–0097 (8)	
F-15A-9-MC	73-0098–0107 (10)	
F-15B-7-MC	73-0108–0110 (3)	(73-0087/0093/0094/0101/0102/0104/0105/0107/0110–0113 sold to Israel, 1992)
F-15B-8-MC	73-0111–0112 (2)	
F-15B-9-MC	73-0113–0114 (2)	
F-15A-10-MC	74-0081–0093 (13)	(74-0085/0088/0093/0097/0101/0107/0109/0122/0125/0137 sold to Israel, 1992)
F-15A-11-MC	74-0094–0111 (18)	
F-15A-12-MC	74-0112–0136 (25)	(74-0119 to GF-15A, Sheppard AFB)
F-15B-10-MC	74-0137–0138 (2)	
F-15B-11-MC	74-0139–0140 (2)	
F-15B-12-MC	74-0141–0142 (2)	(74-0142 to GF-15B, Sheppard AFB)
F-15A-13-MC	75-0018–0048 (31)	
F-15A-14-MC	75-0049–0079 (31)	
F-15B-13-MC	75-0080–0084 (5)	
F-15B-14-MC	75-0085–0089 (5)	
F-15A-15-MC	76-0008–0046 (39)	
F-15A-16-MC	76-0047–0083 (37)	(76-0054/0067/0079/0083 to GF-15A)
F-15A-17-MC	76-0084–0113 (30)	(76-0110 to GF-15A, Sheppard AFB)
F-15A-18-MC	76-0114–0120 (7)	
F-15B-15-MC	76-0124–0129 (6)	
F-15B-16-MC	76-0130–0135 (6)	(76-0135 to GF-15B, Sheppard AFB)
F-15B-17-MC	76-0136–0140 (5)	(76-0136 to GF-15B, Sheppard AFB)
F-15B-18-MC	76-0141–0142 (2)	
F-15A-18-MC	77-0061–0084 (24)	
F-15A-19-MC	77-0085–0119 (35)	(77-0085 to GF-15A, Sheppard AFB)
F-15A-20-MC	77-0120–0153 (34)	(77-0125/0150 to GF-15A)
F-15B-18-MC	77-0154–0156 (3)	(77-0154/0156 to GF-15B, Sheppard AFB)

MODEL	SERIALS	LOCATION
F-15B-19-MC	77-0157–0162 (6)	
F-15B-20-MC	77-0163–0168 (6)	

Cancelled blocks: 74-0143–0157 (F-15B-12-MC), 75-0090–0124 (F-15A/B), 76-0121–0123 (F-15A-18-MC).
FMS production: 76-1505–1514 (F-15A-17-MC, *ten aircraft*), 76-1515–1523 (F-15A-18-MC, *nine*), 76-1524–1525 (F-15B-16-MC, *two*.) All for Israel, *Peace Fox II*.

MODEL	SERIALS	MODEL	SERIALS	MODEL	SERIALS
F-15C-21-MC	78-0468–0495 (28)	F-15C-29-MC	80-0039–0053 (15)	F-15C-36-MC	83-0035–0043 (9)
F-15C-22-MC	78-0496–0522 (27)	F-15C-27-MC	80-0054–0055 (2)	F-15D-35-MC	83-0046–0048 (3)
F-15C-23-MC	78-0523–0550 (28)	F-15C-28-MC	80-0056–0057 (2)	F-15D-36-MC	83-0049–0050 (2)
F-15D-21-MC	78-0561–0565 (5)	F-15C-29-MC	80-0058–0061 (4)	F-15C-37-MC	84-0001–0015 (15)
F-15D-22-MC	78-0566–0570 (5)	F-15C-30-MC	81-0020–0031 (12)	F-15C-38-MC	84-0016–0031 (16)
F-15D-23-MC	78-0571–0574 (4)	F-15C-31-MC	81-0032–0040 (9)	F-15D-37-MC	84-0042–0044 (3)
F-15D-24-MC	79-0004–0006 (3)	F-15C-32-MC	81-0041–0056 (16)	F-15D-38-MC	84-0045–0046 (2)
F-15D-25-MC	79-0007–0011 (5)	F-15D-30-MC	81-0061–0062 (2)	F-15C-39-MC	85-0093–0108 (15)
F-15D-26-MC	79-0012–0014 (3)	F-15D-31-MC	81-0063–0065 (3)	F-15C-40-MC	85-0109-0128 (20)
F-15C-24-MC	79-0015–0037 (23)	F-15C-33-MC	82-0008–0022 (15)	F-15D-39-MC	85-0129–0131 (3)
F-15C-25-MC	79-0038–0058 (21)	F-15C-34-MC	82-0023–0038 (16)	F-15D-40-MC	85-0132–0134 (3)
F-15C-26-MC	79-0059–0081 (23)	F-15D-33-MC	82-0044–0045 (2)	F-15C-41-MC	86-0143–0162 (20)
F-15C-27-MC	80-0002–0023 (22)	F-15D-34-MC	82-0046–0048 (3)	F-15C-42-MC	86-0163–0180 (18)
F-15C-28-MC	80-0024–0038 (15)	F-15C-35-MC	83-0010–0034 (25)	F-15D-41-MC	86-0181–0182 (2)

Cancellations: F-15C-23-MC 78-0551–0560 (ten), F-15D-23-MC 78-0575 (one),
F-15C-32-MC 81-0057–0060 (four), F-15D-32-MC 81-0066*–0067 (two),
F-15C-36-MC 83-0044–0045 (two), F-15D-36-MC 83-0051 (one),
F-15C-38-MC 84-0032–0041 (ten), F-15D-38-MC 84-0047–0048 (two).

*to Saudi Arabia as 81-0003 and replaced in USAF order by F-15C 81-0056.

MODEL	SERIALS	MODEL	SERIALS
F-15E-41-MC	86-0183–0184 (2)	F-15E-49-MC	90-0227–0244 (18)
F-15E-42-MC	86-0185–0190 (6)	F-15E-50-MC	90-0245–0262 (18)
F-15E-43-MC	87-0169–0189 (21)	F-15E-51-MC	91-0300–0317 (18)
F-15E-44-MC	87-0190–0210 (21)	F-15E-52-MC	91-0318–0335 (18)
F-15E-45-MC	88-1667–1687 (21)	F-15E-53-MC	91-0600–0605 (6)
F-15E-46-MC	88-1688–1708 (21)	F-15E-53-MC	92-0364–0366 (3) c/n E207–209. War attrition batch.
F-15E-47-MC	89-0471–0488 (18)	F-15E-58-MC	96-0200–0205 (6) attrition batch.
F-15E-48-MC	89-0489–0506 (18)	F-15E-61-MC	97-0217–0222 (6) attrition batch.
		F-15E-62-MC	98-0131–0135 (5)

Ten new aircraft entered production on 5 October 2000 as E227 -236 for delivery from May, 2002 to mid-2004.

FMS PRODUCTION AND TRANSFERS

MODEL	SERIALS

Peace Eagle *to Japan*
79-0280–281(2) as F-15J-24-MC 02-8801–8802; 79-0282–0285 (4) as F-15DJ-26-MC 12-8051–8054; 79-0286–0287 (2) as F-15DJ-29-MC 22-8055–8056; 81-0078–0069 (2) as F-15DJ-32-MC 32-8057–8058; 81-0070–0071 (2) as F-15DJ-33-MC 42-8059–8060; 83-0052–0053 (2) as F-15DJ-36-MC 52-8061–8062.

MODEL	SERIALS	MODEL	SERIALS	MODEL	SERIALS
Peace Sun *to Saudi Arabia*		F-15C-32-MC	80-0100–0106 (7)	F-15D-31-MC	80-0118–0119 (2)
F-15C-28-MC	80-0062–0067 (6)	F-15D-27-MC	80-0107–0110 (4)	F-15D-32-MC	80-0120–0121 (2)
F-15C-29-MC	80-0068–0074 (7)	F-15D-28-MC	80-0111–0112 (2)	F-15C-32-MC	81-0002 (1)
F-15C-30-MC	80-0075–0085(11)	F-15D-29-MC	80-0113–0114 (2)	*(plus F-15C-32-MC 81-0056, sold as 81-0003)*	
F-15C-31-MC	80-0086–0099 (14)	F-15D-30-MC	80-0115–0117 (3)		

MODEL	SERIALS		MODEL	SERIALS
Peace Sun VI			*Transfers of USAF stock to Saudi Arabia*	
F-15C-49-MC	90-0263–0267 (5		F-15D-24-MC	79-0004–0006 (3)
F-15C-50-MC	90-0268-0271 (4)		F-15D-25-MC	79-0010 (1)
F-15D-50-MC	90-0272–0274 (3)		F-15C-24-MC	79-0015, 0017, 0018, 0019, 0023, 0024, 0028, 0031, 0033
			F-15C-25-MC	79-0038, 0039, 0043, 0045, 0051, 0052, 0055
			F-15C-26-MC	79-0060, 0062, 0063

USAF/RSAF F-15C/D SERIAL CONVERSIONS

USAF/RSAF	USAF/RSAF	USAF/RSAF	USAF/RSAF	USAF/RSAF
80-0078/501	80-0103/502	80-0070/503	80-0081/504	80-0104/505
80-0064/506	80-0067/507	80-0085/508	80-0068/509	80-0087/510
80-0089/512	80/0094/513	80-0093/515	80-0120/516	80-0116/517
80-0109/518	80-0118/519	80-0119/520	80-0062/601	80-0092/602
80-0095/603	80-0090/604	80-0073/605	80-0069/606	80-0071/608
80-0100/609	80-0102/611	80-0079/612	80-0082/613	80-0088/614
80-0106/615	80-0115/616	80-0121/617	80-0111/618	80-0117/619
80-0108/620	80-0083/1301	80-065/1302	80-066/1303	80-084/1304
80-086/1305	80-096/1306	80-080/1307	80-072/1309	80-097/1310
80-091/1311	80-075/1312	80-076/1313	80-077/1314	80-098/1315
80-107/1316	80-113/1318	80-112/1319	80-110/1320	81-003/1321
81-002/1322	79-015/4201	79-023/4202	79-031/4203	79-045/4204
79-063/4205	79-017/4206	79-024/4207	79-033/4208	79-051/4209
79-055/4210	79-060/4211	79-039/4212	79-043/4213	79-018/4214
79-019/4215	79-078/4216	79-032/4217	79-038/4218	79-052/4219
79-062/4220	79-005/4221	79-006/4222	79-004/4223	79-010/4224

(Data via Norman Taylor)

MODEL	SERIALS		MODEL	SERIALS		MODEL	SERIALS
Peace Fox III *to Israel*			F-15C-36-MC	83-0056–0062 (7)		**Peace Fox IV** *to Israel*	
F-15C-27-MC	80-0122–0124 (3)		F-15D-27-MC	80-0131–0132 (2)		F-15D-50-MC	90-0275–0279 (5).
F-15C-28-MC	80-0125–0127 (3)		F-15D-28-MC	80-0133–0136 (4)		(These were actually F-15Es used in an	
F-15C-29-MC	80-0128–0130 (3)		F-15D-35-MC	83-0063–0064 (2)		evaluation programme for the F-15I)	
F-15C-35-MC	83-0054–0055 (2)						

MITSUBISHI HEAVY INDUSTRIES F-15J PRODUCTION

MODEL	SERIALS
F-15J	02-8803–8804 (2) (from kits); 22-8805–8810 (6) (from kits); 22-8811-8815 (5); 32-8816–8827 (13); 42-8828–8844; 52-8845–8863 (19), 62-8864–8870 (15); 72-8871 -72-8895 (17); 82-8896–8905 (10); 92-8906–8913 (8); 02-8914 -028922 (9); 12-8923–8928 (6); 22-8929–228940 (12); 32-8941–8943 (3); 42-8944–8950 (7); 52-8951–8957 (7); 62-8958–8959 (2); 72-8960 (1)

MITSUBISHI HEAVY INDUSTRIES F-15DJ PRODUCTION

MODEL	SERIALS
F-15DJ	52-8061–8062 (2); 82-8063–8066 (4); 92-8067–8070 (4); 02-8071–8073 (3); 12-8074–8079 (6); 32-8080–8087 (9); 52-8086 (1), 62-8089 (1); 72-8090 (1)

Peace Sun IX *to Saudi Arabia*

MODEL	SERIALS
F-15S-54-MC	93-0852–0863 (12)
F-15S-55-MC	93-0864–0875 (12)
F-15S-56-MC	93-0876–0887 (12)
F-15S-57-MC	93-0888–0899 (12)
F-15S-58-MC	93-0900–0911 (12)
F-15S-59-MC	93-0912–0923 (12)

Peace Fox V *to Israel*

MODEL	SERIALS
F-15I-56-MC	94-0286–0294 (9)
F-15I-57-MC	94-0295–0306 (12)
F-15I-57-MC	94-0500–0503 (4)

WING	SQUADRON	CODE/COLOUR	TYPE	TRANSITION FROM/DATES	
56th FW Luke AFB	461st TFTS/FS *Deadly Jesters*	LA (y/bl)	F-15E		1/4/94–4/8/94
	550th FS *Silver Eagles*	LA (bl)	F-15E		1/4/94–/3/95
	555th TFTS *Triple Nickel*	LA (gn)	F-15E		to Aviano with F-16C post-1/4/94

The 56th FW was formed by the renumbering on 1/4/94 of the 58th FW, which had absorbed the F-15E units of the 405th TTW on 29 August, 1991. F-15E training finally passed from the 550th FS to the 333rd FS in March, 1995.

WING	SQUADRON	CODE/COLOUR	TYPE	TRANSITION FROM/DATES	
57th FWW/WG	433rd FWS *Satan's Angels*	WA (y/bl)	F-15A/B F-15C/D/E	F-4	1/11/76 1982 (assets to F-15 Division on 1/6/81)
	422nd FWS/TES	WA (y/bl)	F-15A/B F-15C/D F-15E		1977 1/7/83–current 1990–current

From late-1992 the F-15 Division of the Fighter Weapons School was reorganized into an F-15C/D Division and an F-15E Division.

WING	SQUADRON	CODE/COLOUR	TYPE	TRANSITION FROM/DATES	
58th TTW Luke AFB	461st TFTS *Deadly Jesters* (was 4461st CCTS)	LA (bl/y)	F-15A/B		1/7/77–29/8/79
	550th TFTS *Silver Eagles*	LA (bl)	F-15A/B		25/8/77–29/8/79
	55th TFTS *Triple Nickel*	LA (gn)	F-15A/B		14/11/74–29/8/79

(Assets to 405th TTW from 29/8/79)

WING	SQUADRON	CODE/COLOUR	TYPE	TRANSITION FROM/DATES	
78th Air Base Wing Robins ALC	3339th Test Sqn (engineering evaluation test flight)	RG (was WR)	F-15A/C/D/E		various–current
79th Test & Evaluation Group (single examples at various times for test purposes at Tactical Air Warfare Center)	85th TES (4485th TES)	OT	F-15A/B/C/E		
325th TTW/FW Tyndall AFB	1st TFTS/FS *Griffins*	TY (r)	F-15A/B F-15C/D		15/10/83 early 1994–current
	2nd TFTS/FS *Unicorns*	TY (y)	F-15A/B F-15C/D		-/1/84 -/5/94–current
	95th TFTS/FS *Mr Bones*	TY (b)	F-15A/B F-15C/D		-/1/88 -/10/93–current
366th Wing Mountain Home AFB	390th FS *Wild Boars*	MO (bl)	F-15C/D EF-111A		25/9/92–current
	391st FS *Bold Tigers*	MO (tig)	F-15E	F-111A	13/3/92–current
405th TTW	461st TFTS *Deadly Jesters*	LA (bl/y)	F-15A/B F-15E		29/8/79 (from 58th TTW) 1/8/87

WING	SQUADRON	CODE/COLOUR	TYPE	TRANSITION FROM/DATES	
	550th TFTS *Silver Eagles*	LA (gn)	F-15A/B F-15E		29/8/79 (from 58th TTW) 12/5/89
	555th TFTS *Triple Nickel*	LA (gn)	F-15A/B F-15E		29/8/79 (from 58th TTW) late-1992
	426th TFTS *Killer Claws*	LA (r)	F-15A/B F-4C		1/1/81–29/11/90

(405th TTW took over F-15 training from 58th TTW on 29/8/79. The 58th resumed this role with the F-15E on 29/8/91 and was then renumbered as the 56th FW on 1/4/94).

412th Test Wing/OG	AFFTC	445th FLTS ED	F-15A/B/C/D/E		1993–current

(Continues the work of the original Eagle Combined Test Force [CTF] at Edwards AFB since the early 1970s and the 6512th Test Squadron of the 6510th Test wing in the 1980s.)

AIR DEFENSE COMMAND (ADC) UNITS
(Became ADTAC Units after being transferred to Tactical Air Command on 1/10/79 and then became 1st Air Force from 6/12/85.)

	5th FIS Minot AFB	–	F-15A/B	F-106A/B	-/4/85–1/7/88
	48th FIS *Tasmanian Devils* Langley AFB	LY	F-15A/B	F-106A/B	5/4/82–30/9/91
	57th FIS/FS *Black Knights*	IS (bl/w)	F-15C/D	F-4E	-/7/85–1/3/95
	318th FIS	TC	F-15A/B	F-106A/B	-/9/83–7/12/89

AIR NATIONAL GUARD

	101st FS, 102nd FG, Massachusetts ANG Otis ANGB		F-15A/B F-106A/B		-/9/87–current
	110th FS, 131st FW, Missouri ANG SL *Lindbergh's Own*, Lambert-St Louis		F-15A/B F-4E		IOC 15/9/91–current
	114th FS, 173rd FW, Oregon ANG *Eager Beavers*, Klamath Falls	–	F-15A/B F-16A		-/6/98–current
	122nd FS, 159th FG, Louisiana ANG *Coonass Militia/Bayou Militia*, New Orleans	JZ	F-15A/B	F-4C	-/6/85–current
	123rd FS, 142nd FW, Oregon ANG *Redhawks* Portland International Airport	OR	F-15A/B	F-4C	-/5/89–current

WING	SQUADRON	CODE/COLOUR	TYPE	TRANSITION FROM/DATES	
	128th FS, 116th FW, Georgia ANG *Vincet Amor Patrias*, Dobbins AFB.	GA	F-15A/B	F-4D (to B-1B Lancer)	-/5/86–8/95
	158th FS, 125th FW, Florida ANG Jacksonville International Airport	FL	F-15A/B	F-16A	-/10/95–current
	[188th FS, 150th FW, New Mexico ANG *Tacos*, Kirtland AFB.]		began transition to F-15A/B, 1991 then converted to F-16A		
	199th FS, 154th FW, Hawaii ANG Hickam AFB	–	F-15A/B	F-4C	-/3/87–current

FMS OPERATORS
Israel (Heyl Ha'Avir)

	133 Sqn *'Double Tail Squadron'* Tel Nov AB			F-15A/B	-/12/76–current
	106 Sqn *'Second Baz Squadron'* Tel Nov AB			F-15C/D	1981–current
	69 Sqn *'Hammers'* (Tayeset Ha' Patisham) Hatzerim AB		F-15I		19/1/98–current

148 (R) Sqn: special operations/recce unit at Tel Nov; probable F-15 user

Japan Air Self Defence Force (Nihon Koku Jietai) F-15J/DJ Units

2nd Kokudan: 201 Hikotai (from 4/86); 203 Hikotai (from 13/4/83)	Chitose AB	
5th Kokudan: 202 Hikotai (from 12/81)	Nyutabaru AB	
6th Kokudan: 303 Hikotai (from 4/87); 306 Hikotai (from 1994)	Komatsu AB	
7th Kokudan: 204 Hikotai (from 4/84), 305 Hikotai (from 1993)	Hyakuri AB	
8th Kokudan: 304 Hikotai (from 4/90)	Tsuiki AB	
Hiko Kyodotai (Aggressor Unit)	Nyutabaru AB	

Royal Saudi Arabian Air Force

5 Sqn King Fahad AFB, Taif	F-15C/D	8/81–current	
6Sqn King Khaled AFB, Khamis Mushayt	F-15C/D	8/81–current	
13 Sqn King Abdul Aziz AFB, Dhahran	F-15C/D	8/81–current	
42 Sqn King Abdul Aziz AFB, Dhahran	F-15C/D	1990–current	
55 Sqn King Khaled AFB, Khamis Mushayt	F-15S	9/95–current	

(RSAF F-15Cs shot down two Iranian F-4Es on 5/6/84 during the Iran/Iraq War.)

Experimental Eagles

The AEDC tested models for the STOL Eagle derivatives for several years before the S/MTD Eagle flew. AEDC

Although many of the proposed alternative roles for the F-15, including F-15N 'Sea Eagle', Wild Weasel, and so on came to nothing the aircraft has played an important role in developing new technologies. Several of these projects were undertaken by NASA, whose first Eagle was F-15A 71-0287, a Block 4 airframe that went to the Dryden Flight Research Center as '835' on 5 January 1976. It received full test instrumentation for over twenty-five projects at NASA's Flight Research Facility.

DEEC/ADECS
Several of these projects concerned digital engine controls that greatly improved jet engine fuel consumption and stall resistance following research in the USA and UK in the early 1980s. For the F-15, these additions made the F100 a much more reliable power source. Digital Electronic Engine Control (DEEC) and Advanced Digital Engine Control (ADEC) were tested in '835' from late 1982 (DEEC) and 1986 (ADEC). This work resulted in the F100-PW-220/229 series, giving a smoother transonic acceleration,

easier restart and lower fuel consumption. ADEC concentrated on monitoring and adjusting the engine's stall margin (keeping turbine pressures safely below the point where a stall could occur). As a result, thrust could be safely increased when required and acceleration improved by between 14 and 24 per cent. Fuel flow and temperature figures could also be optimized, with reductions in fuel consumption of up to 15 per cent.

SRFCS
One of the most innovative NASA projects was Self-Repairing Flight Control Systems, also tested in '835'. It originated from the HIDEC (Highly Integrated Digital Electronic Control) programme of 1989 in the same F-15. The aim was to engineer a system that could automatically recognize any damage or failure to a component in the aircraft's flight controls (a rudder, flap, aileron, and so on) and then reconfigure the remaining controls to enable the F-15 to compensate and remain in flight. In the cockpit, the pilot of an SRFCS-equipped aircraft

would also get an MFD-displayed diagram indicating the new control configuration and telling him of any limitations on performance or pilot-induced control inputs that resulted. The Israeli Air Force's experience in recovering an F-15 with a complete wing missing showed incredulous Macair engineers how well their flight control computer already worked and SRFCS aimed to extend this capability. In addition, the system was expanded to allow it to identify faults in other hydraulic, electrical and mechanical systems as they occurred. This reduced the need for 'fixers' to try and replicate the fault post-flight in the time-honoured way – usually an enormously time-consuming business. Trouble-shooting the traditional way could also have its frustrations. One laconic maintainer, in response to a USAF pilot's post-flight write-up complaining that, 'The autopilot in "altitude hold" mode produces a 200ft (61m) per minute descent rate', replied 'Cannot reproduce problem on the ground!' However, another fixer who noticed a glitch-sheet comment: 'IFF inoperative' and wrote in his reply box, 'IFF always inoperative when in OFF mode' would not have needed SRFCS!

PSC stood for Performance Seeking Control and took the digital management of flight controls, engine inlet and powerplant a stage further in 1990 by integrating all three within '835'. Optimum engine and manoeuvring performance were therefore obtainable in all areas of the mission. As a bonus, PSC monitoring could also flag up any engine components that were at risk of in-flight failure.

The **PCA** (Propulsion Controlled Aircraft) programme developed the idea that basic control of the aircraft could be retained after major loss of flight controls by using engine thrust alone. A number of US pilots had used this trick to coax wounded jets out over the Tonkin Gulf during the Vietnam War so that they could eject overwater. The F-4, in particular, could be made to climb by piling on the power, and dive by reducing it, assuming that the controls were in 'neutral'. Using F-15A '835' with its refined digital engine control, courageous test pilots were able to develop techniques that enabled the blue and white '835' to fly at 170kt with all flight controls at neutral. Eventually, they took the aircraft to within 10ft of landing using only thrust controls. After the installation of a couple of thumbwheel controls in the cockpit, one supplying flightpath commands and the other bank angle commands, the programme climaxed with a full 'hands off' landing. The basic signals to the digital engine control system were 'Climb' (more power), 'Dive' (less power) and 'Turn' (differential thrust on the two engines). Engine response times were the crucial factor in the final stages of the approach and landing.

NASA's other F-15A, 78-0281 (still with its original untrimmed wing tips) was used to test thermal tiles for the Space Shuttle, operating from 1975 to 1983. Also on strength was F-15B 74-0141 '836', kept flying with parts from '835' when that was withdrawn in 1996. This aircraft carried the Flight Test Fixture (FTF-II) on its centreline pylon as a box-like structure that could house a variety of experiments in connection with the Space Shuttle and other reuseable launch vehicles.

House Eagles

More drastic modifications were made to one of McDonnell Douglas's two 'tame' Eagles, the first two F-15Bs. 71-0290 tested aluminium-lithium and other composite wing panels, yielding valuable data for the AV-8B and F/A-18 programmes. Later, it was fitted with composite bonded titanium/boron fibre horizontal stabilizers. The aircraft was then more majorly modified as the **F-15S/MTD** (Short Take-off/Manoeuvre Technology Demonstrator) beginning in October1984. In conjunction with Pratt and Whitney, General Electric, National Water Lift (hydraulic actuators) and Cleveland Pneumatic (landing gear), McDonnell Douglas experimented in four new areas. Primarily, the project sought to enable the aircraft to survive that most basic of problems in wartime, how to operate from damaged runways. The two-seater received beefed-up 'rough field' landing gear with eight

new components, later modified for use in the F-15E. Totally new engine nozzles were designed and the whole package was aimed at giving pilots the ability to take off and land on a 50ft-(15m-) wide runway area 1,500ft (460m) in length in 30kts crosswinds, at night. The aircraft also had to be able to carry full internal fuel and up to 10,000lb (4,500kg) of external load. Rectangular-section, two-dimensionally vectoring nozzles were fitted to F100-PW-220 engines in place of the standard round-section units, allowing thrust to be vectored +/– 20 degrees from the normal thrust line to give short take-off. There was a reverse thrust facility for a 72 per cent reduction in landing roll.

In normal flight the nozzles behaved similarly to the standard convergent/divergent models but their vectoring could be employed to provide spectacularly improved manoeuvrability in the vertical plane. In addition, the S/MTD had a pair of modified F/A-18 tailplanes attached ahead of its forward wing-root as powerful canard foreplanes. Offering extra pitch and roll control they also gave added lift for high-aoa manoeuvres, with the vectoring nozzles also acting like a large additional tailplane. Control was further enhanced by the Integrated Flight/Propulsion Control (IFPC) system using General Electric 'fly-by-wire' without mechanical back-up. IFPC used position sensors linked to the throttles, stick and rudder pedals, analysing the signals and devising the best combinations of flight control, engine nozzle (or on the ground, even brakes and steering) to fulfil the pilot's commands most effectively. It operated in five selectable modes: conventional, short take-off/short landing, cruise and combat. Pilots could even select an 'auto glide' mode for landing approach in which throttle movements would affect only speed, not glide-slope. Tests showed that S/MTD conferred a 33 per cent increase in pitch rate at Mach 0.3 and up to 67 per cent better roll rate at Mach 1.4. Installation

of APG-70 radar and the LANTIRN navigation pod assisted with precise short landings where ground-based navigational aids were not available.

With the successful conclusion of this programme in August 1991 the next phase, **NF-15B ACTIVE** began. Again, 71-0290 was used but this time with P&W multi-directional thrust-vectoring nozzles. More closely resembling standard F100 nozzles in appearance these 'pitch/yaw balanced beam' variants could vector +/– 20 degrees in any direction to enlarge the manoeuvring envelope beyond the horizontal plane, though they lacked thrust reversing. Strengthening of the engine fan casings and changes to the F-15B rear fuselage were needed but the new configuration yielded manoeuvrability improvements throughout the performance range up to Mach 2. Although this technology is unlikely to find application in the operational F-15 fleet it has added to the F-22A Raptor's bag of tricks and enabled it to duel with the new generation of Russian fighters.

Other F-15s in use as test vehicles at St Louis included the shark-mouthed F-15A 71-0282, used to flight-test the Eagle's Advanced Environmental Control System **(AECS).** This enhanced the reliability of the electronics by controlling humidity, temperature and dust ingestion into the avionics bays as well as providing one of the most comfortable cockpit environments ever provided in a US fighter. Another early F-15A and F-15B 77-0166 tested the integrated flight fire-control system **(IFFC)**. This allowed the aircraft to be flown up to weapons release point against air-to-air targets using a sensor that could lock on to the target and steer the aircraft. General Electric's **Firefly III** system was also tested and provided valuable background to LANTIRN. It used a podded, laser acquisition/tracking sensor (Martin Marietta ATLIS II) for bomb drops against ground targets.

Assigned to Major Bob Bryan this F-15A was in use by the Eglin Operational Test wing, the 3246th TW, in June 1982. Norm Taylor

F-15 Attrition

Write-offs and Selected Incidents Involving Major Damage

DATE	TYPE	SERIAL	SQUADRON	REMARKS
1975				
14 October	F-15A	73-0088	–	Crashed at Gila Bend Gunnery Range, AZ at low altitude. Both engines flamed out when generators turned off due to smoke in cockpit. This also took out main fuel tank boost pump but emergency pump did not cut in soon enough to restore fuel flow and low altitude prevented engine restart. USAF pilot ejected.
1976	–	–	–	Nil.
1977				
28 February	F-15A	74-0129	57th FWW 'WA'	Mid-air collision with F-5E 'Red Force' Aggressor during ACEVAL/AIMVAL testing over Nellis ranges. F-15 pilot ejected.
6 December	F-15B	75-0085	57th FWW 'WA'	Crashed at Nellis AFB during ACT killing CO of 433rd FWS.
1978				
8 February	F-15A	73-0097	58 TFTW 'LA'	Severe damage in ground accident.
17 April	F-15A	75-0059	36th TFW 'BT'	During DACT with 527th TFTAS off Cromer, pilot reported 4,000lb (1,814kg) fuel remaining but none in feed tank. Both engines flamed out. Pilot ejected.
7 June	F-15A	76-0073	36th TFW 'BT'	Damaged by fire when left engine failed after selecting afterburner.
15 June	F-15A	76-0047	36th TFW 'BT'	During DACT while returning to Bitburg from Bentwaters one engine stalled and the other refused to restart after a stall. Pilot ejected. Wreck recovered and dumped at Alconbury.
6 July	F-15A	76-0053	36th TFW 'BT'	Crashed near Daun, W. Germany while on an instrument departure, killing pilot.
1st September	F-15A	75-0018	1st TFW 'FF'	Crashed off coast of Virginia; the Wing's only loss between this date and March 1980.
19 December	F-15A	75-0063	36th TFW 'BT'	Fire in starboard engine during ACT. Crashed in field nr. Ahlhorn, Germany. Pilot ejected.
28 December	F-15A	75-0064	36th TFW 'BT'	Crashed nr. Daun, W. Germany. Pilot ejected.
29 December	F-15A	74-0136	57th FWW 'WA'	Crashed at Nellis AFB during DACT.
1979				
16 February	F-15A	77-0107	49th TFW 'HO'	Crashed at Nellis AFB during training exercise.
13 March	F-15A	77-0076	49th TFW 'HO'	Crashed, circumstances unknown.
25 April	F-15B	77-0167	MACAIR	Crashed 6mi from Frederickstown, Missouri on its second test flight.
2 June	F-15A	76-0041	36th TFW 'BT'	Involved in accident near Bitburg; circumstances unknown.
3 June	F-15A	76-0035	36th TFW 'BT'	Severely damaged on landing at Bitburg.
13 September	F-15A	76-0085	57th FWW 'WA'	Crashed near Nellis AFB.

DATE	TYPE	SERIAL	SQUADRON	REMARKS
3 October	F-15A	77-0072	49th TFW 'HO'	Crashed after mid-air collision with 77-0061 (same unit) which recovered to MCAS Fallon minus most of its left vertical and horizontal stabilizers. Pilot of -0072 ejected.
12 December	F-15A	–	36th TFW 'BT'	Involved in accident in W. Germany, circumstances unknown.
1980				
4 March	F-15A	75-0070	36th TFW 'BT'	Crashed 5mi south of Baden-Baden, W. Germany.
6 March	F-15A	76-0082	36th TFW 'BT'	Crashed 7mi north of Bitburg.
10 March	F-15A	75-0023	1st TFW 'FF'	Destroyed by fire on the flightline at Langley AFB.
25 July	F-15A	76-0013	36th TFW 'BT'	Crashed during training exercise.
1981				
21 January	F-15B	77-0164	57th TTW 'WA'	Mid-air crash with an F-5E during DACT involving two F-15s and six F-5Es. All three crew killed.
13 February	F-15A	76-0065	405th TTW 'LA'	Crashed in Pacific.
19 March	F-15A	–	IDF/AF	Hit flock of storks during climb-out from base and sustained engine fire but pilot managed to recover to base.
23 June	F-15C	79-0040	525th TFS, 36th TFW 'BT'	Crashed 15mi from Bremen, W. Germany. Pilot killed.
11 September	F-15C	80-0001	36th TFW 'BT'	Crashed on final approach to Soesterburg Open House display. Pilot unhurt.
2 November	F-15A	75-0051	33rd TFW 'EG'	Crashed near Panama City, Fla. after mid-air with another F-15A during in-flight refuelling from a KC-135A.
15 December	F-15A	73-0106	405th TTW 'LA'	Crashed near Phoenix, Az.
1982				
6 April	F-15C	78-0524	18th TFW 'ZZ'	Lost 40nm north-west of Kadena after severe fuel leak.
22 December	F-15C	80-0025	53rd TFS, 36th TFW 'BT'	Impacted mountain peak after a Zulu Alert scramble, killing pilot (Capt Geoffrey Roether) who had a Bitburg Alert Facility named in his memory.
28 December	F-15C	78-0481	18th TFW 'ZZ'	Mid-air collision with F-15C 78-540 92 NM north-east of Okinawa, over the sea. Pilot ejected.
1983				
4 January	F-15C	80-0036	1st TFW 'FF'	Crashed during training exercise.
4 February	F-15A	76-0081	33rd TFW 'EG'	Crashed, pilot ejected.
1st May	F-15D	957	IDF/AF	Collided with A-4N over Negev Desert during ACM. Right wing torn off. Pilot maintained control and landed, taking the arresting cable at 260kt. Aircraft (named *Markia Shchakm*) repaired and later scored its fifth MiG kill.
9 May	F-15A	77-0094	49th TFW 'HO'	Crashed at White Sands, NM. Pilot ejected.
1st June	F-15C	79-0071 and 80-0008	36th TFW 'BT'	Both crashed after a mid-air collision 20mi west of Ramstein. One pilot killed, one ejected.
6 October	F-15A	75-0076	33rd TFW 'EG'	Collided with a 57th FWW F-5E (74-01509) 45mi north-west of Cold Lake, Alberta. Pilot ejected.
20 October	F-15J	12-8053	202 Hikotai, JASDF	Crashed into Pacific 110mi east of Nyutabaru AB.
1984				
10 April	F-15C	79-0044	525th FS, 36th TFW 'BT'	Crashed near Lommersdorf, Germany. Pilot ejected.

DATE	TYPE	SERIAL	SQUADRON	REMARKS
17 August	F-15B	75-0087	325th TFW 'TY'	Crashed in Gulf of Mexico after mid-air collision with an 86th TFW F-4E (68-0535/RS).

1985

DATE	TYPE	SERIAL	SQUADRON	REMARKS
24 June	F-15A	74-0087	21st CW 'AK'	Crashed into Yukon River, Alaska after an explosion shortly after take-off from Elmendorf AFB. Pilot killed.
10 July	F-15D	79-0010	36th TFW 'BT'	Lost a main-gear wheel during touch-and-go landings at Bentwaters and ran off runway, snapping off port gear strut after aircraft's hook missed the arresting gear. No injuries, repaired.
29 August	F-15C	79-0017	32nd TFS 'CR'	Damaged in heavy landing at Stavanger, Norway.
31 August	F-15C	81-0039	1st TFW 'FF'	Crashed on landing at Tinker AFB. Pilot uninjured.
9 September	F-15A	74-0094	21st CW 'AK'	Crashed in Alaska.
5 November	F-15A	74-0090	21st CW 'AK'	Crashed in Alaska.
16 December	–		33rd TFW 'EG' (or ADTC markings)	Crashed into Gulf of Mexico 40mi off the US coast.

1986

DATE	TYPE	SERIAL	SQUADRON	REMARKS
2 January	F-15C	80-0037	57th FIS 'IS'	Crashed into Atlantic 130km south of Iceland. Replaced by 80-0030 (ex-1st TFW).
7 January	F-15C	79-0061 and 80-0032	36th TFW 'BT'	Both crashed after mid-air collision near Rimschweiler, W. Germany.
15 January	F-15A	76-0023	5th FIS	Crashed in Guadalupe Mountains, Texas during an air defence exercise while on attachment to Holloman AFB. Pilot killed.
7 March	F-15A	76-0055 and 76-0074	–	Involved in mid-air collision.
13 June	F-15A	77-0138	49th TFW 'HO'	Engine fire when afterburner engaged for take-off. Pilot escaped and fire suppressed but broke out again. Aircraft returned to USA via C-5A for repair.
12 September	F-15A F-15B	77-0083 77-0153	49th TFW 'HO'	Involved in mid-air collision near Alamagordo, NM. The F-15B crashed; the damaged F-15A landed.
September	F-15C	610 and 611	16 Sqn., R Saudi AF	Involved in mid-air collision nr. Khamis, Saudi Arabia. Both landed with considerable damage and one aircraft burned out after landing.
15 November	F-15A	76-0111	318th FIS	Port main landing gear collapsed on landing at McChord AFB. Aircraft repaired.

1987

DATE	TYPE	SERIAL	SQUADRON	REMARKS
9 March	F-15A	77-0075	49th TFW 'HO'	Crashed 3mi south-east of Holloman AFB. Pilot killed.
13 March	F-15J	42-8840	204 Hikotai, JASDF	Crashed into sea 100nm east of Hyakuri AB after its pilot became disorientated during DACT and died in the crash.
2 April	F-15C	–	IDF/AF	Maj Iftah More lost control of the aircraft during ACM and died in the crash after a seat malfunction.
19 May	F-15C	78-0495	18th TFW 'ZZ'	Crashed into the Pacific.
8 June	F-15C	81-0056	1st TFW 'FF'	Crashed in Virginia.
1st October	F-15A	–	48th FIS	Crashed near Sumatra, Florida while on Alert at Tyndall AFB. Pilot ejected.
24 November	F-15A	75-0056	128th TFS Ga ANG	Mid-air collision with AFRES F-16B during an air-to-air photo sortie. F-15 crashed in Jefferson County after the pilot ejected.

1988

DATE	TYPE	SERIAL	SQUADRON	REMARKS
29 June	F-15J	22-8804 and 22-8808	303rd Hikotai, JASDF	Crashed into Sea of Japan after a mid-air collision during ACT. Both pilots killed.

DATE	TYPE	SERIAL	SQUADRON	REMARKS
15 August	F-15A 672 and 684		IDF/AF	Crashed after a mid-air collision during ACT. Both pilots (including Lt Col Ram Caller, CO of 133 Sqn) and three civilians on the ground were killed. ACMI system in F-15B subsequently modified to show a collision warning indication on the back-seat VDU.
30 August	F-15C	511	13 Sqn R. Saudi AF	Crashed near Al Hesa, Saudi Arabia after control loss, killing pilot.
8 November	F-15C	80-0017	21st TFW AK	Crashed 5mi north-west of Kodiak, Alaska, killing pilot.
1989				
1st May	F-15B	76-0138	95th TFTS, 325th TTW 'TY'	Crashed into Gulf of Mexico 65mi north-east of Tyndall AFB, killing pilot.
18 May	F-15A	–	2nd TFTS, 325th TTW 'TY'	Hit guy-wire supporting radio broadcast tower near Clarksville, Fla. Tower fell over. F-15 returned to Tyndall, departing runway due to undercarriage damage. Pilot escaped, aircraft repaired.
8 July	F-15C	85-0109	33rd TFW 'EG'	Crashed near Lamison, Alabama. Pilot ejected.
10 August	F-15A	–	49th TFW 'HO'	Crashed 60mi north of Holloman AFB. Pilot ejected.
6 November	F-15C	–	43rd TFS, 21st TFW 'AK'	Crashed 60mi north of Las Vegas during a *Red Flag* exercise. Pilot ejected.
28 December	F-15C	–	59th TFS, 33rd TFW 'EG'	Crashed into Gulf of Mexico 40mi south-east of Apalachicola, Fla. killing pilot.
1990				
18 January	F-15C	–	43rd TFS, 21st TFW 'AK'	Destroyed in a crash at Elmendorf AFB.
21 January	F-15C	–	58th FW 'LA'	Crashed on ranges 75mi from Nellis AFB. Pilot ejected.
24 January	F-15C	–	18th TFW 'ZZ'	Crashed in South China Sea 50mi north-west of Clark AFB during *Cope Thunder* Exercise. Pilot killed.
26 January	F-15J	22-8808	JASDF	Crashed in Japan.
15 March	F-15A	–	426th TFTS, 405th TFW 'LA'	Crashed near Wenden, Arizona after control loss during ACT. Pilot ejected.
19 March	F-15C	81-0054	3rd Wing, 'AK'	Hit by inadvertently launched AIM-9M missile from another F-15C causing Class B damage to tail, engine exhaust and wing. Port stabilator shot off. Returned to Elmendorf AFB. Wing Commander replaced shortly afterwards.
25 April	F-15C	81-0049	32nd TFS 'CR'	Crashed into North Sea off Spurn Head during DACT. Pilot ejected.
12 June	F-15A	77-0096	7th TFS, 49th TFW 'HO'	Tyre burst and port undercarriage collapsed on landing at Gilze-Rijen. Pilot uninjured.
2 July	F-15J	–	204 Hikotai, JASDF	Lost in training accident.
30 September	F-15E	87-0203	4th TFW 'SJ'	Hit ground during low-altitude practice intercept by RAF Jaguars while operating from Thumrait, Oman. Maj Peter S. Hook and Capt James 'Boo Boo' Poulet both killed.
24 October	F-15C	79-0067	525th TFS, 36th TFW 'BT'	Crashed into Mediterranean during DACT while detached to Decimomannu.
11 November	F-15C	–	43rd TFS, 21st TFW 'AK'	Crashed into Big Mount Susitana, 30mi south-west of Anchorage, killing pilot.
1991				
18 January	F-15E	88-1689	4th TFW 'SJ'	*Desert Storm* combat loss. Maj Thomas F. 'Teek' Koritz and Maj Donnie R. Holland KIA.
19 January	F-15E	88-1692	4th TFW 'SJ'	*Desert Storm* combat loss. Col David Eberly and Maj Thomas E. Griffiths Jr. POW.

DATE	TYPE	SERIAL	SQUADRON	REMARKS
10 February	F-15C	821	IDF/AF	Details unknown.
14 February	F-15C	80-0074/514	5 Sqn R. Saudi AF	Crashed near Khamis Mushayt, Saudi Arabia.
27 March	F-15C	78-0526	18th FW 'ZZ'	Crashed during training in Japan.
16 September	F-15E	–	461st FS, 58th FW 'LF'	Destroyed in accident. No injuries.
13 December	F-15DJ	12-8079	201 Hikotai, JASDF	Destroyed at Komatsu AB in accident.

1992

15 January	F-15A	–	128th TFS, Ga ANG	Crashed (pilot ejected) after mid-air collision with another F-15A, which landed safely. ANG F-15s stood down for two days to review training procedures.
15 April	F-15C	–	22nd FS, 36th FW 'BT'	Crashed near Stuttgart after engine explosion and fire. Pilot ejected.
22 April	F-15C	–	22nd FS, 36th FW 'BT'	Crashed near Roseburg, W. Germany. Pilot killed.
13 July	F-15C	–	33rd FW 'EG'	Crashed into Gulf of Mexico 90mi south of Eglin AFB. Pilot ejected.
13 July	F-15C	–	33rd FW 'EG'	Overran and damaged on landing at Eglin AFB.
10 August	F-15E	–	57th FW 'WA'	Crashed near Carp, Nevada 80mi from Nellis AFB killing both crew.
17 October	F-15J	72-8884	JASDF	Crashed into Pacific 55mi north-east of Tokyo killing pilot.
30 November	F-15C	83-0021	71st FS, 1st FW 'FF'	Crashed in Saudi Arabia during training for *Southern Watch*. Pilot ejected.

1993

15 March	F-15C	79-0027	95th FS, 325th FW 'TY'	Crashed into Gulf of Mexico 100mi off Tyndall AFB, Fla. Pilot ejected.
12 June	F-15A	77-0117	122nd FS, Louisiana ANG.	Crashed 30mi east of New Orleans NAS. Pilot ejected. Wreck recovered to New Orleans NAS.
6 October	F-15DJ	82-8064	2nd Air Wing, JASDF	Crashed into sea 30mi south of Chitose AB. Crew rescued.
17 December	F-15A	–	122nd FS, Louisiana ANG	Crashed after mid-air collision with Arkansas ANG F-16C 82-0927 which also crashed, killing pilot. F-15 pilot recovered.

1994

12 January	F-15C	–	18th Wing 'ZZ'	Damaged by engine fire at Kadena AFB.
31 January	F-15C	81-0055	57th FW 'WA'	Ran off runway at Nellis AFB after landing with left undercarriage leg retracted. No injuries, aircraft repaired.
4 April	F-15C	78-0530	44FS, 18th Wing 'ZZ'	Crashed after take-off from Kadena AFB. Pilot ejected.
5 May	F-15C	85-0116	33rd Wing 'EG'	Crashed in Gulf of Mexico after loss of control.
6 May	F-15C	78-0497	67th FS, 18th Wing 'ZZ'	Crashed into Yellow Sea off Boryong, nr. Kunsan after mid-air collision with 80th FS F-16C. Pilot killed.
16 September	F-15E	91-0601	494th FS, 48th FW 'LN'	Canopy shattered by duck-strike during low-level sortie over mid-Wales. WSO Capt Mike Panarassi ejected and was recovered by RAF Sea King. Pilot, Brad Robert, landed aircraft at RAF Valley. Aircraft had minor damage to right intake lip and inner surface of vertical stabilizer caused by canopy separating.

1995

18 April	F-15E	89-0504	336th FS, 4th FW 'SJ'	Pilot, Capt Brad Udell, became disorientated during steep dive at night during a practice intercept and ejected. Aircraft crashed and WSO, Capt Dennis White, killed.

DATE	TYPE	SERIAL	SQUADRON	REMARKS
30 May	F-15C	79-0068	53rd FS, 52nd FW 'SP'	Flight control rods were inadvertently installed in reverse during maintenance causing total loss of control after take-off from Spangdahlem. Pilot killed when aircraft crashed on golf course. Base Open Day cancelled and two NCOs charged.
3 August	F-15C	78-0537	18th Wing 'ZZ'	Crashed in Yukon National Reserve, Alaska during *Cope Thunder* exercise. Pilot ejected.
10 August	F-15C	–	1st FW and 33rd FW	Landed at Eglin with damage after mid-air collision over Gulf of Mexico during ACT.
10 August	F-15D	–	IDF/AF	Crashed south of Sde Boker, Israel after bird ingestion caused an engine fire at low altitude. Both crew killed.
11 September	F-15	–		Damaged by hitting approach lights at Portland, Oregon. No injuries.
6 October	F-15J	–	JASDF	Failed to become airborne due to power loss on take-off at Komatsu AB. Overran runway and burned out.
18 October	F-15C	–	3rd Wing 'AK'	Reported crashed in Alaska.
18 October	F-15C	78-0529	44th TFS, 18th Wing 'ZZ'	Crashed into Pacific 65mi south of Kadena AB. Pilot ejected.
8 November	F-15A	–	159th FS, Florida ANG	Ran off runway at Jacksonville. Repaired.
9 November	F-15A	–	131st FW, Mississippi ANG	Overran runway at Whiteman AFB and recovered from field for repair.
22 November	F-15J	52-8846	303rd Hikotai, JASDF	Hit by AIM-9L inadvertently fired from wingman's F-15J. Crashed off Hegura Head. Pilot rescued.
1996				
21 March	F-15C	84-0023	1st FW 'FF'	Crashed on take-off from Nellis AFB during *Green Flag* exercise. Pilot ejected.
3 July	F-15C	–	R. Saudi AF	Two aircraft crashed after mid-air collision, killing both pilots.
27 August	F-15E	–	390th FS, 366th Wing 'MO'	Crashed in Idaho. One crew ejected.
1997				
10 January	F-15C	–	58th FS, 33rd FW 'EG'	Pilot aborted take-off after severe engine fire and escaped. Aircraft severely damaged.
19 January	F-15B	137	IDF/AF	Hit flock of storks near Revivim Kibbutz, Negev Desert causing loss of control. Crew ejected.
11 July	F-15E	89-0491	334th FS, 4th FW 'SJ'	Crashed near Dare County Bomb Range while on range sortie with BDU-33s. Pilot, Maj Pete Whelan and student WSO, Capt Ramiro Martinez ejected.
24 November	F-15C	–	94th FS, 1st FW 'FF'	Crashed 60mi off Virginia Beach. Pilot, 1st Lt David Kyikos, ejected and rescued by USCG.
1998				
1st March	F-15B	73-0112/142	IDF/AF	Crashed on Mt. Eival, West Bank after hitting a 260ft radio antenna during a low-level simulated attack. Crew, Maj Uriel Kolton and Capt Uri Manor, killed when aircraft flew into mountain.
5 June	F-15A	–	122nd FS, Louisiana ANG	Crashed on take-off from NAS New Orleans. Pilot ejected.
6 June	F-15C	85-0112	33rd FW 'EG'	When Eglin AFB was caught in a tornado the aircraft was picked up, turned through 45 degrees and carried 225ft, coming to rest across a concrete barrier causing nose-gear damage. Another F-15C had similar damage.

DATE	TYPE	SERIAL	SQUADRON	REMARKS
16 June	*F-15E*	*91-0327*	*494th FS, 48th FW 'LN'*	Aborted take-off after engine fire following uncontained turbine failure which ruptured fuel tanks. Crew evacuated aircraft. Fire caused runway damage and closed runway for three days. Aircraft returned to Robins AFB in C-5A 68-0222, 12 December, for repairs costing $1.5m and test-flown on 7 August 2000 for eventual delivery to Nellis AFB.
21 October	*F-15E*	*89-0497*	*391st FS, 366th Wing 'MO'*	Crashed in bad weather during a two-ship training mission near McDermott, Oregon. Pilot, Lt Col William E. Morel III (366th OSG Ops Officer) and WSO Capt Jeffrey Fahnlander (366th OSG StanEval Officer) both killed.

1999

DATE	TYPE	SERIAL	SQUADRON	REMARKS
15 January	*F-15E*	*–*	*90th FS, 3rd Wing 'AK'*	Wing tank, pylon and leading edge of port wing severely damaged by bird-strike on approach to bombing range. Aircraft recovered to Elmendorf for repair.
28 January	*F-15C*	*82-0020 and 84-0011*	*85th TES, 53rd Wing*	Mid-air collision over the Gulf of Mexico during DACT with three F-16s. Lt Col Curtis Rackley and Maj Joseph Hruska ejected from '020.
26 March	*F-15E*	*–*	*48th FW 'LN'*	Damaged after running off runway at Istrana AB, Italy during an emergency landing.
29 April	*F-15C*	*–*	*18th Wing 'ZZ'*	Landed using arresting gear after right landing gear failed to extend. Pilot uninjured, aircraft repaired.
15 June	*F-15C and F-15D*		*422nd TES, 53rd Wing*	Both crashed in two unrelated adjacent incidents on Tonopah range, Nellis AFB. Two crew ejected, one with minor injuries.
19 August	*F-15A*	*76-0117 and 77-0118*	*110th FS, 131st FW Missouri ANG*	Mid-air collision during ACM near Round Springs, Salem. Pilot of '117 (Capt Richard Wedan) ejected and was recovered by highway patrol helicopter. Maj Brian Kemp landed '118 at Lambert Field with minor wing damage.
5 November	*F-15C*	*80-0024*	*58th FS, 33rd FW 'EG'*	Damaged by 96th Security Forces Sqn Chevrolet police car, which became wedged under the aircraft when the driver failed to notice the aircraft during a search for his mobile phone on the car's floor.

2000

DATE	TYPE	SERIAL	SQUADRON	REMARKS
3 August	*F-15C 86-0173*		*493rd FS, 48th FW 'LN'*	Crashed en route to Nellis range during *Green Flag*. Capt Christopher Kirby ejected.
11 August	*F-15E 91-0335*		*494th FS, 48th FW 'LN'*	During engine tests the aircraft's arresting hook became detached from the holdback mechanism in Lakenheath's 'hush house' due to improper connection. The aircraft surged forward and its nose penetrated the doors of the building causing Class A ($1 million plus) damage to the F-15E.
12 September	*F-15E 96-0203*		*492nd FS, 48th FW 'LN'*	Tyre burst on landing during return from *Green Flag* to Lakenheath. Aircraft ran off runway at mid-length point and stopped some 100ft onto grass with severe damage to forward fuselage. Left main wheel had failed to align correctly after undercarriage extension and port leg had broken off. Nose section to be rebuilt into a spare F-15E rear fuselage. WSO, Capt Don Jones, had broken arm.

2001

DATE	TYPE	SERIAL	SQUADRON	REMARKS
26 March	*F-15C 86-0169 and 86-0180*		*493rd FS, 48th FW 'LN'*	*Both crashed on Ben Macdui, Scotland, in bad weather conditions. Lt Col Kenneth Hyvonen and Capt Kirk Jones killed.*

Glossary

AAA	anti-aircraft artillery		DAS	direct air support
ABCCC	airborne battlefield command and control centre		DEAD	destruction of enemy air defences
ACC	Air Combat Command		DECU	digital engine control unit
ACEVAL	air combat evaluation		DEEC	digital electronic engine control
ACM	air combat manoeuvring		DMPI	desired mean point of impact
ACMI	air combat manoeuvring instrumentation		DRF	dual role fighter
ACT	air combat training		DTM	data transfer module
ADC	Aerospace Defence Command			
ADI	attitude direction indicator		ECM	electronic countermeasures
ADTAC	Air Defense, Tactical Air Command		ECCM	electronic counter-countermeasures
AEF	Aerospace Expeditionary Force		EGBU	enhanced guided bomb unit
AEW	airborne early warning		ELINT	electronic intelligence
AEZ	air exclusion zone		EMDS	engine monitoring display system
AGL	above ground level			
AIMVAL	air intercept missile evaluation		FDL	fighter data link
AIR	air inflatable retard		FEBA	forward edge of the battle area
ALC	Air Logistics Centre		FIS	Fighter Interceptor Squadron
AMRAAM	advanced medium-range air-to-air missile		FS	Fighter Squadron
ANG	Air National Guard		FLIR	forward-looking infra-red
AOA	angle of attack		FMS	foreign military sales
APAM	anti-personnel, anti-material		FOTD	fibre-optic towed decoys
ASAT	anti-satellite		FTD	field training detachment
ATEGG	advanced turbine engine gas generator		FW	Fighter Wing
ATO	Air Tasking Order			
AWACS	airborne warning and control system		GCI	ground controlled interception
			GIUK	Greenland, Iceland, United Kingdom (gap)
BAI	battlefield air interdiction		GPS	global positioning system
BARCAP	barrier combat air patrol			
BAS	battlefield air superiority		HARM	high-speed anti-radiation missile
BDA	bomb damage assessment		HOTAS	hands on throttle and stick
BFM	basic flight manoeuvres		HUD	heads-up display
BIT	built-in test		HVA	high-value asset
BVR	beyond visual range		HVACAP	high-value asset combat air patrol
CALCM	conventional air launched cruise missile		IADS	integrated air defence system
CAP	combat air patrol		ICS	internal countermeasures set
CAS	close air support		ICT	integrated combat turnaround
CBITS	computer-based integrated training systems		ID	identification
CBU	cluster bomb unit		IDF/AF	Israel Defence Force/Air Force
CCIP	continuously computed impact point		IFF	identification friend or foe
CEM	combined effects munitions		IIR	imaging infra-red
CFE	contractor-funded equipment		INS	inertial navigation system
CFT	conformal fuel tank		IOC	initial operational capability
CFS	concept formulation study		IOT&E	initial operational testing and evaluation
CMD	countermeasures dispenser		IP	initial point
CO	commanding officer		IPE	improved performance engine
CONUS	continental United States		IR	infrared
CRT	cathode ray tube		IRST	infra-red search and track
CSAR	combat search and rescue			
			JASSM	joint air-to- surface strike missile
DACT	dissimilar air combat training		JDAM	joint direct attack munition

JFS	jet fuel starter		RAM	raid assessment mode
JSOW	joint stand-off weapon		RESCAP	rescue combat air patrol
JSTARS	joint surveillance target attack radar system		RFP	request for proposals
JTIDS	joint tactical information distribution system		RGH	range gated high
			RIO	radar intercept officer
Kt knot	(1Kt = 1 nautical mile per hour)		ROE	rules of engagement
			RSAF	Royal Saudi Air Force
LANTIRN	low altitude navigation and targeting infrared for night		RWR	radar warning receiver
LCOSS	lead computing optical sight system		RWS	range while search
LDGP	low-drag general purpose (bomb)			
LGB	laser guided bomb		SA	situational awareness
LPI	low probability of intercept		SAM	surface to air missile
LRS	long-range search		SAR	synthetic aperture radar
LRU	line-replaceable unit		SCAMP	supersonoc cruise and manoeuvring prototype
			SDT	secondary designated target
MANI	multiple air navigation indicator		SEAD	suppression of enemy air defences
MANPADS	man-portable air defence system		SP	Sparrow
MEL	mobile erector/launcher		SRS	short-range search
MER	multiple ejector rack		SRAAM	short-range air-to-air missile
MFD	multi-function display		STT	single target tracking mode
MFF	mixed fighter force		SW	Sidewinder
MND	maintenance non-delivery			
MRM	medium-range missile		TAC	Tactical Air Command
MSIP	multi-stage improvement programme		TACAN	tactical aid to navigation
MTBF	mean time before failure		TARPS	tactical air reconnaissance pod system
MTI	moving target indication		TAM	Tactical Air Meet
			TDC	target designator control
NCTR	non-cooperative target recognition		TDPU	tactics, discussions and procedures update
NORAD	North American Aerospace Defence (Command)		TDY	temporary duty
NVG	night-vision goggles		TEL	transporter/erector/launcher
			TEWS	tactical electronic warfare system
OCA	offensive counter-air		TFR	terrain following radar
ONW	Operation Northern Watch		TFS	Tactical Fighter Squadron
ORI	operational readiness inspection		TFW	Tactical Fighter Wing
OSW	Operation Southern Watch		TISEO	target identification system, electro-optical
OT&E	operational test and evaluation		TLP	Tactical Leadership Programme
			TOSS	television optical scoring system
PACOM	Pacific Command		TSD	tactical situation display
PACS	programmable armament control system		TVSU	TV sight unit
PDF	precision direction finding		TWS	track while scan
PDM	programmed depot maintenance			
PDT	primary designated target		VID	visual identification
PGM	precision-guided munition		VITAS	visual target acquisition system
PLO	Palestine Liberation Organisation		VS	velocity search
PMEL	precision measurement equipment laboratory		VSD	vertical situation display
PPI	plan position indicator		VTAS	visual target recognition system
PRF	pulse repetition frequency			
PSP	programmable signal processor		WCMD	wind corrected munitions dispenser
			WSO	Weapons Systems Officer
QRA	quick reaction alert		WTD	weapons training detachment

Index